The Origins of the Authoritarian
Welfare State in Prussia

Social History, Popular Culture, and Politics in Germany

Geoff Eley, Series Editor

The Origins of the Authoritarian Welfare State in Prussia

Conservatives, Bureaucracy, and the
Social Question, 1815–70

Hermann Beck

Ann Arbor
THE UNIVERSITY OF MICHIGAN PRESS

Copyright © by the University of Michigan 1995
All rights reserved
Published in the United States of America by
The University of Michigan Press
Manufactured in the United States of America
☉ Printed on acid-free paper

1998 1997 1996 1995   4 3 2 1

A CIP catalogue record for this book is available from the British Library.

Library of Congress Cataloging-in-Publication Data

Beck, Hermann, 1955–
    The origins of the authoritarian welfare state in Prussia :
conservatives, bureaucracy, and the social question, 1815–70 /
Hermann Beck.
        p.   cm. — (Social history, popular culture, and politics in
Germany)
    Includes bibliographical references and index.
    ISBN 0-472-10546-9 (alk. paper)
    1. Public welfare—Germany—Prussia—History.
2. Authoritarianism—Germany—Prussia—History. I. Title.
II. Series.
HV279.P9B43   1994
361.943—dc20   94-35186
                                                              CIP

To the memory of

Wilma Schmitt
(1913–93)

Preface

Prussia was in many respects formative for later German history. Its institutions, political culture, and values molded Imperial Germany, the Weimar Republic, and the Third Reich. After unification, Prussia accounted for roughly two-thirds of the Empire's size and population, but its weight within Germany was perhaps even greater, since the German identity after 1871 was in large part a Prussian identity. To a substantial degree, Prussia shaped not only the public tone of the Empire but also—despite Germany's abounding regional diversity—the German image abroad.

Even though the history of nineteenth-century Prussia before the unification of Germany was in many regards the immediate prehistory of the Empire, our knowledge of the Prussian past in the crucial half-century before 1871 barely goes beyond the well-worn clichés of Prussian militarism. In becoming part of a larger entity, however, and as a result of its newly acquired military glory and political might, Prussia changed profoundly. What held true for Prussia during the Wilhelminean Empire thus cannot be tacitly assumed for Prussian society and politics in the earlier decades of the nineteenth century. Prussia before Bismarck does not fit common stereotypes. Still, after two world wars and the Allied Control Council's decision in 1947 to abolish the Prussian state as the "stronghold of reaction and militarism in Germany," soldiers with spiked helmets have largely come to dominate our image of Prussia. The reputation Prussia acquired in the twentieth century has thus led to the wholesale condemnation of its history in the nineteenth, reducing a complex past to a simplified case study of repression and militarism. In the last twenty-five years, German historians, in a long overdue effort to come to terms with a past too long idealized, have been tempted to overemphasize the negative sides of their Prussian heritage, and in the United States, Prussian history has attracted little interest since 1945—not least because of its reputation. Yet given its significance for later nineteenth-century and twentieth-century Germany, it is important that the Prussia before unification be rescued from oblivion in all its

complexities. It is a topic likely to receive attention in the future, as in the wake of the second German unification, some energy will undoubtedly be redirected in scrutinizing the prehistory of the first.

Prussia's influence on Germany was most pronounced in the sphere of bureaucracy. Perhaps even more than its army, its civil service made Prussia into what it was. In Otto Hintze's words, Prussia was the classical country of modern bureaucracy, and it is no accident that the foremost theoreticians of bureaucracy from Hegel to Max Weber took an intense interest in Prussian development. Built up during the eighteenth century, the Prussian civil service reached the apex of its power between the reforms beginning in 1807 and the Revolution of 1848, a period historians appropriately labeled "the age of bureaucratic absolutism." The representative institutions that grew out of the Revolution of 1848 curtailed bureaucratic omnipotence, but the high official remained a figure who commanded unanimous respect and influence, and most ministers of the king continued being recruited from the upper echelons of the higher civil service. In Prussia the existence of a sophisticated bureaucracy thus predated industrialization as well as the formation of parties. Both the industrial enterprise and the party apparatus soon evinced characteristics of bureaucratic organization, as Max Weber and Robert Michels were quick to discover.

The official represented the two sides of the Prussian *Staatsgedanke:* the notion of control and order on the one hand, manifesting itself by a high degree of state interference, and the state's claim to work for the welfare of its citizens on the other. Authority and benevolence are the terms that capture best the Prussian state's attitude toward its subjects. State interventionism, in turn, derived its legitimation from the bureaucracy's claim to work for the good of the population. Bismarck's social legislation of the 1880s, which blazed the trail for the modern welfare state, has come to epitomize this. Though Bismarck's legislation has become an integral part of the history of Imperial Germany, there is no study that probes into the origins of the authoritarian welfare state in Prussia, that is, no analysis of the social, ideological, and political preconditions that led to the rise of the specifically Prussian welfare state mentality, which later left so indelible a mark on Germany.

The present monograph tries to close this gap. It is an attempt to investigate the complex tradition of ideas, institutions, and social policy measures that lay at the root of the Prussian welfare state. I have not endeavored to write a prehistory of Bismarck's social legislation or a history of Prussian *Sozialgesetzgebung*. What interested me was the mental makeup of Prussian conservatives and officials, their approach to social problems and the lower classes, the hidden motivations underlying their social involvement, the strange duality of *Wohlfahrt* and *Staatsautorität* that characterized their ideas, and finally the way their social ideas reflected back on their politics or, in the

case of officials, on the institution of bureaucracy. This study consists of three
parts: an introduction on the social preconditions and perceptions of the social
question in nineteenth-century Prussia; part 1 on conservatives and the social
question; and part 2 on the Prussian bureaucracy, its internal structure, the
prevailing political currents within it, and the social policy measures it
adopted. This investigation thus combines approaches in social history (introduction), intellectual history (the examination of conservative social thought),
and political-administrative history (the discussion of bureaucracy).

The Social Question: Between the 1820s and 1840s central Europe was in
the throes of a profound social crisis. Social misery in most member states of
the German Confederation had become so widespread that, in hindsight, the
entire period has been labeled "the age of pauperism." Contemporaries were
equally aware of the potential political explosiveness of this social crisis; the
ever swelling mass of *Pauperismusliteratur* (tracts and pamphlets on social
misery) in the 1830s and the "Hungry Forties" bears witness to that. Fear of
social upheavals was bound to engender political responses, and conservatives,
liberals, and Hegelians tried in their own ways to grapple with the problem.

Conservative social thought, though least noticed by historians, was perhaps the most fascinating political response, for not only did it influence
Bismarck's social legislation, but the main topics of conservative social theory
between the 1830s and 1860s also set the standards of conservative social
discourse that remained valid until the end of the Weimar Republic. The
concept of a "social kingdom," for example, propagated by such conservatives
as Josef Maria von Radowitz, who held the office of foreign minister after the
1848 Revolution, and Hermann Wagener, Bismarck's adviser on social issues,
later resurfaced in the political discourse of the Weimar Republic. Its underlying notion was that the lower classes could be used as an instrument to keep
down the liberal bourgeoisie by tying the lower orders closer to the "social
monarchy," which, in turn, would actively take up the cause of the lower orders
by supporting their material and political demands. The non-German historian
may not always be familiar with such conservative thinkers as Ludwig von
Gerlach, Viktor A. Huber, Carl Rodbertus, or Hermann Wagener, but their
ideas exerted a powerful influence on nineteenth-century Germany. They
evinced strong social concerns, far exceeding those of contemporary liberals,
and they endowed later welfare legislation with its pronounced patriarchical
slant.

At first sight, the *Prussian bureaucracy* has less in common with the
conservatives than one might assume. After the Napoleonic wars, Prussian
officials emerged as spokespersons of laissez-faire liberalism, and the preceding reform period had earned the civil service a liberal reputation. Liberal
convictions soon waned, however, when confronted with the exigencies of the
day-to-day demands of running a state like Prussia. Financial difficulties,

which resulted in a decrease of the number of higher officials, soon forced the bureaucracy to resort to the proven panacea of repression and control. To curb the rising numbers of the rural and urban proletariat, civil servants felt compelled to interfere in economy and society and embark on a piecemeal program of social legislation. A factory bill to curb child labor was introduced in 1837, and the Poor Laws of 1842 created a system of registration for rural paupers that became formative for Germany's strict system of citizen registration in the twentieth century. The officials' attitude toward the lower classes was revealing insofar as it forces us to reevaluate our knowledge of nineteenth-century German bureaucracy.

The professional mentality of the Prussian civil servant was characterized by certain implicit, unwitting assumptions that had been inculcated in the course of a long process of professional socialization. It is safe to assume that the longer the profession-specific training, the more complex and deeply rooted the profession-specific mentality. Accordingly, the "professional mentality" of the nineteenth-century Prussian bureaucrat was sophisticated and complex, for many restrictive criteria applied, and numerous hurdles had to be overcome to become a full-fledged member of the administrative branch of the bureaucracy. During the course of their obligatory studies, for example, countless officials were undoubtedly influenced by the idealism that pervaded Prussian universities after the reforms. Here lies the root of the often postulated symbiosis of *Bildung* and *Bürokratie*.

It is naturally difficult to filter out these unspoken assumptions, precisely because they were not made explicit but taken for granted, "natural" so to speak. How can these subconscious mental structures be laid bare? The historiography of mentality has often focused on attitudes toward religion or death. In the case of officials, their position toward specific problems or specific social groups seems the most promising approach. My focus was thus on how officials dealt with social problems and on how they treated the problem of pauperism. In the course of this investigation, it will become clear that the officials' mode of functioning in regard to social problems approximated that of conservatives, despite the latter's deep hostility toward the "leveling" influence of the bureaucrat. The examination of the ideas of conservatives and officials brings out a peculiar "welfare state mentality" of benevolence and patriarchical concern pervaded by authoritarian streaks, which is unique in nineteenth-century Europe. In no other European country was there such a strong tradition of social conservatism, even if it must be added that conservative motivations covered the whole spectrum from genuine concern for the welfare of the impoverished to tactical considerations of how the lower classes could be used to perpetuate the power of aristocracy and monarchy. The role of bureaucracy was equally exceptional in that bureaucratic rule was more highly developed and officials were freer in their decisions and had greater authority

than elsewhere. Our topic has therefore an undeniable relevance for the problem of continuity in German history, a theme that runs like a leitmotif through my treatment of conservative and bureaucratic thought and policy. In a long epilogue, I have tried to integrate my own empirical findings into the larger frame of the debate on continuity and discontinuity in German history.

It will become clear that Prussian traditions had positive as well as negative sides, though I have put greater stress on the "liability" of the Prussian past for German history. The ultimate value judgment, however, depends on one's individual perspective and approach to the historically contentious values of "freedom" and "order."

Acknowledgments

I wish to express my gratitude for the intellectual support of colleagues and the financial support of institutions that allowed me to complete this study. A dissertation fellowship from the UCLA department of history permitted me to develop the foundation upon which this book is based. The University of Miami provided generous support through a series of Max Orovitz Summer Awards in Arts and Humanities and General Research Support Awards for travel to archives; its department of history provided equally generous leave time for this project. It is my special pleasure to thank the Berliner Historische Kommission, especially Wolfram Fischer and Otto Büsch, for affording me an ideal physical and intellectual setting in which to complete the final manuscript. Of the many archivists who facilitated my research in various archival collections, special thanks must go to Heinrich Waldmann, the former director of the Merseburg Archives, for his untiring assistance in helping me locate documents. Numerous friends and colleagues gave generously of their time and energy in furthering my work on this project. Kenneth Barkin, Christoph Conrad, Edward Dreyer, Amos Funkenstein, Kirk Hall, Günther Höpfner, and David Sabean read all or parts of the original manuscript and offered suggestions, criticisms and incisive comments. Anne Hausen spent countless hours improving its style. David Barclay, James Retallack and Geoff Eley, the editor of the series in which this book appears, closely read the manuscript at various stages of its development and provided detailed suggestions for improving its substance. Their efforts and rich knowledge of German history have made this a better book. It goes without saying that any shortcomings or flaws remain the responsibility of the author. My greatest debt of gratitude, however, goes to two historians of European history, Eugen Weber and Robert Wohl, both of UCLA, who gave me the encouragement and freedom necessary to pursue less traditional lines of inquiry in analyzing the complexities of German history. I can only hope that the present study positively reflects their influence.

Contents

The Problem: Pauperism and the Social Question in Prussia, 1815–70

Since the early 1820s, most states in the German Confederation found themselves in the throes of a deep social crisis that threatened to engulf ever larger sections of the population. Social misery caused by rising prices (German secondary literature refers to these crises as *Teuerungskrisen*) had been a recurring phenomenon in European history since the fifteenth century, and there had been periodic crises in the sixteenth, seventeenth, and eighteenth centuries.[1] But to contemporaries of the early nineteenth century in Germany, the widespread pauperism signified an essentially new phenomenon. Whether this was solely due to the sharpened sensitivities of modern man, to the widening of his *Bewusstseinshorizont,* as one historian maintained, or to the objective deterioration of living conditions for the lower classes in general, as most specialists now claim, was a contentious issue among historians in the 1950s and 1960s.[2] The severity of pauperism varied regionally; while some provinces, such as East Elbian Prussia, were harder hit than others, no region of the German Confederation was completely spared.[3] Mass poverty and destitution

1. See Michel Mollat, *Die Armen im Mittelalter* (Munich, 1984); Wolfram Fischer, *Armut in der Geschichte* (Göttingen, 1982); Bronislaw Geremek, *Geschichte der Armut,* DTV ed. (Munich, 1991); Wilhelm Abel, *Massenarmut und Hungerkrisen im vorindustriellen Deutschland,* 2d ed. (Göttingen, 1977).

2. See Rudolf Stadelmann, *Soziale und Politische Geschichte der Revolution von 1848,* 3d ed. (Munich, 1973)—the chapter on "Soziale Ursachen der Revolution von 1848" is reprinted in Hans-Ulrich Wehler, ed., *Moderne deutsche Sozialgeschichte* (Königstein, 1966), 137–55; Werner Conze, "Vom Pöbel zum Proletariat," *Vierteljahresschrift für Sozial- und Wirtschaftsgeschichte* 41 (1954): 333–64, reprinted in Wehler, *Sozialgeschichte,* 111–36.

3. Several collections of primary sources that bear witness to the vast regional distribution of poverty have been published. See Ernst Schraepler, *Quellen zur Geschichte der sozialen Frage*

were so widespread in Restoration and pre-March Germany that German social historians labeled the entire period the "age of pauperism."

This "age of pauperism," a category from social history, overlapped with the Restoration (1815–30) and *Vormärz* (1830–48 or 1840–48) periods (though no consensus exists among historians about the precise delineation among them). During the last ten years, when the period between 1815 and 1848 attracted considerable interest, the term *Vormärz* has frequently been applied to characterize the entire epoch between the Congress of Vienna and the 1848 Revolution.[4] The use of the term *Vormärz* indicates that the thirty-three years after 1815 are viewed solely as a prehistory of the 1848 *Märzrevolution*. This poses a conceptual problem, since the whole age was not orientated toward revolution. The 1820s, for example, dominated by the Carlsbad Decrees in German politics and by the Holy Alliance in international affairs, was clearly a decade of "restoration."[5] And the "pre-March" period is specific to Germany, where the revolutions commenced in the month of March. There is similar overlap of terminology with regard to the discussion of social problems. During the 1830s and 1840s, *Pauperismus* was the most frequently used expression. In the 1850s and 1860s, when poverty turned into a problem of the industrial proletariat, the term was superseded by *Arbeiterfrage* or the more general *Soziale Frage*. *Social question* was also used during the first half of the century, but the expression was limited to German-speaking countries. In Western Europe the discussion of social problems was dominated by different concepts, such as *organisation du travail* in France.[6]

in Deutschland (Göttingen, 1955); Carl Jantke and Dietrich Hilger, *Die Eigentumslosen* (Freiburg, 1965). See also two volumes published in the series *Quellen zum politischen Denken der Deutschen im 19. und 20. Jahrhundert* by Hartwig Brandt, *Restauration und Frühliberalismus 1814–1840* (Darmstadt, 1979), and Hans Fenske, *Vormärz und Revolution* (Darmstadt, 1976).

4. In addition to the *Gesamtdarstellungen* by Thomas Nipperdey, *Deutsche Geschichte 1800–1866* (Munich, 1983), Hans-Ulrich Wehler, *Deutsche Gesellschaftsgeschichte 1815–1845/49*, vol. 2 (Munich, 1987), and James Sheehan, *German History 1770–1866* (Oxford, 1989), a host of other general works on the period after 1815 has been published in the 1980s. See especially Dieter Langewiesche, *Europa zwischen Restauration und Revolution 1815–1849* (Munich, 1985); Peter Burg, *Der Wiener Kongress*, DTV (Munich, 1984); Reinhard Rürup, *Deutschland im 19. Jahrhundert 1815–1871* (Göttingen, 1984); Heinrich Lutz, *Zwischen Habsburg und Preussen: Deutschland zwischen 1815 und 1866* (Berlin, 1985); Wolfgang Hardtwig, *Vormärz: Der monarchische Staat und das Bürgertum*, DTV (Munich, 1985), covering the entire period between 1815 and 1848; Hagen Schulze, *Der Weg zum Nationalstaat*, DTV (Munich, 1985); Rainer Koch, *Deutsche Geschichte 1815–1848: Restauration oder Vormärz?* (Stuttgart, 1985); Manfred Botzenhart, *Reform, Restauration, Krise: Deutschland 1789–1847* (Frankfurt, 1985); Dieter Grimm, *Deutsche Verfassungsgeschichte 1776–1866* (Frankfurt, 1988); Hans Boldt, *Deutsche Verfassungsgeschichte: Von 1806 bis zur Gegenwart*, vol. 2, DTV (Munich, 1990).

5. In the present study, the usage of the term conforms to recent practice among historians, i.e., *Vormärz* will be used as all-encompassing (including "the age of restoration").

6. French and British authors used *social question* mostly with reference to Germany. See

Pauperism after 1815 was politically significant insofar as it was conceived as an explanation for the social unrest of 1848, that is, the revolts of the nascent urban proletariat and the rural lower classes.[7] In 1848 the lower classes were more unruly than at any time in nineteenth-century Germany. Correspondingly, when pauperism first became a topic of historical investigation after 1945, it was viewed as part of the prehistory of either the 1848 Revolution or the German socialist movement. In his history of the 1848 Revolution, Rudolf Stadelmann focused on the social revolutionary potential in the lower classes, whereas Werner Conze placed his examination ("Vom Pöbel zum Proletariat") in the context of the history of socialism. Later research on German pauperism shifted its focus to the social composition of the pauperized masses, raising questions about the relationship between the traditional poor and the emerging industrial proletariat, about the reasons for widespread proletarization, and about the uniqueness of early nineteenth-century pauperism.[8] Beginning with the 1970s, deviant behavior, crime, and social protest became increasingly important corollaries of pauperism research. The Silesian weavers' uprising of 1844 and the "hunger revolts" of 1847 and 1848 were obvious cases in point.[9] The 1840s, the "Hungry Forties," brought with them a

---

Wolfram Fischer, "Soziale Spannungen in den Frühstadien der Industrialisierung," in *Wirtschaft und Gesellschaft im Zeitalter der Industrialisierung* (Göttingen, 1972), 224–42; Werner Conze, "Proletariat, Pöbel, Pauperismus," in *Geschichtliche Grundbegriffe,* vol. 4, ed. O. Brunner, W. Conze, R. Koselleck (Stuttgart, 1984), 27–67. *Cum grano salis* one might say that in the German context *Pauperismus* primarily refers to rural paupers and *Arbeiterfrage* to the nascent industrial proletariat (though the two are not fully compatible, as *Arbeiterfrage* also denotes a political problem), while *Soziale Frage* is the larger, generic term including both.

7. For example, in Stadelmann, *Revolution,* or Helmut Bleiber's study of rural rebellions in Silesia, *Zwischen Reform und Revolution* (Berlin, GDR, 1966).

8. The more important ones include Wolfram Fischer, "Soziale Unterschichten im Zeitalter der Frühindustrialisierung," in *Wirtschaft und Gesellschaft im Zeitalter der Industrialisierung* (Göttingen, 1972), 242–57; Fischer, "Das deutsche Handwerk in den Frühphasen der Industrialisierung," *Wirtschaft,* 315–37; Fischer, "Soziale Spannungen in den Frühstadien der Industrialisierung," *Wirtschaft;* Fischer, "Innerbetrieblicher und sozialer Status der frühen Fabrikarbeiterschaft," in *Die wirtschaftliche Situation in Deutschland und Österreich um die Wende vom 18. zum 19. Jahrhundert,* ed. Friedrich Lütge (Stuttgart, 1964), 192–222; Wilhelm Abel, "Der Pauperismus in Deutschland," in *Wirtschaft, Geschichte und Wirtschaftsgeschichte. Festschrift für Friedrich Lütge* (Stuttgart, 1966), 284–98; Abel, *Der Pauperismus in Deutschland am Vorabend der industriellen Revolution* (Dortmund, 1966); Abel, *Massenarmut;* Carl Jantke's introduction to Jantke and Hilger, *Die Eigentumslosen,* 7–48; Werner Conze, "Das Spannungsfeld von Staat und Gesellschaft im Vormärz," in *Staat und Gesellschaft im deutschen Vormärz,* ed. W. Conze (Stuttgart, 1962), 207–69; Theodore S. Hamerow, *Restoration, Revolution, Reaction* (Princeton, 1958), 1–95; Donald G. Rohr, *The Origins of Social Liberalism in Germany* (Chicago, 1963), 50–78.

9. See Dirk Blasius, *Bürgerliche Gesellschaft und Kriminalität: Zur Sozialgeschichte Preussens im Vormärz* (Göttingen, 1976); Dirk Blasius, *Kriminalität und Alltag* (Göttingen, 1978); Richard Tilly, ed., *Sozialer Protest: Geschichte und Gesellschaft,* vol. 3 (Göttingen, 1977); Richard Tilly, *Kapital, Staat und sozialer Protest in der deutschen Industrialisierung* (Göttingen,

deepening of the crisis, since poverty became more widespread after 1844, and hunger increasingly turned into a political problem.[10]

One recurring theme in the German secondary literature is that rural pauperism was even more common than its urban variety—in stark contrast to the situation in England. Bruno Hildebrand's well-known review of Friedrich Engels' *Die Lage der arbeitenden Klassen in England* is frequently cited (e.g., by Wilhelm Abel and Wolfram Fischer) to make that point.[11] Hildebrand sharply rejected Engels' thesis that the proletariat was primarily a creation of industry. The comparison with England is bound to be lopsided, since England was already an industrialized country in the 1840s, while the industrial takeoff in Germany occurred only during the 1850s. But taking up Hildebrand's argument, historians of pauperism, such as Wilhelm Abel, Werner Conze, and Wolfram Fischer, concur that social problems in the German *Vormärz* were not the product of industrialization as Marxists from Friedrich Engels to Jürgen Kuczynski (as well as nineteenth-century conservatives) repeatedly emphasized. Abel and Fischer in particular emphasize the continuity of mass pauperism in preindustrial Europe. In their opinion, the *Pauperismus* of the first half of the century was largely an agrarian "hunger crisis." According to Wolfram Fischer, it was "the last *Ausläufer* of the old, preindustrially determined poverty, sharpened by rapid population growth in agriculture and industry on the one hand, and by heightened sensibility toward social questions on the other."[12]

Agreement on this particular point was due to more than the mechanical solidarity of non-Marxist authors. The economic historians Wilhelm Abel and Wolfram Fischer asserted that central Europe had been afflicted by periodic crises since the late Middle Ages. Fischer pointed to the multitude of *Armenhäuser* in the German states and to the concern governments in western

1980); Wolfgang J. Mommsen and Gerhard Hirschfeld, *Sozialprotest, Gewalt, Terror* (Stuttgart, 1982); Heinrich Volkmann and Jürgen Bergmann, eds., *Sozialer Protest: Studien zu traditioneller Resistenz und kollektiver Gewalt in Deutschland vom Vormärz bis zur Reichsgründung* (Opladen, 1984); Helmut Reinalter, *Demokratische und soziale Protestbewegungen in Mitteleuropa 1815–1848/49* (Frankfurt, 1986); Arno Herzig, *Unterschichtenprotest in Deutschland 1790–1870* (Göttingen, 1988); Manfred Gailus, *Strasse und Brot: Sozialer Protest in den deutschen Staaten unter besonderer Berücksichtigung Preussens, 1847–1849* (Göttingen, 1990).

10. See Richard Tilly, *Vom Zollverein zum Industriestaat*, DTV (Munich, 1990), 9–39, as well as the articles by Karl Obermann, "Die Volksbewegung in Deutschland von 1844–1846," *Zeitschrift für Geschichtswissenschaft* 5 (1957): 503–25, and "Wirtschafts- und sozialpolitische Aspekte der Krise von 1845–1847 in Deutschland, insbesondere in Preussen," *Jahrbuch für Geschichte* 8 (1972): 143–74. See also Hamerow, *Restoration* and Sheehan, *German History*, 637–55.

11. See Bruno Hildebrand, *Die Nationalökonomie der Gegenwart und Zukunft und andere gesammelte Schriften* (Jena, 1922), 137–49; excerpts are reprinted in Hans Fenske, *Vormärz und Revolution*, 248–53.

12. Wolfram Fischer, *Armut in der Geschichhte* (Göttingen, 1982), 56.

Europe evinced on the issue as reflected in poor law legislation or in provisions on how to deal with mendicancy (*Bettlerordnungen*). Abel demonstrated through his investigation of wages and prices that the standard of living of Germany's working population experienced a steady decline since the late Middle Ages. Between the sixteenth and the nineteenth century, prices rose consistently faster than corresponding wages, resulting in a constant diminution of the *Nahrungsmittelpielraum* since 1500.[13] But here common ground among non-Marxist historians ends. Disagreement arose in the 1950s and 1960s about the nature and uniqueness of pauperism in early nineteenth-century Germany. Had *Pauperismus* been just another "hunger crises" of early modern Europe, or did it, by dint of its severity, constitute an essentially new phenomenon, intrinsically different from the crises of earlier centuries? To tackle this question and develop a more comprehensive view of the social question in Germany, it is imperative to examine the main components of its historiography, the contemporary literature on pauperism, the specific nature of social problems in Prussia, and finally, population growth and the composition of the lower classes.

The Main Components of Its Historiography

In his "social and political history" of the 1848 Revolution, Rudolf Stadelmann argued that the lower classes were no worse off in the 1830s and 1840s than in previous centuries. What had changed was merely their "degree of awareness."[14] Stadelmann's interpretation of lower-class living conditions was based on testimonies of a personal nature, such as petitions, popular songs, secret diaries, and other sources that provided information on the daily habits of the population. On the basis of these sources, he put forth the proposition that the sensibility of the lower classes, not objective circumstances, had undergone a change. The decades preceding the revolution bore witness to a new kind of dissatisfaction and insubordination; as a result, social injustice was felt

---

13. See Wilhelm Abel, *Massenarmut.* There are few works of synthesis on the poor in early modern Europe, virtually none on Germany per se. Mollat's *Die Armen im Mittelalter,* Geremek's *Geschichte der Armut,* and Fischer's *Armut* are the only more general works. In the last ten years, however, some research has been done on the urban poor, see Robert Jütte, *Obrigkeitliche Fürsorge in den deutschen Reichsstädten der Frühen Neuzeit: Städtisches Armenwesen in Frankfurt am Main und Köln* (Cologne and Vienna, 1984); Martin Dinges, *Stadtarmut in Bordeaux 1525–1675: Alltag, Politik, Mentalitäten* (Bonn, 1988); and, more general, the dissertation by Michael Doege, *Armut in Preussen und Bayern (1770–1840)* (Munich, 1991). On recent publications see the review article by Frank Rexroth, "Recent British and West German Research on Poverty in the early Modern Period," *Bulletin of the German Historical Institute London* 12 (Summer, 1990): 3–11. There is a wealth of studies on early modern England, conveniently summarized in Paul Slack, *The English Poor Law 1531–1782.*

14. See Stadelmann, "Soziale Ursachen der Revolution von 1848," in Stadelmann, *Revolution,* and Wehler, *Sozialgeschichte.*

more acutely. Notably the socially transient class of wandering *Hand-werksgesellen* (journeymen), unintegrated because not part of any estate, contributed to revolutionary ferment. The insecurity of their ambiguous position between artisans and factory workers was an ideal breeding ground for political discontent. These journeymen, together with restless journalists and "activists among the lower orders" (as Stadelmann referred to tailors and shoemakers), were the forces behind social protest.

There can be no doubt that Stadelmann is too optimistic in his assessment of material conditions when assuming that the first half of the nineteenth century in Germany had not been a time of material hardship.[15] He tends to distort reality when generalizing from a *Pfarrchronik* of 1851 (cited as giving a representative sample of living conditions in Germany), in which the author stated that "the years of about 1830 to 1848 belong to the most pleasant of world history." For the lower classes this hardly held true. Stadelmann was probably more attuned to the new, petty bourgeois self-satisfaction of the *Biedermeier* than to the material conditions of the lower classes. And while he could not completely ignore the problem of pauperism, he limited it to the 1840s, when the crisis reached its culmination.

Werner Conze, in contrast, emphasized the objective deterioration of the material position of the lower classes.[16] Rapid population growth, lack of employment opportunities, and an industrial sector still in its infancy, were all responsible for the crisis. The dissolution of the traditional *Ständegesellschaft* by the reforms of the early nineteenth century and the concomitant *Dekorporierung, Disproportionierung,* and *Entsittlichung* of society lay at its root.[17] The novel element of pre-March *Pauperismus* was thus the destruction of the *ständisch* order, which was most complete in Prussia, where the social crisis was most severe. In his *Preussen zwischen Reform und Revolution,* Reinhart Koselleck in like manner postulated a causal link between the Prussian reforms and the rising numbers of the lower classes, which, through the reforms, lost the safety net of the traditional *ständisch* order.[18] As Werner Conze maintained, the growth of the underclass below the *ständisch* order was disproportional, for it grew faster than other strata of the Prussian population. While the

---

15. Or, for example, when he writes, "Der Lebensstandard hat eine Höhe und Konstanz gewonnen, wie sie wahrscheinlich in allen Jahrhunderten zuvor nicht bestanden hat." See Stadelmann, reprinted in Wehler, *Sozialgeschichte,* 141.

16. See Conze, "Vom Pöbel zum Proletariat," in Wehler, *Moderne;* Conze, "Das Spannungsfeld."

17. Conze, "Das Spannungsfeld," 246–61.

18. See Reinhart Koselleck, *Preussen zwischen Reform und Revolution,* 2d ed. (Stuttgart, 1975). Koselleck subsequently argued that the Prussian bureaucracy, which had been instrumental in implementing the reforms, later (in the 1840s) proved unable to allay the spirits it had conjured up by setting society free from its *ständisch* shackles. According to Koselleck, the Prussian *Beamtenstaat,* incapable of solving the social question, thus perished at the hands of its own creation.

Pöbel ("rabble," a term popularized by Hegel) of *ständisch* society was automatically curbed by the increase in marriage restrictions and other limitations, the proletariat, having shaken off the *ständisch* shackles, was unchained and unleashed. With the abolition of serfdom, the inner bonds to the local *Herrschaft* and to the church became looser as well, which made the proletariat seem especially dangerous in the eyes of contemporaries. Conze concurs with Stadelmann that the industrial revolution in the 1850s provided needed employment for the landless and propertyless poor and essentially ended the crisis. In his essays from the early 1960s, Stadelmann's former collaborator Wolfram Fischer deemphasized the effectiveness of the estates in containing poverty. Fischer stressed the existence during the eighteenth century of a vast mass of extra-*ständisch* paupers who were partially swallowed up by the large standing armies in the age of absolutism.[19] But Conze's and Fischer's position are not mutually exclusive, since Fischer concedes a steep growth of the rural underclass between the late eighteenth and mid-nineteenth century.[20]

By the late 1950s, American scholars had become equally interested in the problem of pauperism; Theodore S. Hamerow was the first to devote attention to it.[21] Hamerow attributed impoverishment to the advance of capitalism in industry, which spelled ruin for the artisan class. The situation of the artisanate was further aggravated by the introduction of industrial freedom (*Gewerbefreiheit*), while peasant emancipation, according to Hamerow, rendered destitute many of the poorer peasants. It was thus the liberal reforms of the early nineteenth century in combination with the rise of industry that were held responsible for the plight of the lower classes. Hamerow charged that the factory took away markets from the artisan, reduced his income, and threw him out of work, while the material conditions among factory workers were relatively good.[22] He emphasized that industrial freedom and the rise of the factory

---

19. See Wolfram Fischer, "Soziale Unterschichten im Zeitalter der Frühindustrialisierung," in *Wirtschaft.*

20. In his review essay, *"Pauperismus* in Germany during the *Vormärz," Central European History* 2 (1969), 77–88, Frederick Marquardt overaccentuated differences between Stadelmann and Fischer, on the one hand, and between Stadelmann and Conze, on the other, and presupposes the existence of camps (i.e., with Theodore Hamerow taking sides with Conze, while Donald Rohr sides with Fischer) that were not as neat in their actual delineation. Werner Conze, for example, would have hardly supported Hamerow's contention that the rise of industry was in part responsible for widespread pauperization. In the estimate of Klaus-Jürgen Matz, *Pauperismus und Bevölkerung* (Stuttgart, 1980), 19, more recent research seems on the whole to support Conze's argument that the destruction of *ständisch* ties and the corresponding change in mentality were a watershed in social development (though Wolfram Fischer has written much on pauperism since and has continuously refined his own position).

21. Hamerow, *Restoration.*

22. See "The Decline of the Handicraft System," in Hamerow, *Restoration,* 21–38. Hamerow was the only historian of pauperism who attributed poverty to the rise of industry.

system not only led to the artisan's destitution but also caused the artisan to break with established authority and seek salvation in a new political order. In this respect, Hamerow's argument is reminiscent of Stadelmann's, though Hamerow differs from Stadelmann otherwise by arguing that the material status of the lower classes had declined sharply.

On that score Hamerow is attacked by Donald G. Rohr, who charges that he painted too uniformly bleak a picture of lower-class life.[23] According to Rohr, Hamerow underemphasized the role of population growth as a cause of social misery, ignored evidence of rising living standards, and overlooked that the distress of the 1840s was local and temporary in character. Rohr chiefly takes issue with Hamerow's depiction of social liberals as advocating "unrestricted industrialism," which, given the strong social concerns of many prominent liberals, was far from accurate.[24] According to Rohr, Theodore Hamerow misread liberal intentions because he had basically misinterpreted the social problem itself. In his own analysis of the social crisis, Rohr relied mainly on literary sources and the accounts of foreign travelers, which conveyed a more optimistic portrait of the situation than the contemporary pauperism literature. To travelers from England, the extremes of rich and poor were less pronounced than at home. The life of the average low-class German compared favorably to the drab existence of his counterpart in England.[25] Most of these travelers remained, however, on the beaten (and affluent) tracks of the Rhineland and Baden and never ventured into the truly unrelieved areas of the Prussian East, where poverty was starkest. In contrast to Stadelmann, Rohr is far from denying the depths of poverty and readily admits that "the hardships which many Germans suffered in the late 1840s were more acute and widespread than any in memory."[26] In view of his own position, Rohr's sharp criticism of Hamerow's depiction of the crisis seems exaggerated, especially since Hamerow himself interpreted pauperism largely as a problem limited to the 1840s (though the decline of the handicraft system and the agrarian problem were seen as gradually unfolding crises).[27] Rohr may have been misled by Hamerow's colorful prose, since–especially when allowing for contemporary pauperism literature–Hamerow can hardly be said to have painted too bleak a picture.

In the 1970s, Wilhelm Abel, doyen of German economic historians, argued that pre-March pauperism was the last major crisis of the preindustrial

---

23. Donald S. Rohr, *The Origins of Social Liberalism in Germany* (Chicago, 1963), 12–72.

24. As indicated by its title, Rohr's study essentially concentrates on what he terms "social liberalism" in Germany.

25. Rohr, *Social Liberalism,* 58.

26. Ibid., 76.

27. See Hamerow, *Restoration,* in his chapter "The Hungry Forties," 75–93. It is true, however, that German liberals were not as socially indifferent as Hamerow claimed.

world and that it was necessary to retrace the history of economic crises since the late Middle Ages to see it in perspective.[28] Between the fourteenth and the nineteenth centuries, Abel claimed, wages had been inversely related to the development of the population. Population growth since the late Middle Ages was thus accompanied by declining real wages and dwindling purchasing power, an assertion Abel based on his extensive investigation of wages and prices since the fifteenth century. The lower classes' standard of living had been incomparably higher in the late Middle Ages than in the early nineteenth century.[29] The general diet of the common people deteriorated in equal measure, and meat, a staple in the late Middle Ages, disappeared virtually completely from the tables of the lower orders of society. Not only did the price revolution of the sixteenth century gnaw at the real income of a simple worker, but the great crises of the seventeenth and eighteenth centuries (e.g., the *Teuerungskrise* of 1770–74) diminished it further. Eighteen forty-seven was then the last year of need in the old system in central Europe, before the breakthrough of industrialization provided sufficient employment for the growing population. But the pauperism of the 1840s was not just the last of a series of periodic crises since early modern times. It was unique because it was perceived by contemporaries as a permanent crisis from which there seemed to be no escape.[30] In contrast to Friedrich Engels and Jürgen Kuczynski, Abel emphasized that by its origins and development, early nineteenth-century poverty belonged to the last crises of the agrarian age. Industrialization did not cause it but on the contrary provided the necessary impetus for overcoming it.

Wolfram Fischer, involved in the pauperism debate almost since its inception, fully agrees with Abel on this point. In a recent attempt to sum up "poverty in history,"[31] Fischer took a position of mediation between Stadelmann and his critics. Like Wilhelm Abel, Fischer stressed the ubiquitousness of poverty in early modern Europe, the fateful incongruity of slow economic growth and more rapid population growth, of lagging employment opportunities and a potentially large labor force, which resulted in perennial underemployment.[32] Since pauperism was so widespread during preindustrial

---

28. Abel, *Massenarmut.*

29. In the fifteenth century, the income of a master artisan, for example, was five times that of an artisan in the 1840s. See Abel, *Massenarmut,* 19.

30. In this context, Abel and others (e.g., Wolfram Fischer) referred to the *Brockhaus Real-Encyclopädie* of 1846 and its definition of *Pauperismus.* "Der Pauperismus ist da vorhanden, wo eine zahlreiche Volksklasse sich durch die angestrengteste Arbeit höchstens das notdürftigste Auskommen verdienen kann, . . . und dabei immer noch sich in reissender Schnelligkeit ergänzt und vermehrt." See Abel, *Massenarmut,* 61.

31. Wolfram Fischer, *Armut.*

32. Wolfgang Köllmann, *Bevölkerung in der industriellen Revolution* (Göttingen, 1974), also emphasizes that population growth in the nineteenth century could not be handled by the preindustrial economy.

times, it can hardly be regarded as the result of industrialization as Marxists (and nineteenth-century conservatives) have charged. Industry did not create the underclass; industrial wages were higher from the start. But it led to the concentration of the underclass in urban centers. At the end of the eighteenth century and especially at the beginning of the nineteenth century, poverty appeared greater, for it was perceived more acutely. But even in objective terms, poverty grew worse as the century progressed. The lower classes were harder hit in the second half of the 1840s than during the famine of 1816/17, as Fischer demonstrated with the example of Cologne.[33] In the 1850s and 1860s, however, with the takeoff of industrialization, poverty receded. The pauperism of the first half of the nineteenth century has therefore been interpreted not as the beginning of a new social question but as the culmination—and, at least for Europe, as the end—of one of humankind's perennial problems.[34] All sections of the lower classes in Germany, even artisans, profited from industrialization, as rising wages clearly show.

The Contemporary Literature on Pauperism

As topics of historical research, pauperism and the social question were discovered relatively late, and even then rarely in their own right, but rather as telling indications of future developments. This is surprising in view of the fact that for literate contemporaries of the 1830s and 1840s, the social question was considered to be a problem of the first magnitude. Between the Congress of Vienna and the Revolution of 1848, it was, together with the "national question" and the "constitutional question," the foremost preoccupation of its day and age. This concern with social issues manifested itself in an ever growing body of literature, the *Pauperismusliteratur.* That term refers to books, tracts, pamphlets, or political treatises dealing with the problem of pauperism. A considerable number of these originated as submissions to public prize questions promoted by royal academies of different states of the German Confederation. In 1835, for example, the royal academy at Erfurt initiated such a competition, soliciting answers to questions of whether "complaints about increasing impoverishment and lack of nourishment [*Nahrungslosigkeit*] in Germany" were justified and how the evil could be redressed.[35] This competition of 1835 elicited only seventeen submissions; a similar event, initiated by

---

33. See Wolfram Fischer, *Armut,* 58.
34. Fischer, *Armut,* 62.
35. See Klaus-Jürgen Matz, *Pauperismus,* 59–60; Paul Mombert, "Aus der Literatur über die soziale Frage und über die Arbeiterbewegung in Deutschland in der ersten Hälfte des 19. Jahrhunderts," *Archiv für die Geschichte des Sozialismus und der Arbeiterbewegung* 9 (1921): 169–227; Jürgen Kuczynski, *Die Geschichte der Lage der Arbeiter unter dem Sozialismus,* vol. 8 (Berlin, 1960), 109–57.

the new king of Bavaria shortly after the revolution, when perception of the social crisis was most acute, met with far greater response (656 submissions).[36] Already the crisis of 1770–74 knew a *Teuerungsliteratur* with dozens of authors commenting on it,[37] but the bulk of works published in the eighteenth century concentrated on *Armenpolizei*, mendicancy, problems associated with workhouses, or legal questions and issues of organization.[38] *Pauperismusliteratur* refers more specifically to the literature on pauperism and the social question of the nineteenth century.[39]

The vast body of *Pauperismusliteratur* has been investigated from different points of view.[40] In 1921, Paul Mombert, using the extensive holdings of a private collection, analyzed 277 titles, mostly from the 1830s and 1840s.[41] Mombert's declared intention was to rescue from oblivion a body of sources that was virtually unknown, and he thus deliberately eliminated from consideration better-known publications, such as the writings of Marx, Engels, and Lorenz von Stein. Because Mombert intended to blaze the trail for a history of the German labor movement, his selection of sources was slanted more toward problems associated with the incipient industrial proletariat than toward rural laborers, though he acknowledged that the question of the industrial proletariat emerged only during the 1840s as a distinctly new phenomenon. As interest in the *Arbeiterfrage* rose, the literature on pauperism in general decreased to the same degree.[42] Mombert also noted a tremendous increase in the literature after 1844–45, when the social crisis deepened.

Similar observations were made by Liselotte Dilcher, who examined 380 titles on pauperism published between 1800 and 1850. The bulk of them appeared in the second half of the 1840s: while the decade between 1821 and 1830 saw only 32 publications on pauperism, the number rose to 55 in the 1830s, and finally to over 200 in the 1840s, 154 alone between 1846 and 1850.[43] Dilcher focused on the suggested solutions to the problem of pauper-

---

36. Matz, *Pauperismus;* Mombert, "Aus der Literatur," 210.

37. See Abel, *Massenarmut,* 59.

38. See Matz, *Pauperismus,* 53.

39. According to Wilhelm Abel it was only in Germany that *Pauperismusliteratur* formed a coherent body of sources. See Abel, *Massenarmut,* 302.

40. In addition to Mombert and Matz, see especially the dissertation by Liselotte Dilcher, "Der deutsche Pauperismus und seine Literatur" (Ph.D. diss., Johann Wolfgang Goethe Universität Frankfurt, 1957); the bibliography by Ruth Hoppe in Jürgen Kuczynski, *Die Geschichte der Lage der Arbeiter unter dem Kapitalismus: Bürgerliche und halbfeudale Literatur aus den Jahren 1840 bis 1847 zur Lage der Arbeiter,* vol. 9 (Berlin, GDR, 1960), 267–85; the anthologies by Ernst Schraepler, *Quellen zur Geschichte der sozialen Frage in Deutschland* (Göttingen, 1955), and Carl Jantke and Dietrich Hilger, *Die Eigentumslosen* (Freiburg, 1965); and the excerpts in Kuczynski, *Geschichte,* 31–236.

41. The literature is cited in Mombert, "Aus der Literatur," 224–36. His article basically offers an elaborate annotated bibliography.

42. See Mombert, "Aus der Literatur," 177.

43. See Dilcher, "Der deutsche Pauperismus," 156.

ism, and on how contemporaries viewed the stringent measures of contemporary poor relief, workhouses, and prisons. In her analysis of the geographical distribution of the *Pauperismusliteratur,* she noted that a larger number of titles was published in northern Germany (except for Württemberg), with Berlin and Leipzig as the main centers of publication. Despite the large volume of literature investigated, Dilcher's list was still far from complete. In collaboration with Jürgen Kuczynski, Ruth Hoppe compiled a list of 400 titles for the mere twenty-nine years between 1822 and 1850, even though she deliberately excluded all socialist authors.[44] Altogether the three bibliographies by Mombert, Dilcher, and Hoppe contain about 600 titles.

Who were their authors? According to Dilcher, most of them were university graduates who had studied *Staatswissenschaft,* jurisprudence, philosophy, medicine, or theology. Few had known poverty through personal experience, but they were interested in the fate of the lower classes by dint of their positions as professors, teachers, doctors, or high-ranking civil servants.[45] And there was a minority of estate owners and merchants among them. Klaus-Jürgen Matz, concentrating on a smaller sample of authors, is more precise.[46] According to him, about one-third of the authors were civil servants, judges, officers, or politicians; a quarter professors or teachers; about 17 percent journalists and writers; and the rest merchants, doctors, and parsons.

Matz notes an increasing politicization of the literature in the wake of the July Revolution of 1830. For the next two decades, *Pauperismusliteratur* acquired a sharp political edge, because now the political consequences of poverty shifted to the center of attention. The public perception of poverty had acquired a new shape as a result of the gradual change in mentality. While the pauper had still been regarded as an integral part of society in the Middle Ages, poverty had become morally tainted in the wake of the Reformation and was considered a social danger after the French Revolution.[47] In the Middle Ages, poor relief had been an ecclesiastical matter, and asylums and hospitals for the poor lay in the hands of the church. After the Reformation, which occasioned a crisis for ecclesiastical poor relief since funds were no longer forthcoming, the poor increasingly became a public burden, and municipal poor relief was soon a financial strain for many communities.[48] Correspondingly, poverty acquired

---

44. See, Kuczynski, *Geschichte,* 267–85. As suggested by the subtitle, Hoppe concentrated on *Bürgerliche und halbfeudale Literatur.*

45. See Dilcher, "Der deutsche Pauperismus," 160–62.

46. Matz's sample is based on eighty-eight authors, mostly from southern Germany. See Matz, *Pauperismus,* 62.

47. See Wolfram Fischer, "Soziale Unterschichten im Zeitalter der Frühindustrialisierung," in *Wirtschaft,* 242–57; Fischer, *Armut,* 33–56; Nipperdey, *Deutsche Geschichte 1800–1866,* 220; Matz, *Pauperismus,* 45–50; Geremek, *Geschichte der Armut.*

48. In contrast to England, where poor relief was at least partially regulated by national poor laws, the administration of the poor in early modern Germany large devolved on the munici-

the odium of laziness and moral depravation. The "honest pauper" became the exception, as poverty was increasingly associated with malevolence, idleness, and even crime. Early modern poor relief thus contained an element of the attempt to better paupers and reform their attitudes toward work. Work was often considered the main panacea against the moral degeneration of poverty. This positive view of the remedying effect of work and industry survived into the nineteenth century and still helps to explain why even philanthropists defended child labor in factories. This negative view of the poor became intensified after the French Revolution and was, if possible, accentuated further during the 1830s and 1840s, when contemporaries increasingly feared that impoverishment might provoke social and political upheaval.

In the first half of the nineteenth century, a cluster of negative developments thus coincided. There was first the objective deterioration of material conditions of the lower classes.[49] The underdevelopment of industry provided a second unfavorable circumstance. On the territory of the German Confederation, the relative lateness of industrialization was due to the absence of national unity and a national market, the lack of available capital, an untrained labor force, and a system of transport that was still in its infancy. The majority of historians of pauperism agree, as indicated above, that with the final takeoff of industry in the 1850s, the crisis subsided.[50] A further novelty was undoubtedly the increased awareness on the part of those who suffered misery. This heightened awareness of their miserable lot may in part have been due to the revolutionary ferment spread by wandering journeymen, as Stadelmann alleged, but mainly it was fostered by the *Pauperismusliteratur,* that is, by the fact that social misery was one of the foremost topics of the age. Contemporaries were acutely aware that they were living in an age of transformation, especially when they became conscious of the profound social changes brought about by the reforms. Concerning social change, the single most visible result of the reforms was the new *Bindungslosigkeit,* the increasing atomization of the lower classes. Most notably in Prussia, the old estates had been broken open, and the vast masses of peasants, formerly under the strict tutelage of the estate owners, were now left to their own devices. This state of affairs was particularly deplored by conservatives, who denounced the resulting atomization of society as an ill omen for the future. Lastly, one might cite the increasingly negative view of poverty, the belief (intensified by the advent of liberalism)

---

palities. The main supralocal measure was the *Bettlerordnungen* of the Holy Roman Empire. See the literature cited in n. 13.

49. Their composition will be discussed later in the Introduction.

50. Recent research demonstrated that the German industrialization in the Rhineland was prepared in a long incubation period during the 1830s and 1840s, when Rhenish merchants and entrepreneurs were involved in a debate on how to industrialize Germany successfully. See Rudolf Boch, *Das rheinische Wirtschaftsbürgertum und seine Industrialisierungsdebatte* (Göttingen, 1991).

that man was the master of his own fate, and that starvation and hunger signified above all else inability or unwillingness to work. And there was widespread fear of certain attitudes contemporaries imputed to the poor. Already Hegel had alleged that poverty in itself debased no one [macht keinen zum Pöbel]; it was "the attitude associated with poverty, the inner rebellion against the rich, against society, against government,"[51] that gave the poor their dangerous quality. It was thus a mixture of changes in the mentality of the poor themselves and in how they were perceived by contemporaries, on the one hand, and of social changes, temporarily accentuated by government measures (such as the reforms), on the other, that characterized the *Vormärz*.

Never before had solutions to social problems been sought as ardently as in those decades. Warnings that social misery was the precursor of revolution lay in the air, for most of the authors of *Pauperismusliteratur* were not disinterested, free-floating intellectuals but staunch defenders of the existing order in which they had a vested interest. The Prussian conservatives, on whom this study focuses, were therefore component parts of a larger debate and tradition, not solitary warners in the wilderness. And Prussian officials still committed to the economic liberalism of earlier years felt called on to enact, or at least discuss, social policy measures, despite the severe and perennial financial plight under which Prussia labored after the Napoleonic Wars.

How did contemporaries in the public discussion of the first half of the nineteenth century explain the problem? There are virtually no systematic analyses of what *Pauperismusliteratur* believed to be the root causes of the social plight. Far and away the best study was made by Klaus-Jürgen Matz, who arrived at roughly five complexes of reasons that constitute recurring themes and resurface time and again in the literature.[52]

A leitmotif in a great many studies was that overpopulation lay at the root of the social crisis.[53] During the *Vormärz*, governments not only tried to restrict marriage by legislation to keep down further population growth but even actively encouraged overseas emigration. In contrast to eighteenth-century mercantilism, which had regarded surplus population as a source of strength, the authors of *Pauperismusliteratur* viewed population growth as a drain on national wealth. A further increase of the population was bound to increase poverty. Matz refers to the all-pervasive influence of Thomas Robert Malthus, who had claimed that, if unchecked, the population of a country would grow in

---

51. "Die mit der Armut sich verknüpfende Gesinnung, durch die innere Empörung gegen die Reichen, gegen die Gesellschaft, die Regierung." See Hegel, *Grundlinien der Philosophie des Rechts,* Suhrkamp ed. (Frankfurt, 1970), 389, article 244, Zusatz.
52. See Matz, *Pauperismus,* 63–84. His examination was based on a sample of about 130 titles.
53. See also Dilcher, "Der deutsche Pauperismus," 81–92; and Mombert, "Aus der Literatur," 222.

geometric progression, while foodstuffs increased only in arithmetic (linear) progression. As the educated German observer kept his eyes riveted on England, Malthus's teaching soon gained widespread currency in Germany.[54] Of Matz's sample, only 8 percent of the authors categorically denied that Germany suffered from overpopulation. Fear of excessive population growth was thus the largest common denominator of the *Pauperismusliteratur.* But there were others.

Religiously motivated and conservative authors lived in constant fear that the increasing emancipation of the lower classes and the dissolution of the traditional ties of *Herrschaft* might lead to chaos. Such Catholics as the Bavarian Franz von Baader and the Baden deputy Franz Josef von Buss saw the dissolution of traditional bonds and the breakdown of the old *Ständegesellschaft* as evil forebodings.[55] These authors deplored the retrogression of Christian beliefs and the corresponding decline in the morals of the lower classes—"*Entsittlichung*" became the frequently used catchword in this context. The seemingly unstoppable loosening of social and human ties might lead to a gradual erosion of values, to work shyness, and to immorality.

Gewerbefreiheit (freedom of trade) was regarded by many as a root cause of the impoverishment of artisans. Criticism of freedom of trade was buttressed by constant complaints about the pernicious effects of unfettered competition by members of the artisanage.[56] Pauperism authors on their part blamed free competition for the impoverishment of the vast mass of the population, as it automatically entailed the "ruin of the weak" and meant the decline of the handicraft system through the overpowering pressure of industrial production. Arguments against freedom of trade were frequently coupled with an idealization of the past, when the strong arm of the guild system still regulated the urban economy. This idealization of previous ages, notably late medieval times, was also a recurring theme with Prussian conservatives, and general criticism of freedom of trade was especially widespread in Prussia.[57]

---

54. See Matz, *Pauperismus,* 95–113. Thomas R. Malthus's *An Essay on the Principle of Population* (London, 1798), which quickly went through several editions, had already been translated into German by 1807.

55. On Baader and Buss see Karl Spreng, "Studien zur Entwicklung der socialpolitischen Ideen in Deutschland auf Grund der Schriften Franz von Baaders und Franz Josef von Buss" (Ph.D. diss., University of Giessen, 1932).

56. The arguments against *Gewerbefreiheit* are well summarized in a petition by fifteen artisan guilds of the town of Görlitz to the ministry of trade and commerce in Berlin. See "Petition der 15 Innungen der Stadt Görlitz," Staatsarchiv Merseburg, rep. 120 B, I, 1, no. 62.

57. This was due to the fact that freedom of trade had been most consequently realized in Prussia. *Gewerbefreiheit* naturally applied only to those provinces that were under Prussian jurisdiction when it was introduced in 1810 and 1811 (i.e., in East Prussia, Pomerania, Brandenburg, and Silesia). In the Rhine Province and parts of Westfalia, freedom of trade had been implemented during Napoleonic occupation, but in the provinces of Saxony (which became part of Prussia in

In the same vein, industrialization was blamed for the increasing proletarization of the lower classes. This argument was popular not only with early socialists but also with conservatives, to whom the social change that came in the wake of industrialization was anathema. Criticism of industrial capitalism was often beset by moral overtones: industry was accused of devaluing human labor and giving rise to usury and exploitation. Friedrich Engels' stirring study of the proletariat in Manchester served many conservatives as a warning example. In popular imagination, the factory system naturally offered itself as a likely culprit, while the English model served as a vision of horror, one to be avoided at all cost.

Finally, contemporary analysts of pauperism found fault with the existing poor law, which mostly lay in the hands of local communes, and with a tax system that often overburdened impecunious peasants. Catholic authors had stigmatized Protestant poor relief legislation since the sixteenth century as "midwife and godfather of pauperism, that plague of locusts."[58] There was much opposition to giving paupers a legal right to poor relief, which might lead (as the English example seemed to indicate) to the perpetuation and growth of poverty. In this regard, Malthus, who had attacked this very principle in his writings, exerted formative influence as an opinion leader.[59] The fear that a general legal claim to poor relief would lead to the growth of the underclass because it only encouraged natural slothfulness was also widespread within the ranks of the bureaucracy. It was a stock-in-trade argument that was current at the time.[60]

The Nature of Social Problems in Prussia

Social problems were more pronounced in Prussia than in most other states of the German Confederation.[61] The shape social problems assumed in Prussia was ultimately determined by the destruction of its traditional social organization molded in the eighteenth century. For us to appreciate the nature of social problems in nineteenth-century Prussia, a short appraisal of eighteenth-century Prussian society is thus necessary.

More than any other contemporary state, Frederican Prussia corresponded

---

1815) and Posen, the old guild system lived on. Uniformity in legislation was not established until the passing of the *Allgemeine Gewerbeordnung* in 1845. See Ulrich Ritter, *Die Rolle des Staates in den Frühstadien der Industrialisierung: Die preussische Industrief=rderung in der ersten Hälfte des 19. Jahrhunderts* (Berlin, 1961); Ilja Mieck, *Preussische Gewerbepolitik in Berlin 1806–1844* (Berlin, 1965).

58. See Matz, *Pauperismus,* 71.

59. Malthus opposed a legal claim to poor relief, believing it contributed to an augmentation of poverty, as it encouraged the poor to have families they could ill afford to support.

60. See the discussion of the 1842 Poor Laws in part 2.

61. As was partially indicated by the regional distribution of *Pauperismusliteratur,* though few works appeared in the Prussian east, which was denuded of towns and opportunities to publish.

in its social and political organization to the political program of its ruler. In the conception of Frederick II, the main social groups within the state— aristocracy, bourgeoisie, and peasants—had their precisely allocated functions.[62] The aristocracy was trained (and, if necessary, forced) into becoming a service elite.[63] In contrast to the English aristocracy, for example, Prussian nobles were barred from entering trade or the service of a foreign power (as was customary practice then among the European nobility); instead they were expected to serve as officers in the Prussian army and to occupy the highest positions in the bureaucracy.[64] The Frederican officer corps and civilian administration thus experienced a "refeudalization," since Frederick's simple and more down-to-earth father, the "Soldiers' King" Frederick William I, had preferred bourgeois advisers. As a result, there had been a large number of non-nobles in high positions when Frederick mounted the throne in 1740. In contrast to that of his predecessors on the *Hohenzollern* throne, Frederick's relationship with his aristocracy—*l'élite de la nation,* as he characterized them—was marked not by antagonism but by collaboration and mutual support. In return for service, the aristocracy was guaranteed its possessions, since

---

62. It is of course problematic to use the term *bourgeoisie* for the numerically and socially weak *Stadtbürgertum* of eighteenth-century Prussia. In our context, the term will be used interchangeably with *town burghers.*

63. Frederick's political program is most clearly enunciated in Friedrich der Grosse, *Das Politische Testament von 1752* (Stuttgart, 1976). On the role of the aristocracy see pages 15, 37, 41–42. On Frederick's relationship with his nobility see Elisabeth Schwenke, "Friedrich der Grosse und der Adel" (Ph.D. diss., University of Berlin, 1911); Otto Hintze, "Die Hohenzollern und der Adel," in *Regierung und Verwaltung,* vol. 3 of *Gesammelte Abhandlungen,* (Göttingen, 1967), 30–56; Hintze, "Das Politische Testament Friedrich des Grossen von 1752," in *Gesammelte Abhandlungen,* 3: 429–48; Fritz Martiny, *Die Adelsfrage in Preussen als politisches und soziales Problem* (Halle, 1938); Hans Rosenberg, *Bureaucracy, Aristocracy, and Autocracy: The Prussian Experience 1660–1815* (Cambridge, Mass., 1958), 88–175; Gerd Heinrich, "Der Adel in Brandenburg-Preussen," in *Deutscher Adel 1555–1740,* ed. Helmut Rössler (Darmstadt, 1965), 259–314; Günter Birtsch, "Zur sozialen und politischen Rolle des deutschen, vornehmlich des preussischen Adels am Ende des 18. Jahrhunderts," in *Der Adel vor der Revolution,* ed. Rudolf Vierhaus (Göttingen, 1971), 77–95; Hubert C. Johnson, *Frederick the Great and his Officials* (New Haven, 1975); Francis L. Carsten, *Geschichte der preussischen Junker* (Frankfurt, 1989).

64. On the Prussian bureaucracy in the eighteenth century see, in addition to Rosenberg, *Bureaucracy,* and Johnson, *Frederick the Great and His Officials,* the older, but still valuable studies by Wilhelm Naudé, "Zur Geschichte des preussischen Subalternbeamtentums," *Forschungen zur brandenburgisch und preussischen Geschichte* 18 (1905): 1–22; Johannes Ziekursch, *Beiträge zur Charakteristik der preussischen Verwaltungsbeamten in Schlesien* (Breslau, 1907); Otto Hintze, "Der österreichische und preussische Beamtenstaat im 17. und 18. Jahrhundert," in *Staat und Verfassung,* vol. 1 of *Gesammelte Abhandlungen,* (Göttingen, 1962), 321–59; Hintze, "Der preussische Militär- und Beamtenstaat im 18. Jahrhundert," in *Gesammelte Abhandlungen,* 3: 419–29; Walter L. Dorn, "The Prussian Bureaucracy in the Eighteenth Century," *Political Science Quarterly* 46 (1931): 403–23, and 47 (1932): 75–94, 259–73; Reinhold A. Dorwart, *The Administrative Reforms of Frederick William I of Prussia* (Cambridge, Mass., 1953); Henri Brunschwig, *Enlightenment and Romanticism in Eighteenth-Century Prussia* (Chicago, 1974).

non-nobles were debarred from purchasing estates, the possession of which remained the privilege of the aristocracy. As he put it himself, Frederick endeavored to "maintain the balance between peasant and nobleman."[65] In practice this meant that aristocrats were prevented from *Bauernlegen* (i.e., the forcible eviction of peasants and confiscation of their land) and instead were expected to provide a certain amount of protection for their unfree peasants. But the king's policy aimed at the perpetuation of dependence, believing that the bonded peasant would be easier to control as a soldier in his army. Town burghers and peasants could not acquire estates, precisely because Frederick deemed them unfit for the *métier d'honneur,* that is, to become officers in his army. As Otto Büsch has convincingly shown, the entire civilian system was relegated to a service function for the army.[66] The aristocrat was needed as officer in the army, just as the unfree peasant was required to serve as common soldier. The two systems, civilian and military, dovetailed at the local level, where the bonded peasant was frequently the subject of the very same nobleman in whose company he was forced to serve in the army, and the aristocratic officer commanded the same peasants in his military unit that worked his estate at home.[67] In this system of almost total social control, the military and the bureaucratic sectors intersected as well. Superannuated officers often became high-ranking officials, for they "knew how to obey and command respect."[68] And about two-thirds of the income of Frederick's small, but well-administered, state was used for military purposes.[69]

Even though, in Frederick's conception, the aristocracy formed "the foundation and the pillars of the state,"[70] the peasants and the town burghers had their function as well. Peasants paid for the bulk of state revenue (in the form of the *Kontribution,* a kind of rural property tax) and provided cannon fodder for the army. Town burghers, a small minority of about 20 percent of the population, enjoyed a virtual monopoly in trade (the nobility was prohibited from en-

---

65. Friedrich II, *Politisches Testament,* 43.

66. Otto Büsch, *Militärsystem und Sozialleben im Alten Preussen 1713–1807* (Berlin, 1962).

67. This dovetailing of the civilian and military sectors was made possible through the *Kantonsystem,* an invention of Frederick William I. In 1733 Prussia was subdivided into districts for military recruitment to end the steady drain on the civilian population caused by the forcible enlistment of soldiers. Each district, or *Kanton,* was under obligation to enroll enough soldiers to fill a regiment, whereby estate owners within that district often served as company commanders, and their bonded peasants as soldiers in their companies.

68. Friedrich II, *Politisches Testament,* 15.

69. With a population of fewer than five million (in 1740), Prussia ranked thirteenth in Europe, but it had Europe's fourth largest standing army (after France, Russia, and Austria). During the eighteenth century, almost 4 percent of the Prussian population was under arms, and military expenditures were a heavy burden on a basically poor state.

70. Friedrich II, *Politisches Testament,* 41.

tering commerce) and were heavily taxed as well. Town burghers were largely exempt from the universally dreaded and unpopular military service. Civilian life and military service were thus interlocked to an extent unknown elsewhere. Viewing Frederican Prussia from this vantage point, it is difficult to deny the validity of Mirabeau's dictum about Prussia as an army without a country.

This precise allocation of functions of the different estates and the interlinking of the civilian and military sectors (the latter being the raison d'être of Frederick's keen interest in the Prussian economy) had far-reaching consequences for Prussian society. As a result, Prussia was an unusually static country, its society was socially arrested, and there was but little social change. The eighteenth-century Prussian social cosmos was motionless but stable. In his model study, based on primary sources edited in the *Acta Borussica,* Otto Büsch has vividly depicted the inner functioning of a system that largely served to maintain the Prussian army. The functions performed by the landed aristocracy for the military were the justification of the cluster of privileges associated with ownership of an estate. There, the Junker not only decided on the life and fate of the peasant, who enjoyed neither freedom of movement nor the right to marry without his overlord's consent, but also supervised the local school and parish. In eighteenth-century Prussia, the state had no business interfering in the *Gutswirtschaft* (manorial social system). The peasant was at the mercy of the estate owner, for better or worse, since state administration reached down only to the *Landrat,* who was in charge of a *Kreis* (local district). But the overwhelming majority of *Landräte* were estate owners themselves. Though poor when compared to the English and French nobility,[71] the Prussian aristocracy enjoyed considerable social privileges. In the small realm of their estates, they were virtually sovereign. Frederick the Great was interested in perpetuating these privileges as long as the aristocrat performed his duty as an officer in the army. The nobleman's social position (in fact, Prussia's entire social system) thus rested on the military.

The social organization of eighteenth-century Prussia serves to explain the peculiar shape pauperism assumed in the first half of the nineteenth century.[72] The social reforms in Prussia were more comprehensive than those in other German states, and, at least in the short run, they brought upheaval and chaos to a country formerly characterized by its unusually rigid social organization. The reforms unbound the arrested society of the eighteenth century,

---

71. An interesting illustration of this are the memoirs of one of East Prussia's most renowned families and its exceedingly frugal lifestyle, in Marion Gräfin von Dönhoff, *Namen die keiner mehr kennt* (Köln, 1962), and Dönhoff, *Kindheit in Ostpreussen* (Berlin, 1988).

72. This is valid mainly for the old provinces of East and West Prussia, Pomerania, Silesia, and Brandenburg, not for the new acquisitions in West Germany (Westfalia and the Rhine Province) or for the province of Saxony. Posen, however, largely followed the eastern pattern, although the aristocracy there (being largely Polish) enjoyed fewer privileges.

undermined the very root of its social system—namely, the interlinkage of the civilian and military sectors—and dispensed with *Bauernschutz* and the old guild system. The implementation of the agrarian reforms, which began with the famous *Oktoberedikt* of 1807, was a gradual process, drawn out over more than half a century and still incomplete by 1848. The revolution and the new agrarian legislation that followed it (in 1850) accelerated completion. Even though the final word on the root causes of pauperism and the social question in Prussia has not yet been spoken, it is clear that there is a causal connection between the reforms and pauperization.[73] Impoverishment of the rural lower classes was severest in East Elbian Prussia, where, at least temporarily, the removal of such protective prohibitions as *Bauernschutz* wrought havoc. The stated purpose of the high-echelon officials who conceived the reforms was to do away with all obstacles and impediments that could hinder the released energies of an unbound society. The bureaucracy had thus "created" pauperism to a greater extent in Prussia than elsewhere.

The edict of October 9, 1807, pronounced the abolition of serfdom (*Erbuntertänigkeit*) for all peasants by 1810. It created a new legal status for the erstwhile bonded peasant but failed to regulate the pressing issue of property relationships between the estate owners and the different classes of peasants—specifically, how services, dues, and tributes were to be compensated for, and how the future tenure of land was to be regulated.[74] Before these matters were addressed in the *Regulierungsedikt* of 1816[75] and the

---

73. One of the central theses in Reinhart Koselleck's *Preussen zwischen Reform und Revolution* is that with the reforms, the bureaucracy had created a social problem it was unable to master afterward.

74. On the liberation of the peasantry and the implementation of the agrarian reforms see Friedrich Lütge, *Geschichte der deutschen Agrarverfassung vom frühen Mittelalter bis zum 19. Jahrhundert,* 2d ed. (Stuttgart, 1967), 222–46; Koselleck, *Preussen zwischen Reform und Revolution,* 134–43; Hanna Schissler, *Preussische Agrargesellschaft im Wandel* (Göttingen, 1978); Klaus Vetter, *Kurmärkischer Adel und preussische Reformen* (Weimar, 1979); Nipperdey, *Deutsche Geschichte 1800–1866,* 33–69, 159–78; Hartmut Harnisch, "Die kapitalistischen Agrarreformen: Ihre Bedeutung für die Herausbildung des inneren Marktes und die industrielle Revolution in den östlichen Provinzen Preussens in der ersten Hälfte des 19. Jahrhunderts," in *Preussische Reformen 1807–1820,* ed. Barbara Vogel (Königstein, 1980), 111–32; Christof Dipper, *Die Bauernbefreiung in Deutschland* (Stuttgart, 1980); Josef Mooser, *Ländliche Klassengesellschaft 1770–1848* (Göttingen, 1984), 93–146; Wehler, *Gesellschaftsgeschichte,* 1:409–28; Robert M. Berdahl, *The Politics of the Prussian Nobility: The Development of a Conservative Ideology 1770–1848* (Princeton, 1988), 115–58; Francis L. Carsten, *Geschichte der preussischen Junker* (Frankfurt, 1989), 80–105; Sheehan, *German History,* 298–310; Ilja Mieck, "Preussen von 1807 bis 1850: Reformen, Restauration und Revolution," *Handbuch der Preussischen Geschichte: Das 19. Jahrhundert,* ed. Otto Büsch (Berlin and New York, 1992), 16–286.

75. The *Deklaration des Regulierungsedikts* of 1816 served to clarify and tighten the original *Regulierungsedikt* of 1811 which, in the opinion of estate owners unilaterally favored the peasants. Consequently, the edict of 1816 was geared toward the interests of estate owners.

Gemeinheitsteilungsgesetz of 1821, *Bauernschutz* was dispensed with. With the nullification of the *Bauernschutz* (which had been introduced by Frederick II to ensure the steady flow of army recruits), the Junkers were now given the opportunity to evict small peasants or buy them out for a pittance to round off their estates.

Roughly outlined, the agrarian reforms consisted of three parts in their final implementation. The *Regulierung* regulated compensation in land and money for the better-off *spannfähige* peasants, who could lay claim to ownership of land before 1763. The *Ablösung* pertained to the poorer peasants. And the *Separation* regulated the partitioning of the vast common lands in villages, woods, meadows, and pastures. The *Separation* meant the dissolution of the *Allmende* (common lands), from which estate owners profited most; the lowest class of peasants, who hitherto had used the common land to graze their cows or feed their pigs,[76] most keenly felt its loss.

There is general agreement that the estate owners were the winners of the reforms, and that the peasants, though they lost a great deal of land, survived the reforms and even emerged strengthened as a result. Those peasants able to exist independently consolidated their position and even grew in number, which was made possible by the enormous *Landesausbau,* the increase of tillable land.[77] Gains in land for the *Rittergüter* came through the *Regulierung* of the larger *spannfähige* peasants, who lost about one-third of their holdings on average, through the buying up and confiscation of smaller farmsteads (*Bauernlegen*), and especially through the *Separation.*[78] The Junkers thus enlarged and consolidated their possessions, the value of which rose considerably during the first half of the century. Increase in the value of their land, as well as sizable monetary benefits reaped by the *Ablösung,* enabled many estate owners to become agricultural entrepreneurs and successful speculators.[79]

---

76. Or to collect food for the winter. Throughout the Vormärz, wood remained the primary heating material, and after the *Gemeinheitsteilungen,* stealing wood became the most common (and steadily rising) offense in Prussia. Before the *Separation,* it could be collected by everybody; afterward collection became a punishable offense. See Dirk Blasius, *Bürgerliche Gesellschaft und Kriminalität: Zur Sozialgeschichte Preussens im Vormärz* (Göttingen, 1976).

77. See Wehler, *Gesellschaftsgeschichte,* 1:420–23, 417; Gunther Ipsen, "Die preussische Bauernbefreiung als Landesausbau," *Zeitschrift für Agrargeschichte und Agrarsoziologie* 2 (1954): 29–54; Nipperdey, *Deutsche Geschichte,* 159–61. Wehler cites figures according to which the amount of arable land almost doubled between 1815 and 1864, while waste land was cut by 83 percent.

78. The *Separation* was virtually carried out as an indemnity for lost feudal rights and privileges. Consequently, 86 percent of the land of the former *Gemeinheiten* went to the estates, only 14 percent to the free peasantry.

79. Schissler, *Preussische Agrargesellschaft im Wandel;* Nipperdey, *Deutsche Geschichte 1800–1866,* 162; Wehler, *Gesellschaftsgeschichte,* 1:422–24; Ilja Mieck, "Preussen von 1807 bis 1850," in Büsch, *Handbuch* 138–42.

Between the 1820s and 1870s, more than two-thirds of all East Elbian estates are alleged to have changed ownership by either sale or auction.[80] In addition to obvious material benefits reaped by the reforms, the Junkers largely retained their social privileges, such as *Patrimonialgerichtsbarkeit* (local jurisdiction), local police powers, supervision of school and church, the *Kirchenpatronat,* the right to appoint village mayors, and other privileges that entailed monetary fringe benefits, such as a decisive voice about the location of thoroughfares and roads, and the right to grant concessions, such as excise licenses. Even after the reforms, social control over the now legally free peasants, the village inhabitants, and the rural proletariat, the *Landarbeiter,* was still ensured. In the wake of the revolution, some of these privileges were discontinued (e.g., patrimonial justice and hunting rights), but the social position of the East Elbian aristocracy remained unshaken at least until 1872, when a new *Kreisordnung* curtailed their local perquisites.

In his landmark study on *Bauernbefreiung,* which set standards for generations to come, Georg Friedrich Knapp claimed that the foremost social result of the agrarian reforms was the creation of a vast rural proletariat, the *Landarbeiterschaft.*[81] Today there is a general consensus that the rural proletariat antedated the reforms and that there was a landless, impoverished substratum of the rural population well before 1800.[82] But the reforms exacerbated the problem and were responsible for a substantial growth of this lowest rural class. Peasants too indigent to be considered by the *Ablösung* and others whose plots had been bought up and who were subsequently evicted swelled the rural proletariat. Then there were those who had to redeem their corvée[83] by regular monetary payments in the form of an annual rent, which frequently exceeded their means and led to their eventual destitution. With these small peasants, estate owners could choose between buying them up and confiscating their

---

80. And after midcentury, about half of all estates were owned by non-nobles, though the rich bourgeois were deliberately kept at bay when it came to sharing power in the local and regional diets, the *Kreistage* and *Landtage,* which continued being dominated by the aristocracy.

81. Georg Friedrich Knapp, *Die Bauernbefreiung und der Ursprung der Landarbeiter in den älteren Teilen Preussens,* 2 vols. (Leipzig, 1887). On the older historiography of the reforms see also Bernd Faulenbach, *Ideologie des deutschen Weges* (Munich, 1980), 140–52; 200–208; Walter Hubatsch, *Die Stein-Hardenbergschen Reformen,* 2d ed. (Darmstadt, 1989). For a representative survey of the more recent literature see Barbara Vogel, *Preussische Reformen 1807–1820* (Königstein, 1980), and Ilja Mieck, "Preussen von 1807 bis 1850," in Büsch, *Handbuch,* 19–31.

82. See, Wehler, *Gesellschaftsgeschichte,* 1:424–28; Nipperdey, *Deutsche Geschichte 1800–1866,* 165–67; Mieck, "Preussen von 1807 bis 1850," in Büsch, *Handbuch,* 92–95. On the lower orders before the reforms see also Jürgen Kocka, *Weder Stand noch Klasse: Unterschichten um 1800* (Berlin, 1990).

83. *Frondienste* is the German term commonly used for the compulsory labor that had to be performed by the bonded peasant.

farmsteads or continuing to request compulsory labor.[84] After the reforms, the *Landarbeiterschaft* therefore not only grew in numbers but also changed its composition, being fed by new and different tributaries.

The *Landarbeiterschaft* consisted of several groups, which were distinct from each other by virtue of their different property status.[85] There were the *Eigenkätner*, who owned a *Kate* (hut), some land, and worked additionally for the estate; the *Instleute*, who worked a plot of estate land, had some possessions of their own, but were in the regular employ of the estate owner (and wholly dependent on him); the *Tagelöhner*, *Einlieger*, and *Heuerlinge*, who were without possessions and a clearly defined service contract; and finally, the *Gesinde*, or farmhands.[86] The *Gesinde* was composed of the sons and daughters of small peasants and the family members of other *Landarbeiter*. Its members had free board and lodging, but no possessions and no stake in the estate. The *Gesindeordnung* of 1810 made certain that they were at the mercy of the landed squirarchy. In 1839 the *Instleute* equally became subject to the *Gesindeordnung*, and in 1846, service books (*Gesindedienstbücher*) for all farmhands were introduced, tightening control even further. As a result of the partition of common lands, those only loosely associated with the estate without defined terms of employment, such as the *Eigenkätner*, *Tagelöhner*, *Einlieger*, and *Heuerlinge*, suffered most. Before the reforms, they had lived off the village community, since they could freely use the common lands to graze their cows, pigs, or sheep. Now these common lands had vanished. In times of need, those more closely connected with the estate, such as the *Instleute* or *Gesinde*, could rely more on their *Herrschaft*, in whose interest it lay to provide for them. The servants and farmhands on the estate, for example, while completely without rights and subject to the whims of the master, were less exposed to the vicissitudes of the market than, for example, the "better-off" *Eigenkätner*.[87]

---

84. See Nipperdey, *Deutsche Geschichte 1800–1866*, 161.

85. There are different typologies in the literature, largely supplementing each other. The most detailed ones are to be found in Wehler, *Gesellschaftsgeschichte*, 1:170–71, 426–28, 2:166–68; Nipperdey, *Deutsche Geschichte 1800–1866*, 165; Hardtwig, *Vormärz*, 77–84.

86. See Nipperdey, *Deutsche Geschichte 1800–1866*, 165; Wehler, *Gesellschaftsgeschichte*, 1:170–71, 2:166–69; Christoph Dipper, *Die Bauernbefreiung in Deutschland 1790–1850* (Stuttgart, 1980). In the winter months, when there was little work on the estate, the *Eigenkätner* usually supported himself by protoindustrial cottage industries.

87. It is hazardous to translate such terms as *Tagelöhner*, *Instleute*, etc., because social conditions in nineteenth-century England were not comparable to those in Prussia. The English language has therefore no expression exactly corresponding to, e.g., *Instmann*. It did not seem advisable to translate *Eigenkätner* as "sharecropper", though their legal and economic positions were similar. "Sharecropper" is usually used as a translation for the French *métayer*, whose position corresponded in many ways to that of the small peasant in the Prussian east. See Emile

Population Growth

This multifaceted substratum beneath the free peasantry grew dispropor-
tionately during the *Vormärz* and was largely responsible for the population
explosion in the Prussian east. In East Prussia, for example, the numbers of
Eigenkätner, Inste, and *Tagelöhner* grew on average five to six times as fast as
that of independent peasants; the *Landarbeiterschaft* as a whole more than
tripled in size.[88] To contemporaries, this homeless and atomized class seemed
to be particularly dangerous precisely because of its rootlessness. And for the
overpopulation of the countryside, no relief was in sight, since migration to the
larger cities was virtually impossible before the 1860s. Not only would it have
been difficult to find employment before the onset of industrialization, but
urban poverty, too, was widespread. There were few large cities in Prussia to
begin with.[89] And cities had the power to keep out unwelcome strangers. Until
1867 it was almost impossible for the rural pauper to obtain the right of
domicile, or *Niederlassungsrecht.* Only large sums of money, influential spon-
sors with municipal citizenship (*Bürgerrecht*), and the guarantee that the newcomer would not become a charge on municipal poor relief could open to him
city gates that otherwise remained firmly bolted.[90] It naturally lay in the cities'
own interest to keep out paupers, who would not only constitute a potential

---

Guillaumin, *The Life of a Simple Man* (Middletown, Conn., 1986). In some instances the original
meaning of the term throws light on the legal and economic positions, such as in *Inste*
(*Eingesessener* in medieval low German).

88. See Nipperdey, *Deutsche Geschichte 1800–1866,* 166. On the growth of the German
population after 1815 see in addition to Nipperdey, *Deutsche Geschichte 1800–1866 ,* 102–14;
Peter Marschalk, *Bevölkerungsgeschichte Deutschlands im 19. und 20. Jahrhundert* (Frankfurt,
1984); Rürup, *Deutschland im 19. Jahrhundert, 1815–1871,* 22–33; Hardtwig, *Vormärz,* 67–70;
Wehler, *Gesellschaftsgeschichte,* 2:7–25.

89. On population figures of Prussian cities before 1850 see "Die über den preussischen
Staat gesammelten statistischen Nachrichten," Staatsarchiv Merseburg, rep. 77, titel 94. Prussian
cities of more than 20,000 inhabitants (in 1846) included the following: Berlin, 408,502; Breslau,
112,194; Köln, 90,246; Königsberg 75,234; Danzig, 66,827; Magdeburg, 55,816; Aachen, 48,557;
Stettin, 45,807; Posen, 43,058; Potsdam, 39,551; Elberfeld, 38,249; Barmen, 34,932; Krefeld,
33,548; Halle, 33,072; Erfurt, 31,277; Frankfurt/O., 30,432; Düsseldorf, 26,309; Münster, 24,193;
Koblenz, 23,431; Elbing, 22,246.

90. On the *Ständeschranken* to keep out foreigners and the difficulties of obtaining domicile, let alone citizenship, see Jürgen Reulecke, *Geschichte der Urbanisierung in Deutschland*
(Frankfurt, 1985); Lothar Gall, *Bürgertum in Deutschland* (Berlin, 1989); Wehler, *Gesellschaft-
geschichte,* 2:18–20; and the well-documented example of Frankfurt/M. in Koch, *Deutsche
Geschichte 1815–1848,* 161–68. Even the wealthy newcomer could not expect to succeed rapidly
in a new city; someone born in Hamburg, for example, could not get very far in Frankfurt or
Cologne within one generation. On urban life and its privileges in Hamburg see Percy E. Schramm,
Neun Generationen, vol. 2 (Göttingen, 1964); and on how that city organized poor relief see Mary
Lindemann, *Patriots and Paupers: Hamburg 1712–1830* (New York and Oxford, 1990).

menace for public security but also deplete local poor relief funds.[91] The valve of domestic migration was opened fully only when freedom of movement was introduced on the territory of the North German Confederation in 1867, and by then the advent of industrialization allowed cities to absorb new populations.[92]

There were three main reasons for the disproportionate growth of the rural proletariat, all of which were causally connected with the reforms. First, the most impecunious peasants, considered by neither *Regulierung* nor *Ablösung*, augmented the *Landarbeiterschaft*. Second, the increased amount of soil under cultivation combined with a growing demand for labor (due to intensified and differentiated tillage and new crops) temporarily heightened demand for rural labor. And third, marriage restrictions were removed—notably the landlord's consent was no longer needed to start a family.[93] All these explain the much faster population increase in Prussia's eastern, predominantly agrarian provinces, which were primarily affected by the reform legislation.[94] With the sole

---

91. On public security in Prussian cities see the study by Elaine G. Spencer, *Police and the Social Order in German Cities: The Düsseldorf District 1848–1914* (De Kalb, 1992).

92. To a limited extent, overseas migration provided an escape valve: from the territory of the future Empire, 210,000 emigrated during the 1830s, 480,000 in the 1840s, and 1,161,000 in the 1850s. See Nipperdey, *Deutsche Geschichte 1800–1866*, 114; Wehler, *Gesellschaftsgeschichte*, 2:17.

93. In contrast to a majority of historians on this subject (from Werner Conze to Thomas Nipperdey), Hans-Ulrich Wehler—while conceding that "in some German states the effects of the reforms sooner or later accelerated the demographic processes" (*Gesellschaftsgeschichte*, 2:9)—makes it clear that he does not believe that the population explosion can mainly be ascribed to the reforms. In his eyes, this argument was but an "ausserordentlich zählebige Legende" (ibid., 7). Wehler argues that the expansion of the European population started well before the mid-eighteenth century and that this expansion was mostly agrarian. As major reasons for population growth, Wehler puts forward the "ubiquitous protoindustrial cottage industry" (ibid., 8), the development of a more differentiated agriculture, and the improved economic situation after the Seven Years' War. These reasons, however, do not explain why the population increase in Prussia's eastern provinces was so much steeper than in the west.

94. On comparative population growth in different Prussian provinces see Wehler, *Gesellschaftsgeschichte*, 2:11; Nipperdey, *Deutsche Geschichte 1800–1866*, 103; Wolfram Fischer et al., eds., *Sozialgeschichtliches Arbeitsbuch: Materialien zur Statistik des deutschen Bundes 1815–1870* (Munich, 1982), 42; for smaller towns, "Die über den preussischen Staat gesammelten statistischen Nachrichten," at *Staatsarchiv Merseburg*, rep. 77, titel 94; and for differences between *Stadt-* and *Landkreise*, "Vergleichende Zusammenstellung der Einwohnerzahl des Preussischen Staates in den Jahren 1840–1855," *Archiv für Landeskunde der Preussischen Monarchie* 4 (1856): 212–27. Between 1816 and 1865, population growth was steepest in the eastern provinces—West Prussia, 121 percent, Pomerania, 111 percent; East Prussia, 100 percent; and Posen, 87 percent—while the population of the western provinces grew at a slower rate—Province Saxony, 72 percent; Westfalia, 57 percent, Rhine Province, 81 percent (see Nipperdey, *Deutsche Geschichte 1800–1866*, 103). During the *Vormärz*, differences were even more pronounced: between 1816 and 1846 the population of East Prussia grew by 67.88 percent, that of West Prussia by 80.26 percent, and the Pomeranian population by 71.17 percent, while population

exception of the kingdom of Saxony, Prussia was the fastest growing German state after 1815. Its population rose from 10.4 million in 1816 to almost 20 million in 1865, and after the annexations within Germany following the war of 1866, Prussia's population (24 million) had even overtaken England's (23.2 million).

The most important reason for the growth of the lower classes in Prussia was undoubtedly the abrogation of marriage restrictions. Between 1815 and 1867, Prussia was virtually the only state within the confines of the future empire that imposed no limitations on marriage. Restrictive regulations were in force in the southern German states of Bavaria, Württemberg, and Baden, and in Saxony and the duchy of Holstein, marriage was prohibited for those who received poor relief. In Mecklenburg, the old checks remained in force, and in practice, marriage was conditional on the consent of estate owners; but despite these limitations, pauperism was rampant in primarily rural Mecklenburg. In the kingdom of Hannover, proof of sufficient food supply (*Nahrungsstand*) and acceptance by a commune was required for matrimony, while in most of the smaller principalities, such as Sachsen-Weimar, Sachsen-Coburg-Gotha, Sachsen-Altenburg, and Schwarzburg-Sondershausen, communes remained powerful, because it lay in their jurisdiction to decide issues concerning the acceptance of newcomers and marriage licenses. Against this backdrop of other German states, Prussian legislation appeared exceedingly liberal.[95]

During the *Vormärz*, the urban poor were as badly off as the rural poor, but urban poverty remained numerically far less significant, as most of the Prussian population lived in the countryside. The few Prussian cities were small by European standards. By the mid-nineteenth century, according to a recent estimate, only 20 percent of the Prussian population were members of the bourgeoisie in the wider sense, that is, including lower ranking civil servants and municipal employees.[96] Even within the larger context of the German Confederation, no city could equal the metropolises of Western Europe, such as London (2.3 million inhabitants in 1850) or Paris (over 1 million inhabitants). Vienna and Berlin had just over 400,000 inhabitants (450,000 and 420,000, respectively), Hamburg had 175,000, Munich and Breslau had just over 100,000 and Dresden and Cologne were getting close to the 100,000 mark.[97]

---

growth in the Rhine Province was a mere 42.10 percent, and in Westfalia only 35.84 percent (see Staatsarchiv Merseburg, rep. 77, titel 94).

95. Matz, *Pauperismus*, 175–81.

96. Jürgen Kocka, "Zur Schichtung der preussischen Bevölkerung während der industriellen Revolution," in *Geschichte als Aufgabe: Festschrift für Otto Büsch*, ed. Wilhelm Treue, (Berlin, 1988), 357–90. For population figures of Prussian cities see n. 89 above.

97. On population figures see Wolfgang Köllmann, ed., *Quellen zur Bevölkerungsstatistik Deutschlands 1815–1875* (Boppard, 1980), 225–27; Reulecke, *Geschichte der Urbanisierung in Deutschland*, 203; Wehler, *Gesellschaftsgeschichte*, 2:11–18; Wolfram Siemann, *Gesellschaft im*

In Saxony, the Prussian Rhineland, and Berlin, an urban proletariat emerged during the 1840s, but industrialization did not begin changing urban life until a decade later. According to the Prussian statistician Dieterici, there were exactly 553,542 "factory workers" in Prussia (in 1846), most of them working in small establishments hardly deserving the name factory.[98] Still, in the contemporary discourse on pauperism and the social question, urban poverty and notably the nascent industrial proletariat played a role far greater than mere numbers might indicate. This was due to the concentration and crowding of paupers in cities and to their greater visibility there, combined with fear that the atomized and restless urban proletariat was more dangerous politically than its rural equivalent. The urban poor also seemed to constitute a greater danger to the moral order of society. Between 1815 and 1850, well over 50 percent (in some cases as much as 75 percent) of the population in Prussian cities belonged to the lower classes. For Germany as a whole, the percentage was generally higher in towns dominated by trade and commerce than in administrative centers, and it grew with the deepening of the social crisis in the 1840s.[99]

Prior to industrialization, the urban lower classes were complex and multifaceted in their composition. They naturally differed in accordance with the type of town they lived in. A Hanseatic seaport like Rostock had a different social composition than a *Residenzstadt* like Weimar or a larger center of commerce like Cologne. By and large, however, diversity can be reduced to five distinct categories: those formerly employed in protoindustrial cottage industries, underemployed master artisans and journeymen, domestic servants, day laborers and other unskilled workmen without steady employment, and those urban poor who existed on poor relief.[100] Among the most destitute were

---

Aufbruch: Deutschland 1849–1871 (Frankfurt, 1990), 243–49; Mieck, "Preussen von 1807 bis 1850," in Büsch, *Handbuch,* 90; and, for more detailed information, "Vergleichende Zusammenstellung der Einwohnerzahl der Städte des preussischen Staates von 1840–1855," *Archiv für Landeskunde der Preussischen Monarchie* 4 (1856): 228–46.

98. Koselleck, *Preussen zwischen Reform und Revolution,* 698. This is not a significant percentage, given that a total population of sixteen million had just been reached in 1846.

99. See Kocka, *Weder Stand noch Klasse,* 96–108. Kocka shows that at the end of the eighteenth century, the proportionate share of the lower classes in the total population was higher in *Handelsstädte* and *Gewerbestädte,* such as Rostock and Barmen, than in *Verwaltungstädte* and *Regierungsstädte* of comparable size, such as Koblenz. On the urban lower classes see also the articles by Antje Kraus and Bernd Weisbrod in Hans Mommsen and Winfried Schulze, *Vom Elend der Handarbeit: Probleme historischer Unterschichtenforschung* (Stuttgart, 1981), 243–57; 334–57; Nipperdey, *Deutsche Geschichte 1800–1866,* 219–48; Wehler, *Gesellschaftsgeschichte,* 1:193–202, 2:241–81; Wolfgang Kaschuba, *Lebenswelt und Kultur der unterbürgerlichen Schichten im 19. und 20. Jahrhundert* (Munich, 1990); Mieck, "Preussen von 1807 bis 1850," in Büsch, *Handbuch,* 152–57.

100. In the Rhine Province with the best communal relief system, one out of twelve persons were supported by communal poor relief. See Mieck, "Preussen von 1807 bis 1850," in Büsch, *Handbuch,* 155; Siemann, *Gesellschaft im Aufbruch,* 164. For the lower classes in pre-March

not only beggars, orphans, and disabled soldiers (and in seaports, out-of-work sailors), but also the very lowest class of civil servants, the so-called *Unterbeamte*.[101]

The most ambiguous group was that of the artisans, many of whom had descended only during the *Vormärz* into the pauperized substratum of urban life. In Prussia, numbers of master artisans, journeymen, and other assistants associated with the artisanate more than doubled between 1815 and 1850, a disproportionate rise with regard to the overall Prussian population.[102] This increase was due largely to the introduction of freedom of trade, and many craftsmen were pauperized as a result of it. Most members of the artisanate thus remained adamantly opposed to freedom of trade, industrial capitalism, and factories and mass-produced articles, in which they viewed a mortal threat to their own existence. As a result, they found themselves in a political quandary. During the *Vormärz,* many artisans were part of the vanguard of the liberal movement, fighting for constitutional government, freedom of the press, and political rights for the people at large, and against the bureaucratic state. In their social and economic demands, however, they aimed at the restoration of a preindustrial, *ständisch*-regulated order, and they displayed deep suspicion toward the capitalist economy. They feared social change, unfettered competition, and the factory system, and they resented the destruction of guilds, for all these changes brought in their wake the very real danger of social decline. The artisan dreaded nothing more than decline into the industrial proletariat, even if, as members of a skilled work force, many artisans soon counted among the industrial proletariats' better-paid members.[103]

Berlin see the vivid descriptions (both originally published in 1846) by Friedrich Sass, *Berlin in seiner neuesten Zeit und Entwicklung* (Berlin, 1983), 147–83, and Ernst Dronke, *Berlin* (Berlin, GDR, 1987), 209–30.

101. Such as the *Zuträger, Aktenhefter,* and *Einheizer,* who gained fifty taler a year or less, while the subsistence level lay at well over one hundred taler. On the industrial proletariat see also Werner Conze and Ulrich Engelhardt, eds., *Arbeiterexistenz im 19. Jahrhundert* (Stuttgart, 1981); Mommsen and Schulze, *Vom Elend der Handarbeit;* Jürgen Kocka, *Lohnarbeit und Klassenbildung: Arbeiter und Arbeiterbewegung in Deutschland 1800–1875* (Berlin and Bonn, 1983); Helga Grebing, *Arbeiterbewegung: Sozialer Protest und kollektive Interessenvertretung bis 1914* (Munich, 1985), 37–66.

102. Their numbers rose from 404,289 in 1816 to 942,373 in 1849; that is, from 3.8 percent to 5.7 percent of the total Prussian population. See Nipperdey, *Deutsche Geschichte 1800–1866,* 211.

103. These generalizations are to be taken with a grain of salt, since regional differences in the artisans' material conditions were great and political preferences varied accordingly. Yet there is a startling discrepancy between the artisans' economic and social demands and their political views. See Wolfram Fischer, "Das deutsche Handwerk in den Frühphasen der Industrialisierung," in *Wirtschaft,* 315–37; Nipperdey, *Deutsche Geschichte 1800–1866,* 210–19; Hardtwig, *Vormärz,* 84–88; Wehler, *Gesellschaftsgeschichte,* 2:54–64; Sheehan, *German History,* 771–75.

The salient feature of the emerging industrial proletariat was its heterogeneity. The social recruitment base of the urban and rural lower classes was so diverse and the wage differences so great that, as Wolfram Fischer put it, there was originally no "common economic class condition."[104] Even in smaller factories, the best paid laborers, often former artisans with a specialized skill, could earn twelve times the amount of the lowest paid youths or children working in the same establishment. The perpetuation of preindustrial traditions, the continued differentiation between lesser and better occupations (which stemmed from the old guild system), regional and linguistic differences between factory workers (reflected in different customs and dialects), and antagonisms between those from towns and others from the countryside combined with huge wage differentials hardly fostered sentiments of belonging to a common class. The absence of a "common economic class condition" entailed lack of class consciousness.[105] In the recruitment of the industrial proletariat from the rural and urban lower classes, four main groups can be distinguished: craftsmen, that is, impoverished masters and journeymen; those formerly employed in protoindustrial cottage industries; untrained day laborers without steady employment in the towns; and the vast group of former rural laborers, which, after the 1850s, migrated west to populate the growing cities in the Ruhr. Not until the 1860s did the industrial proletariat constitute itself as a distinct social class, with all the changes in mentality and social circumstance that entailed.[106]

Nowhere were the profound social changes that destroyed traditional Prussian society perceived more acutely and nowhere did they cause greater concern than with conservatives in Prussia, whose identity was dependent on the established patterns of life. Liberal entrepreneurs, notably in Westfalia and the Rhineland, as well as members of the Hegelian School, equally deliberated on the subject and published their thought on the social question, but the issue did not cut as close to the bone as it did with conservatives, whose existence

---

104. Fischer spoke of the absence of a "gemeinsame wirtschaftliche Klassenlage." See Wolfram Fischer, "Soziale Unterschichten im Zeitalter der Frühindustrialisierung," in *Wirtschaft*, 255.

105. In the early stages of industrialization, more complex articles continued to be fabricated by craftsmen, while the factory specialized in simpler mass-produced articles. As a result, work in the factory, requiring less skill, enjoyed little prestige, though it was, for the most part, better remunerated. See Fischer, "Soziale Unterschichten" in *Wirtschaft*, 242–57.

106. For a case study see Hartmut Zwahr, *Zur Konstituierung des Proletariats als Klasse: Strukturuntersuchungen über das Leipziger Proletariat während der industriellen Revolution* (Berlin, GDR, 1978); for a briefer orientation see Zwahr, "Zur Konstituierung," in *Ein anderer historischer Blick: Beispiele ostdeutscher Sozialgeschichte*, ed. Georg Iggers (Frankfurt, 1991), 41–56.

was more immediately affected and who seemingly had the most to lose. There was an astonishing continuity of conservative social thought from the early 1830s until the unification of Germany. And their ideas were especially pertinent because they were close to the centers of power, so that there was a greater chance of thought being translated into action.

PART I

Prussian Conservatives and the Social Question

The Berliner Politisches Wochenblatt and the Beginnings of Social Conservatism in Prussia, 1830–41

The term *Prussian conservatism* evokes a whole array of mostly negative images. One may think of haughtily smiling officers, commonly associated with Wilhelminean Germany; of the square, dull faces of East Elbian Junkers; of thin-lipped authoritarian schoolmasters who were the terror of their pupils; or of seemingly incorruptible Prussian bureaucrats whose decisions, as critical scrutiny often revealed, tended to favor their own class. For the late Empire, the term may conjure up the even more familiar cliché of industrialists from the Ruhr with huge bellies, huge fortunes, and consciences as malleable as the ores consumed by their furnaces. And, of course, there are the goose-stepping soldiers with their oversized moustaches and spiked helmets.

Our negative images of possible embodiments of Prussian conservatism are countless. Though politically vastly outnumbered, conservatives epitomized the Prussian type, for they were commonly associated with the *staatstragende* classes, notably the Junkers, who, in foreign eyes, seemed to dominate political life in Prussia and even the German Empire. In the decade before the First World War, Prussians, those descendants of "mongrel Slavonic savages," in Chesterton's succinct phrase, had become universally feared and hated in the West.[1] In England and France (and to a certain extent also in

---

1. Günther Blaicher, *Das Deutschlandbild in der englischen Literatur* (Darmstadt, 1992), 22. After 1871, these clichés frequently did correspond to the reality of life in Wilhelminean Germany, but they gained international prominence through allied propaganda only during the First World War. In the trenches, English soldiers were repeatedly reminded that their principal foe was Prussia.

Russia), Prussia was held responsible for turning Germany, that erstwhile heaven of "poets and thinkers," as Madame de Staël had characterized it, into a belligerent great power. But then Prussia itself had undergone a sea of change in foreign opinion. Before 1866–71 it was looked upon fondly by England, whose politicians, if anything, faulted it for excessive caution in foreign affairs. During the height of the Seven Years' War, England's ally Prussia, hailed as a "bastion of Protestantism," and its universally admired king, Frederick II, experienced a rare popularity unequaled by any other country.[2] The generally high opinion in which Prussia was held in western capitals during the first two-thirds of the nineteenth century depended on its timid reserve in foreign affairs. After 1815 Prussia was the least significant of Europe's five great powers and a serious threat to no one. This changed abruptly, first with the French, through Prussia's unexpected victory in the war against Austria (1866), and then with England, by dint of the Franco-Prussian war.[3]

But before these clichés arose, there was a Prussia quite different in character, and not only to the foreign eye. Even to critical Prussians, the country (notably its upper classes) seemed different before it merged into a larger Germany; it was shaped by frugal habits, modest in outward display, measured in tone.[4] And Prussian conservatism, too, was different in character than its later negative image. The most obvious difference was in its foreign policy orientation. Until 1866 conservatives were for the most part antinational in orientation, opposed to the creation of a nation state, opposed to all foreign policy adventures, and staunchly clinging to an alliance with Austria and Russia, even if this turned out to the detriment of Prussia's position in Europe, as in the case of the Olmütz treaty.

There are several possible typologies to classify German conservatives before 1870. Among the better-known ones are those of Klaus Epstein and Hans-Ulrich Wehler.[5] Epstein differentiated between the "status quo conservative," who clings to what he has; the "reform conservative," who is prepared to make some concessions to permit gradual change; and the "reactionary," who

2. See Manfred Schlenke, "Das friderizianische Preussen im Urteil der englischen öffentlichen Meinung 1740–1763," in *Geschichte in Wissenschaft und Unterricht* 14 (1963): 209–20. Schlenke argued that the early years of the war saw a "Preussenbegeisterung wie ihn kein anderes Land zu irgendeiner Zeit je erlebt hat." For more details see also Manfred Schlenke, *England und das friderizianische Preussen 1740 bis 1763* (Freiburg, 1963).

3. For France see Claude Digeon's brilliant study of French opinion toward Germany, *La Crise Allemande de la Pensée Française* (Paris, 1959), which clearly shows the rupture of 1866, and Klaus Rudolf Wenger's *Preussen in der öffentlichen Meinung Frankreichs 1815–1870* (Göttingen, 1979); for England see Blaicher, *Das Deutschlandbild in der englischen Literatur.*

4. See Marion Gräfin Dönhoff, *Preussen: Mass und Masslosigkeit* (Berlin, 1987).

5. See Klaus Epstein, *The Genesis of German Conservatism* (Princeton, 1966), esp. 3–29; Hans-Ulrich Wehler, *Deutsche Gesellschaftsgeschichte*, vol. 2, (Munich, 1987), 442–55.

is bent on restoring an earlier condition.[6] Wehler distinguished between *Beamtenkonservatismus*, which, according to him, increasingly came to dominate the civil service after 1820; the unbending *altständisch-patrimonialer* conservatism, for which Friedrich Ludwig von der Marwitz was a typical representative; the *legitimistisch-neuständischer* conservatism, which was more flexible and open to reform; the *pragmatischer Staatskonservatismus*, which was geared toward "preservation of the existing, 'narcotization,' repression of conflicts, if necessary;"[7] and finally the *Reformkonservatismus*, which displayed not only a tendency toward reconciliation with the modern constitutional state but also an openness toward the social question and efforts "to defuse it with the help of political intervention."[8] These typologies, though interesting and stimulating, do little to elucidate differences among social conservatives in Prussia, who, by dint of the narrow definition, already constitute a group by themselves. In the case at hand, the introduction of abstract categories might cloud rather than highlight differences among them.[9]

Relatively little has been written on social conservatism per se after 1945. There are a number of monographs on individual figures and two articles dealing with the phenomenon in general, though partly focusing on a later period.[10] Before 1939 the topic attracted greater interest, reflected in a number of dissertations on social conservatism in Prussia.[11] Loss of interest in social conservatism after the Second World War may well be part of a larger trend that signified dwindling interest in German conservatism before 1870. Was this seemingly intrinsic lack of interest due to the wholesale condemnation of

---

6. Epstein applied this typology in his discussion of conservative political attitudes in Germany between 1770 and 1806.

7. Wehler, *Gesellschaftsgeschichte*, 2:451.

8. Ibid, 2:452.

9. In part 1, chapter 4, Epstein's typology will be applied to different types of conservatives within the bureaucracy.

10. See, e.g., Wolfgang Saile, *Hermann Wagener und sein Verhältnis zu Bismarck: Ein Beitrag zur Geschichte des konservativen Sozialismus* (Tübingen, 1958); Wolfgang Scheel, *Das "Berliner Politische Wochenblatt" und die politische und soziale Revolution in Frankreich und England* (Göttingen, 1964); Sabine Hindelang, *Konservatismus und soziale Frage* (Frankfurt, 1983); Johann Baptist Müller, "Der deutsche Sozialkonservatismus," in *Konservatismus—Eine deutsche Bilanz,* ed. Helga Grebing et al. (Munich, 1971), 67–98; Jacques Droz, "Préoccupations Sociales et Préoccupations Religieuses aux Origines du Parti Conservateur Prussien," *Revue d'Histoire Moderne et Contemporaine* 2 (1955); 280–300.

11. See, e.g., Hildegard Goetting, "Die sozialpolitische Idee in den konservativen Kreisen der vormärzlichen Zeit" (Ph. D. diss., University of Berlin, 1920); Karl E. Femerling, "Die Stellung der konservativen Partei zur gewerblichen Arbeiterfrage in der Zeit von 1848–1880" (Ph. D. diss., University of Halle, 1927); Ingwer Paulsen, "Viktor A. Huber als Sozialpolitiker" (Ph.D. diss., University of Berlin, 1937); Walter Früh, "Radowitz als Sozialpolitiker: Seine Gesellschafts- und Wirtschaftsauffassung unter besonderer Berücksichtigung der sozialen Frage" (Ph. D. diss., University of Berlin, 1937).

German conservatism after 1945, or did renewed probing into the earlier conservatism before 1870 simply promise too few new revelations? Since the mid-1960s, the conservative *Verbände* of the Empire, especially of Wilhelminean Germany, have attracted the attention of critical historians. Those (few) German historians interested in the conservatism before 1870 seem mostly to have identified with Prussian conservatism themselves.[12] Recently a more critical tone has come to pervade the discussion.[13] For those historians who wrote on Prussian conservatism in the prewar period, it frequently had a *Leitbildfunktion*—they hoped to derive from its teachings implicit lessons for the present time. The fact that conservatives in Prussia evinced strong social inclinations underlined their sense of obligation toward the lower classes and pointed to the strength of the Prussian-German model. After 1945 this was of no more consequence. Yet with the inner concern and cause for research, mere interest seems to have vanished as well. In regard to conservatism, other questions (e.g., conservatives' relationship to different social groups in society or questions of organization) predominated, and "social conservatism" seemed to have become almost immaterial.

Robert Berdahl's recent *The Politics of the Prussian Nobility* offers an excellent analysis of the agrarian reforms, a discussion of the changing social position of nobility and peasantry in East Elbian Prussia, and a sophisticated examination of Adam Müller's conservative thought, but it pays little attention to the pronounced social concerns so paradoxically evinced by Prussian conservatives. Even in his chapter on the *Wochenblatt* circle, Berdahl focused on religion and politics and virtually ignored their social preoccupations.[14] But Berdahl's book contains instructive evaluations of the conservative thought of

---

12. This may not be entirely accurate, as I am especially thinking of Hans-Joachim Schoeps, whose numerous articles on the Gerlachs, Hermann Wagener, and the *Berliner Politisches Wochenblatt* remained for decades the only publications on these topics. Some of the more recent works, such as Frank-Lothar Kroll's *Friedrich Wilhelm IV und das Staatsdenken der Deutschen Romantik* (Berlin, 1990), certainly do not fall in this category.

13. See the examination of conservatism in Thomas Nipperdey, *Deutsche Geschichte 1800–1866* (Munich, 1983) 313–20, 732–34; Panajotis Kondylis, *Konservatismus: Geschichtlicher Gehalt und Untergang* (Stuttgart, 1986); Hans-Ulrich Wehler, *Deutsche Gesellschaftsgeschichte*, 2:409–12, 440–57, 464–65, 575–77; Wolfgang Schwentker, *Konservative Vereine und Revolution in Preussen 1848/49* (Düsseldorf, 1988); Eckhard Trox, *Militärischer Konservatismus: Kriegervereine und "Militärpartei" in Preussen zwischen 1815 und 1848/49* (Stuttgart, 1990).

14. Robert Berdahl, *The Politics of the Prussian Nobility: The Development of a Conservative Ideology 1770–1848* (Princeton, 1988). This is of course not meant to belittle the interesting chapter, "The Gerlach Circle and das Berliner Politische Wochenblatt," (ibid., 246–63) where, among other things, Berdahl offers an interesting discussion of the *Wochenblatt*'s criticism of capitalism.

Haller and Stahl, which this one, insofar as it deals exclusively with those conservatives who focus on social issues, virtually omits.

Before 1848 there was no parliament and there were no parties in Prussia—none of the Catholic, conservative, liberal, or socialist groupings of later years. The country was governed by a Hohenzollern king (Frederick William III, 1797–1840; Frederick William IV, 1840–58), whose nominal powers were virtually absolute. He set the long-term political goals, while the day-to-day political decisions were made by a bureaucracy that was the most highly developed of its day and age. Between 1815 and 1848, the Prussian bureaucracy was at the zenith of its power, and historians agree that the officials' authority was practically absolute; some have even gone so far as to speak of a dictatorship of the bureaucracy.[15] The country had no written constitution until December 1848, even though Frederick William III had promised one, first during the Napoleonic Wars, then again after 1815. Later it conveniently occurred to the Hohenzollern that they did not want to have "a piece of paper" between themselves and their people. To the dismay of many liberals, Prussia thus remained without a constitution despite unceasing pressure from the liberal bourgeoisie for the earlier redemption of the king's promise, until the Revolution of 1848 wrested it as a reluctant concession from the monarchy.

After 1815, Europe's governing circles lived in permanent fear of a repetition of the events of 1789. Especially within the territory of the German Confederation, where Metternich's system was firmly established, those in power were stricken with terror when remembering 1793. The Carlsbad Decrees of 1819 had nipped in the bud the liberal political movement. Professors and students, standard bearers of liberal and national aspirations, were kept under surveillance. The press was chained. And in Mainz a "Central Investigating Committee" for the "suppression of subversive activities" had been created. In short, authorities searched, interrogated, and suppressed. Anyone who delivered revolutionary speeches and was said to have attacked the system of restoration by turning against the prevailing power structure in word or deed was sent to a fortress or, if of lower social standing, thrown into a common jail. Police records in most European countries contained detailed information about illustrious personalities, but none were kept more meticulously than those of Prussia. Travelers were shadowed, conversations at table reported, and countless letters tampered with. Thousands of suspects fell victim to the Carlsbad Decrees (which continued in effect until April 1848). Two thousand were snared by the different principalities in the period between 1833

---

15. On the power of Prussian officials between 1815 and 1848 see Hermann Beck, "The Social Policies of Prussian Officials: The Bureaucracy in a New Light," *Journal of Modern History* 64 (1992): 263–98, esp. 264–65.

and 1839 alone. Most were arrested. Some were sentenced to death. The former Prussian state archives house a myriad of files on these clandestine goings-on, all of which were diligently recorded.[16]

A convenient excuse for these repressive measures was the murder of August von Kotzebue, a popular playwright and best-selling author of the time. Kotzebue's books sold better than those of his contemporary Goethe, but he was also widely despised for being an agent of the Czar and a symbol of reaction. Kotzebue was stabbed on March 23, 1819, in Mannheim, then a center of liberal politics, by theology student Carl Ludwig Sand, a onetime member of the "Giessener Schwarzen," one of the first and most active *Burschenschaften,* which were then at the forefront of the struggle against reaction.[17]

Sand's deed brought an end to an era, for between 1819 and 1830, political discussion ended, and the silence of a graveyard descended over the forty-one member states of the German Confederation. The 1820s were marked by the Heidelberger *Romantik,* by the longing for the lost world and values of the Middle Ages. Above all, the period was characterized by the politically tranquil *Biedermeier,* the age of the content *Kleinbürger.* Nothing symbolizes this epoch's outlook on life better than Caspar David Friedrich's painting *Two Men in Contemplation of the Moon.* Contemplation of nature, absorption in the observation of the sunset, petty bourgeois portliness, a comfortable complacency often referred to as *Gemütlichkeit,* a promenade on a Sunday afternoon (well captured in another of Friedrich's paintings), and the savoring of the little joys of everyday life were the characteristic features of the 1820s. During this decade, virtues, values, and habits of the petty bourgeoisie were formed, and the furniture of the *Biedermeier,* the interior decor of the epoch, remained the ideal-typical manifestation of the spirit of the German bourgeoisie until well into the twentieth century. A mode of living, later contemptuously referred to as *spiessbürgerlich,* or philistine, was formed during that time. During the Biedermeier, the *Spiessbürger* was in his element; he was the epitomy of his time, politically as abstemious as is his whole age.

All this changed drastically with the July Revolution of 1830 in Paris. In Chemnitz and Vienna, there were riots because of dearth and unemployment. Constitutions were promulgated in Braunschweig, Saxony, Hanover, and Kurhessen. Only Prussia remained calm.

---

16. Still one of the best studies on the overall mood of the period is Frederick B. Artz's volume in the "Rise of Modern Europe" series, *Reaction and Revolution, 1814–1832* (New York, 1963).

17. For a lively (and very sympathetic) account of Sand's deed, see Gustav Wiederkehr, *Mannheim in Sage und Geschichte,* 5th ed. (Mannheim, 1958).

The first news of the successful revolution in Paris reached Berlin on the second of August. During that evening, those gathered at the soirée in the royal palace conceived a plan to found a new, conservative newspaper. This select dinner circle included the crown prince (later Frederick William IV), the privy councillor von Ancillon, and Count von Voss-Buch, who later was to become an active member in Prussia's first conservative circle of political significance. The group had become dismayed at how revolutionary events in Paris had been represented in the two existing Berlin newspapers, the *Vossische Zeitung* and the *Haude- und Spenersche Zeitung.* The indignant gentlemen gathered in the tea room at Monbijou saw an urgent need for a press organ defending the interests of the antirevolutionary party. Their meeting eventually resulted in the foundation of the *Berliner Politisches Wochenblatt,* and with it of a group of conservative thinkers, who formed the vanguard of Prussian conservatism.[18]

The conservative groupings that existed in Prussia before 1830 were of little consequence for social conservatism. They were part of either political romanticism or the so-called *altständisch* opposition against the reforms, notably the agrarian reforms, spearheaded by Friedrich August Ludwig von der Marwitz. In Berlin a small circle of *konservative Romantiker,* as they came to be called, had come into existence during the time of French occupation. This was the *Christlich-deutsche Tischgesellschaft,* with Achim von Armin and Adam Müller as presiding members, founded on January 18, 1811, the anniversary of the Prussian coronation day (1701), when Frederick I, "king in Prussia" (i.e., only in East Prussia and not in the boundaries of the Holy Roman Empire) had been crowned in Königsberg. Other significant members of the group were Heinrich von Kleist, Clemens von Brentano, Johann Gottlieb Fichte, Karl von Clausewitz, and Friedrich Karl von Savigny. This first conservative circle was continued between 1816 and 1818 in the so-called *Maikäferei,* a coterie of conservatives, who met at an inn in Berlin (run by an innkeeper named Mai).[19]

---

18. See the literary bequest of Graf Carl von Voss-Buch, *Staatsarchiv Merseburg,* rep. 92, no. 32. Voss-Buch's *Nachlass* contains autobiographical notes referring to the foundation of the *Berliner Politisches Wochenblatt.* These are partially reprinted in Robert Arnold, "Die Aufzeichnungen des Grafen von Voss-Buch über das Berliner Politische Wochenblatt," *Historische Zeitschrift (HZ)* 106 (1911): 325–41; for a different interpretation see Carl Varrentrap, "Rankes historisch-politische Zeitschrift und das Berliner Politische Wochenblatt," *HZ* 99 (1907): 33–119.

19. On political romanticism in Prussia see Sigmund Neumann, *Die Stufen des preussischen Konservatismus* (Berlin, 1930), 68–112; Karl Mannheim, "Conservative Thought," in *From Karl Mannheim,* ed. Kurt H. Wolff (New York, 1971), 132–222, and for a more complete version of the text, David Kettler, Volker Meja, and Nico Stehr, eds., *Karl Mannheim: Konservatismus* (Frankfurt, 1984); Friedrich Meinecke, *Weltbürgertum und Nationalstaat* (Munich, 1962); Carl Schmitt, *Politische Romantik,* 3rd ed. (Berlin, 1968); Alfred von Martin, "Weltanschauliche Motive im altkonservativen Denken," and Jakob Baxa, "Romantik und konservative Politik," in *Konser-*

The *altständisch* conservatives, a small group of Junkers from the Mark Brandenburg, inextricably linked with the name Marwitz, originated as an opposition group against the reforms. Their protest fell, however, on deaf ears with their fellow noblemen, most of whom were quick to perceive the material opportunities proffered to them by the reforms. Marwitz was violently opposed to the bureaucratic rule that emerged in the wake of the reforms, to agrarian capitalism, and to the emerging modern state, which he believed would gradually erode the position of the aristocracy. Essentially, Marwitz wanted to turn the clock of time back to the sixteenth century, when the political might of the Prussian aristocracy was at its height, and when Junkers were bargaining on an equal footing with their sovereign over levying taxes. His most significant contributions to conservatism were probably the articulation of his deep-seated fear of social disintegration and atomization following the reforms, and a cultural criticism well captured in Robert Berdahl's study of Prussian conservatism.[20]

The *Christlich-Deutsche Tischgesellschaft* and the *Maikäferei* exerted some influence on the formation of the politically more influential circle that, after 1830, formed around the *Berliner Politisches Wochenblatt*. This *Wochenblatt* group (not to be confounded with the later *Wochenblattpartei*, led by Moritz August von Bethmann-Hollweg) included some active members of the former *Maikäferei*. Leopold von Gerlach, who later achieved fame as friend and councillor of Friedrich Wilhelm IV, was the connecting link between these circles. In the *Christlich-Deutsche Tischgesellschaft*, he already sat at the same table with Adam Müller and Fichte, and after 1816 he became one of the leading members of the *Maikäferei*. The latter group was pervaded by a more political spirit, in contrast to the mere aesthetic and literary ideals of the *Tischgesellschaft*, whose most prominent members, such as Achim von Arnim

vatismus in Europa, ed. Gerd-Klaus Kaltenbrunner (Freiburg, 1922), 139–81, 443–69; Henri Brunschwig, *Enlightenment and Romanticism in Eighteenth-Century Prussia* (Chicago, 1974); Ernst Klein, "Die Auseinandersetzungen Adam Müllers mit den wirtschaftstheoretischen und wirtschaftspolitischen Auffassungen seiner Zeit," in *Katholizismus, konservative Kapitalismuskritik und Frühsozialismus bis 1850*, ed. Albrecht Langner (Paderborn, 1975), 99–123; Hans-Joachim Schoeps, *Deutsche Geistesgeschichte der Neuzeit*, vol. 4 (Mainz, 1979), 9–47; the introduction to the collection of primary texts by Klaus Peter, ed., *Die politische Romantik in Deutschland* (Stuttgart, 1985), 9–75; Robert Berdahl, *The Politics of the Prussian Nobility: The Development of a Conservative Ideology 1770–1848* (Princeton, 1988), 158–82; Wilhelm Ribhegge, *Konservative Politik in Deutschland: Von der französischen Revolution bis zur Gegenwart* (Darmstadt, 1989), 54–58; Kurt Lenk, *Deutscher Konservatismus* (Frankfurt, 1989), 71–87.

20. See Berdahl, *The Politics of the Prussian Nobility*, 134–43; Martin Greiffenhagen, *Das Dilemma des Konservatismus in Deutschland* (Munich, 1977), 150, 228; Madelaine von Buttlar, *Die politischen Vorstellungen des F.L.A.v.d. Marwitz* (Frankfurt, 1980); Panajotis Kondylis, *Konservatismus: Geschichtlicher Gehalt und Untergang* (Stuttgart, 1986); Francis L. Carsten, *Geschichte der preussischen Junker* (Frankfurt, 1989), 80–105; Ribhegge, *Konservative Politik in Deutschland*, 44–45; Wehler, *Gesellschaftsgeschichte*, 2:442–45.

and Clemens von Brentano, are primarily remembered for their poetic works.[21] Adam Müller, the "conservative romantic," had been the political authority of the *Tischgesellschaft*. The more radical Karl Friedrich von Haller determined the political course of the *Maikäferei*, which was mostly frequented by officers and jurists; literary men were the exception rather than the rule.

These modest beginnings were to little avail. It can hardly be said that either group exerted any political influence beyond the narrow circle of its members. More important, neither of the two groups had a press organ at its disposal. The *Berliner Politisches Wochenblatt*, which started publication on October 8, 1831, was the first conservative paper in Prussia that voiced the opinions of "Old Prussia," that is, of conservative landowners and everyone who favored stemming the tide of revolution. "Nous ne voulons pas la contrerévolution, mais le contraire de la révolution," a phrase often used by De Maistre, became the slogan of the conservative weekly.[22]

Historians are not unanimous about exactly how the paper came into being. According to the notes of Carl von Voss-Buch, one of its founding members, the plan for the paper was conceived during the soirée on August 2, 1930, between the crown prince and some of his conservative advisers. In Voss-Buch's version, Josef Maria von Radowitz was not involved at all, even though Radowitz eventually became one of the most influential members of the *Wochenblatt* circle. In his short autobiography, Radowitz claims he himself conceived the idea of founding the paper.[23] The secondary literature is equally split on the issue. In his monograph on the *Berliner Politisches Wochenblatt*, Wolfgang Scheel favors Radowitz's account, whereas Hans-Joachim Schoeps, doyen of conservative pro-Prussian historiography, lends more credence to Voss-Buch. Neither of the two has strong arguments in favor of his own view. Because the *Wochenblatt* had difficulties with the rather rigid Prussian censorship from the very beginning, one might doubt whether the plan for the paper originated within official circles. That Ernst Carl Jarcke, the first editor-in-

21. See Ludwig von Gerlach, *Aufzeichnungen aus seinem Leben und Wirken,* vol. 1 (Schwerin, 1903); Hildegard Goetting, "Die sozialpolitische Idee in den konservativen Kreisen der vormärzlichen Zeit" (Ph.D. diss., University of Berlin, 1920); Baxa, "Romantik und konservative Politik"; Meinecke, *Weltbürgertum und Nationalstaat.*

22. See Hans-Joachim Schoeps, "Neue Briefe zur Gründung des *Berliner Politischen Wochenblattes,*" *Zeitschrift für Religions- und Geistesgeschichte* 13 (1961): 114–27; Heinrich von Treitschke, *Deutsche Geschichte im Neunzehnten Jahrhundert,* vol. 4 (Leipzig, 1928) 165, 199, 200; Wolfgang Scheel, *Das Berliner Politische Wochenblatt und die politische und soziale Revolution in Frankreich und England* (Göttingen, 1964).

23. See "Aufzeichnungen des Grafen Carl von Voss-Buch über das Berliner Politische Wochenblatt," Staatsarchiv Merseburg, rep. 92, no. 32, Carl von Voss-Buch (cited in n. 18 above); Paul Hassel, *Josef Maria von Radowitz, 1797–1848* (Berlin, 1905). See also Carl Varrentrap, "Rankes Historisch-politische Zeitschrift," 33–119; Robert Arnold, "Aufzeichnungen des Grafen," 325–41.

chief of the *Berliner Politisches Wochenblatt,* was prohibited from using the names originally envisaged, *Allgemeine Staatsanzeigen* or *Preussische Annalen,* casts doubt on the account of Voss-Buch, which, incidentally, was not written until twenty years after the paper's foundation.

The committee of editors, initially composed of Wilhelm and Leopold von Gerlach, Carl von Voss-Buch, Joseph Maria von Radowitz, and Karl von Canitz, quickly raised the money necessary for the foundation of the paper: eight hundred taler, roughly the equivalent of the annual salary of a councillor in the ministry of the interior.[24] Other important members were soon to include Ernst Carl Jarcke, a legal scholar from Berlin University who, despite his youth, was famous for his pungent formulations, sarcastic wit, and trenchant pen; the historian Heinrich Leo from Halle University; and Ludwig von Gerlach, soon to emerge as one of the most eminent conservative Prussians in his century. Jarcke left the group after only one year to become a full professor at the University of Vienna, which, in the Protestant Prussian capital, had proved to be difficult, if not impossible, for a Catholic. But despite his short tenure, he exerted a strong influence on the paper.

The contributors to the *Wochenblatt* were split into an orthodox Protestant and a Catholic section. The brothers Gerlach, Heinrich Leo, and Voss-Buch were orthodox Lutherans, while Karl Ludwig von Haller and Jarcke, both recent converts to Catholicism, formed the Catholic section, together with Radowitz and Philipps, who later gained some renown through his collaboration in Goerres's *Historisch Politische Blätter.* These divisions were significant in an age when religious differences and issues often predetermined political controversies, and when the quest for political freedom manifested itself in attacks on Protestant or Catholic orthodoxy. *Religionskritik* and political criticism were thus often intertwined in a German Confederation dominated by Metternich's police state, since religious issues could provide the cover necessary for voicing one's true opinion in the stiflingly censored print media. The early political philosophy of the Young Hegelians in the 1830s (which largely

---

24. See Hassel, *Radowitz;* Ludwig von Gerlach, *Aufzeichnungen;* Hans-Joachim Schoeps, *Das andere Preussen,* 5th ed. (Berlin, 1981); Ludwig Salomon, *Geschichte des Deutschen Zeitungswesens von den Anfängen bis zur Wiederaufrichtung des Deutschen Reiches,* vol. 3 (Oldenburg and Berlin, 1906). The *Wochenblatt* was published every Saturday on Folioformat, and the yearly subscription was just over six taler. The editor, Jarcke, received a yearly salary of eight hundred taler, whereas Leopold von Ranke, editor of the *Historisch-Politische Blätter,* was paid only six hundred taler (by the state) for his editorial work. Varrentrap and Voss-Buch (see n. 23) both emphasize that the *Wochenblatt* obtained about 1,200 taler annually from the Prussian state, mostly during the later period of the journal's existence. State support became imperative after 1837, when the *Wochenblatt* took sides with the Prussian state (and against the Catholic church) during the *Kölner Kirchenstreit,* thereby losing a substantial number of its subscribers.

consisted of religious disputes) and the political stir created by a religious work, David Friedrich Strauss's, *Das Leben Jesu,* are prominent cases in point. Attacks on established religious doctrine and demands for the separation of the Catholic church from Rome were often implicitly associated with criticism of the police, the bureaucracy, or the censorship of the press. Restoration Europe also witnessed the end of the religious rationalism and indifference that had been the hallmark of the eighteenth-century Enlightenment. After 1815 a wave of re-Christianization swept over Germany, affecting private lives as much as public consciousness. And in Prussia, where the local parson continued being appointed by the landed squire, Protestantism served as a pillar and legitimation for those in power.[25] As a result of the often irreconcilable antagonism in which many religious controversies were fought—combined with the early suppression of political activities—political party disputes in Prussia later displayed a similar implacability. The religious and philosophical antagonisms of the 1830s thus adumbrated an important part of later German political culture.[26]

The *Wochenblatt* group, then, consisted of roughly half a dozen members, who also wrote the most important articles. There were Graf Carl von Voss-Buch, in whose palais in the *Wilhelmstrasse* the group often met (hence their nickname *Club von der Wilhelmstrasse*); Voss's friends and collaborators; and the brothers Leopold and Ludwig von Gerlach, both of whom remained important figures in Prussian politics until Bismarck became prime minister in 1862.[27] Leopold, a staff officer, later became general and an intimate adviser to Frederick Wilhelm IV, whose domestic policy he partially shaped as a member of Frederick Wilhelm's shadow cabinet, the *Camarilla.* Leopold's brother Ludwig, a high-ranking official in the judicial branch of the bureaucracy (*Gerichtspräsident*), was the theoretician among the brothers. He was closely acquainted with Ernst Wilhelm Hengstenberg and a regular contributor to

---

25. The same held true for Catholicism in other German states. Criticism of religion or tendencies toward de-Christianization were therefore noted with alarm. The conservative Friedrich Julius Stahl thus gloomily predicted in 1847: "Nimmt in der Nation die Lossagung vom christlichen Glauben zu, die sich jetzt so mächtig zeigt, so hören die öffentlichen Institutionen auf, vom Christentume bestimmt zu sein, so ist es nicht mehr möglich, das Ansehen des Königtums zu behaupten, wir erhalten in der unvermeidlichen Fortbildung unserer Verfassung nicht einen konstitutionellen Staat, sondern einen demokratischen" (cited in Rainer Koch, *Deutsche Geschichte 1815–1848: Restauration oder Vormärz?* [Stuttgart, 1985], 135).
26. See Franz Schnabel, *Deutsche Geschichte im 19 Jahrhundert,* 4 vols. (Freiburg, 1929–1936), vol. 7, *Die katholische Kirche in Deutschland,* vol. 8, *Die protestantischen Kirchen in Deutschland;* Hans Rosenberg, *Politische Denkströmungen im Vormärz* (Göttingen, 1972); Robert M. Bigler, *The Politics of German Protestantism* (Berkeley and Los Angeles, 1972); Nipperdey, *Deutsche Geschichte 1800–1866,* 403–40; Wehler, *Gesellschaftsgeschichte,* 2:459–77; James Sheehan, *German History, 1770–1866* (Oxford, 1989) 555–72.
27. See also Schoeps, *Das andere Preussen,* 1–70.

Hengstenberg's orthodox Lutheran *Evangelische Kirchenzeitung (EKZ)*, which commanded considerable authority over the moral issues of the time. The sovereign power of the king was vigorously defended in the columns of the *EKZ*, and by the mid-1840s, the name of the paper had become synonymous with reaction in political and religious matters. In the early forties, the *EKZ* had attacked the Left Hegelian *Hallische Jahrbücher*, thus setting itself up as the champion of the old order.[28] Ludwig von Gerlach was very much a man of this old order. He was no mere reactionary, however. His political ideals were braced by religious convictions as well as by active deeds, and as a frequent visitor of prisons in and around Berlin, the Prussian aristocrat could be heard preaching to the inmates. Heinrich Leo, a historian at Halle University, but better known as a member of the Hegelian Right, and Karl Ludwig von Haller, whose *Restauration der Staatswissenschaften* had become the standard work of restoration theory, were other central figures who contributed articles to the journal.

The Gerlachs, Voss-Buch, and Heinrich Leo were rooted in the world of Old Prussia. Their understanding of politics belonged to a prerevolutionary Europe. Within them, the old frondeur, the spirit of the Quitzows, the robber-knights of the fifteenth century who fought against the first Hohenzollern when they came to the Mark Brandenburg in 1415, was still alive. Their ideal state was a *Ständestaat*, a state in which the different estates—knights, town burghers, and free peasants—shared power with the king. Their world was the universe of the late Middle Ages, which they wanted to see restored—a demand that manifested itself by the strong opposition they voiced against the "absolute state" in the columns of the *Berliner Politisches Wochenblatt*.[29]

But this element of Old Prussia was but one ingredient of the conservatism of the *Wochenblatt*. Another was represented by Josef Maria von Radowitz and Carl Ernst Jarcke. Being Catholic, both were alien elements in the tightly knit world of the pietist Protestantism of the Gerlachs and other Prussian conservatives. Josef Maria von Radowitz, who, after a distinguished career in the service of the Hohenzollern dynasty, became foreign minister in 1849, is known mainly as the architect of the ill-fated *Unionspolitik* of 1850, and his name became thus inextricably linked with the humiliation of Olmütz. This and Bismarck's deprecating remarks about him as the "king's lackey" (in

---

28. See the important articles in the *Evangelische Kirchenzeitung*, such as "Über das Verhältnis der Kirche zum Staat," *EKZ* 26 (1840): 444–48; and "Woher kommt die Kirchenscheu der Königlichen Beamten im Preussischen Staat," *EKZ* 29 (1843): 425–31.

29. See *BpW*, April 6, 1833, "Revolution und Absolutismus"; *BpW*, February 22, 1834, "Von der Entwicklung der Gesellschaft"; *BpW*, September 27, 1834, "Absolutismus, Gerechtigkeit und Gemeinwohl"; *BpW*, December 29, 1832, "Die Doktrinen des Wochenblatts"; *BpW*, September 1, 1832, "Die politischen Parteien"; *BpW*, October 29, 1832, "Das Berliner Politische Wochenblatt am Schlusse des ersten Jahres seines Bestehens."

Bismarck's autobiography, *Gedanken und Erinnerungen*) did irreparable harm to his posthumous fame. Radowitz was born outside Prussia. Of Hungarian descent, he attended French military schools as well as the *Ecole Polytechnique* and even fought for Napoleon's armies in Saxony in 1813. At Leipzig, where the tide of battle turned for good against the French emperor, he became an allied prisoner of war and participated on the German side in the campaigns of 1814. His brief allegiance to the French forces earned him the lifelong mistrust of Prussian conservatives. Hengstenberg, for example, warned his friend Ludwig von Gerlach in 1831 not to collaborate with Radowitz, whom he believed to be a proselytizer.

The common denominator between the Gerlachs, Leo, and Voss-Buch, on the one hand, and Radowitz and Jarcke, on the other, was their opposition to any form of revolution. Shared concepts of the Middle Ages, the idea of the *Ständestaat,* and the role of the monarch made for further common ground. The most durable bond among them was their common reasoning with respect to organic growth, right (*Recht*), and law (*Gesetz*). These institutions of state and society, they argued, had matured only gradually, while rights and privileges had developed historically over the course of centuries.[30] Law, they believed, existed only in its given, organically matured form, as did claims, titles, and rights of possession. And only the gradual process of development could endow legitimacy on them.[31] The source of law was seen as twofold: it sprang from historical development (historical "becoming," as it was put) and from divine blessing. Historical development per se conferred divine legitimation.

The members of the *Wochenblatt* were unanimous on one other important point: abstract principles should not be applied to matters of state and society. General principles said to be rooted in natural law, such as "the rights of man" or "the sovereignty of the people," were therefore rejected from the start. Even Haller's restoration philosophy and Savigny's historical school of law, which both stood sponsor to the ideology of the *Wochenblatt,* were sometimes viewed critically. In short, there was an inherent mistrust of all kinds of closed systems, and it was on this foundation that the traditionalism of the *Wochenblatt* was based.[32]

Members of the *Wochenblatt* were men of practical affairs, civil servants, and political advisers. Even the "Right Hegelian" Heinrich Leo saw himself more as a man of action than as an inhabitant of a lofty ivory tower. Years of practical training, exposure to the world of power politics, firsthand knowledge

---

30. *BpW,* October 29, 1833, "Die Kraft und Schwäche des Liberalismus"; *BpW,* October 26, 1833, "Versuch einer systematischen Darstellung der politischen Parteien."

31. *BpW,* December 8, 1832, "Vom deutschen Bauernstande"; *BpW,* May 7, 1835, "Über den erblichen Adel als notwendigen Bestandteil der erblichen Monarchie."

32. *BpW,* February 15, 1834, "Von der Entwicklung der Gesellschaft."

of state affairs, and intimate acquaintance with those who ran the government found expression in their style. They wrote to be read and understood by an audience like themselves. Their foremost concern was not to construct great political and social schemes but to disseminate conceptions and ideas that could be understood by the educated reader. They never counted on popular appeal but catered to a conservative audience of elevated rank. Their discourse was naturally conditioned by the times and by their culture, so the modern reader studying the *Wochenblatt* is not always able to cast off the impression that a vituperative schoolmaster is speaking to him. Yet in contrast to the often impenetrably turgid prose of restoration and pre-March Germany—a prose designed more to conceal, camouflage, and dissemble (to mislead the censor) than to enlighten or inform—the *Wochenblatt* was eminently readable.

It is difficult, if not impossible, to situate the men around the *Wochenblatt* in an intellectual tradition, for they were not scholars, and they knew little of the political philosophy of past ages. Legal tracts, historical works (notably those closely acquainted with Prussian history and customs), and thorough study of the Bible (which also set criteria for right and wrong in everyday life) had been their intellectual fare and had influenced their formation. Haller and Heinrich Leo were undoubtedly well acquainted with contemporary European philosophy, especially with de Maistre and Bonald, but for the others, it was above all the German past, the Middle Ages and Prussian history, that had shaped their ideas. Then, of course, there was the shared hostility toward liberalism, the French Revolution, and the heritage of the Enlightenment. These joint aversions, together with the firm belief in historical development and the "good and vested rights," were the most solid common denominator of the group.

In a programmatic article commemorating the first anniversary of the *Wochenblatt*'s publication,[33] the editors emphasized that the "good and vested rights" were "divine rights, as it was divine will and commandment to hold sacred property and the right of the other." The article continued that

> only in the observation of this sphere of right lies freedom, and just as there is no freedom without *Recht*, so we believe there is no true inviolable right without the belief in divine commandment, which protects the rights and property of men.

Three fundamental political tenets pose a mortal threat to these "good and vested rights." The *Wochenblatt* calls them different forms of "absolutism": first, the concept of "the will of the people," that is, that the majority should determine what is right and wrong; second, the concept of "the dictatorship of

---

33. *BpW,* October 29, 1832, "Das Berliner Politische Wochenblatt am Schlusse des ersten Jahres seines Bestehens," 246–47.

the civil service," leading to "the most highly developed form of absolute officialdom"; and third, the concept of "modern liberal constitutionalism," which constitutes nothing but "the representation of current opinion." With *Absolutismus* (absolutism), the *Wochenblatt* characterized a state of affairs

> in which . . . an absolute principle or authority, be it absolute state-centeredness [*Staatsphilosophismus*], the Zeitgeist, or the will of the people, national glory, or the common weal, is set over duly acquired and vested rights [gute und wohlerworbene Rechte].

In plain speech this meant that everything that existed was sanctified by tradition—a world outlook corresponding to the arrested society of eighteenth-century Prussia. If one follows this line of thought, it suggests that the conservatives of the *Wochenblatt* were intent on absorbing newly developed protuberances of society into the already existing structure. The premises of their worldview rule out social change. This is an ideology ideally suited for the defense of inherited privileges. Nevertheless, one should not succumb to the temptation of lumping it together with the later reactionary conservative ideology of the German Empire. The conservative parties of the Empire were subservient to the crown to such a degree that our view of Prussian and German conservatism seems to imply outright obeisance, if not even servility, toward king or emperor.[34] In stark contrast to such political submissiveness, we read in the *Wochenblatt* of April 6, 1833, that "royal absolutism and revolution are but different aspects of one and the same thing, twin children of the same mother."[35] This rejection of royal absolutism is tightly connected with the *Wochenblatt*'s idealized interpretation of the *Ständestaat*. Just as *Gesetz* (i.e., law and vested rights) had developed organically, so had the *Stände* (the estates). The absolutism of the crown is discarded in favor of a state ruled jointly by estates and king. The existence of the different estates, the *Wochenblatt* asserted, "was based on the naturally determined difference of occupation, ways of life, customs, and interests" of the people; and the estates were "created and conditioned by nature." The diversity of interests in society and all aspects of the common weal (*Gemeinwohl*) were represented by the different estates of the aristocracy, the clergy, and the cities. Among them, that is, in the deliberations of the estates themselves, "the majority of votes did not commit the minority." None of the curiae (*Kurien*) could force a law against the privileges or *Rechtskreis* of the other, "but each curia granted or denied the

---

34. Literary illustrations of this that have also shaped our view of Prussian conservatism can be found in the novels of the imperial era, such as Heinrich Mann's *Der Untertan* (*The Man of Straw*) and Theodor Fontane's *Frau Jenny Treibel*.

35. *BpW,* April 6, 1833, "Revolution und Absolutismus" (third article), 83.

sovereign [the favors] which he alone had asked for."[36] The restoration of these lost liberties and political privileges was one of the foremost political goals of the *Wochenblatt*.

If one judges Prussian conservatism with the standard clichés in mind, one may overlook the fact that originally even the conservatives saw their own power checked by counterbalances. Their conservatism was not totalitarian. There were *Ständevertretungen* and *Ständegerichte* to maintain the good old *Recht*. This *Recht*, this "essential order," was not the same for everyone. It was characterized by inherent inequality: "the equality of law and, as its means, the uniformity of law in the whole country, was and is absolutism's real goal and ambition."[37] Conservatives were opposed to the codification of law and its concomitant rationalization, as this would necessarily result in the obliteration and standardization of naturally evolved differences. Inequality formed part of their identity and was one of their most fundamental tenets, just as the preservation and restoration of the prerevolutionary world was among their declared goals. This entailed automatic mistrust of all-encompassing principles. Such recurring statements as "absolutism has annihilated the autonomous monarchs and republics," that is, the *Grundherrschaften* and independent *Corporationen*,[38] clearly show that the ideology of the *Wochenblatt* was based on the historic experience of the Holy Roman Empire, with its free cities and countless principalities, each possessed of its own legal system and its own independent (*reichsunmittelbare*) *Ritterschaft*. The French and English aristocracies never knew comparable independence.

Profound distrust of the modern state and its bureaucracy were the inevitable by-product of this historic experience. The free ("immediate") *Reichsritter* knew no state above him. Consequently, the conservative Prussian Junker who felt connected to this tradition fought against the leveling forces of the emerging modern state. "If the state has to be the primary source of all law," wrote the *Wochenblatt* in February 1834, "private law loses its firm stance and the only barrier against the arbitrariness of despotism collapses."[39] In anticipation of what much later was to become a real danger, the article continued, "In this case, even the most brutal outrage can be justified by public interest and the maintenance of the state." "True freedom," the title and theme of the article, was considered to lie in the "*Rechts- und Freiheitssphäre jedes einzelnen*

36. *BpW*, March 30, 1833, "Revolution und Absolutismus" (second article), 77.

37. *BpW*, April 6, 1833, "Revolution und Absolutismus" (third article).

38. Ibid.

39. *BpW*, February 22, 1834, "Die Lehre von der wahren Freiheit." It is surely no accident that the most effective resistance group against Hitler's dictatorship stood in the tradition of Prussian conservatism, even though the men around Stauffenberg hardly justified their resistance to national socialism by reference to the ideas of the early Prussian conservatives.

Staatsmitgliedes,"[40] which indicated that it was above all freedom in the social microcosm that counted for conservatives.

Consequently, the *Berliner Politisches Wochenblatt* argued that freedom within the state was based not primarily on the *Regierungsform,* or form of government, but on the relationship between the "*Inhaber und Repräsentanten der Staatsgewalt*" (which could be a royal sovereign, a national assembly, or representatives of the people) and the "*Rechts- und Freiheitssphäre jedes einzelnen Staatsmitgliedes.*" It was the close supervision and scrutiny by the state, the bureaucracy, or the people that was deprecated, and *Wochenblatt* conservatives argued accordingly that "the true defenders of freedom are those who see the sphere of influence of the state limited by the *Rechtssphäre* of each individual member of the state." There was pronounced opposition to Rousseau, the "inventor of popular sovereignty, . . . who teaches that within the *Staatsverband* the individual has to transfer all his personal rights to the state."[41] This antagonism toward state, dynasty, bureaucracy, and the close control bureaucratic rule entailed, is one of the *Wochenblatt*'s salient features. Bureaucratic surveillance, *Wochenblatt* conservatives believed, stifled society's free development. Centralized power was therefore rejected in favor of particularist, regional, and *ständische* powers, such as estates or corporations. Where they prevailed, the individual enjoyed greater freedom. The Gerlachs, Radowitz, and other members of the *Wochenblatt* thus advocated a policy considered to be the hallmark of classical liberalism: as little state as possible. Dozens of articles in the *Wochenblatt* gave vent to their distrust of the monarch, royal absolutism, the bureaucracy, and an all-powerful people.

Despite common opposition to royal absolutism, the *Wochenblatt* conservatives reproached German liberals for being but pale copies of their English and French counterparts. More importantly, they criticized them for wanting to replace the historically grown *Verfassung* (which meant more than constitution; it also included customs and traditional rights) of their country with an artificially imposed one.[42] "What has been acquired naturally and lawfully in the course of time, be it for entire estates, for corporations, or for individuals, all this is the *Verfassung* of a country," Radowitz wrote in the *Berliner Politisches Wochenblatt* in 1832.[43] How, he asked, could an artificial constitution that had been drafted in a few days outlast the work of generations and centuries? A change of constitution, he held, "must always only be a product of a

40. *BpW,* April 19, 1834, "Die Lehre von der wahren Freiheit" (Schluss), 94.
41. Ibid.
42. Ibid.
43. *BpW,* September 1, 1832, "Die politischen Parteien," 221.

natural and lawful process."[44] Thus the members of the *Wochenblatt,* despite their common hostility toward the absolute monarchy, deemed liberalism's approach to reality entirely alien to their own.

According to the members of *Wochenblatt* group, the Prussia of the 1830s possessed a dangerous tendency toward becoming an absolute state (in their interpretation of the concept). For them the absolute state was governed by the rule of abstract law, not by the traditional *Recht. Recht* had its foundation "in the will of God," and man was not qualified to pronounce this divine will. *Recht* could be perceived solely by man's conscience and in the light of divine revelation, the *Wochenblatt* proclaimed. "Laws, i.e., man-made regulations, can therefore not be the source of Recht."[45] Even for positive law (statute law), customs and jurisprudence were seen as sources equally valid as royal decrees (*Verordnungen*). The best institutions for the administration of justice were therefore the instruments of self-government of towns, the *Ständeeinrichtungen,* and *Zünfte* (guilds).[46] These *Ständeeinrichtungen* were seen as natural checks on royal power. And that royal power had to have its narrowly defined limits was a cornerstone in the worldview of the *Wochenblatt* circle:

> The doctrine of the omnipotence of the king with his chambers—even against the command of God and the existing *Recht*—we consider to be slavish and nonsensical.[47]

Instead, the *Wochenblatt* recommended that institutions of private law, such as the guilds, assume again some of the functions the modern state seemed about to usurp.

In a long article on "The Doctrine of True Freedom," conservatives argue that guilds ought to assume policelike functions over their members. An idealized picture of the late Middle Ages is conjured up and elevated into a model worthy of emulation. In hindsight the late Middle Ages become a time of resplendent prosperity, a world without social ills or poverty, in which the individual was firmly integrated into the family. A universe is conjured up in

---

44. "Die Lehre von der wahren Freiheit." In his *Gespräche aus der Gegenwart über Kirche und Staat* (see chapter 2 below), Radowitz even professed an intellectual and emotional affinity to the Young Hegelians, whose aims he rejected, but whose idealism he felt akin to, whereas he completely dismissed everything the liberals stood for. It was especially the autonomy of the individual, proclaimed by the liberals, to which Radowitz was opposed. Radowitz was deeply convinced of the necessity of *Bindung,* of an integrating structure for the individual, which liberals so violently rejected. It was this element of *Bindung* that Radowitz recognized in the philosophy of the Young Hegelians and in the nascent socialist movement.
45. *BpW,* December 29, 1832, 332.
46. *BpW,* December 29, 1832, "Die Doktrinen des Wochenblatts," 331–32.
47. Ibid.

which "corporations of artists and artisans rose in vigorous activity," and where

> everyone celebrated merry evening hours in the guild-hall or the *Her-rendrinkstube* [public house] after a hard day's work, keeping many banquets and feasts throughout the year according to their guild's statutes and by-laws.

In times of hardship, the guilds would provide an instant support network to aid its impoverished members: "widows are not abandoned, their children not deserted."[48] The medieval concept of a regulated, God-given order thus became the foundation for the conservatives' reasoning. They promoted the idea of a closed society, where the individual was a cog in a larger machine, a society whose members were safe and provided for, but at the same time unfree and highly dependent on one another.

From the late 1830s until the demise of the paper in 1841, the conservatives' suggestions for a solution to pauperism reflected this backward-oriented, medieval ideal.[49] In the *Wochenblatt*'s depiction, the late medieval world appeared as an entirely self-regulating social cosmos: corporations and guilds helped their members who had come down in the world to get back on their feet again, the municipal council recruited its members from within the corporations, and "the guild ordinances and corporation bylaws were effectively police laws, the effectiveness of which reached the inner household of the master craftsman."[50] The members of the *Wochenblatt* thus clearly preferred tight supervision by the guilds—believed to be part of a natural social order—to the controlling eye of the state. This sounds reminiscent of Hegel's *Rechts-philosophie,* since in Hegel's conceptions, guilds and corporations also precede the state chronologically. To Hegel the Middle Ages constituted a corporate society without a state, in which the worth of each member was estimated in accordance with the profession he held. The high appreciation in which the Middle Ages were held was a characteristic feature of the times. The 1820s saw the heyday of the romantic movement in Germany that glorified the Middle Ages, and what the modern observer might disapprove of as infringements of personal freedom, contemporaries praised as achievements of late medieval city life. A case in point, for example, was the guilds' power to outlaw any master craftsman who did not abide by their regulations. He would publicly be dishonored (*ihm wurde der Schimpf erklärt*), which might well finish him off

---

48. *BpW,* February 22, 1834, "Die Lehre von der wahren Freiheit"; *BpW,* May 19, 1832, "Betrachtungen über Gewerbe-, Zunft-, und Innungswesen," 131.

49. See their later suggestion that knights' orders should be founded in the thinly populated eastern areas of Prussia to absorb the poor.

50. *BpW,* May 19, 1832, 131.

not only socially but also economically.[51] In the *Wochenblatt*'s representation of the arrested society of the late medieval city, social conflicts did not arise because everyone was firmly tied into the social fabric. Master craftsmen and journeymen were bound by a rigid system of regimentation. They were expected to greet each other according to a fixed ritual, the *Gesellengruss*, and the journeymen's association, the *Gesellenverband*, kept its members under close scrutiny, punishing deviation by instant expulsion, which left the ostracized journeyman the choice between starvation and emigration. The saying *Lehr-jahre sind keine Herrenjahre*, which is still being used today, testifies to the deplorable position of the *Lehrling*, or apprentice, who was at the very bottom of the guild pecking order. He received his orders from the master craftsman and the journeyman, was not allowed to smoke tobacco in public, was barred from frequenting public houses, and was prohibited from carrying a cane, the status symbol of the journeyman.[52]

This close-knit social network of the medieval artisanate naturally absorbed the poor and prevented the emergence of pauperized masses. In a *Wochenblatt* article on "The Teachings of Pauperism," the conservatives therefore argued that it was the government's duty "to favor the artisan profession" and the peasantry and "to do away with the despotism of financial power." The decline of the *Handwerk* was ascribed to the organization of the Prussian *Militärverfassung* in the eighteenth century, according to which "the son of the artisan was born to become a soldier." While traveling from town to town, as prescribed by custom, journeymen were frequently picked up by recruiting officers en route and forced into the army. This, the *Wochenblatt* group argued, undermined the reproduction of the artisanate, which "never regained its former greatness after the Thirty Years' War." Another development fatal to the *Handwerk* was the rise of a "system of factories and workshops" and the introduction of freedom of trade during the Reform Era. The conservatives of the *Berliner Politisches Wochenblatt* were convinced that freedom of trade in combination with the factory contributed to the "pauperization of cloth, linen, and stocking weavers, steel and brass workers, tanners, and others." With the dissolution of journeymen's associations, a corollary of *Gewerbefreiheit*, the traditional craftsman was destined to become extinct and, the *Wochenblatt* group believed, to be replaced by a "multitude of uncouth and dissolute workers."[53]

---

51. *BpW*, May 19, 1832, 131. He was publicly made an outcast, since his fellow guild members would not interact with him any more.

52. Similar economic concepts were discussed by conservatives at the end of the Weimar Republic. Conservatives' fascination with the economic order of the Middle Ages seems to have been rekindled whenever social change was overwhelming.

53. *BpW*, January 12, 1839, "Die Lehren des Pauperismus," 6; *BpW*, May 19, 1832, "Betrachtungen über Gewerbe-, Zunft-, und Innungswesen," 152.

Conservatives pointed out that a salient characteristic of the German craftsman was his knowledge of how to manufacture a product from start to finish—in stark contrast to English and French artisans, who were apprenticed in a factory-like manner.[54] The *Handwerker* was apprenticed in a *zünftig* fashion. After completing a long apprenticeship, he had to remain a journeyman for years before becoming a master craftsman and being admitted to a guild. This admission, in turn, enabled him to open his own shop. In contrast, English and French craftsmen, trained in a factory-like manner, knew how to produce only a part of the finished product.[55] The transition from journeyman to industrial laborer thus presaged a clear decline for the conservatives; while the journeyman was integrated into social groups, the industrial worker was uprooted and devoid of any moral bonds. For the conservatives of the *Wochenblatt,* this constituted the nucleus of the social problem: they were afraid of the "multitude of uncouth and dissolute workers,"[56] afraid that the mass of journeymen, apprentices, and dependent peasants, once freed from the "paternal" tutelage of guild and manorial obligations, would sweep away the existing order. Therefore, a recurring theme in many of the *Wochenblatt's* articles is that it lay "in the nature of man" to realize the "necessity of certain restrictions and limitations."[57]

This very theme has been a leitmotif in conservative thought throughout the nineteenth and twentieth centuries. The so-called "conservative revolutionaries" of the Weimar Republic regarded restrictions on personal liberty as an indispensable precondition for the functioning of society.[58] In 1927, Hugo von Hofmannsthal epitomized this when he said of the German youth that what they wanted above all were "engagements, commitments, and bonds—not freedom."[59] In the context of the 1830s, the restrictions the group around the *Berliner Politisches Wochenblatt* wanted to see imposed on society referred primarily to an undoing of the Prussian reforms and a return to what they considered the natural limitations of the prerevolutionary period. Conservatives argued that freedom of trade should be abolished and that guilds, corpora-

---

54. *BpW,* May 19, 1832, 131.

55. That was one reason why Karl Marx found that factory work alienated the worker from himself, as he was unable to identify with the product he had created. If Marx had been born an Englishman, this very concept of *Entfremdung,* which can be traced in Marx's writings as early as 1843, might well be missing from his philosophy.

56. *BpW,* May 19, 1832, "Betrachtungen."

57. *BpW,* May 13, 1837, "Über den Missverstand der Freiheit in volkswirtschaftlicher Beziehung."

58. See especially Kurt Sontheimer, *Antidemokratisches Denken in der Weimarer Republik* (Munich, 1968); Armin Mohler, *Die konservative Revolution in Deutschland 1918–1932,* 3d ed. (Darmstadt, 1989).

59. Hugo von Hofmannsthal, *Das Schrifttaum als geistiger Raum der Nation* (Munich, 1927), 27.

tions with special privileges, and privileged trading companies should be re-established in its stead. Liberalism as an economic theory and social philosophy was rejected per se, for "dependence is the only cohesive factor in society."[60] The autonomy of the individual was rejected in the same vein, for "to reach higher stages of development, greater or lesser restrictions on personal freedom are necessary."[61]

This notion of mutual dependence in society led conservatives to argue in favor of a neofeudal order. Subordination did have its benefits, they held, because the dependent person derives obvious advantages from the master. Subordination, therefore, must ultimately be considered to be "reasonable and just," as "it is not given to man to provide for his living in complete independence from others." Conservatives predicted that

> the fragmentation of civil society into individuals and the disintegration of all bonds, which give more security to the individual than the state could provide, will have grave results.[62]

They consistently argued in favor of a closed society that would be self-contained, regimented, but secure.[63] It would offer shelter to the individual but would also restrict his personal freedom. If the natural forces of society remained unchecked, widespread pauperization would only be a matter of time, conservatives believed. They also followed Malthus in rejecting the English poor law as a means of curbing poverty, as the poor law "only recognized the unconditional duty of the state to support every pauper." The solution to social problems did not lay within the competence of the state, but the state could restrict freedom of trade and industry, for "the higher the development of industrial freedom in a country, the more rapidly the caste of paupers will grow." A corollary to that was that "individual independence in respect to free competition" would have to be curtailed as a "salutary impediment to growing poverty." Conservatives argued that due to growing competition, "the working

---

60. *BpW*, May 13, 1837, "Missverstand."

61. Another perennial theme in German conservative thought that found a vociferous spokesperson in Thomas Mann, who, in his *Betrachtungen eines Unpolitischen* (1918), compared the "shallow civilization" of the liberal powers of Western Europe with the profound "Kultur" and "community spirit" of the German people, whose superiority he attributed precisely to the high degree of mutual dependence prevalent in German society.

62. "Missverstand."

63. In his *The Open Society and Its Enemies* (1943–45), Karl Popper attacked the concept of a closed society (which he discovered in Plato, Marx, and Hegel) as pretotalitarian. Popper's comparison between the ideal types of an "open" and a "closed" society and the concomitant mentalities is psychologically interesting. Popper's "closed" society has many traits in common with early Prussian conservatism and provides an explanation for their deep-seated fears of social mobility, free trade, economic competition, the atomization of society, and the free exchange of ideas.

class (*Arbeiterstand*) becomes ever more oppressed and dependent on the will of the factory owners."[64] The "unbridled, wild speculative spirit" of the industrial entrepreneur was thus blamed for the misery of the working classes.[65] It therefore had to be the duty of the state, conservatives expostulated, "to restrict competition" and eliminate "the grasping element" [das wegraffende Element], which referred to the industrial entrepreneur, whose ascendancy in society the *Berliner Politisches Wochenblatt* viewed with suspicion. They were not only blamed for "the lowering of the price of labor,"[66] which added to the impoverishment of the industrial worker, but were also seen as a threat to the vested social power of the East Elbian aristocracy.[67]

The growing importance of the industrial proletariat was recognized early on in Prussia. Those Prussians who, in the 1830s and 1840s, were interested in matters of state, society, and economy studied England as the country whose virtues they wanted to emulate and whose vices they wanted to avoid. Hegel had written an essay on the English Reform Bill, Radowitz and Ludwig von Gerlach had traveled to England in the 1840s, and in 1844 the young Friedrich Engels had written a widely publicized book about the condition of the working classes in Manchester. Viktor Aimé Huber, who edited a conservative journal between 1845 and 1847 in Berlin that was sponsored by the Prussian government (the *Janus*), had spent a relatively long period of time in England.[68] Huber was the author of a widely regarded book on English universities that was subsequently translated into English. Even a young, penniless apothecary apprentice, Theodor Fontane, had spent a week in London in the early 1840s.[69]

In Prussia itself a working class hardly existed in the 1830s. There was some industry in Berlin, several factories in the Rhineland, and a handful of large workshops in Prussia's second biggest city, Breslau in Silesia. And in the Silesian mountains, there were thousands of starving weavers, who rose against their exploiters in the uprising in 1844. England thus served as a model of things to come, and numerous articles in the *Wochenblatt* reflected the conservatives' preoccupation with the growing size of the industrial pro-

64. *BpW,* May 13, 1837, "Missverstand." The elimination of free competition became again a prominent issue in the last phase of the Weimar Republic, when conservatives (the DNVP) and national socialists were its strongest advocates.

65. *BpW,* August 28, 1841, "Bericht über die neuesten Zeitereignisse," 191.

66. *BpW,* May 13, 1837, "Missverstand."

67. *BpW,* August 28, 1841, "Bericht über die neuesten Zeitereignisse."

68. Huber's *Janus* was in a sense a successor to the *Wochenblatt* but never achieved its popularity. In its best years, the *Wochenblatt* had over 1,000 subscribers, while *Janus* had a circulation of about 750 copies in 1846, generally deemed to be its best year. It never had more than 200 subscribers. See Ingwer Paulsen, *Viktor A. Huber als Sozialpolitiker,* 2d ed. (Berlin, 1956).

69. A lively account of his visit can be found in the second part of Theodor Fontane's autobiography, *Von Zwanzig bis Dreissig.*

letariat. As a result, polemic onslaughts against "financial despotism,"[70] the "speculative spirit" of factory owners,[71] and liberalism, considered to be a "false religion," became more frequent.[72]

The gravest danger inherent in the new factory system—in addition to the creation of an industrial proletariat—was the threat it posed to the economic and social position of the landed squirarchy. If the aristocrat was to be supplanted by the rising industrial entrepreneur, damage to state and society would be irreparable, the *Wochenblatt* argued, for the state's well-being rested on the interplay of two social forces: the landed nobility in the countryside, and guilds and corporations in the towns. Moreover, behind the factory system—conservatives referred to it as "modern feudalism"—a "thunder cloud of a great social revolution" was lurking. With somber foreboding, the *Wochenblatt* diagnosed "great economic upheavals which have taken place," the "profoundly incisive consequences of which may perhaps surpass all those concussions which we today designate as revolution."[73] That was written at a time when only one railway line was in operation in Prussia. To conservatives, industrialization was the harbinger of a new age of barbarism, with the worker as "the bondsman of the new age." The "aristocracy of money and industry" that had replaced the feudal aristocracy, now exercised "a far more oppressive rule" over the lower classes, which had been "stripped of all the more lenient elements of religious belief and honor." The patriotism and concern for the public weal that the new industrial entrepreneur boasted was regarded to be nothing but a cloak for amassing riches, while the modern worker had been "abandoned to utter misery and moral depravation." Women and children, the *Wochenblatt* wrote, "are forced into servitude," and

> imprisoned in large slave colonies where, deprived of any education whatsoever, they are exposed to any temptation and thousands, whose health is ruined through poisoned air, find a premature death.

And if machines were ever to render the workers' labor power redundant, they would be left to "certain death by starvation or to the charity of the state."

> [The new] feudalism is—in short—the old aristocratic rule . . . that has been resurrected without poetry, faith, love and gallantry—and without humility; it is the old luxury, but without taste and without dignity, the old domination, but without the sacrificing generosity, without the disin-

---

70. *BpW,* January 12, 1839, "Die Despotie des Geldreichtums," 6; "Die Lehren des Pauperismus."

71. *BpW,* August 28, 1841, 191.

72. *BpW,* October 19, 1833, "Die Kraft und Schwäche des Liberalismus," 260.

73. *BpW,* June 6, 1837, "Der moderne Feudalismus," 134.

terestedness, without the voluntary devotion to a higher ideal; it is the old ambition, but without the innate morale [*Sitte*] and without the feeling of high pride, conceit without honor—in one word: it is the power of gold which has replaced the power of iron.[74]

Was all this a smear campaign by one privileged social group that felt in danger of being pushed aside by another? It was much more than that. There is a streak of antimodernism, a protest against the dawning new age in all this. It was a sort of *Kulturkritik*, focusing on contemporary social changes and their worst features. In an article on the railway, the rush and precipitation of modern life were deplored, and the *Wochenblatt* ceaselessly reiterated the theme that all aspects of life have become corroded by money: "where money tinkles, heavenly bells can't be heard." The spirit of the age, conservatives sadly alleged,

> hurries from pleasure to pleasure and pays no attention to nobler admonitions; it will not listen to impulses other than *Sinnenlust und Fleischesfreude.*[75]

The *Wochenblatt*'s antimodernism already indicates that its members were likely to turn to the past when seeking solutions to the social question.[76] Their particular point of view also inclined them to see the plight of industrial workers mostly in terms of moral depravation, in the "monstrous moral corruption" they were exposed to. Should the untamed, uneducated masses ever be in a position to dominate society, then the end of European culture would have come. For the men around the *Wochenblatt*, the potential of "untamed licentiousness, profligacy, and dissoluteness" was greater in modern times than in medieval society, the idealized feudalism of which conservatives much preferred to the *Industriesklaverei* of the modern age.

As early as 1835, conservatives polemicized against the employment of children in factories.[77] Child labor had been an issue in Prussia since 1818,

---

74. *BpW*, June 6, 1837 "Der moderne Feudalismus."

75. *BpW*, April 15, 1839, 82.

76. Antimodernism and antiurbanism were also frequent themes in the popular literature and poetry of the late nineteenth and early twentieth century in Germany, when the ever expanding industrial state seemed to engulf the last vestiges of the often idealized rural life. By 1900 the antimodernist and antiurban *Kulturkritik* had ceased to be a preserve of the political right; by then it had become a preoccupation of the avant-garde as well. See David L. Gross, "*Kultur* and Its Discontents: The Origins of a 'Critique of Everyday Life' in Germany, 1880–1925," in *Essays on Culture and Society in Modern Germany*, ed. Gary D. Stark and Bede K. Lackner (College Station, Tex., 1982), 70–98.

77. *BpW*, October 3, 1835, "Einiges über die sittlichen Zustände der niedrigen Klassen in England," 240.

when an industrialist in the Rhineland was publicly praised by the king for having established a factory school. With the attention of the authorities focused on him, it was soon brought to light that over three hundred children, some as young as six, were employed in the factory of the honored entrepreneur for day and night shifts and had to toil for a fourth of the wages of the adult workers. Since this incident, the attention of the bureaucracy had been drawn to the issue, and after much delay, on April 6, 1839, the *Regulativ zum Schutze jugendlicher Arbeiter in Fabriken* was passed, outlawing child labor under the age of nine.[78] The *Wochenblatt* castigated child labor as "morally shrivelling," as the manifestation of "a brutality that is indescribable," charging that in England, associations of factory workers "bully [and] commit crimes and cruelties," and that they were "killing and maiming deviating members." Factory work as such was considered to be "demoralizing," brutalizing the worker: "trustworthiness, moderation, industry, and domestic virtues seem to be wholly extinct among the lower classes."[79] According to the *Wochenblatt,* the morally demeaning nature of factory work had created the modern working class. It was a *novum* in history, for "only the modern age knows the proletariat," which in the long run "might become the most powerful lever of a social revolution."[80]

The specter of a social revolution is frequently conjured up by the *Wochenblatt,* especially in the later years of its existence. How could this seemingly unstoppable social change be harnessed? The growth of the proletariat was not considered as being solely due to the growth of population.[81] The northern half of Germany had been far more densely populated before the Thirty Years' War, the *Wochenblatt* group argued, and then no proletariat had existed. Conservatives were convinced that the revolutionary tide could be stemmed only if the old beliefs and checks that used to act on the lower classes were restored. The breakdown of Christian faith, the breaking-up of families, and the disintegration of the large family units that tilled the soil jointly had ultimately led to the formation of a proletariat. The instability of modern times, the breakdown of the old order, and the rootlessness of modern man had given the proletariat its restless, dangerous features. "Who is able to stand up for the multitude of the poor?" the *Wochenblatt* asked: "Who takes notice of these unfortunates? The state? Our philosophical state is but a dead idea . . . , offering punishment and discipline, not commiseration. Compassion is only to be found in charity and human sympathy." And these characterized only one

---

78. On factory legislation see part 2, chapter 8.
79. *BpW,* June 6, 1837, "Der moderne Feudalismus."
80. *BpW,* November 14, 1835, "Die Proletarier."
81. *BpW,* February 13, 1841, 35.

social group, the aristocracy, "which has both noble-mindedness and the means to help."[82]

The *Wochenblatt* thus argued that only the aristocracy would be equal to the task of reintegrating the proletariat into society. This could be done through the foundation of an aristocratic order, "molded after the old knight orders," that would have the function of serving and protecting the poor. As a practical matter, it could be implemented by establishing colonies for the poor in the underpopulated eastern provinces of Prussia, where, under tutelage of the aristocracy, paupers would be allocated a fixed amount of property. The benefits of this aristocratic order would be manifold. Not only would it increase the agrarian capacity of the east and reorganize trade and farming (in the medieval sense), but "educational establishments, catering houses, and welfare institutions of all kinds" would be built, and most importantly, "the aristocracy would find itself again in helping others":

> A brotherhood, becoming a knight's shield for poor people, would be [for the aristocracy] the most glorious task of the time, which can be realized only by the German aristocracy.

In the final analysis, the assistance the aristocracy was to give to the poor was thus conceived as an instrument of its own survival. Aristocrats, conservatives argued, ought to congregate in knights' orders "not only for the benefit of others, but also for the benefit of the aristocracy itself," for the "renovation, the conservation of this estate."[83] But this was written in 1841, when the original group had already disintegrated. Radowitz and the other Catholic collaborators of the *Wochenblatt* had become alienated from the circle after the *Kölner Kirchenstreit* and had gone their separate ways.

What then was the uniqueness and intrinsic importance of the *Wochenblatt* conservatism? Like most conservatives of the first half of the nineteenth century, the members of the group stood in an anti-Enlightenment tradition, polemicized against the French Revolution, and were influenced by political romanticism. For them life was governed not by rationality but by history; it was the gradual organic development that mattered, not abstract principles reflected in codified law or a written constitution. Foremost was the struggle against revolution, for in 1789 that monster had shown that moderately liberal beginnings were followed by dictatorship, terror, and the rule of the gutter. Future revolutions might take the same course; it seemed their inner consequence. Typical on a general level, but unique by dint of the vigor with which it was advocated, was the *Wochenblatt* group's idealization of the

---

82. Ibid.
83. Ibid.

Middle Ages; their emphasis on a naturally given order, embodied by *Stände* and *Zünfte,* and on natural inequality, a God-given hierarchy; and their pronounced antiliberalism. Man did not live by himself as an individual but was bound by social ties: family, corporations, estates, and the paternalistic relationship of the *Gutsherrschaft.* And the social and political power of those at the top was naturally based on mutual obligation: peasants performed services for the manorial lord in return for shelter, food, and other kinds of social assistance. Freedom from service and obligation was therefore not true freedom. The individual, conservatives argued, would be isolated and perish in atomistic solitude. Here one senses *Wochenblatt* conservatism's closeness to later socialist theories, equally anxious to tie the individual into larger social entities. And in some respect, the members of the *Wochenblatt* group anticipated later socialist (and conservative) criticisms of modernity. If viewed from this vantage point, their anticapitalism, their anti-industrialism, their antimodernism, and last but not least, their antiliberalism, which was causally connected with the other three, were extremely "modern."

Striking and unique is the strong backward orientation of the group around the *Berliner Politisches Wochenblatt.* Neither other Prussian conservatives, such as Carl Rodbertus or Viktor Aimé Huber, both of whom regarded modern industrial development as a blessing, nor the Left Hegelians, who enthusiastically supported Prussia's development toward a modern *Rechtsstaat,* shared this obsession with the past. The virulent antimodernism *Wochenblatt* conservatives evinced explains their criticism of the bureaucracy, in which they saw a modernizing agent. And the modern *Rechtsstaat,* governed by an abstract, codified law, was naturally not their ideal. They rejected it with everything it entailed. Instead, territorial and particularist powers, such as corporations and estates, were hailed as marking a path toward "true freedom," which could be achieved only outside and against the modern centralized state. Most striking in this context was that the members of the *Wochenblatt* circle rejected "royal absolutism," as they referred to it; that is, the Hohenzollern's absolute power was seen as an infringement on their freedom. Complete, unquestioning submission to the royal will was taken for granted by Prussian conservatives of the last third of the century, but to the men around the *Wochenblatt,* the idea was anathema. The members of the *Wochenblatt* were legitimist only insofar as this did not interfere with their traditional privileges. In their intellectual universe, parts of the medieval *Widerstandsrecht* against infringements of the crown had survived. They were deeply rooted in the Prussian traditions of early modern times, when the Mark Brandenburg was effectively governed by the nobility, and when the Hohenzollern elector, having come to the Mark in 1415, was tolerated at best as *primus inter pares.*[84]

---

84. Due to its paradoxical complexities, *Wochenblatt* conservatism is occasionally mis-

The narrow fixation on Prussian traditions by the members of the *Wochenblatt* group was the reason many features of their brand of conservatism were already outdated at the time they originated and the reason the group fell apart without further ado after 1841. Yet important features of their ideology survived to influence members of a later generation of conservatives, such as Hermann Wagener, and were disseminated in modified form by the *Wochenblatt*'s most prominent renegade, Josef Maria von Radowitz.

---

judged in general surveys of German conservatism—for example, in a survey on the history of German political parties, where Hans-Jürgen Puhle wrote: "Der Consensus des konservativen Legitimismus (z.B. der Brüder Gerlach oder der Gruppe um das Berliner Politische Wochenblatt) bestand aus einer Synthese aus Gehorsam gegenüber der gottgewollten Obrigkeit, Gottesgnadentum des legitimen Herrschers, antitraditionalistischer Gläubigkeit, Bündnis von Thron und Altar, ausgedrückt in der preussischen unierten Staatskirche, universalistischer Ständelehre, Mystifizierung eines verklärten Mittelalters und grossdeutschen Sympathien." See Walter Schlangen, ed., *Die deutschen Parteien im Überblick* (Königstein, 1979), 35. Here, specific features of *Wochenblatt* conservatism are lumped together with characteristics of late nineteenth-century conservatism, of which Puhle is a specialist. When reading the paragraph, one cannot help getting the impression that *Wochenblatt* conservatism is virtually identical with the conservatism of late nineteenth-century Germany. The "legitimism" of the members of the *Wochenblatt* group was quite different from that of later conservatives. And there were few "grossdeutsche Sympathien" among members of the group, as this would have meant the end of Prussia. It is astonishing that Puhle distinguishes between "Brüder Gerlach" and the "Gruppe um das Berliner Politische Wochenblatt" as if the former had not been part of the latter. There was great variety among conservatives in the first half of the nineteenth century, and there were profound differences between them and later German conservatives. One should not subsume all of them—from de Maistre, Bonald, Görres, and Baader to the *Wochenblatt* group—under the heading "legitimistischer Konservatismus" (as Puhle does), since historic reality was more complex than that.

CHAPTER 2

A Social Kingdom to Save the Monarchy: The Social Philosophy of Josef Maria von Radowitz, 1830–53

Josef Maria von Radowitz, born in 1797 in the Harz Mountains, came to Prussia in 1823. At that time the twenty-six-year-old sojourner hardly suspected that the country in whose service he was entering would determine the course of the remaining thirty years of his life. Even less would he have surmised that he, too, would some day exert a formative influence on politics in his adopted homeland. Radowitz was of Hungarian descent.[1] His grandfather had become a Prussian prisoner of war after the battle at Hohenfriedberg and chose never to return to his native land. In keeping with his cosmopolitan background, the young Radowitz studied in Mainz, in Chaleroi, and at the Ecole Polytechnique in Paris, where Ampère and Cuvier were among his teachers. Throughout his life Radowitz pursued the interests in natural sciences and mathematics he had acquired during his formative years. His first published work in 1827 was a mathematical treatise.

In the German Wars of Liberation, Radowitz had initially fought on the French side. In 1813, the sixteen year old already commanded a battery, and after the battle at the Katzbach, Napoleon himself bestowed the cross of the Legion d'Honneur on him. This was a rare distinction for someone who later in life, among many other achievements, was also to become a Prussian general.[2]

---

1. For more biographical information see chapter 1.
2. Radowitz's autobiography, "Aus meinem Leben," reprinted in Paul Hassel's *Josef Maria von Radowitz, 1797–1848* (Berlin, 1905), is indispensable for any knowledge of Radowitz's life. See also the short article on Radowitz in the *Allgemeine Deutsche Biographie* and Wilhelm Corvinus's introduction to Corvinus, ed., *Radowitz ausgewählte Werke*, 3 vols. (Regensburg, 1911). After 1945, interest in Radowitz's social thought has ebbed considerably. His ideas are briefly alluded to or discussed in the recent *Gesamtdarstellungen* of nineteenth-century German

His early allegiance to the French forces made other Prussian conservatives later doubt his motives and qualifications to advise the king and represent Prussian interests abroad. But Radowitz became a turncoat out of conviction. A close friend and adviser of the Prussian crown prince, whom he first met in 1823, he soon held important positions within the Prussian general staff, which he entered as captain in 1823. In 1836 he became the Prussian military plenipotentiary at the German Diet in Frankfurt; in the 1840s, he served as the Prussian envoy to various Southern German courts; and in May 1848, the district of Arnsberg in Westfalia sent him back to Frankfurt, this time as deputy to the revolutionary parliament, where he soon made a name for himself as one of the most prominent members of the far Right. After the failure of the revolution, in 1850, Radowitz, the longtime friend and esteemed adviser of his king, became Prussian foreign minister. His *Unionspolitik,* aiming at the creation of a *Kleindeutsches Reich* under Prussian leadership, remained unsuccessful due to the resistance of Austria and Russia. Its failure, leading to Prussia's humiliation at the treaty of Olmütz, brought Radowitz's political career to a sudden and inglorious end. On December 25, 1853, three years after Olmütz, he died, deserted by almost everyone but his king, whose friendship he never lost.

Radowitz's relationship to Prussia was not as unambiguous as that of the Gerlachs or of other East Elbian aristocrats. His loyalty was divided between his Prussianism and his Catholicism. "Whoever is a member of the Catholic Church and at the same time a Prussian, belonging to both out of profoundest conviction and with all his heart, will have a hard time of it," he once wrote.[3] To eliminate doubts concerning his loyalty, he attached himself all the more fervently to the country of his adoption. "Prussia," he wrote in 1839, "has become my true fatherland, my sole home, the abode of so many joys and sorrows, of so many kindnesses."[4] The *Kölner Kirchenstreit* of 1837 consequently became a matter of great distress for him, since he was among the few important Catholics in Prussia who did not openly speak out against the politics of the Prussian government when it arrested the archbishop of Cologne,

---

history, especially by Hans-Ulrich Wehler, *Deutsche Gesellschaftsgeschichte,* vol. 2 (Munich, 1987), 267–68, or in Panajotis Kondylis, *Konservatismus: Geschichtlicher Gehalt und Untergang* (Stuttgart, 1986), but most of the literature dates from before 1939. See especially Walter Früh, "Radowitz als Sozialpolitiker: Seine Gessellschafts- und Wirtschaftsauffassung unter besonderer Berücksichtigung der sozialen Frage" (Ph.D. diss., University of Berlin, 1937); Hildegard Goetting, "Die sozialpolitische Idee in den konservativen Kreisen der vormärzlichen Zeit" (Ph.D. diss., University of Berlin, 1920); Friedrich Meinecke, *Radowitz und die deutsche Revolution* (Berlin, 1913).

3. "Der preussische Katholik," in Josef Maria von Radowitz, *Gesammelte Schriften,* vol. 4 (Berlin, 1853), 301. Hand in hand with his religious beliefs went his enthusiasm for the German romantic movement, especially for Novalis, for Gothic architecture, and for the Christian German Middle Ages.

4. Radowitz, *Gesammelte Schriften,* vol. 4 (Berlin, 1853), 94–95.

Droste-Vischering, for refusing to cooperate with the authorities on the question of mixed marriages. Radowitz thus became subject to hostilities from the Catholic side, without being immune to suspicion from Protestant conservative Prussians.[5]

The fact that Radowitz essentially remained an alien among Prussian conservatives, set apart by provenance and denomination, facilitated his detachment from the narrowly aristocratic milieu of the *Wochenblatt* circle. Although there was never an open break between him and the other members of the group, growing mutual estrangement had been evident since the public dispute over mixed marriages in 1837. In the 1840s, after the dissolution of the paper, Radowitz went so far as to question the fundamental tenets of conservatism itself. "Standing firm in one's opinion if one is convinced of the righteousness of one's cause is a duty," he wrote in his *Gespräche aus der Gegenwart über Kirche und Staat;* "persevering in something merely because it has been there, is wrong and unwise."[6] In this, his most popular and widely read literary work,[7] he contrasted the ideologies of the time in the form of a dialogue. In doing so, he displayed extraordinary intuition and a great deal of sympathetic understanding for his political opponents.

In the *Gespräche,* the reader became confronted with five different political mentalities. Protestant-conservative pietism was represented by the aristocrat Arneburg, whose brother Detlev personified the Left Hegelian democrat; Detlev's future father-in-law, the industrialist Crusius, acted as the spokesperson of liberalism and constitutional monarchy; and the bureaucracy was represented by *Ministerialrat* Oeder (counselor in a ministerial department). The political and social views of Radowitz himself were propounded by the hu-

---

5. In the 1840s, Prussia was primarily a Protestant country—and so it remained for the rest of its history. The Catholic parts of the population lived primarily in the province of Posen (mainly inhabited by Poles), in parts of Westpreussen (with a strong Polish minority), in Silesia (which had been Austrian until Frederick the Great occupied it in 1740), and in the newly acquired provinces of Westfalen and Rhineland, which, for the most part, became Prussian only in 1815. In 1849 the Catholic percentage of the population in Prussia was Prov. Ostpreussen, 12.32 percent; Prov. Westpreussen, 46.91 percent; Prov. Posen, 63.03 percent; Prov. Pommern, 0.92 percent; Stadt Berlin, 3.66 percent; Prov. Brandenburg, 0.99 percent; Prov. Schlesien, 47.69 percent; Prov. Sachsen, 6.44 percent; Prov. Westfalen, 55.79 percent; Prov. Rhineland 75.21 percent; Preussen insgesamt, 37.23 percent (see Wolfram Fischer et al., *Sozialgeschichtliches Arbeitsbuch: Materialien zur Statistik des deutschen Bundes 1815–1870* [Munich, 1982], 43).

6. Radowitz, *Gespräche aus der Gegenwart über Kirche und Staat,* 4th ed. (Stuttgart, 1851), 361.

7. It quickly ran through four editions and was supplemented after the revolution by the *Neue Gespräche aus der Gegenwart über Kirche und Staat* (Stuttgart, 1851). The first edition of the *Gespräche* appeared in April 1846, the second in October 1846, the third in February 1847, and the fourth in March 1851.

mane nobleman von Waldheim.[8] Throughout his *Gespräche,* Radowitz distanced himself from his former conservative brothers-in-arms. Over the course of decades, former friends even turned into adversaries, since the *Kreuzzeitung,* the conservative organ founded by Ludwig von Gerlach during the Revolution of 1848, attacked his policies relentlessly. While Ludwig von Gerlach barely modified his political ideas as previously expounded in the *Wochenblatt,* Radowitz soon became convinced that "the monarchy based on estates [*die ständische Monarchie*] is extinct in the consciousness of the masses." The majority of Prussian conservatives continued to cling to the concept of a "*ständisch* renewal," whereas Radowitz expostulated that "the state, based on estates, has lost its foundation in public opinion." Public opinion now demanded representatives other than estates, Radowitz believed, and more authority for those representatives of the future. The consciousness of the masses would nevertheless remain "monarchical conservative," and, he maintained, "it is our duty to erect constitutional monarchy on this foundation."[9] This belief in the inherent conservatism and monarchism of "the consciousness of the masses" was shared by Carl Rodbertus and later by Hermann Wagener. The conviction of the innately conservative tendency of the lower classes became an important prerequisite for the concept of a "*Sociales Königtum,*" a "social kingdom," and, in the 1860s, the basis of Wagener's demand for universal suffrage.

    Along with these evolving differences in political thought between Radowitz and the other members of the *Wochenblatt* circle, concomitant changes in Radowitz's social philosophy emerged. An unfailing indication of this change lay in Radowitz's criticism of the existing ownership of property. "The organization of property relations which has existed heretofore is as untenable as existing political organization," he wrote after the revolution.[10] The members of the aristocracy should, accordingly, not possess the power to dispose of their property without limit; on the contrary, they ought to be bound by certain obligations toward their dependents.[11] Radowitz's concept of property is, in turn, conditioned by his view of the proletariat. The threat posed to

---

8. Radowitz displayed much insight in his representation of the political views of the democrat Detlev, the spokesperson for Left Hegelianism, whose uncompromising attitudes Radowitz traced with much empathy—for example, in statements such as "Darum weisen wir jede Gemeinschaft zurück mit den falschen Freunden des Fortschritts, mit allen, die nicht den Mut und die Konsequenz eines Prinzips haben" (Radowitz, *Gespräche,* 4th ed., 108).

9. Radowitz, *Gesammelte Schriften,* vol. 4 (Berlin, 1852–53), 247–49.

10. Ibid., 4:242. "What is it that still holds the social system together?—Only the potential for violence!" (ibid., 243).

11. This idea that the usufruct of one's property entailed an automatic commitment to aid those who were dependent on the property (which is most clearly applicable to the estate of a nobleman) can also be found in Ludwig von Gerlach's writings. With Gerlach, however, it was religiously motivated. See chapter 3.

society by the growing numbers of the dispossessed appeared more imminent to him than to the members of the *Wochenblatt* in the 1830s: "with the proletariat, a fourth estate has arisen. How many comparisons does this invite with the history of the rise of the third estate?"[12] And shortly after the revolution, the failure of which he witnessed in Frankfurt, he wrote that "whoever wants to truly restore society will first have to drain and cultivate the morass of the proletariat from which the deadly fumes ascend."[13]

This daunting task should be shouldered by the state, according to Radowitz—and herein lies the most pronounced divergence to the *Wochenblatt*. Together with Lorenz von Stein, Radowitz thus became the first in a line of conservative social thinkers who believed the state to be responsible for the solution of the social question. Carl Rodbertus had developed this idea in an article as early as 1839, but the article was not published until the 1870s, when it had lost all originality. The "Old Prussian" line of conservative thought, embodied by the *Wochenblatt* and Ludwig von Gerlach, openly disapproved of state intervention. To them the state smacked of bureaucracy, which was a red flag for the conservative Junkers. After the revolution, Hermann Wagener, who largely owed his career to Ludwig von Gerlach, again advocated state action to help the proletariat (for the expressed purpose of binding it closer to the monarchy). But Wagener only made full use of the ideas of Rodbertus, Stein, and Radowitz and suited them to his own ends. Through his study of French social movements, Lorenz von Stein had been among the first to realize that future revolutions would mainly have a social, not merely a political, character.[14] Strongly influenced by Hegel, Stein was convinced that freedom was realized only in the sphere of the state, not in society, and that only the complete independence of state power could guarantee unhampered and peaceful social development. Stein believed that the independent and strong position of the state was realized in the Prussia of his time. Stein's practical contribution to the power of the Prussian state consisted in his activities as a secret agent for the Prussian government during his stay in Paris.[15] His image of Prussia was an idealized one, shaped by Hegel's *Philosophy of Law*. Accordingly Stein's concept of a social kingdom was not an outgrowth of his own knowledge of Prussian affairs but a theoretical construction. The social philosophy of Radowitz on the other hand, sprang from experience. In sharp

12. Radowitz, *Gesammelte Schriften*, 4:149.
13. Ibid., 4:211.
14. Lorenz von Stein, *Der Sozialismus und Communismus des heutigen Frankreich* (Leipzig, 1842); its third edition was published as *Geschichte der sozialen Bewegung in Frankreich von 1789 bis auf unsere Tage*, 3 vols. (1850), and was later edited by Gottfried Salomon (Munich, 1921).
15. Joist Grolle, "Lorenz von Stein als preussischer Geheimargent," *Archiv für Kulturgeschichte* 50 (1968): 82–84.

contrast to Radowitz, however, Stein's attitude toward the bureaucracy was positive—in the Hegelian tradition. He was convinced that only the bureaucracy was capable of solving the social question. And Stein would naturally have rejected any solutions outside and against the state, such as those propagated by the *Berliner Politisches Wochenblatt.*

In his *Gespräche,* Radowitz advanced the idea that the state should terminate "the heathen unrestrictedness of property . . . and replace it by the inveterate principle that all possessions are but borrowed, each proprietor but a steward of his property, for the use of which he shall be held accountable not only toward the eternal judge but also toward his fellow humans."[16] To Radowitz, property thus entails an obligation or, as he succinctly put it, *"Je höher die Schicht, je weiter die Pflicht."*[17] Now that "the two great pillars on which the community of men used to rest, now that the two great forces, the idea of justice and ecclesiastical discipline have forfeited their sway over the masses," he reasoned, it would no longer be possible to maintain the "unlimited conception of property."[18] And to restrict this absolute ownership was one of the state's most urgent duties: "the state will be driven to meet its social mission or else it will be bowled over by it."[19]

In fewer than ten years after the dissolution of the *Wochenblatt,* the social question had thus become the most pressing problem of the day and age for Radowitz. He believed that the tackling of the social problem would eventually call forth "as many systems and parties" as the political problem had produced. The "pitiable squabble over political forms" was utterly unimportant in Radowitz's judgment "in comparison to the colossal challenges of pauperism, the proletariat, the solidarity of misery, the relationship between capital and labor." "Already in our own day," he noted, "when the existing authorities are still in the full possession of their power," it is high time that the state embark on "the solution of the social task," as otherwise it will be forced on the authorities later "when the government will be powerless and haplessly confronted with an anarchy."[20] With his view of the intervening state as the agent responsible for the solution of the social question, Radowitz distanced himself vigorously from earlier ideas when he, like the other members of the *Wochenblatt,* had sought solutions to social ills in the return to the *Ständestaat.* Now

---

16. Radowitz, *Gespräche aus der Gegenwart über Kirche und Staat,* 2d ed. (Stuttgart, 1846), 428.

17. "The higher the social stratum, the greater one's [social] duty." See Radowitz, *Gespräche,* 2d ed., 429. This very concept is also advanced by Ludwig von Gerlach.

18. Radowitz, *Gesammelte Schriften,* 4:265, "Nochmals die sociale Aufgabe und das Repräsentativsystem."

19. Ibid., "Der Staat wird dazu getrieben werden, der socialen Aufgabe zu genügen, oder sie wird ihn über den Haufen werfen."

20. Radowitz, *Gesammelte Schriften,* 4:265–66.

social problems were best tackled in the overall framework of the state, albeit an authoritarian, patriarchical one. This is astonishing in view of the fact that he shared the traditional mistrust of the Prussian conservative for bureaucracy; in the Prussia of the 1840s, "state" was almost synonymous with officialdom.

The growing urgency of the profound social malaise Radowitz perceived did not allow him to ban the industrial laborer from his field of vision. The more legally independent and politically equal the worker became, Radowitz speculated, the quicker he would be aware of the oppressiveness of his grinding poverty, aggravating further an already strong sense of destitution: "Equality before the law [for the worker] and material inequality, that is the expression of our distressing reality; and herein lies the great danger."[21] As a result of this realization, Radowitz intended to withhold political equality from the workers. Their interests, he believed, would best be safeguarded by a "social kingdom" (*soziales Königtum*), a form of government that would be compatible with the patrimonial principle in the solution of the social question.[22] In this "social kingdom," the monarch would actively support the demands of the "fourth estate" and try to better their material position—he would become a king of the poor, so to speak—and his own position would in return be strengthened by the lower classes, who would support him against the demands of the liberal bourgeoisie. Arneburg, the spokesperson of conservatism in Radowitz's *Gespräche,* expounded on this idea, suggesting an alliance between prince and proletariat:

> not all support for our princes has been exhausted to come off victorious against triumphant mediocrity. May they have the courage to turn to the masses. There, in the lowest and most numerous class of the people, still are their natural allies, still reside unspent resources, there still are natures capable of gratitude, deference and improvement.[23]

This image of the lower classes as being fundamentally conservative and royalist, waiting only for a chance to seize the helping hand of the monarch, had become increasingly popular with conservatives from the 1840s on. Lorenz von Stein, Carl Rodbertus, and Hermann Wagener exemplified that position in Germany, Disraeli in England.[24] In contrast to Hermann Wagener,

---

21. Radowitz, *Gesammelte Schriften,* 4:225.

22. The theory of the "social kingdom" was also put forth by Lorenz von Stein.

23. Radowitz, *Gespräche,* ed. by Wilhelm Corvinus, 270.

24. On Rodbertus see also Carl-Valerius Herberger, *Die Stellung der preussischen Konservativen zur sozialen Frage 1848–1862* (Meissen, 1914); on the "social kingdom" Hermann Wagener wrote (in Hermann Wagener, *Die kleine aber mächtige Partei* [Berlin, 1885], 9): "Alles Königtum wird fortan entweder ein leerer Schatten oder eine Despotie werden oder untergehen in Republik, wenn es nicht den hohen sittlichen Mut hat, ein Königtum der sozialen Reform zu werden." For more on Wagener's social thought see chapter 4, below.

Stein and Radowitz were thereby more interested in salvaging the institution of monarchy than in alleviating the misery of the lower classes.[25] In his propagation of the "social kingdom," Radowitz's main purpose was to use the propertyless masses as an instrument against the liberal bourgeoisie to salvage the monarchy and the conservative status quo, for he saw corruption and decline coming from the liberals.

In the *Gespräche*, for example, the pietist conservative Junker Arneburg praised the usefulness of the lower classes as "an unexpected ally . . . against the usurpation of the middle classes,"[26] that is, as a de facto counterrevolutionary force against a liberal-bourgeois uprising. Governments had better make an effort, Arneburg went on, to render distinct "the ever present conflict" between the interests of the bourgeoisie and those of the fourth estate. This could best be accomplished if the princes gave "priority to the still rather neglected bare necessities of the lowest classes."[27] When, in a different passage, the spokesperson of bureaucracy, Oeder, mockingly cut short Arneburg, inquiring whether he, the conservative aristocrat, intended to preach "a *Bundschuh*, a struggle between rich and poor," Arneburg retorted that it was not the proletariat that posed the most imminent threat to the monarchic system in Germany but the liberal middle classes. A certain way out of the dilemma could be found if the government "accepted the interests of the unpropertied estates as its main objective; if it governed [and] administered on their behalf."[28] In Radowitz's view—and in this he resembled all other Prussian conservatives—the main enemy was the liberal bourgeoisie, which seemed infinitely more menacing than the fourth estate.[29] The *Wochenblatt* conservatives of the 1830s had seen themselves and their position more directly challenged by the growing might of the bourgeoisie than by the proletariat of their time, which was still small and without any political rights. Radowitz still stood in their tradition, for deep-seated antiliberalism linked him to his former collaborators. The rule of the liberal middle classes, with their demands for constitutional monarchy, free trade, a centralized nation state with a free market economy, and the expansion of industries, would naturally mean the end of the paternalistic state, to which Prussian conservatives, including Radowitz, felt committed. To preserve the social status quo, Radowitz was thus prepared to integrate the pro-

---

25. Hermann Wagener is the exception insofar as he displayed genuine concern about the fate of the industrial laborer. Lorenz von Stein, however, emphasized that the institution of monarchy would hardly be able to survive, unless it became a "*Königtum der sozialen Reform.*"

26. Radowitz, *Gespräche*, ed. by Wilhelm Corvinus, 330.

27. Ibid., 332.

28. Ibid., 271. Oeder's analogy is taken from the German Peasant Wars (1524–25).

29. The infamous union of "iron and rye" between Rhenish heavy industry and the East Elbian aristocracy was a matter of future generations.

letariat into the existing state by using state and bureaucracy to redress some of its social grievances.

Immediately before and during the Revolution of 1848, when he himself witnessed the explosive force of social upheavals in Frankfurt, the social question became the focal point of public policy for Radowitz. The future of the monarchy and the future configuration of society and state depended on its solution. As Lorenz von Stein had recognized before him, Radowitz came to realize that "the next revolution will not be a political but a social one." The war cry of this revolution "will not be some hollow political theory but hunger versus gluttony, bareness versus luxury, the rights of man versus the rights of the citizen."[30] Detlev, the Left Hegelian democrat of the *Gespräche*, who made this prediction, accused the present, since "during no time the dependence of the poor on the rich had been so oppressive, so merciless."[31] Even though he was diametrically opposed to conservatives ideologically, Detlev equally recommended state intervention to eliminate the misery of the working class, whereby he specifically referred to the urban proletariat that was still in its infancy at the time the *Gespräche* were written.[32] The Left Hegelian democrat then proceeded to set himself up as champion of the prince, who should become the greatest entrepreneur, while the state itself would make its debut "as manufacturer, as industrialist."[33] Private enterprise could be eliminated through public competition and the profit of publicly owned enterprises "would devolve upon the workers that belonged to them; initially in part and in future years fully." The Left Hegelian went on to recommend that "an ever larger share in the management and administration of the public institution" [i.e., the publicly owned factory] should be handed over to the workers "until it passes over completely into their property."[34] In Detlev's conception, workers of state-owned factories should "form an association, administering their own

---

30. Radowitz, *Gespräche,* ed. by Wilhelm Corvinus, 137.

31. Ibid., 139.

32. An urban industrial proletariat developed during the 1840s in Prussia's larger cities, such as Breslau (see, e.g., Alexander Schneer, *Der Zustand der arbeitenden Klassen in Breslau* [Berlin, 1844]); Cologne, Prussia's third largest city (see Pierre Ayçoberry, *Cologne entre Napoleon et Bismarck* [Paris, 1981]), with a population of about 90,000; and above all Berlin (see especially Ernst Dronke, *Berlin,* 2 vols. (Frankfurt, 1846); Friedrich Sass, *Berlin in seiner neuesten Zeit und Entwicklung* (Leipzig, 1846).

33. Radowitz, *Gespräche,* ed. by Wilhelm Corvinus, 145. The Young Hegelians themselves wanted to implement their ideas within the framework of the Prussian monarchy, until they became disillusioned with the policies of Friedrich Wilhelm IV. But this was not until 1842–43. An interesting analysis of their relationship to the state can be found in Gustav Mayer, "Die Junghegelianer und der preussische Staat," *Historische Zeitschrift* 123 (1920): 413–40. See also part 2, chapter 8, below.

34. Radowitz, *Gespräche,* ed. by Wilhelm Corvinus, 146.

affairs."[35] The liberal entrepreneur Crusius, with whom Detlev held this conversation, dismissed his proposals as unrealistic, for who would "provide the assets for the first necessary investments?" The capital should be made available from "public funds," the Left Hegelian responded, adding that the people should not turn to "Solon and Lycurgus," that is, to great codifiers of constitution and law, but to "the absolute rulers."[36] This is a variation of the theme of a "social kingdom," only this time advanced from the Left, a first indication that Radowitz had more in common with the "idealistic" Left Hegelians than with liberals.

Radowitz's antiliberalism has a complementary element in his opposition to industrialization, for in his opinion, industry was the cause for one of the miseries of the contemporary age—the creation of an urban proletariat: "the great merchant, the factory owner, the speculating entrepreneur—they engulf hundreds of self-supporting social elements." Detlev lamented that

> out of that a species of man has grown, multiplying in dreadful progression, what we, characteristically enough, simply call "worker." The proletariat stands there in its gigantic figure, and with it the bleeding sore of the present becomes unleashed: pauperism.[37]

The sympathetic understanding that the conservative author of the *Gespräche* displayed for the standpoint of the Left Hegelian democrat, in whose mouth he put statements of euphoric eloquence, discloses the author's own preferences. As repeatedly emphasized in his writings, Radowitz felt more akin to the idealism of the Hegelian Left (which had become a symbol of the idea of democracy in Prussia) than to rationally calculating liberalism. The potential threat coming from the bourgeoisie outweighed his fear of the democratic Left and of revolution. One might even go so far as to explain Radowitz's spiritual affinity to the Left Hegelians in terms of the allure that the idea of revolution exerts on the romantic character.

While there were vehement disagreements between the conservatives Arneburg and Waldheim and the democrat Detlev on questions of religion and politics in general, there was frequently a startling concurrence of opinion on social issues. The views Radowitz expressed in his *Fragmente* in regard to antiliberalism, state intervention, and the concept of a "social kingdom" were

---

35. The idea of an association of workers was also advanced by Victor A. Huber. This "Genossenschaftsgedanke" dominated the sociopolitical discussion of the 1850s and was mostly propagated by liberals, of whom Hermann Schulze-Delitsch is the best known. But, as the example of V. A. Huber shows, the notion of the association can also be found among conservatives, with Huber as the one notable exception.

36. Radowitz, *Gespräche,* ed. by Wilhelm Corvinus, 148.

37. Ibid., 141.

largely congruent with the convictions expressed by Detlev in the *Gespräche*. Next to the shared concept of the *Soziales Königtum,* the most significant common denominator between them touched on the question of state intervention. "Who can and may exert such coercion?" Detlev was asked by Crusius when the Hegelian spoke of "breaking the hard-hearted selfishness . . . to secure proportionate consumption of worldly goods for all men." That, Detlev answered, lay within the power of the one authority that has become the heir to the church, "the state."[38]

There is further common ground in the mutual criticism of the industrial age and its deforming influence on humankind. The "servitude of money," with which the poor were afflicted, was even harsher than the bondship of the Middle Ages, Detlev lamented in the *Gespräche:* the "proprietors of money are the feudal lords; the workers, regardless of their ability, are their bondsmen."[39] Statements like these are reminiscent of the *Wochenblatt,* whose language was similar and whose anticapitalism pointed in the same direction. In a similar vein, Radowitz predicted in 1842 that industry would be "idolized" and "treated like the most important affairs of state in industrial exhibitions, while anyone seeking nothing but his own advantage with all means is fawned upon by kings down to their lowest servants and showered with decorations and honors."[40] Radowitz was naturally opposed to the promotion of industrial establishments, the *Gewerbeförderung,* a policy inaugurated by the Prussian bureaucracy in the 1820s.[41] In the *Gespräche,* the conservative Junker Arneburg chimed in with the polemics against the "idolatry of industry."[42] In this context, the enemy common to all Prussian conservatives was the liberal bureaucrat (in the *Gespräche,* the councillor Oeder) who represented the policy of rapid industrialization.[43]

---

38. Ibid., 136.

39. Ibid., 139.

40. Radowitz, *Gesammelte Schriften,* 4:113, "Industrie und Zölle." The industrial fair of 1844 in Berlin was in preparation at the time.

41. Responsible for the *Gewerbeförderung* was Peter Christian Beuth in the ministry of trade and commerce. See also William O. Henderson, *The State and the Industrial Revolution in Prussia 1740–1870* (Liverpool, 1958); Ulrich P. Ritter, *Die Rolle des Staates in den Frühstadien der Industrialisierung: Die preussische Industrieförderung in der ersten Hälfte des 19. Jahrhunderts* (Berlin, 1961); Ilja Mieck, *Preussische Gewerbepolitik in Berlin 1806–1844* (Berlin, 1965); Wolfgang Radtke, *Die preussische Seehandlung zwischen Staat und Wirtschaft in der Frühphase der Industrialisierung* (Berlin, 1981).

42. Radowitz, *Gespräche,* ed. by Wilhelm Corvinus, 343.

43. In some instances, however, state interference in the economy could also hinder the process of industrialization. See, for example, Friedrich Zunkel, "Die Rolle der Bergbaubürokratie beim industriellen Ausbau des Ruhrgebietes 1815–1848," in *Sozialgeschichte Heute,* ed. Hans-Ulrich Wehler (Göttingen, 1974), 130–47; Richard Tilly, *Kapital, Staat und sozialer Protest in der deutschen Industrialisierung* (Göttingen, 1980).

In addition to ingrained hostility toward industry, the reader of Radowitz's works encounters a pronounced aversion to some of the features of modern life in general. Radowitz deplored greatly that everything could be bought with money. According to him, "the great social transformation of modern times" was that it had become primarily "capital and money that characterizes the citizens," not social standing, descent, or ethnic affiliation. "Formerly a Jew could never become truly powerful, however much money and mortgage bonds he might have possessed"; now it happened all the time. Radowitz deplored the disintegration of town guilds, the automatic corollary of which was the end of the preferential treatment hitherto enjoyed by local citizens. In olden days "a resident alien never grew powerful in Lübeck or Frankfurt," he mused wistfully.[44] All these attitudes were very much in line with the teachings of the *Wochenblatt* in the 1830s.

Therefore, despite the progressive elements of Radowitz's thought that alienated him from his former brothers-in-arms of the *Wochenblatt* and, in some instances, drew him close to Left Hegelian democrats, his thought essentially remained conservative. The leitmotif of conservative thought, opposition to social change, remained a prevailing theme for him. Even though Radowitz endorsed state interference on behalf of the industrial proletariat, he did not relinquish the idea of the state as an essentially paternal institution. He thus favored a solution that kept the lower classes in a form of tutelage, albeit a benevolent one. In his understanding, it was the task of the state to forestall social change and blunt the lower classes' edge.

An unfailing indicator of the suspicion with which Radowitz viewed the modern state and its achievements was what one might call his *Zivilisationskritik*. In Radowitz's writings, the reader meets with a critique of modern culture and civilization that is considered typical of turn-of-the-century *Lebensphilosophie*, with its vociferous protest against urbanization, the metropolis, modern industry, technology, and the power of money. This latter subject also exerted a perennial fascination on Radowitz. Already in 1826 he castigated the "slavery of mammon," which in his opinion was the most insidious of all forms of slavery, "since it pretends to a kind of freedom that does not exist." Because of "the power of money," the proper understanding of "working and serving" had been lost. "The submission to objects, needs, wants, and money" would become the worst possible degradation of man.[45] At times his *Zivilisationskritik* assumed almost absurd features, as when, for example, he maintained that railroads would destroy the experience of traveling, because the traveler ceased being a person "for the duration of the conveyance" and

---

44. Radowitz, *Gesammelte Schriften*, 4:143, "Geld."
45. Ibid., 4:5.

turned into "an object, an ordinary freight" instead.[46] This romantic-conservative critique of and attack on the modern state and its achievements formed a strange contrast to his understanding, even sympathy, for the socialistic ideas of his time.

In the *Gespräche,* Radowitz, by way of his alter ego Waldheim, conceded that the socialist and communist demands "are imperative consequences of the whole essence of the modern state."[47] The demands socialists placed on the state were justified after the decline of the church, Waldheim argued. Yet socialism's most repelling feature was that it "bases the whole of society solely on the crude sensual and material needs of the body," which excluded "the transcendental eternal, the core root of all law and all belief."[48] Waldheim conceded, however, that he could understand "the reasoning of men such as Grün, Hess, Drohnke, Püttmann, Wolff, Engels, Schmidt, . . . ,"[49] whom he preferred to bourgeois liberals.[50] For Radowitz, socialism and communism symbolized the "longing for the perfection of the absolute state and absolute reason," and he saw in them "nothing else than the struggle and urging of an unhappy generation for the personal God they have deserted."[51]

Other conservative social theoreticians, such as the Bavarian Franz von Baader and the Baden deputy von Buss, considered apostasy from religion to be the root and origin of the brutalization of the masses. A renewed turning toward religion was thus propagated in many of the later *Arbeitervereine.* In this context, religion was also viewed as a "deactivating element" to appease the dangerous crowd. Already in 1842, Radowitz had turned sharply against what he considered the leftist extremism of the "Hegelian system" and its "teachings of the autonomy of the human mind," which would turn into "genuine disbelief . . . in the field of religion . . . and equally crude absolute radicalism in the field of politics."[52] The *Wochenblatt* had railed even more violently against the Young Hegelians and their *Hallesche Jahrbücher,* accusing them of corrupting an entire generation of young people by "injecting the

---

46. Ibid., 5:340.
47. Radowitz, *Gespräche,* ed. by Wilhelm Corvinus, 149.
48. Ibid., 152.
49. Ibid., 367. Karl Grün and Moses Hess were early collaborators of Marx and better known than Marx within the confines of the German Confederation in the 1840s. Ernst Dronke had gained notoriety through his book on Berlin. Wilhelm Wolff was known to a wider public through his writings on social misery in Silesia, *Die Schlesische Milliarde;* and the man hidden behind the common name "Schmidt" was the Left Hegelian Max Stirner, whose *Der Einzige und sein Eigentum* is still discussed in philosophical seminars today.
50. Waldheim let no opportunity pass to belittle liberalism, the main purpose of which was "to exchange gentlemen by the grace of God through gentlemen by the grace of mammon" (*Gespräche,* 367).
51. Radowitz, *Gespräche,* 367.
52. Radowitz, *Gesammelte Schriften,* 5:179.

poison of their political and ecclesiastical heresy deep into the hearts of our youths."[53]

Though the critique of religion (which had become the hallmark of Young Hegelian philosophy since David Friedrich Strauss's book on the *Leben Jesu*) turned Radowitz against the Hegelian Left, he felt drawn to it for the sake of its idealism. In 1837 Radowitz had written that, like himself, the republican acknowledged "that it is not the material well-being which matters with the individual or within the social sphere of the state, but the realization of an eternal idea." That was the reason

> we respect the consistent republican, the *"Mann der Bewegung"* more highly than his materialistic companion [i.e., the liberal]; we can credit his thoughts, however erroneous they may be, with moral value, and believe more in the possibility of his achieving true understanding.[54]

It is thus a common mode of viewing the world that unites the conservative with the Left Hegelian democrat across the seemingly unbridgeable chasm of the content of their ideas. There could, however, be absolutely no community with the "materialists" in politics (as Radowitz calls the liberals), even though they were closer to him in social position and probably shared many of the paraphernalia of education and wealth with him. The main dividing line, "in politics as in all other things," lay for Radowitz in the "principal antagonism between idealists and materialists."[55] This antagonism between idealists and materialists in politics has remained a perennial theme in German political life since that time. In political discourse, it was the idealistic element that was associated with the "German character," while the materialist later became equated with the "civilization of the West," a line of reasoning that reached its height in the ideological struggle at the beginning of the First World War, with Thomas Mann, Ernst Troeltsch, and Friedrich Meinecke among the more prominent contenders on the German side.

When Radowitz wrote this in the late 1830s, the term *Republikaner* (those advocating a republican form of government) was synonymous not only with Left Hegelianism but also with Heine, Börne, Freiligrath, Herwegh, and other poets and writers of the *Junges Deutschland.* Toward them he felt a close

---

53. *BpW,* July 14, 1838, 159, "Die Halleschen Jahrbücher für deutsche Wissenschaft und Kunst." There the *Wochenblatt* charged that Young Hegelians, "Die Grundmauern alles historisch Gewordenen und durch die Sitte Geheiligten auswühlen, den Glauben verachten und Wissen predigen, die Gediegenheit aber des wirklichen Wissens von Thatsachen verhöhnen, dem Staate das Prinzip ihrer selbstischen Freiheitsmanie unterlegen und dadurch ihn gewinnen wollen, als seyen sie selbst die Vernunft und Wahrheit: das sind die Zwecke und Bestrebungen dieser unruhigen linken Seite."

54. Radowitz, *Gesammelte Schriften,* 4:82.

55. Ibid., 4:81, "Idealismus- Materialismus in der Politik."

affinity, since for them, as for himself, "the perceptible and tangible world was only a cloak of eternal ideas and the manifestation of these ideas the most noble object of existence."[56] What separated him from the *Republikaner* in this common quest, according to Radowitz, was that with them "the idea, under which the visible is subordinated" was a wrong one. Liberalism, however, "the materialistic principle,"[57] which he saw dominant in France in 1837, was solely interested "in this tangible world and the enjoyments it is capable of offering to the senses."[58] Liberalism was simply alien to his nature. Besides, the liberal interpreted the role of the state differently, taking "every higher principle that is inherent in the state or realizable through it for a chimera, as for him nothing possesses substance, only that which appeals to the senses." To the liberal, the sole functions of the state were "enlightenment, industry, credit, commerce, trade."[59]

Despite a similar "idealistic" view of state and society, Radowitz evinced strong reservations about the Left Hegelians, as they saw "in administrative despotism the very form of the absolute state which, at present, is most suited to the realization of their political demands."[60] Here one again encounters the conservative aversion to the omnipotence of bureaucracy, and the hostility toward a centralized power that had often been raised in the *Wochenblatt* and in Radowitz's *Gespräche aus der Gegenwart über Kirche und Staat.* Oeder, the *Ministerialrat* of the *Gespräche,* the representative of officialdom, constantly faced the conservative opposition of Arneburg and Waldheim. The "administrative absolutism of the Prussian state"[61] was odious to Radowitz, because it threatened to level naturally developed differences. In 1844 he went so far as to compare "the regiment of the officials" with "Russian despotism,"[62] and in 1847 he called on the king "to liberate himself and his country resolutely from the shackles of the administrative machine, the rule of officialdom."[63] In 1848 he went on to repudiate the *"Beamtenstaat"* as being tantamount to "absolutism from above,"[64] and in 1852, a year before his death, he wrote with great relish that the world of the *"Beamtenregiment"* had perished.[65]

56. Ibid.
57. Ibid., 4:84.
58. Ibid., 4:81.
59. Ibid., 4:82.
60. Ibid., 5:315, "Die Hegelinge."
61. Ibid.
62. Ibid., 4:141, "Deutschlands Gefahren." The term Radowitz used was "russischer Sultanismus."
63. Ibid., 4:152.
64. Ibid., 4:198.
65. Ibid., 4:285.

The central theme in Radowitz's social thought is the idea that an alliance between the monarchy and the proletariat, brought about by a social policy favoring the industrial and rural lower classes, would guarantee the future of the Prussian monarchy by providing an effective protection against the demands of the liberal middle classes. Radowitz did not favor a solution of the social question within a modern constitutional state, nor did he support the bureaucracy in its attempt to regulate social life. This would have meant either the rule of liberal constitutionalism or that of the all powerful official, and he had little sympathy for either one. Since estates were no longer a reflection of modern political life, he rejected as antiquated suggestions for the restoration of the *Ständestaat* and for the setting up of aristocratic orders to provide for the poor—both of which had been proposed by the *Wochenblatt*.

Like the conservative Hegelian Lorenz von Stein, Radowitz regarded the establishment of a social kingdom—"a kingdom of social reform," as Stein put it—as the ideal solution. This solution was especially suited to the needs of the upper classes, since it would prolong the existence of the *patriarchalischer Obrigkeitsstaat*. The preservation of this form of state, which everywhere seemed to be in the throes of death, was Radowitz's main concern. Neither the aristocracy nor the industrial entrepreneur nor the proletariat itself should act as champion of the socially downtrodden. That privilege should be reserved for the authoritarian state, dominated by the firm, but benevolent, social kingdom.

CHAPTER 3

Property, Association, and the State: The Social Conceptions of Ludwig von Gerlach, Viktor A. Huber, and Carl Rodbertus in the 1840s and 1850s

The other dominating figure of the *Wochenblatt* circle, Ludwig von Gerlach, remained firmly rooted in the idea of the *Ständestaat* until the revolution, and even beyond. In 1848, Ludwig von Gerlach became one of the founding fathers of the conservative party.[1] Gerlach is entitled to lay claim to lasting impact on the further development of conservative social thought due to the intellectual guidance and nourishment he lavished on Hermann Wagener, who became the commanding mind of conservative social thought in the 1850s and 1860s.[2]

As to Gerlach's own social ideas, one can only note the persistence and obstinacy with which he clung to such outdated notions as *Patrimonial-gerichtsbarkeit*, a manorial jurisdiction by dint of which the local Junker held supreme judicial authority, and which remained in force until 1848. From here

---

1. See, e.g., Erich Jordan, *Die Entstehung der konservativen Partei und die preussischen Agrarverhältnisse von 1848* (Munich and Leipzig, 1914); Hans-Joachim Schoeps, *Das andere Preussen*, 5th ed. (Berlin, 1981); Marjorie E. Lamberti, "The Rise of the Prussian Conservative Party, 1840–1858" (Ph.D. diss., Yale University, 1966); and especially Wolfgang Schwentker, *Konservative Vereine und Revolution in Preussen* (Düsseldorf, 1988).

2. Gerlach exerted formative influence on Wagener in his position as *Gerichtspräsident* in Magdeburg at the time Wagener received his juridical training at the Magdeburg law courts. Gerlach may even have been instrumental in bringing Wagener to Magdeburg, where Gerlach and Wagener had a close personal relationship. Wagener used to call on Gerlach at least once a week. See Wolfgang Saile, *Hermann Wagener und sein Verhältnis zu Bismarck* (Tübingen, 1958); Ludwig von Gerlach, *Aufzeichnungen aus seinem Leben und Wirken* (Schwerin, 1903).

it was but a small step to Gerlach's incessant advocacy of *Erbuntertänigkeit,* the serflike tutelage for the peasants, which had been abolished de jure with the October edict of 1807 but was de facto allowed to linger on in some regions until after 1848.[3] The experience of the revolution, even if it ultimately failed to leave a lasting imprint on his thought, modified some of his political views. The proletariat, looming large as a political force during the spring of 1848 (probably larger than ever again in nineteenth-century Germany) should be permitted to constitute itself as an estate, Gerlach conceded. But this was a concession designed to domesticate the beast rather than nourish it. In a memorandum for the king, November 23, 1848, Gerlach wrote that "all estates, all interest groups, even the proletarians should be admitted to the assembly of estates through their representatives . . . but [only] in their function as an estate, as an interest group, as proletarians, not as mere numbers of persons."[4]

Gerlach's pietistic Protestantism, which was unaffected by the revolutionary upheavals, remained the main pillar of his social and political beliefs. He epitomized the type of Prussian conservative equally influenced by pietistic and feudal-aristocratic beliefs, a phenomenon that was, if not common, certainly not exceptional in Prussia.[5] There was, however, one central issue on which Gerlach's ideas concurred with those of Radowitz, namely, a similar conception of the nature of property. With Gerlach, as with Radowitz, it was not the private component of property that was sacrosanct but the public one— the obligations attached to it. As Gerlach put it in a speech to the upper Prussian chamber:

> If property is not linked to an office, it becomes untenable. If you convince me that property does not entail an official duty vis-à-vis the state, or the obligation towards voluntary service, to consume oneself in sacrifice [*zur Aufopferung*], you will make a communist out of me.[6]

One year previously, on August 18, 1848, Gerlach had already proclaimed before the so-called *Junkerparlament* that

---

3. On the *Regulierung* and *Ablösung,* etc., see the introductory chapter on the social question.

4. Schoeps, *Das andere Preussen,* 41.

5. The best-known conservative pietist circle in pre-March Prussia was the one around Thadden-Trieglaff, of which the young Otto von Bismarck also was a member. See the informed description by Ernst Engelberg, *Bismarck: Urpreusse und Reichsgründer* (Berlin, 1985), 183–206.

6. November 10, 1849, in Schoeps, *Das andere Preussen,* 38. The disputes between Radowitz and Gerlach became more acrimonious during the revolution. Gerlach was disgruntled about what he considered to be Radowitz's compromising attitude toward the revolution and his negative influence on the king. See Gerlach, *Aufzeichnungen aus seinem Leben und Wirken,* vol. 1 (Schwerin, 1903), 477.

property is but a political concept, an office established by God, in order to keep God's law for the state alive; it is only in connection with the obligations engraved on it that property is sacrosanct; merely as a means to enjoyment, property is not sacred, but squalid. In respect to property without obligation, communism is right.[7]

In the final analysis, it was the obligation tied to property that sanctioned the aristocracy's claim to it, thereby justifying the aristocracy's innate privileges to hold the highest offices in the kingdom. For it was the possession of land, of estates, that, through obligation, created the eligibility for high office. On the basis of these ideas, Gerlach repeated a proposition in 1848 that was made by the *Wochenblatt* seven years before, namely, that the aristocracy, for the sake of its own renewal, should devote itself to its social mission: "It would be a noble task . . . of the great landed property to help the cities redeem a portion of their proletariat."[8]

At first sight, Viktor Aimé Huber seems to be the antithesis to Gerlach in virtually every respect, not only by dint of his origins and his own aloofness toward the group of "Old Prussian" conservatives around the Gerlachs, but also because Huber generally endorsed industrial capitalism and further development of industry, both of which were anathema to the Gerlachs. In one respect, however, they are compatible, for both have frequently been associated with the Protestant social movement. In Huber's case the bulk of the *Forschungsliteratur* tends to interpret his ideas in this tradition,[9] and he is thus often lumped together with Johann Hinrich Wichern among others.[10] The

---

7. Gerlach, *Aufzeichnungen*, 541. Gerlach went on to emphasize that the privileges currently threatened, "*Patronat, Polizei, Gerichtsbarkeit*" must not be given up, as they constituted obligations and duties rather than rights. It was clear that Gerlach wanted to preserve those elements as necessary for the justification of the aristocracy's position, the raison d'être of which was service to the state, "*Adelig ist, wer dem Staate umsonst dient.*"

8. Quoted in Schoeps, *Das war Preussen*, 3d ed. (Berlin, 1966), 143: "Es wäre eine edle und vielleicht wohl ausführbare Aufgabe des grossen Grundbesitzes, den Städten einen Teil ihres Proletariats tilgen zu helfen." In 1841, the *Wochenblatt* had suggested that the Prussian aristocracy should found colonies for the poor in Prussia's East Elbian regions (see chapter 1).

9. Most of the literature on Huber is from long before the Second World War, originating between the mid-1870s and 1933; there is one recent study on Huber's social activities, Sabine Hindelang's dissertation, *Konservatismus und soziale Frage* (Frankfurt, 1983). Important older works on Huber include Rudolf Elvers, *Viktor Aimé Huber: Sein Werden und Wirken*, 2 vols. (Bremen, 1872–74), and Ingwer Paulsen's 1937 dissertation, *Viktor Aimé Huber als Sozialpolitiker*, 2d ed. (Berlin, 1956).

10. Those interpreting Huber's thought and action as part of a Protestant social movement include, e.g., Paul Göhre, *Die evangelisch-soziale Bewegung, ihre Geschichte und ihre Ziele* (Leipzig, 1896); Fritz Fischer, "Der deutsche Protestantismus und die Politik im 19. Jahrhundert," *Historische Zeitschrift* 171 (1951): 473–518; Hans Christ, "Christlich-religiöse Lösungsversuche der sozialen Frage im mittleren 19. Jahrhundert" (Ph.D. diss., University of Erlangen, 1951);

present analysis, however, focuses exclusively on Huber's social and political ideas.

In this regard we meet in him one of those rare Prussian conservatives who did not advocate the restoration of guilds and the suppression of freedom of trade or beat the drum for the reintroduction of other features of medieval life. Huber's background and career were atypical for a Prussian conservative.[11] Huber's mother, Therese Huber, had been praised by Wilhelm von Humboldt as "one of the most outstanding women of the time."[12] She was first married to the famous Jacobin Georg Forster of Mainz, and she may well have laid the groundwork for her son's initial liberalism. Huber himself, born in Stuttgart on March 10, 1800, was the total opposite of the native Prussian Junker rooted to the soil. Huber spoke French, English, Spanish, and Italian as fluently as his native German tongue. In the 1820s, he traveled extensively throughout western Europe, spending several months in England, half a year in Paris, and much time in Spain, where he actively took up the liberal cause and fought against the Carlists. The fruit of his travels to England became a two-volume study of the English university system that was subsequently (1843) translated into English and hailed as a seminal work in its field.[13] In the 1830s, Huber settled down as professor of history and occidental languages in Rostock (1832) and Marburg (1834).

In the early 1840s, when the criticism of state and society, advanced by the Left Hegelians in their *Hallesche Jahrbücher,* gathered momentum as a result of accumulated frustration over the new king's failure for decisive reform,[14] Huber made his first public appearance as a conservative spokesperson. His sixty-page pamphlet, *Über die Elemente, die Möglichkeit oder Nothwendigkeit einer konservativen Partei in Deutschland* (1841), attracted attention in the Prussian capital.[15] Huber's treatise was directed against "the development of the so-called Young Hegelian school and its journalistic organ, the *Hallesche Jahrbücher,*"[16] since the journal corrupted the "moral founda-

Walter Bredendieck, *Christliche Sozialreformer des 19. Jahrhunderts* (Leipzig, 1953); William O. Shanahan, *German Protestants Face the Social Question* (Notre Dame, Ind., 1954).

11. On his life see Elvers, *Huber;* Paulsen, *Huber;* and Hildegard Goetting, *Die sozialpolitische Idee in den konservativen Kreisen der vormärzlichen Zeit* (Ph.D. diss., University of Berlin, 1920).

12. Wilhelm von Humboldt, *Briefe an eine Freundin,* part 2 (brief 5 and 6).

13. Viktor A. Huber, *Die englischen Universitäten,* 2 vols. (Kassel, 1839–40); Elvers, *Huber,* 2:133–34.

14. Frederick William IV mounted the throne in 1840.

15. *On the Elements, the Possibility or Necessity of a Conservative Party in Germany* (Marburg, 1841).

16. Huber, *Elemente,* 4. The *Hallesche Jahrbücher* later changed its name to *Deutsche Jahrbücher* after the Left Hegelians were expelled from Prussia, and the journal could no longer appear in Halle.

tions of Christian education."[17] According to Huber, the conservative party was "the opposite of torpor and stagnation"[18] and should include "all those views, ways of thinking, convictions, and interests that are still somehow conscious of their connection with the foundations of Christian education [*Bildung*] . . . and moral [*sittlich*] life."[19] In Huber's catchword, "whoever is not against us, will be with us."[20] As he conceived it, the conservative party was not just an elite but a broadly based movement of the people, which accounted for his approximation of "the conservative point of view" and "the popular one."[21]

A comparable interpretation of the social basis of conservatism would have been unthinkable for the *Wochenblatt* circle, as their understanding of conservatism was based on leadership and doctrinal exegesis as the preserve of a select few. Even Radowitz would have been wary of identifying conservative and popular standpoints, despite his belief in the innate conservatism of the masses. In Radowitz's intellectual world, it was taken for granted that the masses had to be led by people far above their own station. Huber thus became the first among Prussian conservatives to expressly state the idea that conservatism was not just rooted in the masses but harbored in their womb. In his follow-up pamphlet, *Die Opposition,* published in 1842, Huber declared that "the development of Prussian affairs will, for better or worse," exert great influence "on the whole of Germany," since already "the person of the prince, bearing the Prussian crown, forms a spiritual center for all sane elements of German folklife."[22]

Huber became Prussian only by elective affinity when he moved to Berlin in 1843, but he believed in Prussia's German mission with greater fervor than most native Prussians. Most conservative Prussians at the time still preferred remaining Prussian and had no intention of ever becoming German. But exaggerated pride in the ability and "mission" of the country of one's adoption is often a characteristic of the homeless intellectual. A similar phenomenon occurred with Radowitz, another *Vernunftpreusse* and advocate of Prussian virtues. Their very conservatism may well have been reinforced by the zeal inherent in any stranger, craving recognition in his adopted land. In the German Empire, it later became proverbial that the most ardent Berliners were born in Breslau.

Huber's political writings drew the Prussian king's attention to him, and

17. Huber, *Elemente*, 5.
18. Ibid., 12.
19. Ibid., 13.
20. Ibid., 12.
21. Ibid., 44.
22. Viktor A. Huber, *Die Opposition: Ein Nachtrag zu der conservativen Partei* (Halle, 1842), 11.

in court circles of the Prussian capital his name was mentioned as that of a possible candidate to edit a conservative press organ intended as a counterweight to Arnold Ruge's *Deutsche Jahrbücher.*[23] After other contenders for the position of editor, including Ranke and Dahlmann, showed little interest, Radowitz, by order of the king, started negotiations with Huber.[24] Finally, during a meeting in Kassel, Radowitz managed to persuade Huber that he would be the right man "to foster the good cause of right and truth on the literary field."[25] In the autumn of 1843, Huber was thus appointed professor of occidental languages at Berlin's Friedrich Wilhelms University, to a chair especially established for him. The political motive for Huber's nomination was almost immediately apparent to professors and students alike. His status as political appointee made professorial colleagues reluctant to accept him as one of their own, while students, who had at first regarded Huber and the political controversies surrounding him with some interest, soon stayed away from his lectures, deterred by the new professor's awkward oral delivery.[26]

With the help of government funds, a new conservative journal, *Janus,* was finally created, its name symbolizing the unity of past and present in one. It appeared between January 1845 and March 1848. Even though *Janus* was seen by many as the successor to the *Berliner Politisches Wochenblatt,* a mere sixty-six copies were sold during the first half-year of its publication. In 1846, the year of its greatest success, only 174 copies out of a total circulation of 750 reached their intended destination. Commercial failure was due, at least in part, to lack of collaboration with other conservatives. Huber had especially hoped that higher officials would join in his venture,[27] but despite official backing, Huber was not fully integrated into Berlin's conservative circles. In the second half of the 1840s, he entertained a cordial relationship with Friedrich Julius Stahl, who became a leading theoretician of the conservatives in the 1850s;[28]

---

23. See Rudolf Elvers's article on Huber in the *Allgemeine Deutsche Biographie* (Leipzig, 1881) 13:249–58 and Hans-Joachim Schoeps's article in the *Neue Deutsche Biographie* (Berlin, 1972) 9:688–89.

24. See Max Lenz, *Geschichte der königlichen Friedrich Wilhelms Universität zu Berlin,* vol. 2 (Berlin, 1918), 60–68; Elvers, *Huber,* 2:119.

25. See Walter Früh, *Radowitz* (Berlin, 1937), 43; and Lenz, *Geschichte.* Ranke and Dahlmann had been the first choice for the position of editor of a conservative journal, but negotiations between them and the Prussian government remained inconclusive, for each of them wanted to direct the paper according to his own ideas.

26. Huber's written style proved to become even more convoluted, which contributed to the commercial failure of his conservative *Janus.* His later student and biographer Rudolf Elvers ascribes this obvious shortcoming to the pressure of having to produce too much. Huber virtually wrote the journal all by himself, which, according to Elvers, made it impossible for him to polish his style. (See Elvers, *Huber,* 2:188–90.) Before he settled down as a professor, Huber had been a popular *Reiseschriftsteller* with a facile pen, whose prose was eminently readable.

27. See Elvers, *Huber,* 188; Paulsen, *Huber,* 51.

28. See Paulsen, *Huber,* 49. The revolution, however, put an abrupt end to their friendship.

with Heinrich Leo, conservative historian and former collaborator of the *Wochenblatt;* and with Karl Friedrich von Eichhorn, the minister of culture, who had been instrumental in ousting the Left Hegelians from Prussia. He had virtually no contact with the Gerlachs and Radowitz.

Since 1840, Huber had occasionally contributed short reviews to Hengstenberg's *Evangelische Kirchenzeitung,* and in the columns of this paper, he first commented on social issues in Prussia. The occasion was provided by the projected reestablishment of the medieval *Schwanenorden* by the king. Huber welcomed the fact that "one of the first monarchs in our world and time recognizes publicly and solemnly the cause of poverty as his own, as the cause of the great and powerful of this earth." Prompt action was needed, as poverty "had grown into a formidable public sore," and it was thus more than fortunate "that the king himself" constituted "the commercial center" of the organization.[29] Huber's first public pronouncement on social issues was already suggestive of the strange mixture of ideas he advocated. The central idea toward which he gravitated was the concept of an association in which the poor congregated for mutual protection. In stark contrast to this were his sympathies for the notion of a social king, alluded to in the article for the *Evangelische Kirchenzeitung.* With his theory of association, Huber soon occupied a precarious position in conservative thought, for he was in danger of being placed on a level with early French socialists, who offered similar panaceas for poverty.[30] But the concept of the social kingdom (for, according to Huber, it was the king who ought to lead the social order, the *Schwanenorden*) placed Huber in the "Old Prussian" line of conservative thought ranging from Radowitz to Hermann Wagener.

In Huber's conception, the organization of the laboring masses should take place "under protection and supervision of the state . . . and with substantial support of state funds." Ultimately, however, the working masses could be

---

29. "Auch ein Wort über den Schwanenorden und dessen mögliche Bedeutung," *EKZ* 11 (February 7, 1844): 81–88.

30. Though with radically different premises underlying their ideas. Even before Lorenz von Stein had introduced them to a wider German audience through his study of early French socialists, Fourier, Cabet, and later also Louis Blanc were known in Prussia. Not only were Börne, Heine, and others whom strict censorship had forced into exile familiar with them, but also more conservative men of letters, such as the Hegelian Eduard Gans and Karl Rosenkranz, discussed French socialism in their correspondence. In the 1850s, "Association" became a slogan of liberal social policy, which was to lead to further misunderstandings and hostility between Huber and other Prussian conservatives who dismissed "Association" (or "Assoziation," which is the more modern spelling) in favor of "Corporation." See, e.g., Karl Rosenkranz, *Briefwechsel zwischen Karl Rosenkranz und Varnhagen von Ense* (Königsberg, 1926); Karl Rosenkranz, *Von Magdeburg bis Königsberg* (Königsberg, 1873); Eduard Gans, *Rückblicke auf Personen und Zustände* (Berlin, 1836). Huber's theory of association is outlined in his article "Ueber innere Colonisation," *Janus* 1 (1846): 193–255.

effectively organized only through "free unions . . . on the material basis of common property that will have to be established."[31] And there were two other recurring themes that surfaced for the first time in Huber's 1844 article for the *Evangelische Kirchenzeitung:* there was his thought that the unions (later referred to as associations) should be based on "moral-religious foundations," which foreshadowed Huber's preoccupation of pauperism being an inherently moral problem, a problem of *Bildung* and styles of life;[32] and interrelated was his concern for "the autonomy of family life,"[33] the integrity of which had to be preserved. One of the foremost tenets of the associations that were to be founded for the protection of the proletariat was "the safeguarding of a Christian family life within the proletariat."[34]

The idea that the *Bindungslosigkeit* (that is, the absence of a supportive social fabric for the individual and the lack of integration into a larger whole) was the core of the social problem, a notion familiar from the *Wochenblatt* and Radowitz, reappeared in Huber's thought in modified form. The main purpose of "associations of a greater or smaller number of proletarian individuals and families,"[35] which Huber planned to create, was redemption of the individual "from his existence in atomistic masses." Association would prove "the advantage of organic groupings in comparison to the atomistic mass."[36] It is this moralizing and psychological approach to social problems that marked the dividing line between Huber's organic concept of association, on the one hand, and the liberal "help through self-help" concept of association, on the other. The latter gained prominence through Hermann Schulze-Delitzsch in the 1850s. For the liberals, the association was a means to an end; for Huber, it was an end in itself. In his conception, association was tightly interwoven with the idea of the Christian state, intent on furthering the moral and religious foundations of the lower classes. In contrast to the liberal concept of association, the federation of workers Huber had in mind aimed at maintaining the conservative status quo and the integration of the proletarian into family and association. "Redeeming" workers from mass existence also implied disarming them, thereby rendering innocuous the social danger they might present.

In the summer of 1844, Huber ventured on a journey through England to study the industrial proletariat in situ. There he spent several months in Manchester to examine the conditions of the working classes. As was to be expected, the account of Huber's impressions differed considerably from

---

31. Huber, "Schwanenorden," *EKZ* 11 (February 7, 1844): 81–88.
32. Especially visible in Huber, "Manchester: Das Proletariat," *Janus* 2 (1845): 641–78, 705–27.
33. Huber, "Schwanenorden," *EKZ* 11 (February 7, 1844): 87.
34. Huber, "Ueber innere Colonisation," *Janus* 1 (1846): 204.
35. Ibid., 205.
36. Ibid., 215.

Friedrich Engels's *Conditions of the Working Classes in England*, even though both appeared in 1845.[37] No doubt, the conservative professor was initially shaken by the sight of the misery around him. According to his own account, he labored under the spell of a "ponderous, dreary impression,"[38] remembering the massacre of Peterloo, the traces of which were "with indelible letters written in the memory, even in the faces of these people."[39] Eventually, however, Huber came to the conclusion "that with more thrifty habits the workers could . . . in each respect be better off." When all was said and done, the misery was the proletarians' own fault: they were "too dull-witted or too careless, too thoughtless, too disheartened."[40] Here the prevalence of a moralizing approach becomes obvious again, an approach that basically ignores material preconditions. It is thus to be expected that for Huber the causes of poverty lay with the persons concerned.[41]

Nevertheless, the danger embodied by the proletariat remained great. In England and Wales alone, there were "among its population of sixteen million men at least six million who, in demeaning brutality or else in declared hostility, stand outside political and social civilization." For the present, Huber noted with relief, "these starving millions" had not yet found the means "to endanger the existing status quo and the people favored by it."[42] But the problem could not be ignored. Material improvements were secondary, for "the amelioration of the conditions of the English manufacturing proletariat is completely independent of that." What truly counted were improvements "in the domain of moral and religious life."[43] Even when allowing for Huber's moralizing approach, his callousness regarding the material conditions of the proletarians remains astounding: "To me children appear to be the most pitiable ones of all," he wrote, "having to crawl under rattling and humming looms, but they will get used to it too."[44]

While Huber perceived some features of urban proletarian life as repugnant, his sketches of the existence of rural paupers were almost idyllic.[45] The "hundreds of men, women, girls, and children" living in the factory settlements around Bolton were characterized as being "of healthy, content appearance, conspicuously well dressed, well fed; the women and children are partly like

---

37. Huber, "Manchester: Das Proletariat," *Janus* 2 (1845): 641–78, 705–27.
38. Ibid., 643.
39. Ibid., 647.
40. Ibid., 676.
41. Ibid., 677.
42. Ibid., 652.
43. Ibid., 678.
44. Ibid., 673.
45. Huber described the living conditions of the rural proletariat in his second article on England, in "Das Proletariat," *Janus* 2 (1845): 705–27.

milk and bread."[46] The fact that it was possible to lead "a Christian and materially tolerable existence sheltered from hardship" was demonstrated by the example of the English rural proletariat.[47] Accordingly, the organization of the rural proletariat in England provided the model for Huber's own associations.[48] To avoid being lumped together with "Fourier's Phalanstères, Owen's Social Colonies, or Cabet's Ikaries,"[49] Huber set himself a modest goal: "Each worker shall in the sour sweat of his brow acquire enough during six weekdays that he and his dependents can safely count on satiating themselves in pleasure and gratitude . . . and rest the seventh day."[50] The "acquisition of so-called political rights and liberties for the proletarians" was, however, no matter of urgency; fulfillment of modest material needs for the "infinite majority of proletarians" claimed greater priority.[51] He therefore focused on describing "an ideal image of such proletarian quarters,"[52] guided by the impressions received during his visit to England: "The English cottage system is, if correctly understood and diligently carried out, the only one to safeguard the necessary independence for the proletarian family without excluding essential advantages of the associations."[53] Given that "the expense of such buildings is usually far too great to be covered by the future inhabitants themselves,"[54] who would finance the project? According to Huber, the key to its success lay with the state, which should bestow "annually a couple of hundred thousand thaler on such enterprises," while "municipal corporations will also have a very natural obligation to become partners in manifold ways."[55] It would be unwise, Huber argued, "to execute great things without the state in our present status quo"[56]—an argument that testifies to the pervasive influence his Prussian environment had exerted on him. In Prussia, bureaucratic rule had made the state omnipresent, which may explain why even associations of workers that by their very nature gravitated toward private management were in Huber's conception financed in part by the state.

---

46. Ibid., 708.

47. Ibid., 715.

48. Huber, "Über innere Colonisation," *Janus* 1 (1846): 193–255.

49. Ibid., 197.

50. Ibid., 198.

51. Ibid., 199.

52. Ibid., 202, 227: "Wir legen ein ganz entscheidendes Gewicht auf den Punkt der Wohnung, der Baulichkeiten, der lokalen materiellen Anstalten."

53. Ibid., 206. Huber's plans for the implementation of his association project bear witness to the influence English and French early socialists must have exerted on him, despite his own violent denunciations of this (e.g., ibid., 211).

54. Ibid., 228. Huber hastened to add that these inhabitants were "for the greater part, totally without property."

55. Ibid., 229.

56. Ibid., 251.

In this regard Huber was a victim of Prussian conditions, since, in contrast to conservatives like Radowitz, he sought an alternative to direct state involvement. Huber was well aware of his plight: "We will be reproached with an inherent contradiction against often proclaimed principles if we involve the state to this degree," he wrote. He would always welcome "the most extensive development of free activity for the individual and association." But he "could not and did not want to exclude organs of the state from competition," for "we [must] in any case accept matters as we find them."[57] Probably to a larger extent in Prusssia than elsewhere, the nature of the state thus directed the thought and ideas of any social thinker intent on implementing his theories into predefined tracks. A certain amount of state participation had to inhere in a social philosopher's concepts from the beginning. Since Frederick William I and Frederick II had shaped it in the eighteenth century, the state apparatus exerted paramount influence on all sectors of life. In the Prussia of Frederick the Great, for example, the state apparatus—that is, monarch and bureaucracy—controlled and directed the Prussian economy and society to an extent unparalleled at the time. When Huber conceived his plans for workers' associations, this state of affairs had changed only insofar as the formerly dominant role of the monarch had been absorbed by higher-ranking officials. In 1846, the year Huber published his ideas, the rule of officials was still unbroken. This may explain in part why Huber went so far as to envision the establishment of a *Ministerium des Armen-und Proletariatswesens,* a ministry of poor relief,[58] arguing that in the long run "no civilized state could exist without its own agency, . . . a ministry for these things."[59]

Even though Huber had been appointed to his Berlin position semiofficially, he was denied ultimate success among the broader masses and among his fellow conservatives. In part, official sponsorship may have alienated other conservatives, but ultimate blame for Huber's failure lay with the man himself. His inability to formulate ideas clearly and succinctly, his predilection for impenetrable prose that heaped one involved period on the other, and the imperviousness of his lectures were not conducive to public success.[60] The lukewarm reception his ideas found with other Prussian conservatives was a cause for personal dismay. Huber complained publicly that conservatives had shown for his proposals "neither understanding nor approval—that would have been asking for too much—nor even serious consideration or critical examination."[61] Huber's rejection by other conservatives undoubtedly had to do with his being a non-Prussian; having been born in southern Germany and

---

57. Ibid.
58. Ibid.
59. Ibid., 252.
60. See Elvers, *Huber,* 2:109–10.
61. See *Janus* 2 (1847): 290–91 (Anmerkung).

having traveled throughout western Europe for years, the foreigner remained strong in him. Huber, for example, never discontinued his old habit of interspersing his articles with Spanish, Portuguese, or English figures of speech. He thus never got used to glorifying the emotional symbols dear to Prussia, such as the Hohenzollern, the officer corps, and the virtues of the landed aristocracy (as a Junker indigenous to the Mark Brandenburg would have done); and his heart did not beat faster at the sound of the Leuthen chorale. For the "Gerlachsche Clique,"[62] Huber had only mistrust, and in a letter to his father-in-law, he dismissed Radowitz as nothing but a "beau parleur." These conservatives, in turn, could not warm up to his "Assoziation," which they automatically associated with the liberal archenemy.

The gulf widened in the 1850s, when it came to "an almost irreconcilable struggle"[63] between the adherents of the concept of *Korporation,* represented by both the *Kreuzzeitung* and those advocating the reintroduction of guilds, and the supporters of the "Assoziation," most of whom were liberals. Prussian conservatives from the *Berliner Politisches Wochenblatt* to the *Kreuzzeitung* (founded in 1848) considered "*Autorität,*" the "authority ordained by God,"[64] to be the salient characteristic of the corporation, by which the apprentice acknowledged the authority of the journeyman, who, in turn, respected the master craftsman as his superior. In the 1850s, a great number of conservatives endorsed feudalization of industrial establishments, where discipline and order were to be maintained by means of a strict hierarchy. To conservatives this central idea of authority and patriarchal rule seemed absent from Huber's concept of association, whose members were basically equal in standing and whose fundamental doctrines focused on self-help. The *Staats- und Gesellschaftslexikon,* an encyclopedia with a strong conservative bias, published by the erstwhile *Kreuzzeitung*'s editor Hermann Wagener, defined "association" as "a revolutionary order, which artificially masses former guildsmen, now deteriorated into factory workers, into groups for the purpose of political agitation."[65] As Huber became identified with the concept of association, he inevitably incurred other conservatives' suspicion.

An additional factor that separated him from his conservative peers was Huber's attitude toward industry and progress. He shared neither their well-known hostility toward the seemingly unstoppable advance of industrialization nor their criticism of modernity and its achievements. Before 1848, these concepts were conspicuously absent from Huber's political teachings. On the contrary, he professed to favor industrial development and rejected the purely

---

62. Paulsen, *Huber,* 53.

63. See Karl V. v. Herberger, *Die Stellung der preussischen Konservativen zur Sozialen Frage 1848–1862* (Meissen, 1914), 40.

64. See *Neue Preussische Zeitung: Kreuzzeitung* 112 (1850); Herberger, *Konservativen,* 40.

65. *Staats- und Gesellschaftslexikon,* vol. 8 (1861), 323.

agrarian orientation of the Gerlachs and their followers.[66] Before the revolution, Huber was far from advocating a return to a precapitalistic economy, in which the work of the artisan and the farmer would be extolled as "ethical" and industry was seen as "corrupting." In the same vein, he rejected the idolization of the Middle Ages and guild life.

At the beginning of the 1850s, however, Huber conceived ideas that approximated those promulgated by the *Berliner Politisches Wochenblatt*. In his *Bruch mit Revolution und Ritterschaft,* he argued that the management of associations was, after all, a task best accomplished by the aristocracy. The aim of his pamphlet was "to give prominence to the true and highest calling of the *Ritterschaft* [i.e., the aristocracy], which lies in the social sphere."[67] The lower the aristocracy valued its social mission, the less convincing would be its claim for political rights. As with the *Wochenblatt,* Radowitz, and Ludwig von Gerlach, the assumption of social obligations had become a justification for the political power of the aristocracy. Huber specifically addressed the "aristocracy of birth, of possession, of office, of intellect."[68] This new elite, he argued, could and should act as a counterweight to the selfishness and acquisitive instincts of the bourgeoisie and to the rigid and ossified spirit of officials.[69] As other conservatives before him, Huber turned against the "rampant growth of bureaucracy,"[70] whose "mechanisms threaten to fossilize political life."[71] Huber saw the main function of the aristocracy in threefold service: service for the Lord, service for the dynasty, and "above all service for the poor, the underprivileged, the ailing of our age."[72] In the same vein, Huber suggested a "timely revival of knights' orders," for "now as before, the younger generation, not only of the aristocracy but also of the dynasty, could find a field of dignified activity in them, the scarcity of which is only too noticeable."[73] Like the *Wochenblatt* before him, Huber intended to create a new elite capable of leading the country and able to imbue it with new vigor. In opposition to the group around the *Wochenblatt,* however, he wanted to recruit this new aristocracy not just from the members of the landed aristocracy but from a wider pool. Even though Huber spoke, like Gerlach, of "the obligation property imposes, with its grave responsibility towards God,"[74] he reproved the theoreticians of the *ständische Monarchie* for their preoccupation with carrying out "a

---

66. Paulsen, *Huber,* 66.
67. Viktor A. Huber, *Bruch mit Revolution und Ritterschaft* (Berlin, 1852), vii.
68. Ibid., 37.
69. Ibid., 38–39.
70. Ibid., 15.
71. Ibid., 32.
72. Ibid., 34.
73. Ibid., 46.
74. Ibid.

doctrinaire program [after Haller and Adam Müller], rather than simply help-ing the people in the way . . . required by the demands of modern industry."[75]

In many respects, Viktor Aimé Huber is a good example of how an outsider, despite fundamentally different inner predispositions and inclina-tions, adopted some of the underlying assumptions of conservative social theory, such as that of the social mission of the aristocracy, to make himself accepted. In Prussia, there were strong intellectual and social pressures that restrained any deviation from mainstream conservatism. The deviationist could easily be placed in the enemy's (in Huber's case the liberal) camp. But one might argue that for Huber, it was merely the attraction exerted on him by certain concepts (e.g., that of an elite created by dint of service) that made a potential heretic revert back to the mainstream.

Huber's argument that the state should shoulder responsibility for his associations is more easily understandable. It had been virtually unthinkable among conservatives a decade earlier, but by the mid-1840s, demands for state intervention had become common coinage. Rhenish liberals demanded state promotion of industries and, in the case of the Westfalian entrepreneur Friedrich Harkort, went as far as to call for state aid for the poor.[76] Right Hegelians promulgated that the solution of the social question was a duty of the state. In his *Philosophy of Law and of Society,* for example, Heinrich Bernhard Oppenheim suggested that the state could be instrumental in redistributing wealth, and Karl Rosenkranz equally favored state intervention to alleviate social ills.[77] Lorenz von Stein, who is generally considered to have been strongly influenced by Hegel, considered active state intervention as the only possible remedy to cope with the growing proletariat.[78] And in 1849, the Prussian minister of trade and commerce, the formerly liberal Elberfeld banker August von der Heydt, conceded that "to relieve the misery of the people was one of the first tasks of each government."[79]

75. Ibid., 53.

76. See, e.g., Donald Rohr, *The Origins of Social Liberalism in Germany* (Chicago, 1963), 138–39; Hans-Ulrich Wehler, *Deutsche Gesellschaftsgeschichte* (Munich, 1987), 2:266; in general Rudolf Boch, *Grenzenloses Wachstum? Das rheinische Wirtschaftsbürgertum und seine Indus-trialisierungsdebatte 1814–1857* (Göttingen, 1991).

77. Heinrich Bernhard Oppenheim, *Philosophie des Rechts und der Gesellschaft* (Stuttgart, 1850); Karl Rosenkranz, "Die mögliche Verfassung Deutschlands und Preussens Verhältnis zu derselben im Sommer 1848," *Neue Studien* 3 (1877): 291–314; see also Hermann Lübbe, "Die politische Theorie der Hegelschen Rechten," in *Politische Philosophie in Deutschland,* DTV (Munich, 1974), 27–83.

78. See his *Geschichte der sozialen Bewegung in Frankreich von 1789 bis auf unsere Tage,* 3 vols. (Munich, 1921), originally published in 1850. See also Stein, *Der Sozialismus und Kom-munismus des heutigen Frankreich,* 2d ed. (Leipzig, 1848).

79. July 7, 1849, "Votum des Ministers für Handel und Gewerbe . . . ," in *Vorschläge zur Lösung der sozialen Frage und Massnahmen wegen Abwendung eines Nothstandes, 1848–1860,* Staatsarchiv Merseburg, rep. 120BB, VII, no. 2, 85.

The first Prussian conservative to advocate state intervention as the main panacea was Carl Rodbertus.[80] Rodbertus was born on August 12, 1805, in the old university town of Greifswald on the Baltic, which was still under Swedish domination at the time of his birth. Unlike his father and grandfather, both of whom had been well-known professors (his grandfather was the famous Physiocrat Schlettwein), Rodbertus displayed little inclination toward winning academic laurels. After several years as an official in the judicial branch of the bureaucracy,[81] Rodbertus quit the civil service to study history and economics in Heidelberg, a decision prompted by the outbreak of the July Revolution of 1830 in Paris. He then ventured on extensive journeys through Switzerland, France, and Holland, before finally settling down in Jagetzow, a manor he had bought for himself in Pomerania in 1835. Henceforth, Jagetzow was his home and his point of departure, for his position as gentleman farmer influenced his life considerably. Even as political writer and essayist, Rodbertus henceforth remained removed from the political struggles of his day. His livelihood never depended on royal favor or a temporary political appointment. Nevertheless, Rodbertus's future political involvement, though short-lived, was by no means insignificant. During the Revolution of 1848, he became a member of the Prussian national assembly and minister of culture in the cabinet of Auerswald, a post from which he resigned, however, after having served for only two months.

---

80. It was thus for good reason that Friedrich Engels's bon mot about Rodbertus's *preussischen Bürosozialismus* gained such notoriety.

81. See the long article by Moritz Wirth in the *Allgemeine Deutsche Biographie* for a detailed outline of Rodbertus's life. Rodbertus is one of the lesser known conservatives of nineteenth-century Germany, since his conservative state socialism met with no interest in either East or West Germany after 1945. The secondary literature on him dates mostly from before 1930; Erich Thier's *Rodbertus, Lassalle, Adolph Wagner: Ein Beitrag zur Theorie und Geschichte des deutschen Staatssozialismus* (Jena, 1930) was among the last independent studies devoted to his ideas, while Walter Vogel's, *Bismarck's Arbeiterversicherung: Ihre Entstehung im Kräftespiel der Zeit* (Braunschweig, 1951) dealt with Rodbertus's theoretical contribution to Bismarck's social legislation. For references to his ideas in the more recent literature see Thomas Nipperdey, *Deutsche Geschichte 1800–1866* (Munich, 1983), 520; Panajotis Kondylis, *Konservatismus: Geschichtlicher Gehalt und Untergang* (Stuttgart, 1986), 446; Hans-Ulrich Wehler, *Gesellschaftsgeschichte*, 2:265–66. On his role in the revolution see Wolfgang Schwentker, *Konservative Vereine und Revolution in Preussen* (Düsseldorf, 1988), 305–7, 322; Otto Büsch, ed., *Handbuch der Preussischen Geschichte*, vol. 2 (Berlin, 1992), 254, 261. Rodbertus, however, is not mentioned in a number of studies on conservatism, e.g., Sigmund Neumann, *Die Stufen des preussischen Konservatismus* (Berlin, 1930); Martin Greiffenhagen, *Das Dilemma des Konservatismus in Deutschland* (Munich, 1977); Robert Berdahl, *The Politics of the Prussian Nobility* (Princeton, 1988); Kurt Lenk, *Deutscher Konservatismus* (Frankfurt, 1989); Reinhart Koselleck, *Preussen zwischen Reform und Revolution,* 2d ed. (Stuttgart, 1975); James Sheehan, *German History 1770–1866* (Oxford, 1989). This relative neglect is due to the fact that Rodbertus did not form part of a tradition; there is no line of filiation (as, for example, in the case of Ludwig von Gerlach or Hermann Wagener), and Rodbertus's ideas cannot be interpreted in a strictly conservative context.

Since the mid-1830s, Rodbertus had been interested in the social question, to the analysis of which he devoted much of his later life. In contrast to Radowitz and the Gerlachs, who also made a name for themselves as politicians and advisers to the king, Rodbertus is chiefly remembered for his literary contribution and as an advocate of state socialism. Some attributed Rodbertus's high regard for the state to Hegel's influence,[82] which, however, is far-fetched, as Rodbertus never had any contact with Hegel himself or his disciples. Others saw in him the conservative counterpart to Ferdinand Lassalle, the founder of German Social Democracy.[83] With Lassalle, Rodbertus shared not only the predilection for a strong state that takes the lead in social matters but also a pronounced antiliberalism.

Though the bulk of Rodbertus's writings on the social question was produced in the 1860s and 1870s, his first important essay on the issue, written in 1839, already contained all his central ideas.[84] When the *Berliner Revue* published this essay, "*Die Forderungen der arbeitenden Klassen,*"[85] in 1872, Rodbertus wrote to his collaborator, Rudolf Meyer, that he would find "in this article already the entire system which I developed piece by piece in my writings on political economy."[86] Rodbertus's disciple and the coeditor of his collected works, Adolph Wagner, wrote in 1899 that "during his entire future life Rodbertus went beyond his early achievements only in details."[87] For Adolph Wagner, the main accomplishment of Rodbertus's earlier years consisted in his article on "*Die Forderungen der arbeitenden Klassen.*"

---

82. See, for example, Hans-Ernst Jansen, *Das Proletariat im Vormärz in den Anschauungen deutscher Denker* (Kiel, 1928), 53. Carl-V. Herberger, *Konservativen,* 69, saw in Rodbertus "a disciple of Hegel and Fichte . . . , which was the reason why Friedrich Engels mockingly referred to his teachings as Prussian officialdom's socialism."

83. See, e.g., Hans-Joachim Schoeps, *Üb' immer Treu' und Redlichkeit: Preussen in Geschichte und Gegenwart* (Düsseldorf, 1978), 91; or Thier, *Rodbertus.*

84. Rodbertus's literary production reached its highest point in the early 1870s during his collaboration with Rudolf Meyer, the publisher of the conservative journal *Berliner Revue.* Since its foundation in 1855, the *Berliner Revue* had concentrated on social issues. Later Hermann Wagener became the driving force behind the journal. See Adalbert Hahn, *Die Berliner Revue* (Berlin, 1934).

85. Rodbertus's article, "Die Forderungen der arbeitenden Klassen" (the demands of the laboring classes) was written in 1839 and sent to the *Augsburger Allgemeine Zeitung,* then the most highly renowned newspaper within the confines of the German Confederation. The *AAZ* sent it back without further consideration, and it was not until 1872 that an abbreviated version of the article was printed in the *Berliner Revue.* It was reprinted, again in a shortened version in *Briefe und sozialpolitische Aufsätze von Dr. Rodbertus-Jagetzow,* ed. Rudolf Meyer (Berlin, 1895), 575–86, and it was printed completely for the first time in the edition of Rodbertus's writings, *Schriften von Dr. Carl Rodbertus-Jagetzow,* vol. 3, ed. Adolph Wagner (Berlin, 1899), 195–223.

86. From the preface by August Skalweit in Carl Rodbertus, *Die Forderungen der arbeitenden Klassen* (Frankfurt, 1946), 3.

87. Carl Rodbertus-Jagetzow, *Schriften,* 3:3.

This pivotal essay opened with three questions: What do the laboring classes want? Will others be able to withhold it from them? Will the fulfillment of workers' demands entail the end of modern culture?[88] On the first question, Rodbertus commented that the demands of the working classes appeared "in a rather disguised form." Though they were seemingly striving for political recognition,[89] this "craving for political power" was only a pretended goal, merely serving as means to an end; "the end itself is: more property."[90] Behind the working classes' cry for more property stood nothing but their wish "for more participation in the degree of culture of the time, more participation *an den Wohlthaten der heutigen Cultur.*"[91] Regarding the second question, Rodbertus remarked that no one doubted the working classes' resolution to pursue their goals with genuine determination, "the determination historical destiny needs when pursuing its grand designs."[92] The only benefits the working classes drew from modern society were "personal freedom and a kind of formal equality," but theirs was a freedom without subsistence that equaled "a debt claim without debtor."[93]

At the present time, when "the shack is placed in immediate vicinity to the palace, and the silk dress, unable to avoid it, brushes against rags and tatters,"[94] these demands presented a great threat to society due to the ever swelling numbers of the laboring poor. Rodbertus was convinced that in the long run the state could not be solely defended against them "with such weak and purely negative means as bayonets."[95] The full mustering of state authority against the proletariat had to remain an exception and should not be allowed to become a basis for normal conditions, as the existing state of society could not be defended by violence alone. On the contrary, the cohesion of society had to come from within: "What holds society together is of a moral nature, preserved and enhanced by moral [*sittliche*] institutions."[96]

---

88. Rodbertus, *Schriften,* 3:195. For the full version of the article see Rodbertus, *Schriften,* 3:195–224. The fact that Rodbertus refers to the *"Birminghamszenen"* at the beginning of the article shows that it was written in 1839 and not in 1837, as alleged by some.

89. Ibid., 3:195. Rodbertus argued that "such a desire would be disquieting," as it would necessarily lead to a republican form of government.

90. Ibid., 3:196.

91. Ibid., 3:197.

92. Ibid.

93. Ibid., 3:199.

94. Ibid. Rodbertus continued revealingly: "Von der Zahl der arbeitenden Klassen schweigen wir, denn wir mögen keine Inschriften für ihre Fahnen liefern."

95. Ibid., 3:200. The counterforces available against the workers' onslaught were "police and canons, and, if one wants, the stories of Miss Martineau" (an allusion to the English writer Harriet Martineau, 1802–76, an advocate of Malthusian principles, whose works were widely read in Germany).

96. Ibid., 3:201.

In Rodbertus's conception, these institutions could historically be subdivided into the systems of *Zucht* (discipline) and *Bildung* (education). The first of these was based "on subordination"; it was dominant during the Middle Ages and with "the laboring classes of antiquity," in the system of slavery, whereas the second had been prevalent among the free citizens of antiquity. In his own age, Rodbertus found "only the last decaying remnants of the former, and only the crude rudimentary beginnings of the second system."[97] The laboring classes had emancipated themselves from the system of *Zucht* without yet being integrated into the new, modern system of education. In opposition to *Wochenblatt* conservatism, Rodbertus held that the working classes could not be returned to servitude: "A century of history cannot be undone."[98] And that was why the contemporary situation (1839) seemed so precarious: "In the midst of present-day society there is a numerous people of barbarians, barbarians in mind and morals, endowed with the poverty, the boldness, and the savagery of barbarians, covetous of the treasures, the pleasures, and the culture of the others."[99] In former times this lowest class could successfully be used against the *"Rotüre der Mittelklassen"*;[100] in the present struggle, however, one is left only with the choice "to have the barbarians fight each other."[101] With evil foreboding, Rodbertus added that "the barbarians fighting in Rome's armies conquered Rome." The provisional conclusion Rodbertus drew from this was that traditional solutions to social problems had become hackneyed and new answers had to be found.[102]

To find a solution, it was necessary "to keep production always at such a high level of productivity that the workers can profit from it too." It would be reserved for a state-directed economy, able to carry out a "modification of the property status," to implement this program. In all his subsequent proposals, however mitigated they were by obfuscation, Rodbertus essentially beat the drum for a state socialist program. The primary task of the state would be the abolition of the *"rentierende Eigentum,"* the profit-yielding possessions:

Landed property and capital would become the common good of society, but whatever had been produced by the tools of the workman, after

97. Ibid., 3:202.

98. Ibid., 3:204.

99. Ibid., 3:205.

100. The "presumption of the middle classes," that is, the rising bourgeoisie. Rodbertus's concept is reminiscent of Radowitz's suggestion concerning the possible use of the proletariat as a weapon in the struggle against the bourgeoisie (see chapter 2).

101. Rodbertus, *Schriften,* 3:205.

102. "Was bleibt übrig? Nichts als die Ueberwindung des Hindernisses, als die sociale Parole: Weiter!—Denn die Gesellschaft hat ihre Schiffe verbrannt!" (ibid.). This renders it obvious that Rodbertus did not turn to the past as the key to the solution of the social question.

subtracting the reproduction of capital, would become the property of the workers in accordance to their performed labor.[103]

Yet there were major differences between Rodbertus's state socialism and the social conceptions of the early French socialists and Marx. Differences were most pronounced when considering a state of affairs in which "productivity is not yet sufficiently large to grant more to all classes." At the stage where only "handmills are known, slavery has to exist," Rodbertus argued, since antiquity would have never accomplished its mission without it. What ultimately mattered was "that mind [*Geist*] realizes itself somewhere in the nation," which will then be a justification for one class to live at the expense of another, "so that at least the privileged class can execute the will of history."[104] Among other things, this cultural elitism that measured everything according to achievements and results of education and culture separated Rodbertus from socialists, to whom slavery was unacceptable under any circumstances.

In his blueprint of state socialism, Rodbertus expressly acknowledged the influence of Ricardo. Following the Englishman's lead, Rodbertus introduced *Arbeitszeit*, the working hours, as the general yardstick determining all remaining factors. Even the new currency to be established in Rodbertus's system was to be based on the working hours of the individual laborer. An individual worker's share of produced goods would be computed commensurate to the amount of work he put into their creation.[105] The wages of the worker were to be directly related to his working hours and the general level of productivity, and his standard of living should rise proportionately to national wealth.

Rodbertus also anticipated the case, later analyzed by Marx in greater detail, where the industrial worker, by equal or even rising wages, became poorer "in relation to the quantities of goods which other classes draw from the national product."[106] An increase in workers' affluence, to Rodbertus tantamount to the solution of the social question,[107] would be possible only if the government carried out "a legally binding assessment of value for all goods,

---

103. Ibid., 3:208–10.

104. Ibid., 3:207.

105. Ibid., 3:222. Rodbertus and Marx argued along similar lines in this respect, and much of what Marx outlined in *Wage, Labor and Capital* had already been anticipated by Rodbertus ten years earlier.

106. Karl Marx, *Wage, Labor and Capital,* (Chicago, 1986), 218. This happens "when the working classes do not benefit from increasing productivity to the same extent as the propertied classes." Marx analyzed this in a series of articles in 1849.

107. As Adolph Wagner, the long time associate and disciple of Rodbertus, wrote in the introduction to Rodbertus's *Schriften,* 3:xxiv, Rodbertus saw the social question as "only the question of the proportionate share of the working classes in the entire national productive output."

which has to be based on labor."[108] Rodbertus called on the state to create paper money based on this value assessment, with which workers were to be paid. It was also the task of the state to establish a system of storehouses, stocked with provisions by entrepreneurs, where industrial laborers could exchange money for food.[109] With the help of this rigid system of state regulation, the social question—according to Rodbertus, "the vital question of modern civilization" itself[110]—could be solved.

In the radicalism of his proposals regarding state control, the role of industrial workers, and their share in the profits, Rodbertus was unique among conservative social theoreticians in Prussia. It is no wonder, then, that the *Augsburger Allgemeine Zeitung* refused to print his article. Despite some of the extremes reached in detail, however, Rodbertus shared a broad common basis and numerous points of departure with other conservatives. His social ideas were pervaded by a pronounced antiliberal streak. Liberalism, he maintained, like "no other part of the entire national economy," was inspired by "a merely negative character."[111] Liberalism had laid the foundation for the "despotism of profit-yielding property," the very despotism that continually confined the worker "to the standards of minimum subsistence,"[112] even at times of rising productivity. It was due to "Smith's system" that the owners of profit-yielding property acquired absolute power, which they were able to exert at will over "the dispossessed worker." Rodbertus was convinced that owners of the means of production "will grant the laborer only that which is absolutely necessary to maintain his labor power and reproduce it in his children."[113] The liberals' concept of ownership, according to which everyone could use his property at his own discretion (or, if so desired, leave it entirely unused) met with Rodbertus's disapproval, since "changes in the economic conditions could induce the proprietors" to withhold even the bare necessities of life from the workers.[114] Rodbertus's antiliberalism, unlike that of the *Wochenblatt* or Radowitz, was not coupled with a preference for a precapitalistic economic

108. Rodbertus, *Schriften,* 3:222. Naturally, this fixed value for all goods would have "to change from time to time according to changes in productivity."

109. Ibid., 3:222.

110. Ibid., 3:223: "Das Studium der besten Köpfe sollte ihr gewidmet sein; jede Akademie sollte an ihrer Beantwortung arbeiten . . ."

111. Ibid., 3:212.

112. Ibid., 3:213.

113. Ibid., 3:213. This might well be a verbatim quotation from the works of Karl Marx. At the beginning of the 1870s, Rodbertus accused Marx of plagiarism, without, however, being able to substantiate his allegations. After Rodbertus's death, the editors of his works retracted these accusations for the most part. See Rodbertus, *Schriften,* 3:xxix. Like Marx, Rodbertus spoke of a "allgemeinen gewerblichen bellum omnia contra omnes, den die Kapitalisten unter sich zu bestehen haben."

114. Ibid.

order and preindustrial relations of production. On the contrary, Rodbertus maintained that there was nothing that "could change the world more beneficially than the discovery of machines has done. In days to come, machines might be able to take the place of the slaves of antiquity, and all the rest of society represents the free men."[115]

Yet to put the blessings of the machine age to good use, the existing organization of the economy would have to be changed. Rodbertus was convinced that within the liberal system of his day, even "the discovery of the most accomplished machine conceivable, of a perpetuum mobile, . . . could bring in its wake death by starvation or a new servitude for the workers."[116] The liberal system, unable to extricate itself from its "culturally hostile tendencies," should therefore be replaced by a new "system of state-direction."[117] The future, Rodbertus argued, belonged to a state-directed economy. This concept of a strong, almost omnipotent state that would solve the social question through its own authority constituted the common ground Rodbertus shared with conservatives like Radowitz and Hermann Wagener, on the one hand, and with socialists like Ferdinand Lassalle, on the other.

Rodbertus demanded that the government's power be great enough to restrict "the despotism of profit-yielding possessions."[118] The "fate" of the working classes was to be taken out of the hands of "blind societal forces" by intervention of the state, which would then proceed to place it on better and lasting foundations. As for concrete measures, Rodbertus advocated that the government augment "the portion of the national product going to the workers." It would be the government's task "to shelter the laboring classes from the vicissitudes of changing economic conditions,"[119] placing them under the protection of the state.[120] As the lower classes had gone unprotected since the Reforms of 1807, Rodbertus now wanted the state to assert a guardianship over them similar to that which the feudal lord once wielded over his peasants.[121]

---

115. Ibid., 3:215.

116. The idea, later to be developed by Marx, that with increasing industrial output the worker became subject to growing servitude can be found *in nuce* with Rodbertus.

117. Rodbertus, *Schriften*, 3:216.

118. Ibid., 3:217. Whenever he referred to governmental powers, Rodbertus naturally proceeded from realities existing in Prussia. The existing distribution of power in his home country undoubtedly predisposed his theoretical concepts.

119. Ibid., 3:219.

120. According to Rodbertus, the working classes did not have to fear changing economic conditions as long as they were kept in dependence. It was only since their emancipation—an allusion to the Prussian reforms—that they were exposed to the fluctuations of the economy.

121. When speaking of the state's role in alleviating the lot of the lower classes, Rodbertus hoped that the state could help "to find the means so that the laboring classes can profit from the progress of productivity." Like Marx, Rodbertus defined productivity as "*Verhältnis der Masse des*

Even though Rodbertus shared the antiliberalism of the *Wochenblatt* and Radowitz, he opposed the restoration of guilds and the reintroduction of other features of a medieval economic order. In that respect he very much resembled Huber. Rodbertus strongly disavowed romantic tendencies, "which, suspicious of all the achievements of the modern idea of law, are equal to an escape back into the Middle Ages."[122] Accordingly, he was convinced that "whoever turns to the past to redress the social question will never contribute to its solution."[123] State action, the leitmotif of Rodbertus's social thought, was imperative in another field as well, for it was the state that had "to rescue modern culture from the venomous breath of the materialistic system." In his high regard for the state and the pivotal role it was destined to play, Rodbertus surpassed other Prussian conservatives, most notably the *Wochenblatt* group, but also Huber, whose associations, though under conservative auspices, were still partially imbued with the idea of self-help. In his belief in a strong state, Rodbertus approached Hegel; the role he reserved for the state in the solution of the social question was similar to that allotted to it in the social theories of Ferdinand Lassalle. Nevertheless, the eminently conservative traits of Rodbertus's thought predominated. They were epitomized in the importance he attributed to cultural values, for the sake of which he was even prepared to justify the slavery and servitude of the past.[124]

Produkts zu der ihr zum Grunde liegenden Quantität Arbeit" (*Schriften*, 3:220). In both cases it was Ricardo who stood sponsor to the concept. Rodbertus also wanted to express the value of goods in terms of the amount of labor they embodied. So did Ricardo and Marx. Rodbertus held that a product, in which "manorial lord, capitalist, and worker own their share," (221) could be assessed only by the amount of working hours it contained. To make the growth in a laborer's wages directly proportional to the growth in productivity, government intervention would be necessary (222).

122. See Hermann Dietzel, *Carl Rodbertus*, vol. 1 (Berlin, 1886), 20.

123. Ibid., 1:21.

124. In his emphasis on the inherent value of culture and the role education played in elevating the lower classes, Rodbertus very much resembled the Southern German theoreticians Franz von Baader and Ritter von Buss.

CHAPTER 4

Hermann Wagener's Conservative Socialism in the Reichsgründungszeit and Social Conservatism in Prussia from the Restoration to Bismarck

With its rapid growth of an urban proletariat, the decade after the revolution effected a change with which conservatives, given their background, were ill-equipped to deal. Moreover, Prussia had turned into a constitutional state with a liberal party that steadily grew and increasingly broadened its electorate at the cost of conservatives, especially with the beginning of the New Era in 1858. When, with the onset of the constitutional crisis in the early 1860s, the liberals further consolidated their position, the more far-sighted among conservative leaders therefore realized the need for reinforcing their electoral base.

In a conservative party that catered largely to the interests of its natural constituency, the East Elbian estate owners, there was little concern for the fate of those at the other end of the social spectrum. Most of the more social-minded conservatives soon found themselves on the fringes of the conservative party, though ultimately for reasons that had little to do with their social concerns. Josef Maria von Radowitz, the trusted friend and adviser of Frederick William IV (and foreign minister for a brief period after the revolution), soon became persona non grata among mainstream conservatives, due to his anti-Austrian foreign policy. He died deserted by his former conservative peers. Viktor Aimé Huber, who never forgave conservatives for condoning the passing of a constitution and arranging themselves so easily within the constitutional state, cannot be considered a member of the party after 1850. And Ludwig von Gerlach, whose ideas and actions had shaped Prussian conserva-

tism from its earliest beginnings, and who dominated conservative politics in the 1850s (until about 1866), soon renounced his earlier social concerns.

The towering figure of Prussian social conservatism, the man who continued the prerevolutionary tradition inaugurated by the *Wochenblatt*, was Gerlach's onetime protégé Hermann Wagener. Born in 1815, the same year as Bismarck, Wagener grew up in a Protestant parsonage in the Mark Brandenburg, a family background he shared with many famous German men of letters (Nietzsche being the best-known example). In 1835, Wagener took up the study of jurisprudence at Berlin University.[1] He started his legal career as *Referendar* at the higher regional court (*Oberlandesgericht*) at Frankfurt/Oder, where Ludwig von Gerlach held the vice presidency.[2] In 1847, Wagener was appointed higher regional court district judge (*Oberlandesgerichts-Assessor*) in Magdeburg by the good offices of Gerlach, who presided over the Magdeburg Court of Appeal at the time. The "plan to found a conservative paper edited by Wagener,"[3] realized in the *Neue Preussische Zeitung* or *Kreuzzeitung*, which first appeared on July 1, 1848, dated from this period. From virtual obscurity, Wagener thus became an important figure in Prussian politics after the revolution, when he made his appearance as editor-in-chief of the *Neue Preussische und Kreuz-Zeitung*, the main press organ of the conservative party. In a party without an apparatus, this was a key position.[4] Wagener's contentious and polemical style brought him notoriety but also implacable enemies, even among fellow conservatives, which eventually led to his resignation from the editorship in 1853. Yet he soon reemerged as one of the main spokespersons of the conservative party, first in the Prussian *Abgeordnetenhaus*, then in the North German Diet (1867–71), and finally, between 1871 and 1873, in the *Reichstag* of the newly established German Empire.

---

1. In Berlin Wagener hardly studied with the renowned Hegelian Eduard Gans but preferred the lectures of Carl von Savigny, known for his *"historische Rechtsschule"* and as successor to Eichhorn as minister of culture in the 1840s. See Wolfgang Saile, *Hermann Wagener und sein Verhältnis zu Bismarck* (Tübingen, 1958), 4.

2. Each week Gerlach arranged a meeting with his *Referendare* with lectures and discussions. See Ludwig von Gerlach, *Aufzeichnungen aus seinem Leben und Wirken* (Schwerin, 1903), 298: "Hans Kleist, the future *Oberpräsident* of the Rhine Province, and Wagener, the future editor of the *Kreuzzeitung*, came together in my house for lectures on judicial issues or public law with other higher regional court *Referendare*."

3. Gerlach, *Aufzeichnungen*, 477. Gerlach wrote that an "erster Keim der Kreuzzeitung" was conceived in those days.

4. In contrast to other political parties in Germany, conservatives remained a *Honoratioren-partei* without an apparatus until well into the Empire. See James Retallack, *Notables of the Right: The Conservative Party and Political Mobilization in Germany 1876–1918* (Boston, 1988); Thomas Nipperdey, *Die Organisation der deutschen Parteien vor 1918* (Düsseldorf, 1961); Gerhard A. Ritter, *Die deutschen Parteien 1830–1914* (Göttingen, 1985).

Wagener's most important political function was his role as Bismarck's adviser on social issues between 1862 and 1873. Not being a specialist in social affairs himself, the Prussian prime minister and future German chancellor often had to rely on Wagener's expert advice. The host of memoranda that Wagener submitted on the *Arbeiterfrage* testifies to his close collaboration with Bismarck, a collaboration that was also based on a once close personal friendship reaching back to the 1840s.[5] In sharp contrast to the majority of conservative deputies, Wagener continually emphasized the vital importance of the social question. In his memoirs, published in the 1880s, he lamented that if conservatives had only followed his recommendations thirty years ago, they would have found themselves in a much more favorable political position.[6] Wagener's political career, which had started so promisingly, came to a sudden inglorious end in 1873, due to his involvement in a financial scandal of the *Gründerjahre,*[7] the period of promoterism following the foundation of the Second Reich.

Hermann Wagener drew his inspiration from many sources, among which Lorenz von Stein, Carl Rodbertus, and Ferdinand Lassalle were the most important.[8] Radowitz's social ideas may have influenced Wagener as well, though, as editor-in-chief of the *Kreuzzeitung,* he strongly opposed Radowitz's foreign policy. As was already noted by his contemporaries, Wagener was not an original writer, but he was an immensely prolific one. And in contrast to the men from whom he borrowed, he did not have to expound his ideas in writings of a merely academic character, like Lorenz von Stein, or in a series of aphorisms and dialogues, like Radowitz. He incorporated their insights into the policy guidelines he developed for Bismarck. Moreover, by dint of his journalistic activities—as editor-in-chief of the *Kreuzzeitung* (1848–53) and publisher of the conservative *Staats- und Gesellschaftslexikon* (1859–67) and the *Berliner Revue*—he was in a position to exert an immeasurably greater influence on the public than his conservative predecessors. Wagener's great literary undertaking, the *Staats- und Gesellschaftslexikon* (twenty-three volumes) was conceived as a conservative counterweight to existing encyclopedias and their,

---

5. See Hans-Joachim Schoeps, "Hermann Wagener: Ein konservativer Sozialist," *Zeitschrift für Religions- und Geistesgeschichte* 8 (1956): 193–217; reprinted with few alterations in Schoeps, *Das andere Preussen,* 5th ed. (Berlin, 1981), 203–30; Saile, *Hermann Wagener.*

6. Hermann Wagener, *Die kleine aber mächtige Partei: Nachtrag zu Erlebtes* (Berlin, 1885), 3.

7. See Saile, *Hermann Wagener,* 114. Wagener had obtained shares for the *Pommersche Bahn* while lobbying for the concession of this new railroad line. According to Bismarck, Wagener had done only what hundreds of honorable people had done as well. While a parliamentary committee, set up to investigate the affair, later cleared Wagener of all criminal charges, his name remained morally tainted.

8. Schoeps called him "insignificant and resourceless" as a theoretician.

in Wagener's estimation, inherently liberal slant. His most important collaborator in this stupendous publishing enterprise was Bruno Bauer, former prominent Left Hegelian and onetime friend of Karl Marx. Bauer had spearheaded the radical opposition to the Prussian government in the 1840s. Even though Bauer had lost his radical edge after the revolution, it is indicative of Wagener's special brand of conservatism that he selected as collaborator a man who had gained notoriety as a Left Hegelian.

Already during the 1860s, Wagener made the prediction that "if the Conservative Party succeeds in successfully tackling the *Arbeiterfrage,* it will be the end of the Progressive Party."[9] When, with the outbreak of the constitutional conflict in 1861, the number of conservative deputies rapidly dwindled, Wagener was the first to urge that conservatism was in dire need of broadening its popular base. "The *Arbeiterfrage* is essentially a question of power of great significance,"[10] he admonished his peers, an issue that could be used as a lever to fortify the position of both the crown and the conservative party. Like so many conservatives of his time (including Bismarck), Wagener deeply distrusted the civil service,[11] which had effectively ruled the country up to 1848, and he was convinced that "the maggot-infested bureaucracy no longer provided a reliable basis of power for the Prussian crown."[12]

According to Wagener, the social question could be solved only if the Prussian monarchy realized its social vocation and turned into a "social kingdom." He was convinced that the future position of the monarchy depended on the support of the lower classes, just as the material welfare of pauperized craftsmen and industrial laborers could be substantially improved by the helping hand of the monarch. And in the early 1860s, when Wagener advanced the idea in his communications with Bismarck, a social kingdom was more than a mere pipe dream. It seemed politically feasible, since the dispossessed lower classes were believed to be strongly royalist in outlook, only waiting to seize the helping hand of the monarch. They would, therefore, show gratitude for any active material intervention on their behalf. Moreover, the actual political situation was so strained that the matter brooked no delay. In December 1861, before Bismarck became Prussian prime minister, the rising tide of liberalism,

---

9. *Neue Preussische Zeitung* 30 (February 5, 1863), supplement; Gerhard Ritter, *Die preussischen Konservativen und Bismarcks deutsche Politik 1858–1876* (Heidelberg, 1913), 142–43.

10. Adolf Richter, *Bismarck und die Arbeiterfrage im preussischen Verfassungskonflikt* (Stuttgart, 1935), 191.

11. As has been shown above, antagonism toward the civil service was a leitmotif in conservative thought. It was most pronounced with the *Wochenblatt* group and later, in the 1840s, with Josef Maria von Radowitz but it remained strong with conservatives after the revolution as well.

12. Siegfried Christoph, "Hermann Wagener als Sozialpolitiker" (Ph.D. diss., University of Erlangen, 1950), 61.

whose deputies outnumbered conservatives by a ratio of ten to one,[13] seriously jeopardized the hitherto unchallenged position of the crown. Wagener therefore found himself in the position of a conservative forced to realize that his *ständisch*-structured world belonged to an irretrievable past,[14] and his only recourse, under unfavorable political conditions, was to salvage whatever possible. He was well aware that "police state methods" alone would not do. "Petty harassments by the police only embitter without truly helping," he wrote in a memorandum to Bismarck.[15] The survival of the monarchy now depended on the realization of its social mission. "All kingship will henceforth be a hollow shadow," he maintained, "or mere despotism, or it will degenerate into a republic, if it does not muster the high moral courage to become a kingship of social reform."[16] In a long memorandum to Bismarck,[17] Wagener took the view that it should be the first concern of the conservative party "to acquire and secure the sympathy of the wide masses of the population through active intercession on behalf of their material and moral interests."[18] Radowitz had already expressed a similar idea when arguing that the lower classes of society should be tied to the dynasty, so that both could advance jointly against the true enemy of the crown, the liberal bourgeoisie. For both Radowitz and Wagener, this concept was to find its logical conclusion in the propagation of a "social kingdom."

Wagener was even more emphatic in his promotion of the social role of the monarchy than Radowitz. "The European kingships have a future only if they turn into social kingdoms," he wrote.[19] The opposition of the bourgeoisie could be overcome, Wagener argued, only by "creating a political counterweight through the small craftsmen and the working class, whose political needs and wants gravitate towards monarchical power."[20] Early on, Wagener discerned the *"Herrschaftsanspruch,"* as he put it, of the fourth estate, "which

---

13. Election results of December 1861: 14 conservative deputies, 119 deputies of the Progressive Party, 91 *Altliberale*, 50 *linkes Zentrum*.

14. In the early 1850s, as editor of the *Kreuzzeitung*, he still favored a *Ständestaat* along the lines of the *Berliner Politisches Wochenblatt*. Ludwig von Gerlach clung to this notion until the 1870s.

15. Saile, *Hermann Wagener*, 143.

16. Wagener, *Die kleine aber mächtige Partei*, 9, 13. Wagener adopted this sentence almost verbatim from Lorenz von Stein and put it into a draft of a conservative party program in 1855.

17. March 1, 1864, "Denkschrift von Justizrat Wagener vom 1.März 1864," Staatsarchiv Merseburg, Nachlass Zitelmann, rep. 92, no. 91, 10pp. The memorandum is preserved with Bismarck's marginal notes on it.

18. Ibid., 9–10.

19. Ibid., 1.

20. Ibid., 2. This corresponded to Radowitz's idea of fighting the bourgeoisie in alliance with the fourth estate.

has grown into a societal power, naturally striving for political supremacy within the state, just as the first, second, and third estate did when they were in a position to do so."[21] The king had the obligation, Wagener maintained, to be "the protector of the weak, the king of beggars, the savior and patron of the popular masses."[22] Wagener's compassion for destitute workers was more than a convenient veneer; he perceived their exploitation by industrial entrepreneurs as manifest injustice. In a speech before the *Reichstag* of the North German Confederation in 1867, Wagener observed that "in fifty years," no one would be able to understand that "the worker had merely been able to draw a concrete prize from the goods he produced. Gentlemen, such things as serfdom and bondage can be upheld only as long as awareness of their abjectness has not seeped into the masses."[23] Wagener equally emphasized that the monarchy should not link its fate with that of the currently ruling classes, since "for crown and kingdom nothing is more fatal than to identify with the ruling classes and fight off attacks directed against them, as if these had been aggressions against the monarchy itself."[24]

Compared to *Vormärz* conservatives, Wagener's social thought was characterized by increased openness toward socialism. In his short work *Die Lösung der Sozialen Frage* (1878), he interpreted socialism as the continuation of the French Revolution, as "the third act in that great European tragedy of fate."[25] Wagener naturally opposed the revolutionary legacy of 1789, but he also objected to labeling socialism as a mere "system of brutal instincts and desires of the working classes," as most other Prussian conservatives did. In Wagener's eyes, socialism constituted a "very vigorous system, encompassing all facets of the human life and species."[26] Even though the socialist of his own day still behaved as "political partisan and collaborator of liberalism and democracy,"[27] Wagener was convinced that the socialist would turn against those parties once the democratization of state and society had been achieved.[28] To counter the socialist danger effectively, Wagener deemed it

---

21. Ibid., 2 (Anmerkung).

22. Wagener, *Die Lösung der sozialen Frage* (Berlin, 1878), 66.

23. Schoeps, *Das andere Preussen,* 211.

24. Wagener, *Die Lösung der sozialen Frage,* 84.

25. Wagener, *Die Lösung der sozialen Frage,* 3. There was a connection between the French Revolution and socialism, since the root of modern social movements lay in the "Widerspruch zwischen der durch die erste französische Revolution proklamierten rechtlichen Freiheit und Gleichheit und der thatsächlichen sozialen Unfreiheit und Ungleichheit der grossen Masse des Volkes" (ibid., 4).

26. Wagener, *Die Lösung der sozialen Frage,* 19.

27. Ibid., 33.

28. Wagener noted that "der Sozialismus bei uns noch ein Werk zu verrichten vorfindet, welches eigentlich der aus der ersten französischen Revolution geborenen Demokratie gebührt [i.e., the democratization of state and society] . . . um alsdann auch hier zu der eigentlichen

imperative to understand socialism and to attempt to win over the workers for the state.[29] By the end of the 1850s, Wagener had disassociated himself completely from the ideals of the *Ständestaat,* which continued being propagated by Ludwig von Gerlach. In 1865, Wagener pointed out to Gerlach that "estates did not exist any more" and that

> the hallmark of the times is precisely the disintegration and decomposition of all outdated institutions and organisms. . . . The *Arbeiterfrage* has become tantamount to stemming the tide of destruction by founding and shaping timely institutions and organisms . . . in place of what has been lost and cannot be maintained any more.[30]

Wagener immediately considered Bismarck's antisocialist legislation of 1878 a grave political blunder,[31] and in the 1880s he equally rejected the German chancellor's social legislation, because he deemed it insufficient. According to Wagener, a program of social legislation had long been overdue as part of the *"innere Reichsgründung"* and should have been introduced in a more radical and thoroughgoing form.[32]

Even though Wagener displayed a good deal of genuine concern for the fate of the lower classes, one might still argue that his strategic considerations as to how they could be used to buttress the rule of conservative forces prevailed. When, with the emergence of the labor leader Ferdinand Lassalle in 1862, the possibility of an independent working-class party loomed on the horizon, a more active social policy on the part of conservatives became imperative. Consequently, Wagener's prompting toward Bismarck assumed a new degree of urgency. Wagener now became convinced that Prussia's political fate, that is, whether the crown or the parliamentarian system would ultimately be allowed to triumph, depended on which of the two lent the more decisive support to the masses.[33] To win over the lower classes, Wagener was therefore prepared to grant substantial concessions, based on the belief that the laboring poor, from the dispossessed peasant to the unemployed journeyman and industrial worker, were basically royalist and conservative in outlook. The

---

sozialen 'Entwicklung' fortschreiten zu können" (*Die Lösung der sozialen Frage,* 32–33).
   29. Wagener rarely spoke of *Soziale Frage* but used instead the term *Arbeiterfrage.* From the early 1850s on, *Pauperismus* ceased being used.
   30. *Neue Preussische Zeitung-Kreuzzeitung,* 257 (November 2, 1865); also cited in Hans-Joachim Schoeps, *Deutsche Geistesgeschichte,* vol. 4 (Frankfurt, 1980), 388.
   31. Schoeps, "Hermann Wagener," 196.
   32. On *Sozialgesetzgebung,* Wagener wrote to Meyer that "alle unsere sogenannten Sozialreformer teils schon von einem falschen Prinzip ausgehen, teils auf halben Wege stehen bleiben und deshalb keinen anderen Erfolg haben werden . . . , als den Kapitalismus noch zu stärken und zu festigen." See Schoeps, *Deutsche Geistesgeschichte,* 4:402.
   33. Saile, *Hermann Wagener,* 43–44.

most substantial political concession Wagener was willing to make was to grant universal suffrage.

There could be little doubt that the current *Zensuswahlrecht*, Prussia's three-class franchise, represented "the worst possible representation anyone could conceive of,"[34] and if the state was unwilling to grant universal suffrage as a necessary and timely concession now, mass despotism as was already prevalent in contemporary Bonapartist France might well be the result. Wagener explained in a speech before the North German Diet that he would not dare to defend the position "that a merchant here in Berlin, just because his money bags are weightier, would be favored by a three- or even ten-fold franchise in preference to a grenadier returning with a high decoration from the battle of Königsgrätz."[35] Such opinions alienated him from more doctrinaire conservatives like Ludwig von Gerlach.[36] In contrast to them, Wagener never showed any inclination of transferring the patriarchical forms of social rulership practiced in the East Elbian manorial system to industrial relations. He realized that these forms of social dominance belonged irredeemably to the past. It was now high time to make political concessions to industrial laborers to integrate them into the state and turn them into defenders of the existing order. From 1862, Wagener thus demanded that universal suffrage be granted as a "correlate for the heavy toll of lives [*Blutzoll*]" taken in compulsory military service.[37] In his memoirs, Wagener later asserted that with the introduction of universal suffrage the state had shouldered the obligation to implement social reforms.[38]

In an 1862 memorandum to Bismarck, Wagener wrote that "the revolutionary tendency of the masses" would disappear by itself if "the professional honor of the worker were restored, which once, out of ignorance and error, has

---

34. *Neue Preussische Zeitung-Kreuzzeitung* 90 (April 14, 1862); see also Hugo Müller, *Der Preussische Volks-Verein* (Berlin, 1914), 64; *Berliner Revue,* April 25, 1862; Siegfried Christoph, "Hermann Wagener als Sozialpolitiker: Ein Beitrag zur Vorgeschichte der Ideen und Intentionen für die grosse deutsche Sozialgesetzgebung im 19. Jahrhundert" (Ph.D. diss., University of Erlangen, 1950), 99.

35. *Stenographische Berichte des Reichstages des Norddeutschen Bundes,* March 28, 1867, 421; also cited in Christoph, "Hermann Wagener," 132; Schoeps, *Das andere Preussen,* 212.

36. See Adolf Richter, *Bismarck und die Arbeiterfrage im preussischen Verfassungskonflikt* (Stuttgart, 1935), 182–94; Adalbert Hahn, *Die Berliner Revue: Ein Beitrag zur Geschichte der konservativen Partei zwischen 1855 und 1875* (Berlin, 1934), 131.

37. *Neue Preussische Zeitung-Kreuzzeitung,* November 2, 1862; also quoted in Schoeps, *Das andere Preussen,* 212.

38. Hermann Wagener, *Erlebtes: Meine Memoiren* (Berlin, 1884), 42. In his memoirs of 1884, Wagener seemed to have already modified his opinion: "Selbstverständlich war die Einführung des allgemeinen, gleichen, direkten Wahlrechts ein gefährliches und zweischneidiges Experiment, und ich habe seinerzeit wiederholt und auf das Eindringlichste darauf hingewiesen, dass es diesem Stimmenrecht gegenüber nur die eine Alternative gebe: entweder die Sozialreform mit Energie und Consequenz in die Hand zu nehmen, oder aber allmählich in die sociale Revolution hineinzutreiben."

been demolished by the authorities."[39] Wagener essentially recommended establishing a new *Arbeiterstand,* with its own distinct identity, so that the working classes could take their allotted place among the other classes of the state.

In Wagener's writings and speeches, the lower classes often became idealistically transfigured as the unspoiled and pure contrast to the bourgeoisie, and a basically contented working class was juxtaposed with the brutal egotism of their bourgeois social betters. This was the underlying notion that lay at the root of the most perplexing phenomenon in Wagener's social thought: his "flirtation" with socialism and Ferdinand Lassalle. Wagener was intimately familiar with the writings of St. Simon, Marx, and Lassalle, and he repeatedly emphasized how highly he regarded their ethical idealism and their stress on timeless and eternal values, which he compared favorably to the "cold materialism" of the liberal creed.[40] His detailed knowledge of socialist theoreticians, though unusual for a conservative of his day and age, is easily explainable, since Wagener borrowed from the stockroom of socialist ideas as freely as he had pillaged the writings of conservative thinkers. In part, his knowledge was due to practical points of contact with the Left. Wagener's closest collaborator on the *Staats- und Gesellschaftslexikon* was the former Left Hegelian Bruno Bauer, while the socialist Johann Baptist von Schweitzer (who later became Lassalle's successor) cooperated with Wagener on the *Berliner Revue,* a conservative journal with a focus on social affairs.

In addition to personal contacts, similar ideological themes connected Wagener's conservatism with Lassalle's socialism. The opposition of socialists to the increasing atomization of modern society and to the lack of commitment pervading the modern age struck a sensitive chord with Wagener. To Wagener, socialists made a genuine effort to put a new community in the place of the one that had been lost. Above all, it was this strong yearning for community that, in Wagener's opinion, conservatives shared with socialists. Common to both was a collectivist outlook, the belief that the needs of the individual had to be subordinated to those of the larger societal whole. Both favored state capitalism over the private economic enterprise, arguing that the free play of market forces offered undue advantages to their common bogeyman, the industrial entrepreneur, and therefore had to be replaced by a more planned, state-controlled organization of labor. Further common ground consequently lay in their yearning for organization and the establishment of corporations (though the socialist Lassalle referred to them as trade unions) and in their concomitant

39. Hermann Wagener, "Denkschrift an Bismarck vom 18. Oktober 1862," reprinted in Saile, *Hermann Wagener,* 135–37.

40. In this regard his ideas are comparable to those Radowitz advanced in the *Gespräche* (see chapter 2).

rejection of the liberal caretaker state, with its "help through self-help" ideology. An automatic by-product of Wagener's social kingdom was the strengthening of a strong central power, without which neither Wagener nor Lassalle thought it possible to alleviate the social malaise. Their joint belief in a strong state and a strong kingdom constituted an additional bridge between them, especially since Lassalle proved astonishingly receptive toward royal dictatorship. And finally, virulent antiliberalism formed another solid basis of agreement between the conservative Wagener and the socialist Lassalle.

Wagener's favorable predisposition toward the German labor leader was reflected in his writings and public statements. After Lassalle's death, Wagener testified "that his attention for the workers had been good" and that what had been most important to Lassalle "was to get the workers away from the deceptions of the bourgeoisie." Wagener praised Lassalle's "high regard for the state, the misuse of which as a mere caretaker Lassalle opposed energetically."[41] And in parliament, the conservative deputy Wagener referred to the socialist Lassalle as an "ingenious, creative man," who had perpetuated Old Prussian virtues.[42]

Wagener was correct in his assumption that there was a basis for collaboration between himself and Lassalle. Lassalle's letters to Bismarck testify to that. In a note of February 5, 1864, for example, Lassalle, when referring to his latest work, wrote to Bismarck that with it he hoped "to smash our common enemy [i.e., liberalism]."[43] Lassalle's tone of almost chummy familiarity is striking, and other socialists were painfully aware of Lassalle's dangerous elective affinities. In June 1864, only a few months before Lassalle's untimely death, Wilhelm Liebknecht related to Marx a speech Lassalle had given in his house on the occasion of a soirée. Lassalle had referred to the bourgeoisie as "the sole enemy," and Liebknecht wrote, "we should vow to him to fight this enemy in a life and death struggle and in this not even shrink back from an alliance with the kingdom." Here the concept of the "social kingdom" is advanced from the Left, just as Radowitz and Wagener had advanced it from the Right. Liebknecht further recounted his astonishment over "the strangely mild judgments bestowed on Herrn von Bismarck in the circle around Lassalle."[44] Half a year after Lassalle's death, Marx and Engels learned of the serious negotiations he had entertained with the incarnation of reaction, Bismarck. Engels thereupon denounced Lassalle as "quite a common scoun-

---

41. Wagener, *Erlebtes*, 2:39.
42. See Schoeps, *Deutsche Geistesgeschichte*, 4:404.
43. Gustav Mayer, ed., *Bismarck und Lassalle: Ihr Briefwechsel und ihre Gespräche* (Berlin, 1928), 103.
44. Ibid., 53.

drel," while Marx charged that Lassalle had wanted to model himself into "a Richelieu of the proletariat."[45]

Indeed, circumstances permitting, Lassalle would have been prepared to make far-reaching concessions to Bismarck. On June 8, 1863, referring to the statutes of his *Allgemeiner Deutscher Arbeiterverein,* which he had enclosed in his letter to Bismarck, Lassalle wrote:

> from this miniature painting [i.e., enclosed statutes] it will become obvi-
> ous how true it is that the working class instinctively gravitates towards
> dictatorship, provided it [the working class] can rightfully be convinced
> that this dictatorship is exerted in its own interest, and [it will become
> obvious . . .] how much the working class—as I just told you recently—
> will be prepared, despite its republican convictions . . . to accept the
> crown as the natural champion of a social dictatorship.[46]

Radowitz and Wagener could not have put it more drastically, except they would have avoided the term *dictatorship,* which would have smacked too much of dreaded "royal absolutism." The concept of a "social kingdom" thus became the main point of convergence between socialism and conservatism.

The contacts between Wagener and Lassalle foreshadow the possibility of the influence "leftist" elements could bring to bear on conservative thought. Wagener knew that the conservatives' program could appeal to a wider public only by incorporating populist elements that would make it attractive to the masses. He sensed that the feasibility of his "social kingdom" depended on whether or not conservatives could offer substantial advantages to the lower and lower-middle classes. Since Wagener intended to win over the people by means of an active social policy, it was his concern to bring Lassalle and Bismarck to one table. He thereby hoped to enlist Lassalle's support for Bismarck's policy in return for substantial concessions leading to the better-ment of the social and political situation of the proletariat. Wagener's scheme came to naught, partly because of Lassalle's untimely death in a duel.

With Hermann Wagener, as with Radowitz and Rodbertus, all of whom were dyed-in-the-wool conservatives, the leftist elements of his social thought coexisted symbiotically with otherwise eminently conservative ideas. The "leftist" in Wagener emerged when he intimated that his own point of view was closer to Lassalle's than to that of the liberal politician Hermann Schulze-Delitzsch, for example; or when, in a memorandum to Bismarck, he empha-sized that in dealing with the working classes, the principle "continuous col-laboration reflected in co-ownership" would have to be followed.[47] It was thus

---

45. Ibid., 57.
46. Ibid., 60.
47. Saile, *Hermann Wagener,* 137.

not without good reason that August Bebel apostrophized Wagener as "royal Prussian court Socialist,"[48] whose task it was to bait the workers for Bismarck.

By conservative standards, Wagener's sympathy for the workers was exceptional. In a memorandum of April 18, 1863, for example, he advised Bismarck not to let "the traditional organs of state" deal with social problems, as it would be difficult "to solve the *Arbeiterfrage* with the help of men and institutions that are unfavorably disposed or hostile towards it." In this memorandum, Wagener remarked that it was not the masses that threatened the "monarchic principle" but "the oligarchs of finance capital and the Catilinarian failures of literature kept in leading-strings by them, and the affiliated liberal notabilities of bureaucratism."[49] According to Wagener, the chief enemies of the traditional state were found not among the ranks of the proletarians—they could still be won over by the crown—but among the propertied upper bourgeoisie, the intellectuals, and the liberal bureaucracy.[50]

Hostilities had thus remained the same since the *Vormärz.* Wagener's antiliberalism was as pronounced as that of Radowitz, Huber, or Rodbertus, and his fear of the machinations of finance capital was as irrational as the resentments of other conservatives toward "profit-yielding" capital. In Wagener's writings and public pronouncements, antiliberalism was ubiquitous. In his memoranda to Bismarck, the *"liberaler Bürokratismus"* constantly reappeared as the intransigent enemy. Wagener was convinced that industrialists were largely responsible for the widespread social misery. Just as he occasionally idealized the lower classes in their putative *Königstreue,* he passed sentence on the liberal bourgeoisie, whose ideology he held responsible for the social abuses of the present. Wagener's economic policy was naturally diametrically opposed to those of the liberals, which (inter alia) manifested itself in his antagonism to freedom of trade and in his distinct state socialism: the economy had to be subservient to the state, and state interference in the economy to provide for the welfare of the lower classes had to be intensified. In his parliamentary speeches, Wagener repeatedly advocated protective laws for the workers, even defending their right to go on strike (*Koalitionsrecht*), which he saw as a first step on the road toward organizing the workers into a professional estate, thus bolstering their self-confidence.

---

48. Schoeps, *Deutsche Geistesgeschichte,* 4:385. Bebel referred to Wagener as the "Königlich Preussischer Hofsozialist."

49. Handwritten memorandum of Wagener dated April 18, 1863, reprinted in Saile, *Hermann Wagener,* 138–44, especially 142.

50. Suspicion of bureaucratic rule had already been prevalent with the *Berliner Politisches Wochenblatt* and Radowitz, as well as with other pre-March conservatives. It was even more pronounced in Wagener's writings. In the memorandum to Bismarck of April 18, 1863, Wagener cautioned against the power of the bureaucracy, for "the crown will not be able to preserve her constitutional right as executive power . . . with the current insubordination of the civil service."

Wagener's hostility against liberalism was more than a rebellion against economic laissez-faire, more than the resentment of a conservative supporter of the aristocracy who feared that the rising bourgeoisie would supplant the traditional ruling elite. With Wagener it was rather a deep-seated moral hatred sustained by his conviction of the absolute social reprehensibility of the new *Grossbürgertum* and its subversive liberal creed, which, as he believed, had destroyed traditional society and was thus to be held accountable for the increasing atomization and isolation of the individual as well as for the material destitution of the lower classes. In keeping with this, Wagener's antiliberalism and his hostility toward industrial capitalism is pervaded by what historians have termed *Kulturkritik*. Wagener's intellectual "anti-intellectualism," his disdain for all *Literaten,* his occasionally resurgent nostalgia for the Middle Ages, and his brusque rejection of the "Goddess reason," that is, his "anti-rationalism," all fall into this category.

This "cultural criticism" was a recurring theme with most Prussian conservatives and was most distinct with Marwitz, the *Wochenblatt* group, Radowitz, and Wagener, reflecting their common opposition to modernity. Another characteristic Wagener shared with conservatives was his almost paranoid fear of the potential threat the proletariat posed to society, a fear that turned into an obsession after he had witnessed the Commune uprising in the spring of 1871.[51] A further point of contact was Wagener's conception of property, which was reminiscent of Gerlach and Radowitz. In his *Die Lösung der sozialen Frage,*[52] he recommended that the state take over private enterprises, a suggestion conditioned by his view that the property holder should not be able to dispose freely of his possessions, but that, on the contrary, ownership entailed an inherent obligation. By turning the "dispossessed into possessors,"[53] or, as he put it in his memoirs, by elevating the working classes "to the standard of life of the middle classes,"[54] Wagener intended "to liberate labor of the *Lohnknechtschaft* of capital and eliminate the antagonism between capital and labor."[55] Wagener's lasting importance for conservatism lay in his

---

51. On his return from Paris to Berlin in the summer of 1871, Wagener, on a walk with his collaborator Rudolph Meyer near Potsdam, observed: "Wenn sie Paris und St.Cloud sehen sollten und die Trümmer dieses Schlosses, so werden Sie finden, dass es schöner war als das, was sie hier sehen, und dieses Schloss haben französische Arbeiter zerstört im Angesicht des Feindes. Ich fürchte, wenn unsere innere Politik gegenüber dem 4. Stande nicht besser wird als sie war und ist, so werden sie diese schönen Schöpfungen Friedrichs des Grossen und des guten kunstsinnigen Königs Friedrich Wilhelm IV eines Tages ebenso verwüstet sehen." See Maximilian Harden, ed., *Die Zukunft* 12 (Berlin, 1895): 395–96.

52. Wagener, *Die Lösung der sozialen Frage,* 127.

53. Ibid., 150.

54. Wagener, *Erlebtes,* 2:6.

55. Wagener, *Die Lösung der sozialen Frage,* 150. Bismarck himself regarded these ideas not without sympathy, as testified in his remarks toward Schmoller, to whom Bismarck admitted

role as mediator between *Vormärz* social conservatism, which he had absorbed and to a certain degree popularized, and the social legislation of the second half of the century. Central in this context is his impact on Bismarck's social views. That Bismarck had an open ear for Wagener's suggestions in social questions can best be demonstrated by Wagener's above-mentioned memorandum, which was preserved with the Prussian prime minister's marginal notes.[56] In it, Wagener claimed that "European monarchy has a future only as a social monarchy" and that the opposition of the bourgeoisie could best be overcome by satisfying "the justified material demands . . . of the petty bourgeoisie [Bismarck: which ones?]." A political counterweight against the bourgeoisie could be created only by supporting small tradesmen and the "*Arbeiterstände*, . . . whose political needs always gravitate towards monarchical power [Bismarck: by which means?]."[57]

Not being a specialist in social affairs himself, Bismarck naturally had to rely on his collaborator's advice. After Wagener left office in 1873, his influence on Bismarck diminished. In the final analysis, Bismarck may have been too much of a pragmatist and realist to follow to the letter Wagener's carefully predesigned instructions for action. Moreover, his interest in social issues was too limited to adopt Wagener's social schemes wholeheartedly. Bismarck's *Gedanken und Erinnerungen*, where hardly any mention was made of his social legislation, testify to that. Yet Wagener's numerous memoranda on social problems, which he drafted over the years for Bismarck, could not fail to leave a lasting mark in countless details. Wagener had undoubtedly made Bismarck more receptive to the lower classes' plight and had opened up options Bismarck himself may not have deemed viable.

Wagener also had an intellectual and political affinity to later German conservatives, notably to the conservative revolutionaries of the Weimar Republic. The kinship between his ideas and theirs is such that one might suspect Wagener stood sponsor to many of their political concepts. Just as German conservatives of the 1920s, Wagener set *Gemeinschaft* (a term he used inter-

---

that he, too, would be a *Kathedersozialist*, but so far had not had the time for it. See Schoeps, *Üb' immer Treu' und Redlichkeit: Preussen in Geschichte und Gegenwart* (Düsseldorf, 1978), 100. In 1865, when Bismarck had to defend himself before the Prussian *Abgeordnetenhaus* for having initiated an audience for the weavers of Waldenburg with King William, Bismarck proclaimed that "Prussian kings have never been by preference kings of the rich. Already Frederick the Great said as Crown Prince: 'Quand je serai roi, je serai un vrai roi des gueux.' A king of the beggars. He wanted to protect the poor" (Ibid., 146).

56. See "Justizrath Wagener: Denkschrift vom 1. März 1864 betr. die innere Lage," Staatsarchiv Merseburg, Nachlass Zitelmann, rep. 92, no. 91.

57. At the time Bismarck read Wagener's memorandum of March 1, 1864, he was already familiar with the concept of the "social kingdom" and the underlying assumption that the working classes gravitated toward the monarchy. Lassalle had suggested the very same to him in his letter of June 8, 1863. See Gustav Mayer, *Bismarck und Lassalle*, 60.

changeably with *Gesellschaft*) above the individual: like them, he emphasized that to flourish, the individual had to be integrated into the larger whole: family, corporations, and estates. Also like later conservatives, he stressed that property entailed an obligation toward society and, at the same time, a right to rule, which served him as justification for the social domination of the East Elbian aristocracy. Antiliberalism and in part also antirationalism were features he shared with other conservatives of his time. In contrast to them, however, Wagener stressed that it was the right (and even the duty) of the state to limit the individual's freedom, and that the economy had to be subordinated to the state. His interest in social policy and the *Arbeiterfrage* rendered his ideas eminently modern and atypical of the general patterns of conservative thought of his own day and age.

It is a different question altogether whether the conservative revolutionaries of the Weimar Republic were familiar with Wagener's writings and speeches.[58] Yet it is certain that Wagener popularized social-conservative conceptions that experienced an astonishing renaissance later—in the *Lebensphilosophie* of turn-of-the-century Germany and during the "conservative revolution" of the 1920s. They also influenced national socialism. Still, it may be an overstatement to interpret Wagener as one of the intellectual predecessors of Nazism. Yet this conservative bohemian, who bore such little resemblance to the conservative notabilities of his time, was, in many respects, the inventor of a new brand of radical conservatism in Germany, which so far has largely gone unnoticed and has barely been recognized in its profound influence on the further development of German conservatism.[59]

Even though backward-oriented in some of their concepts, such as the *Ständestaat,* Prussian conservatives of the *Vormärz* reacted to something new. They were at the beginning of an intellectual tradition, not epigones of one. Their political philosophy was postrevolutionary, overshadowed and predetermined by their constant fear of a repetition of 1789. Prussian conservatives, from the *Wochenblatt* group to Hermann Wagener, thus had less in common with their predecessors, eighteenth-century German conservatives,[60] than with their great grandchildren of the twentieth century, who used their concepts and elaborated them further.

---

58. On conservatism in the late Weimar Republic see Klemens von Klemperer, *Germany's New Conservatism* (Princeton, 1957); Kurt Sontheimer, *Antidemokratisches Denken in der Weimarer Republik* (Munich, 1968); Arnim Mohler, *Die Konservative Revolution in Deutschland 1918–1932,* 3d ed. (Darmstadt, 1989).

59. In some respects, Wagener's conservatism is comparable to that of Maurice Barrès and the French right after the 1880s, without the rabid nationalism of some of its members. See Zeev Sternhell, *La Droite Révolutionaire 1885–1914: Les Origines Françaises du Fascisme* (Paris, 1978).

60. See Klaus Epstein, *The Genesis of German Conservatism* (Princeton, 1966).

Prussian conservatives between 1815 and 1870 saw themselves as politicians, not as political theorists, even though their main political achievements may have remained of a mere theoretical nature. It is therefore difficult, if not impossible, to trace the philosophical and theoretical influences that acted on their thought. None of them was impregnated with a coherent theoretical system. The influences worth noting were of a practical nature: the government reports Radowitz read about pauperized regions, the slums of Manchester Huber toured, and the experiences Wagener may have collected while serving as judicial official.

Among conservatives, the group around the *Berliner Politisches Wochenblatt* was unique by dint of the absoluteness with which it turned to the past for a solution to the social question. At the beginning of the 1830s, concepts like *Ständestaat* and "guild life" dominated the social discourse, but as time went on, the idealized image of the Middle Ages lost its attraction. A reason accounting for the change was the waning of the German romantic movement in literature. The 1840s were no place for the solemn quest of the "*blaue Blume*" of the romantic age. It was an age of hope; but the realm people hoped for in pre-1848 Prussia was made not of the fantasy and dreamlike stuff of the romantic writers but of something more concrete, such as freedom of the press, freedom from bureaucratic tutelage, and, above all, tangible improvements in material conditions.[61]

Even though concepts like *Ständestaat* or *Zunft* had been either rejected or ignored by such conservatives as Huber and Rodbertus, related ideas were extolled throughout the 1840s and 1850s: there was a streak of antimodernism running through Radowitz's social thought, while Viktor A. Huber praised the idea of an aristocratic order, whose noblest task would be to lead his associations.[62] The notion that the aristocracy—"la fleur de la noblesse, l'élite de la nation," in the words of the francophone Frederick II—was the estate predestined to wield power was not advanced just by the *Berliner Politisches Wochenblatt*. Radowitz and even Huber reverted to this idea, which constituted a leitmotif of Gerlach's thought. Centuries of Prussian history stood behind this concept. There had been no other country in eighteenth-century Europe in which the nobility wielded as much social power as in Prussia. The locally based power of the *Gutsbezirk* had been acquired in return for the renunciation of political influence in the country. Hohenzollern rulers, from the Grand Elector to Frederick II, had endowed their aristocracy with social influence

---

61. Ludwig von Gerlach remained the only major conservative figure to regard a state made up of different estates as the main panacea for the social malaise, but his participation in and influence on the social discussion had been dwindling ever since the failure of the *Wochenblatt*.

62. See Huber's pamphlet *Bruch mit Revolution und Ritterschaft* (Berlin, 1852), discussed in chapter 3.

in the regional sphere as a compensation for the consolidation of royal absolutism.

Concomitant with favoring the aristocracy, conservatives originally professed a pronounced hostility toward the state. This was reflected in mistrust vis-à-vis bureaucratic power and in suspicion toward "royal absolutism." Suspicion of omnipresent officialdom was strong with the *Wochenblatt,* with Radowitz, and especially with Hermann Wagener. Reservations toward the bureaucracy were partly based on the conservatives' view of the upper-echelon civil servant as "liberal bureaucrat," a species epitomized by Councillor Oeder in Radowitz's *Gespräche.* Conservatives feared that the "liberal official" was intent on leveling God-given inequalities, the fruits of which many aristocrats enjoyed. They were concerned that officials would impose a constitution on the country that would be alien to its traditional character. In this, they not only worried about the loss of ancestral privileges and vested rights but also feared the leveling of regional differences and their local strongholds. Finally, animosity toward officials had a good deal to do with simple jealousy of the university-educated official, who had been able to obtain influence and power by dint of mere education.[63]

Only the *Berliner Politisches Wochenblatt* coupled antagonism toward the bureaucracy with warnings against the omnipotence of royal power. Propaganda for a "social kingdom" would have been unthinkable for the *Wochenblatt* circle. This changed markedly with Radowitz, and the change may well have been connected to Radowitz's close personal relationship with the king. Compared to the *Wochenblatt,* Radowitz envisaged a much augmented role of the state to solve social problems, while Huber already considered the establishment of a "Ministry of Poor Relief." In the theories of Rodbertus, the state was viewed as the great beneficial institution. The exclusive reliance on a social kingdom by Radowitz and on the state by Rodbertus went so far that they were prepared to leave it completely to monarch or state to bring about social justice. A rigid system of state regulation seemed the only means of keeping the lower classes in check. As a consequence of this line of thought, the concept of a strong, almost omnipotent state emerged.

At this point, the conservatives had come full circle: from total negation of the state to complete endorsement, even encouragement, of state involvement. Considering the strong antietatist streak of the *Wochenblatt,* this change is astonishing. The frondeur spirit of the early *Wochenblatt* group had quickly evaporated. Fear of the new and persistently growing power of the bourgeoisie and of the ever swelling numbers of the lower classes soon outweighed any

---

63. For reasons of representation, the very highest positions in the bureaucracy, such as the *Oberpräsidenten* (provincial governors) and *Regierungspräsidenten* (district governors), were mostly filled with members of the nobility. See part 2, chapter 5.

dread of "royal absolutism." Faced with the choice between the absolutism of the crown and possible concessions to the bourgeoisie—for fear of this class was initially greater than fear of a still nameless fourth estate that was not yet organized politically—conservatives chose without hesitation the supremacy of the ruler, who was more familiar to them after all.

The "social kingdom" was thus conceived as a device to enhance royal power by collaboration with the proletariat. Radowitz and Wagener sought to legitimize the monarch's authority through his "social mission," and Radowitz's idea of keeping down the bourgeoisie with the help of the fourth estate was a kind of Bonapartism *avant la lettre*.[64] The concept of the "social kingdom" was perhaps the most original idea of social-conservative thought before 1870. It was primarily designed not to help the lower classes but rather to pacify them by integration into the existing state. It also had a virulent antiliberal slant. This antiliberalism was common to all conservatives, from the *Wochenblatt* to Radowitz, Gerlach, Huber, Rodbertus, and Hermann Wagener. It was their largest common denominator. A noteworthy feature of conservatives' antiliberalism was its vindictiveness and hatred of the "oligarchy of finance" and "profit-yielding capital." Wagener even spoke of *Lohnknechtschaft,* a term known through the vocabulary of national socialism. The intensity of the rancor and the space conservatives devoted to it was astonishing, especially when considering how relatively weak and insignificant Prussian liberalism remained until the later 1840s, how rudimentary its party organization was, and how backward industries on the Rhine, Saxony, and Silesia were in comparison to the English competition.

When attacking liberalism, conservatives attacked more than an economic theory or a political creed. To them, liberalism embodied a new form of life, questioning all that had grown organically, and rendering obsolete time-honored traditions. It seemed to bring a new freedom in its wake. The men around the *Wochenblatt* as well as Radowitz dreaded this new kind of freedom, indissolubly linked, it seemed, with industrial development, the constitutional state, and an affluent, self-confident bourgeoisie. As a result, their antiliberalism was coupled with advocacy of a precapitalistic economic order and anti-modernist *Kulturkritik.* It was to be expected that the Radowitzes would be negatively predisposed toward industry, the bourgeoisie, and liberalism from the beginning. But how can the antiliberalism of Viktor A. Huber or Carl Rodbertus be explained, since both favored the achievements of the machine age? With them, a psychological motive was decisive. Both feared the atomization of society—the breaking up of "organic forms" of life, of a "community"

---

64. Analogies to twentieth-century fascist regimes come to mind, but the entirely different circumstances surrounding their rise make the value of direct comparisons questionable.

that seemed endangered through rapid social change fostered by the liberal ideology.

The social question consequently became a moral problem for them, a problem that could be solved by education. This was especially emphasized by Huber. In his isolation, man had no choice but to degenerate into a proletarian. Only in a community, reestablished in Huber's associations, could man be himself again. Here the social question ceased to be an economic and social problem and became purely a moral (*sittlich*) one. *Bindung,* not *Freiheit,* was to be the solution to the problem. Conservatives therefore opposed the Prussian reforms for having created an "atomized" society, engendering pauperism by throwing overboard the element of *Bindung,* that is, the commitments, bonds, and mutual obligations that were indispensable for holding society together. One of their foremost concerns was to reintegrate the working classes into society's larger whole, since the gravest threat emanating from the lower orders lay precisely in their atomized nature. And for the reconstitution of societal bonds, the power of the state was indispensable.

This explains some conservatives' intuitive gravitation toward socialism. Radowitz is a case in point. In his *Gespräche,* he gave vent to the feeling that he was emotionally more akin to socialists than liberals, though the latter were closer to him in rank and social standing. This surprising affinity arose because Radowitz believed that socialist ideology offered shelter to the individual whereas the liberals offered no security whatsoever. Conservatism's strong popular appeal, which both Huber and Wagener emphasized, as well as the lower classes' instinctive gravitation toward royal power that Wagener (and Lassalle) had discerned, belonged in this category as well.

A possibly unique phenomenon was Prussian conservatism's conception of property—its emphasis on obligation and duty toward society and state, believed to be inherent in property. This was stressed by Gerlach, Radowitz, and Wagener alike. There was an underlying antiliberal slant in the assertion of Gerlach and Radowitz that property should not be freely disposable but should entail a responsibility toward society. In former times, the dominance of the aristocracy had been legitimized through landed property and the obligation toward those dependent on it, whereas the bourgeoisie amassed unheard of riches in the face of workers' starvation. To conservatives, the bourgeoisie seemed therefore the unsocial class of society per se, the embodiment of all the baseness of the age. The belief that social misery was due to unrestricted competition was taken as a fact by conservatives, and it was only logical that most of them favored curtailing it.

The increasing openness of conservatives vis-à-vis the lower classes was an equally interesting phenomenon. Whereas the *Wochenblatt* was still bent on leading the lower orders back into feudal dependence, Rodbertus advocated the workers' participation in the achievements of modern culture, and Radowitz

called on royal power to intervene on their behalf. Hermann Wagener even favored granting political rights to the workers, which, of course, was conditioned by the changed social and political situation of the 1860s. Nevertheless, it is fair to speak of a growing social awareness or social conscience. With Wagener, this was further substantiated by his collaborations with the former Left Hegelian Bruno Bauer and with Lassalle (though the latter collaboration was never fully realized as a result of Lassalle's early death). But the amalgamation of Left and Right is foreshadowed in Wagener's ideas. In the spring of 1872, he even made the concrete effort to found a social-conservative party, meant to include the social-democratic *Allgemeine Arbeiterverein,* led by Lassalle's successors Schweitzer and Hasenclever. The intended leader of the new party was Carl Rodbertus-Jagetzow, who, due to his state socialist ideas, would have been acceptable to social democrats as well. After a lengthy to-and-fro, however, Rodbertus refused to leave his ivory tower (in combination with other adverse circumstances), and the project finally foundered. The entire social conservative theory from the Restoration to Bismarck, with its increasingly strong element of state socialism, seemed to lead up compellingly to such a party.

From the vantage point of the later twentieth century, the long-term effect of their contemporary Karl Marx, or even that of Hegel and the left wing of his school, seem to have exerted an incomparably greater influence than the "social conservatives" in Prussia. In regard to nineteenth-century Germany, however, this was different. Not only were their ideas widely known throughout Prussia and influential in the first all-encompassing program of social legislation, but men like Gerlach, Radowitz, and Wagener also epitomized the spirit of their age. In such a thoroughly conservative country as Prussia, it was chiefly the conservatives who shaped the political discourse.

The key to understanding their relevance and importance for the future course of German history is perhaps best encapsulated in Oswald Spengler's little book *Preussentum und Sozialismus.* The Prussian conservatives' worldview lay at the root of what Spengler called Prussian socialism. "The two parties that can be labeled specifically Prussian, the conservative and socialist one," Spengler wrote in the early 1920s, are standard-bearers of the true Prussian spirit. Both were "socialist in a higher sense," pitted in a life and death struggle against liberalism, the intrinsically antisocialist, anti-Prussian principle per se.[65] Socialism and conservatism share unquestioning submission to the *"unbedingte Autorität"* of the state. Spengler contrasted Prussian socialism, that is, the highly developed state, in which everyone served as a cog within a larger machinery and contributed to the blossoming of the whole, with English

---

65. Oswald Spengler, *Preussentum und Sozialismus,* 2d ed. (Munich, 1924), 64.

liberalism, the expression of the "*Seeräuberinstinkt des Inselvolkes*," geared toward individual affluence and devoid of any higher, unifying principle.

According to Spengler, the only form of government that corresponded to the true Prussian spirit was a monarchic one—"a socialist monarchy—for authoritative socialism is monarchic," Spengler wrote, referring promptly to Lassalle, who had extolled the symbiosis between the Prussian kingdom and the working classes to combat liberalism. Spengler could just as well have referred to Wagener or Radowitz, who had elaborated the same concept long before Lassalle. In Germany, Spengler claimed, the two socialist parties, that is, socialists and conservatives, will eventually have to find a common path to combat their common enemy. Spengler adulated the very same tenets as "truly Prussian" and "genuinely socialist" that had been characteristic of the *Wochenblatt*, Radowitz's *Gespräche*, and Hermann Wagener's speeches and memoranda. Society ought to be structured in accordance with professional estates, Spengler held, praising a society "where everyone lived within the system, working with the exactitude of a good machine." He stressed "the idea of an order [*Orden*]" where everyone worked for the good of everyone else and, "according to his practical, moral, and intellectual abilities," had certain responsibilities, a measure of "*Befehl und Gehorsam.*" It was the closed society advanced by the *Wochenblatt* group, in a twentieth-century guise.

Prussian socialism was authoritarian, monarchic, geared toward service for a larger whole, and based on a society structured according to rank (and not wealth). It was an amalgamation of conservatism and socialism, whereby it was unimportant that the former spoke of "the monarchic state," the latter of "the working people." For Spengler this was but "a difference in words in view of the fact . . . that in each case the individual will is subjected to the will of the whole." Property and private riches were viewed with contempt, for true property was public and engendered obligation. Society, therefore, could be structured not according to individual wealth—that was the liberal's, the Englishman's, domain[66]—but according to achievement, to one's membership in a professional order, one's place in the hierarchy of "*Befehl und Gehorsam.*" Spengler claimed that "Old Prussian values and socialist convictions, today fighting each other with the hatred of brothers, are one and the same."

The principal mediators between the world of Old Prussia and the twentieth-century were Prussian social conservatives, such as Radowitz, Ludwig von Gerlach, Huber, Carl Rodbertus, and Hermann Wagener. Their ideas stood sponsor to Oswald Spengler's monarchic, conservative, authoritarian Prussian socialism. Many of their concepts—such as their views on property,

---

66. "When an Englishman speaks of national wealth, he refers to the number of millionaires" (ibid., 49). Spengler quoted Engels, saying, "Nothing is more alien to English sentiment than solidarity," and, "Jeder für sich: das ist englisch: alle für alle: das ist preussisch."

on mutual obligation, and on a strong state supporting the working classes to use them in the fight against the bourgeoisie; their idea of a social kingdom; their antiliberalism; Rodbertus's state socialism; and Wagener's conservative socialism—eventually percolated into the public discourse to become part of a specifically Prussian (and later German) conservative identity, a state ideology, so to speak, that transcended party lines and impregnated wide sections of the population. Many facets of this state ideology experienced a renaissance in the latter part of the Weimar Republic, when it was widely propagated by conservative groups and became a focal theme in the "conservative revolution." It helped make Hitler, who frequently invoked it, "ideologically" acceptable to those Prussians to whom otherwise he might have been too common and uncouth. Early Prussian conservatives had nothing in common with the national socialist movement—they would have looked on its members as rabble, not worthy of serious consideration. But some of their ideas, though modified by the times, became part of Prussian-German political consciousness in the twentieth century and proved a powerful lever to rally conservative Germans behind Hitler.

It might seem absurd to label men like Radowitz and Wagener ideological precursors of the Nazi movement. They certainly would have combated it with everything they had. But one could argue that an inevitable result, a logical final point of a line of development of conservative social thought that started with Radowitz and was continued by Wagener, amounted to a gradual convergence of socialism and conservatism. This conservative Prussian socialism was epitomized in the idea of a social kingdom. And, ironically enough, the only "social kingdom" German history knew was the Third Reich.

PART 2

The Bureaucracy and the
Social Question

The relationship between officials and conservatives was beset with contradictions and paradoxes. In the half-century after 1815, officials and conservative landowners enjoyed uncontested social preeminence. Aristocratic landowners had been the traditionally ruling elite for centuries, while upper-echelon bureaucrats emerged as the embodiment of Prussia's *classe politique* after the reforms. Socially there was much overlap as well. Though more than two-thirds of the members of the higher bureaucracy came from the ranks of the bourgeoisie, noblemen predominated in the highest offices. Members of Brandenburg's oldest aristocratic families, such as the Arnims, devoted themselves entirely to state service.

In their role as "bureaucratic modernizers,"[1] however, officials incurred the irreconcilable wrath of conservatives, who saw the very foundations of their world undermined by bureaucratic action. Prussia's social conservatives, from the *Wochenblatt* group to Hermann Wagener, were united in their profound hatred of officialdom. But this antagonism was paradoxical, since, despite outward hostility, both groups were bound together by a multitude of common elements. These united them at the basis of their relationship, for there was common ground regarding a joint view of how to deal with societal problems. In the final analysis, officials were far from being the ruthless modernizers conservatives saw in them (see chapters 6 through 9).

Coping with the ever-growing social problems was within the range of responsibilities of the higher civil service. By reason of the economic liberalism of many high officials, the civil service was in principle opposed to thoroughgoing state intervention. But a traditional sense of responsibility,

---

1. See the interesting study by Gary J. Bonham, "Bureaucratic Modernizers and traditional Constraints: Higher Officials and the Landed Nobility in Wilhelmine Germany, 1890–1914" (Ph.D. diss., University of California, Berkeley, 1985).

combined with authoritarianism and humanitarian concerns, propelled administrative authorities into some kind of state interference, though it was at first limited to the regulating measures of the police state. To stand idly by and witness an entire generation be physically and mentally crippled by factory work was impossible, even if the authorities' initial concern lay with the growing illiteracy and the physical debility of the next generation of recruits.

Already on September 5, 1817, *Staatskanzler* Hardenberg issued a memorandum to the *Oberpräsidenten* of Silesia, Brandenburg, Saxony, Westfalia, and the Rhine Province,[2] inquiring about the situation of children employed in factories. After 1824, the exchange of notes resumed within the bureaucracy concerning the possible limitation of child labor, which finally led to a law restricting child labor in factories (in 1839). Less intense throughout the 1840s, official correspondence about the issue of child labor continued unabated. Individual violations of the 1839 law were discussed, and the ground was prepared for the second *"Kinderschutzregulativ"* of 1853, which, however, was not solely drafted by the bureaucracy but prepared by the *Abgeordnetenhaus,* the Prussian Parliament. The laws on the "Inclusion of Newcomers" and on the "Obligation to Poor Relief," both dating from December 31, 1842, constituted an attempt to stem the tide of rural paupers. But despite these measures, officials were slow to realize the potentially explosive force inherent in the social question. The term *social revolution,* for example, used by all conservatives from Radowitz to Wagener, was rarely employed in official bureaucratic correspondence.

What interests us here, in the context of the origins of the authoritarian welfare state in Prussia, is not a detailed prehistory of Bismarck's social legislation but an analysis of the inner motives of officials, their deeper social conceptions and underlying political attitudes, in short, their mental makeup. To appreciate fully officials' social policy measures, it is necessary to examine briefly the constituent factors of their mentality, that is, their position in society, social background, privileges, and salaries, and also the constraints under which they labored, such as the strict code of discipline.

---

2. "Runderlass an die Oberpräsidenten" at DZA II, Merseburg, rep. 74, VIII, no. 24; also reprinted in Jürgen Kuczynski, *Die Geschichte der Lage der Arbeiter unter dem Kapitalismus,* vol. 8 (Berlin, 1960).

CHAPTER 5

The Reality of
Bureaucratic Absolutism

The actual power of the Prussian bureaucracy between 1815 and 1848 can hardly be overestimated. Historians agree that its authority was virtually absolute. In his important essay "Zur Genesis der preussischen Bürokratie und des Rechtsstaates," Eckart Kehr spoke of "a dictatorship of the bureaucracy between 1807 and 1848." Hans Rosenberg referred to the period as "the classical age of Prussian bureaucratic absolutism." For the German administrative historian Fritz Hartung, the age was characterized by a "Blütezeit des büro-kratischen Absolutismus." Reinhart Koselleck, generally eschewing labels throughout his very detailed analysis of civil servants' functions, rights, and legal positions, considered the bureaucracy as "the sole true *Staatsstand* that existed in Prussia in those days," which, of course, as Jonathan Sperber observed recently, tells us more about bureaucratic self-perception than the bureaucracy's actual social and political position.[1] In the final analysis, however, the issue was not a controversial one: nearly everyone, including the authors of the great surveys of nineteenth-century Germany, concurs that the power of

---

1. Eckhart Kehr, "Zur Genesis der preussischen Bürokratie und des Rechtsstaates," in Kehr, *Der Primat der Innenpolitik: Gesammelte Aufsätze zur preussisch-deutschen Sozialgeschichte,* ed. Hans-Ulrich Wehler (Berlin, 1965), 45; Hans Rosenberg, *Bureaucracy, Aristocracy, and Autocracy: The Prussian Experience, 1660–1815* (Cambridge, 1958), 202–29; Fritz Hartung, *Staatsbildende Kräfte der Neuzeit* (Berlin, 1961), chap. 4; Reinhart Koselleck, *Preussen zwischen Reform und Revolution,* 2d ed. (Stuttgart, 1975), 202; Jonathan Sperber, "State and Civil Society in Prussia: Thoughts on a New Edition of Reinhart Koselleck's *Preussen zwischen Reform und Revolution,*" *Journal of Modern History* 57 (1985): 295. Otto Hintze, whose specific investigations mainly concentrated on Frederican Prussia, covering the *Vormärz* only in his survey articles, abstained from unequivocal labels but nevertheless made it clear that after 1815 the civil service "der eigentlich herrschende Faktor im Staat geworden war, seitdem der scharf autokratische Charakter des 18. Jahrhunderts einer mehr bürokratischen Verfassung Platz gemacht hatte"; Otto Hintze, "Der Beamtenstand," in *Soziologie und Geschichte,* vol. 2 of *Gesammelte Abhandlungen* (Göttingen, 1967), 92.

Prussian officials was virtually unassailable. Thomas Nipperdey, who in his *Deutsche Geschichte 1800–1866* allotted relatively little space to the powerful civil servants, wrote that "before 1848 Prussia was above all a *Beamtenstaat*" and that officials regarded themselves as "the true mediators between state and society."[2] Nipperdey's view, which oriented itself more toward the actual position of civil servants in the state than toward their self-image, somewhat resembled that of Franz Schnabel, who equally stressed the *Fachkompetenz* of the bureaucracy, emphasizing, in less ambiguous terms than Nipperdey, their absolute authority.[3] And Hans-Ulrich Wehler spoke of the predominance of "bureaucratic absolutism" in his recent *Deutsche Gesellschaftsgeschichte.*[4]

Thus, there is general unanimity about the power and authority of the Prussian state apparatus in the *Vormärz,* even though it might be arguable whether one can speak of a "dictatorship of the bureaucracy" as Kehr did. Royal power continued representing a check on bureaucratic dominance, at least nominally, insofar as the king's veto could forestall implementation of any measure, and even highest ranks had to curry royal favor, for even ministers could be dismissed in disgrace. Minister of Finance Flottwell and Minister of Justice Mühler, both of whom were dismissed during the 1840s, were cases in point.

Between 1815 and 1848, domestic policy decisions thus rested largely on the shoulders of high-ranking civil servants. As Willard Fann has shown, the power of the different departmental ministers, or *Fachminister,* and among them especially that of the minister of the interior, was pivotal.[5] Until his death in 1822, *Staatskanzler* Hardenberg stood above the ministers at the top of the civil service hierarchy. But even Hardenberg's position had not been incontestable, for he could not hold his own against a united front of all the other *Fachminister.* With Hardenberg's demise, the last intermediary instance between king and ministers fell. Ministers continued, at least formally, to depend

2. Thomas Nipperdey, *Deutsche Geschichte 1800–1866* (Munich, 1983), 336, 331.

3. Franz Schnabel, *Deutsche Geschichte im neunzehnten Jahrhundert,* vol. 4, *Die vormärzliche Zeit* (Freiburg, 1964), 120.

4. Hans-Ulrich Wehler, *Deutsche Gesellschaftsgeschichte 1815–1848/49,* vol. 2 (Munich, 1987), 297–322. Willard R. Fann, following Rosenberg, also used the term *bureaucratic absolutism* in his essay "The Rise of the Prussian Ministry 1806–1827," in Hans-Ulrich Wehler, ed., *Sozialgeschichte Heute: Festschrift für Hans Rosenberg* (Göttingen, 1974), 125.

5. Willard R. Fann, "Rise of the Prussian Ministry," 119–29; Fann, "The Consolidation of Bureaucratic Absolutism in Prussia, 1817–1827" (Ph.D. diss., University of California, Berkeley, 1965). For information on the structure of the bureaucracy see also Albert Lotz, *Geschichte des deutschen Beamtentums* (Berlin, 1909); Reinhart Koselleck, *Preussen zwischen Reform und Revolution;* Hartung, *Staatsbildende Kräfte der Neuzeit;* on the functions of key positions within the bureaucracy see Dietrich Wegmann, *Die leitenden staatlichen Verwaltungsbeamten der Provinz Westfalen 1815–1918* (Münster, 1969), Klaus Schwabe, ed., *Die Preussischen Oberpräsidenten 1815–1945* (Boppard, 1981).

on royal favor and the good graces of the monarch. But the king was completely at the mercy of his ministers' expertise and technical knowledge, as is succinctly expressed by one of them: "We know the king's opinions thoroughly, and we can always compose our reports so that we are certain of their approval."[6]

Technically, above the ministers was the Council of State, or *Staatsrat*, a congregation of the royal princes, army commanders, in exceptional cases certain commanding generals, the ministers of the various departments, and, by appointment, several provincial governors, the *Oberpräsidenten*. As indicated by its name, the *Staatsrat* was an advisory council, constituting a kind of senate of the highest dignitaries of the kingdom, and participating as advisory organ in drafting legislation.[7] The actual domestic power within the state was wielded by the *Innenverwaltung*, the civil servants of the domestic administration. These included the *Landräte*, who were in charge of the local district, or *Kreis;* the *Regierungen*, which administered the affairs of a regional district, or *Regierungsbezirk* (roughly the size of an English county, slightly larger than a French *département*); and finally the *Oberpräsidenten* (provincial governors), who had authority over several *Regierungsbezirke*. The regional district government, the *Regierung*, was staffed with *Räte* (councillors) and headed by a *Regierungspräsident*.[8]

Laws were promulgated from the ministry in consultation with the *Oberpräsidenten*, the *Regierungen*, and the provincial diets, the *Provinziallandtage*, which had been established in 1823.[9] In some instances, especially if a local matter was at stake, the *Landrat* was consulted as well. Objections raised against a law or amendments demanded by the provincial diets sometimes led to changes or supplemental legislation. Laws were elaborated jointly by the different ministries that had a stake in the matter at hand. All important legislative drafts were based on the expert opinions of high

---

6. Fann, "Rise of the Prussian Ministry," 121. An example of such influence can be found in the 1844 report of Minister of the Interior Arnim to the king concerning acceptance of the statutes of the "Association for the Welfare of Workers." In his report, Arnim consciously played up to royal fears of an uncontrollable public opinion and managed to change the king's originally favorable predisposition. See December 26, 1844, "Akten betreffend die Bildung von Vereinen für das Wohl der arbeitenden Klassen," Staatsarchiv Merseburg, rep. 120 D, XXII, no. 1, vol. 1, 64–76 verso.

7. The most complete study still is Hans Schneider, *Der Preussische Staatsrat 1817–1918* (Munich and Berlin, 1952).

8. The highest officials in the central body of the administration in Berlin were the minister and the *Direktoren* of the ministry of the interior. They issued directives to the *Regierung* and local *Kreis.*

9. On the *Provinziallandtage* see Herbert Obenaus, *Anfänge des Parlamentarismus in Preussen bis 1848* (Düsseldorf, 1984).

officials in the *Regierungen,* who, in turn, could introduce bills.[10] The final decision, however, always lay with the high bureaucracy, never with the local or provincial diets. The ultimate decision about the fate of a bill was reserved for the highest collegiate councils within the bureaucracy itself. Within these councils, made up of ministers and other high officials, rigid policy lines hardly seem to have existed. Each law was discussed paragraph by paragraph, with constellations of ministers and other high officials opting for or against a specific point, changing according to the issues involved.[11] After having been approved by the *Staatsrat* and the king, drafts of the bill were again presented to the ministry (*Staatsministerium*) for countersignature, a practice that had become customary but not a *conditio sine qua non* for the final enactment of a law.[12] Still, it was a symbol for how great ministerial power had become.

The multitude of groups and opinions within the bureaucracy was an element that mitigated the dictatorship of the bureaucracy. The bureaucracy never reacted en bloc; inside the apparatus there was—if not discord and quarrel, as Karl Twesten once held [13]—at least a diversity of opinions reflected in expert reports that freely contradicted each other. As Thomas Nipperdey appropriately labeled it, the Prussian bureaucracy was a "*diskutierende Verwaltung,*"[14] an administration in whose councils, boards, and committees free discussion reigned supreme, at least on the higher levels. Strongholds of collegial debate were the *Regierungen,* chaired by a *Regierungspräsident,* who was originally only a primus inter pares among other higher officials. His authority was augmented in 1825, and for a time it seemed as if the French prefect system was about to supersede the collegiate principle of Prussian *Regierungen.*[15] Ultimately, the principle of collective responsibility and com-

---

10. See also Reinhart Koselleck, "Staat und Gesellschaft im preussischen Vormärz," in *Moderne Preussische Geschichte 1848–1947,* ed. Otto Büsch and Wolfgang Neugebauer (Berlin, 1981), 378–415.
    11. Illustrative of this point was the final deliberation before the passing of the Poor Laws of 1842. The laws were discussed one last time within the council of ministers, where final alterations were made without consulting with any other body, such as the *Provinziallandtage,* for example. The proposals of the provincial diets were taken into consideration but were still subject to random change within the council of ministers, which therefore exerted practically absolute powers.
    12. Otto Hintze, "Das preussische Staatsministerium im 19. Jahrhundert," in *Regierung und Verwaltung,* vol. 3 of *Gesammelte Abhandlungen* (Göttingen, 1967), 530–619; Ernst Klein, "Funktion und Bedeutung des Preussischen Staatsministeriums," *Jahrbuch für die Geschichte Mittel- und Ostdeutschlands* 9/10 (1961): 195–261.
    13. Karl Twesten, *Was uns noch retten kann: Ein Wort ohne Umschweife* (Berlin, 1861); quoted in Kehr, *Der Primat der Innenpolitik,* 37.
    14. Nipperdey, *Deutsche Geschichte 1800–1866,* 333.
    15. The *Kabinettsorder* of December 31, 1825, amounted to an increase in the power of the *Regierungspräsident.* Jacodus Temme, a former official, wrote in his memoirs that "the president of a collegiate body . . . in Prussia often embodies the driving force behind it." Stefan Born, ed., *Erinnerungen von J. D. H. Temme* (Leipzig, 1883), 178. The regulation of 1825 only gradually

petence prevailed over the French prefect system in Prussia. Based on collegial discussions among all higher civil servants of a *Regierung*, it had the advantage that decisions were arrived at jointly, whereas the prefect system vested the president of the respective administrative body with sole responsibility.[16] Top officials in the bureaucracy argued that the element of bureaucratic self-control inherent in collegiality rendered the *ständische Provinziallandtage* redundant. Reinhart Koselleck even went so far as to argue that the passing of a constitution may have introduced a procrastinating element to further modernization due to the inherent conservatism of a society that was dominated by the aristocracy. Koselleck seems to agree with Barthold Georg Niebuhr's dictum that "liberty has an incomparably stronger foundation in the *Verwaltung* than in a constitution."[17] Given the existence of conflicting opinions on practically all issues, ranging from commerce, trade, and local administration, to the police (for the competence of the *Regierungen* encompassed every sector of society), one might argue that *Regierungen* worked like regional parliaments. That, at least, was a view held by many higher officials.

Yet this line of reasoning overlooked the fact that all the putative parliamentarians had been trained at a university (where they mostly studied jurisprudence), had undergone two civil service examinations, and had pledged allegiance to the Prussian state. This preselection, combined with a relatively homogeneous social recruitment pattern, precluded radically diverging opinions from the start. It was therefore essentially the defenders of Prussia's semi-absolutist government who pointed to the *Regierungskollegien* as a substitute for constitutional government. Historians have often seen in *Vormärz* officials spearheads of a *"bürgerliche Öffentlichkeit,"* a liberal bourgeois public. Werner Conze, for example, contended that the liberal reformist spirit stayed alive "in the provinces, administrative districts, towns, and counties [*Landkreise*], after 1820." According to Conze, the standard-bearer of liberal and reformist ideas was, above all, "the civil service, whose foremost representatives were liberal-minded, reform-oriented, cultivated, and relatively decisive."[18] This positive image, however, was not always justified. The officials serving as parliamentarians in the constitutional states of Southern Germany and later in the Paulskirche also shared the natural advantage of *Abkömm-*

---

changed "den Geist der Regierungen" of which Temme spoke, and collegial discussions remained the rule rather than the exception throughout the *Vormärz*.

16. The collegiate principle had the inherent shortcoming of being slower but offered the advantage of generating support among all members of a *Regierung* who participated in the decision-making process. Decisions reflecting the judgment of several people (usually the majority of the group) tended to be defended by the majority when questioned thereafter.

17. Koselleck, "Staat und Gesellschaft im preussischen Vormärz," 413.

18. Werner Conze, "Das Spannungsfeld von Staat und Gesellschaft im Vormärz," in *Staat und Gesellschaft im deutschen Vormärz*, ed. Conze (Stuttgart, 1962), 207–69, 245.

lichkeit (i.e., they were available to serve in parliament for a number of years, something a merchant might not be).[19]

The Structure of the Bureaucracy and Key Positions within It

After the Congress of Vienna, Prussia was subdivided into ten provinces. In 1824, the two parts of the Rhine Province were merged, and East and West Prussia combined into a single province, so that the kingdom now consisted of eight large regional units. Provinces varied considerably in terms of size, population, population density, and prosperity.[20] The province of "Prussia" (i.e., East and West Prussia combined) was bigger than the kingdoms of Württemberg, Saxony, and the Grand Duchies of Baden and Hesse taken together, whereas Westfalia was about the size of Württemberg. Provinces were subdivided into *Regierungsbezirke* (government districts). Between 1815 and 1848, there was a total of twenty-five to twenty-seven *Regierungsbezirke* (*RB*), which, in turn, were subdivided into *Kreise*.[21] Their number varied with the size of the *Bezirk*, ranging from four in *RB* Stralsund in Pomerania to twenty-two for *RB* Breslau in Silesia. At the head of a province stood an *Oberpräsident*, of a district a *Regierungspräsident*, of a *Kreis* a *Landrat*. Together with the councillors in the ministries and the *Regierungen*, these were the key positions in the Prussian administration.

The position of *Oberpräsident* was designed to represent the government in the province,[22] coordinate the various administrative branches, and supervise all supraregional affairs (exceeding the regional competence of the *Re-*

---

19. Conze mentioned the fact that civil servants offered expertise in a variety of fields. In the parliament of Hesse-Darmstadt, for example, 42 of 50 deputies were state or local officials (Ibid., 228). Out of 830 deputies sent to the Paulskirche, more than 600 had a university education; 312 of these were either judges or state and local officials. Including teachers and professors, there were 436 civil servants in the Paulskirche (see Nipperdey, *Deutsche Geschichte 1800–1866*, 610).

20. Population figures of Prussian provinces in 1843: Schlesien, 2,948,884; Rheinprovinz, 2,679,508; Prov. Preussen, 2,406,380; Brandenburg, 1,935,107; Sachsen, 1,683,906; Westfalen, 1,421,443; Posen, 1,290,187; Pommern, 1,106,350. See "Statistische Nachrichten über den preussischen Staat," Staatsarchiv Merseburg, rep. 77, titel 94, vol. 4; Wolfgang Köllmann, ed., *Quellen zur Bevölkerungs-, Sozial-, und Wirtschaftsstatistik Deutschlands 1815–1875* (Munich, 1985).

21. See *Handatlas des preussischen Königreiches* (Glogau, 1846); *Historischer Atlas für die preussischen Staaten von 1836;* "Vergleichende Zusammenstellung der Einwohnerzahl des Preussischen Staates in den Jahren 1840–1855," *Archiv für Landeskunde der Preussischen Monarchie* 4 (1856).

22. See Georg-Christoph von Unruh, "Der preussische Oberpräsident," in *Die Preussischen Oberpräsidenten 1815–1945*, ed. Klaus Schwabe (Boppard, 1981), 18. The position had been created because the different departmental ministers (created by the reforms in 1808) were not as well versed with the concerns of the province as the provincial ministers of the Frederican age.

gierungen), such as educational matters, public health, state police, and issues concerning provincial diets.[23] Before 1848 *Oberpräsidenten* were often regarded as symbols of their respective province by virtue of long tenure, which, in some instances, lasted four decades.[24] It is a telling example of the preponderance of bureaucratic administration over provincial diets that the *Oberpräsident* chaired these.[25] In Prussia, the state—that is, the bureaucracy— even administered the representative bodies of society. The position of *Oberpräsident* was also a frequent springboard to ministerial office. Out of a total of forty-five *Oberpräsidenten* in the Prussian administration between 1815 and 1866, fourteen were invested with a ministerial post,[26] nine became ministers after serving as *Oberpräsident,* and another three returned after their ministerial term to chair the provincial administration. This highlights a specific feature of the Prussian civil service as noted in 1909 by Otto Hintze, namely, that ministers were recruited from among the most senior officials.[27]

Before entering office, the *Oberpräsident* had passed through a series of administrative positions, which set a career pattern for his position. Ordinarily, he had completed military service, obligatory since 1814, before entering a university to study *Rechtswissenschaften* and *Staatswissenschaften.* A full course of study at a university had been made obligatory in 1804.[28] Training either in the judicial branch of the bureaucracy, in the provincial administration, or at the central level in Berlin was frequently followed by appointment to the office of *Landrat.* Thereafter the future *Oberpräsident* could be nominated

---

23. On Prussian *Oberpräsidenten* see also Lotz, *Geschichte des deutschen Beamtentums,* 355–56; Ferdinand Fischer, *Preussen am Abschlusse der ersten Hälfte des 19. Jahrhunderts* (Berlin, 1876), 113–14; Wegmann, *Die leitenden staatlichen Verwaltungsbeamten der Provinz Westfalen;* Koselleck, *Preussen zwischen Reform und Revolution,* 221–27; Hartung, *Staatsbildende Kräfte der Neuzeit,* 275–318.

24. From the 1820s through the 1840s, Prussia had a number of prominent *Oberpräsidenten* whose names became synonymous with their provinces. Some held their positions for decades: Flottwell in Posen between 1830 and 1840; Merckel in Silesia from 1815 to 1820 and again from 1825 to 1845; Sack in Pomerania between 1816 and 1831; Schön in West Prussia from 1815 to 1824 and in the newly created province of Prussia from 1824 to 1842; Vincke in Westfalia from 1815 to 1844.

25. See Unruh, *"Der preussische Oberpräsident,"* in *Die preussischen Oberpräsidenten,* ed. Schwabe, 19.

26. See Rüdiger Schütz, "Die preussischen Oberpräsidenten von 1815 bis 1866," in *Die preussischen Oberpräsidenten,* ed. Schwabe, 43–44.

27. Otto Hintze, "Der Beamtenstand," in Hintze, *Gesammelte Abhandlungen,* 2:60–125. During the pre-March period, when the country was effectively ruled by officials, this was to be expected. Yet things did not change markedly after Prussia became a constitutional state.

28. Wilhelm Bleek, *Von der Kameralausbildung zum Juristenprivileg: Studium, Prüfung und Ausbildung der höheren Beamten des allgemeinen Verwaltungsdienstes in Deutschland im 18. und 19. Jahrhundert* (Berlin, 1972).

to a position within a district government, before eventually chairing it as *Regierungspräsident,* usually the last step on the road to the provincial governorship.[29] In the absence of a parliament and political parties (before 1848), there were naturally no political appointees, so that access to the highest provincial post was possible only after a distinguished civil service career and a great deal of experience in different levels of the administration. This contributed to a high degree of homogeneity among provincial governors.[30] This changed after the revolution, since with the disciplinary legislation of July 21, 1852, the *Oberpräsidenten* became *politische Beamte,* which meant that they could be ordered to withdraw from active service at short notice.

The aristocratic element predominated among the highest ranks of the bureaucracy, and the *Oberpräsident* was a case in point. Out of thirteen *Oberpräsidenten* who held office between 1815 and 1824, eight (61.5 percent) belonged to the old aristocracy, one had been recently ennobled, and four came from the ranks of the bourgeoisie.[31] In the years preceding the revolution, this proportion shifted in favor of the bourgeoisie, but between 1848 and 1866, during the "constitutional age," the proportionate share of the old aristocracy rose anew. Sociologically, the introduction of a constitution had not led to democratization.[32] Of the forty-five *Oberpräsidenten* holding office between 1815 and 1866, forty-two were Protestant.[33]

The direct administration of the provinces lay within the competence of the *Regierungen.* Even though the *Regierungen* were collegially and not hierarchically structured, the president of the Regierung held a dominant position

---

29. Twenty-eight of the forty-five *Oberpräsidenten* who held the office between 1815 and 1866 chaired a *Regierung* or occupied the equivalent position in the judicial bureaucracy. In cases where the prospective *Oberpräsident* had neither been *Landrat* nor chaired a *Regierung,* he held another high position in the *Innenverwaltung* or the judicial service. In five cases the ministerial position preceded appointment to *Oberpräsident,* in which case the office became a sinecure for former ministers.

30. Among the forty-five *Oberpräsidenten* (1815–1866), there was only one, the Pomeranian conservative Senfft von Pilsach, who belonged to the conservative Protestant *Erweckungsbewegung* and managed to enter the higher civil service without either attending university or passing through basic administrative training. He became *Oberpräsident* of Pomerania in 1852.

31. See Schütz, "Die preussischen Oberpräsidenten," 48.

32. These figures may not reveal much as far as the mentality of the *Oberpräsidenten* is concerned. John R. Gillis has observed that even the members of the old aristocracy serving in the bureaucracy between 1794 and 1848 considered themselves as part of the civil service rather than as offspring of the traditional aristocratic elite. See Gillis, "Aristokratie und Bürokratie im Preussen des 19. Jahrhunderts," in *Preussische Reformen,* ed. Barbara Vogel (Königstein, 1980), 188–206.

33. See Schütz, "Die preussischen Oberpräsidenten," 35.

within it, at least nominally.[34] De facto, most of the *Regierungen* preserved their collegial spirit, and presidents continued to be occasionally outvoted by other high civil servants. In his memoirs, Hans Viktor von Unruh provided a vivid account of the situation in the *Regierung* at Gumbinnen (East Prussia), where a newly appointed *Regierungspräsident* yielded when faced with the opposition of a majority of councillors (despite the president's appeal to the new instructions of 1825). If we follow Unruh, the actual change of formerly independent *Regierungen* into prefecture-like administrative bodies started only during the 1840s.[35] The *Regierung* participated in the making of laws and had as its executive organs *Landräte*, town mayors, and the police authorities at its disposal. Officials in different branches of the civil service, such as revenue officers, forest officers, and members of the board of health, equally fell under the authority of the *Regierung*. Corresponding to the *Regierungen* of the twenty-five government districts were the twenty-two Superior Provincial Courts of the judicial administration.[36] The administrative authority of the *Regierung* was virtually all-encompassing. The jurisdiction of the *Regierung* Münster in Westfalia, for example, comprised all matters of domestic sovereignty, including censorship, district police, poor relief, the revenue system, supervision of trade and commerce, and army-related issues necessitating the participation of the civil administration, such as recruitment and mobilization.[37]

After the revolution, not only *Oberpräsidenten* but also *Regierungspräsidenten* became political appointees under the disciplinary law of 1852, which decreed that both could be forced into retirement after being granted a pension. This was the end of the civil servants' autonomy, however relative it had been. Henceforth the majority of higher civil servants was forced to support the government and its policies. This included the large number of officials serving as deputies in the Prussian legislature, who had no choice but to support the reactionary government policies of the 1850s.

The *Landrat* held a key administrative position at the lowest level of the bureaucracy. He was in charge of a local district and chaired the meetings of the

---

34. According to the new regulations of 1825, the president of a *Regierung* was in a position to decide issues and overrule the collegiate body of councillors. Some interpreted this as a victory of the prefect system over the old Prussian system of joint responsibility.

35. Unruh, *Erinnerungen aus dem Leben von Hans Viktor von Unruh*, ed. H. Poschinger (Stuttgart, 1895).

36. See Lotz, *Geschichte des deutschen Beamtentums*, 364–65 (the so-called *Oberlandesgerichte*). Government districts and superior provincial courts were allocated the same relative rank in the administrative hierarchy; otherwise they functioned in complete independence from each other.

37. Wegmann, *Die leitenden staatlichen Verwaltungsbeamten in der Provinz Westfalen*, 22.

local district council, which was part of the *ständische Selbstverwaltung*. This body also elected the *Landrat*. But a prior selective mechanism operated before nomination, for in the Prussian east it was customary that only landed proprietors were eligible. Moreover, to be confirmed, the *Landrat* needed royal consent, which could amount to a further weeding-out process. In Prussia's eastern provinces, the office was consequently dominated by noble estate owners. For his actions, the *Landrat* was accountable to the *Regierung*, to the meetings of which he had free access. In the official hierarchy, he held the same rank as a councillor (*Regierungsrat*), though he was generally considered to be of more exalted station, for in contrast to a *Regierung* councillor, the position of *Landrat* was an aristocratic preserve. In 1842 the *Rheinische Zeitung* published a survey according to which 234 out of 306 *Landräte* came from the aristocracy, but only 72 came from the bourgeoisie.[38] The majority of *Landräte* was therefore considered to belong to the "strictly monarchical or feudal party."[39] They were the backbones of conservative Prussia, an element obstructing progress at the pivotal place where the administration came into direct contact with the population.

Within his district, the *Landrat*'s powers were virtually unlimited. He had the power of police, supervised the collection of taxes, and controlled the communities in his district. In addition to his official status, he could count on the obedience inspired by the landed aristocrat. The *Landrat* was one of the few higher officials who came in touch with the general public, for he was expected to travel throughout his district and, if necessary, provide relief on the spot. Since he had to represent the state adequately, he was naturally expected to be a man of independent means. Even though the *Landrat* was legally obliged to pass the civil service examination, the requirement could be waived in the *Landrat*'s case by royal decree. It thus frequently happened that former officers were directly appointed to the position,[40] a practice especially popular during the reign of Frederick the Great. Throughout the nineteenth century, the office continued to serve as a source of civil employment for former officers. The effect of this was twofold: on the one hand, it favored the aristocratic element among *Landräte*, as the higher officer corps was to a substantial degree made up of aristocrats; on the other, it contributed to the social militarization of the countryside, to the infiltration of military mannerisms and the parade-ground manners known as *Kasernenhofton*. It also carried the slavish obedience of the military into the lower ranks of the district bureaucracy. This was aggravated by the service, either as policemen or as subordinate officials, of many former

---

38. See Koselleck, *Preussen zwischen Reform und Revolution,* 435.
39. F. Fischer, *Preussen am Abschluss,* 116.
40. Hans Viktor von Unruh, *Erinnerungen,* 58.

corporals and sergeants who were only too well adjusted to the military demeanor of their superior *Landrat* and who were quick to imitate the *Landrat's* brusque vituperative tone when dealing with the "less respectable" elements of society.

Social Composition, Financial Status, and Control: The Limits of Bureaucratic Power

Within the bureaucracy as a whole, aristocratic predominance was the exception rather than the rule, being limited to highest offices that required large-scale representation, such as the positions of minister, *Oberpräsident, Regierungspräsident,* and most positions in the diplomatic service.[41] Aristocratic influence as a whole was more significant in Prussia than in the Southern German states, though even in Prussia the non-noble element prevailed numerically.[42] In 1820, for example, 82 percent of councillors in *Regierungen* came from the ranks of the bourgeoisie, and only 18 percent from the aristocracy.[43] By 1851 the bureaucratic percentage had risen to 27 percent,[44] which was in keeping with the overall increase of the aristocratic quota in the administration after 1825. A major reason for this rise was the aristocratic reaction that set in after the definitive failure of the reforms in 1819. As a result, the proportionate share of the aristocracy in the entire provincial administration rose from about 25 percent to 33 percent between 1820 and 1845, without counting *Landräte.*

---

41. Of thirty members of the higher diplomatic service, twenty-nine were aristocratic. That was to be expected in a Europe still dominated by the aristocracy. A major power like Prussia could ill afford to send a commoner as ambassador to the French or English court. For the figures see *Rheinische Zeitung* 100 (1842); reprinted in Koselleck, *Preussen zwischen Reform und Revolution,* 435.

42. On the social composition of the Prussian bureaucracy see John R. Gillis, *The Prussian Bureaucracy in Crisis* (Stanford, 1971); Schütz, "Die preussischen Oberpräsidenten"; Koselleck, *Preussen zwischen Reform und Revolution; Lotz, Geschichte des deutschen Beamtentums;* Peradovich, *Die Führungsschichten in Österreich und Preussen 1815–1918* (Wiesbaden, 1955); Hans-Joachim Henning, *Die deutsche Beamtenschaft im 19. Jahrhundert* (Stuttgart, 1984); Bernd Wunder, *Die Geschichte der Bürokratie in Deutschland* (Frankfurt, 1985).

43. The term *bourgeoisie* is infelicitous in the German context, where it is commonly applied to the *Grossbürgertum* and therefore a synonym to *haute bourgeoisie.* The term *Bürgertum* (besides being unfamiliar to the Anglo-Saxon reader) is equally problematic, as it can hardly be used without further qualifications, for there is the *Besitzbürgertum,* the propertied bourgeoisie; the *Bildungsbürgertum,* the university trained bourgeoisie (a fitting label for non-noble high officials); and finally the *Kleinbürgertum,* the petty bourgeoisie. If used without further qualifiers, *Bürgertum* refers to middle class; the *Bürger* is definitely below the "bourgeois" on the social scale. A master artisan is a *Bürger,* a banker or rich merchant with international connections a bourgeois. Despite the evident shortcomings of the term *bourgeois,* it is used here in the sense of "non-noble."

44. Henning, *Beamtenschaft,* 44; Nipperdey, *Deutsche Geschichte 1800–1866,* 320–37. In 1840, only eight of the presidents and vice presidents of *Regierungen* were bourgeois; twenty came from the aristocracy.

According to John Gillis, the influx of aristocratic civil servants was so signifi- cant that it destroyed the corporate solidarity of the core bureaucracy,[45] while Reinhart Koselleck pointed out that within the *Regierungen*, higher officials increasingly cultivated an aristocratic code of honor even when they were of bourgeois origin themselves.[46]

Its powerful position within the state gave the bureaucratic profession a degree of social prestige that set it apart from comparable professions in trade, commerce, or education.[47] The judicial branch of the bureaucracy, which carried less prestige than the *Innenverwaltung*, constituted the exception to increasing feudalization. Around 1840, over 60 percent of the highest positions within the judicial branch, the presidents of Higher Regional Courts, or *Oberlandesgerichtspräsidenten*, were bourgeois; and in 1844, ten out of twelve of the highest Superior Counsellors (*Vortragende Räte*) in the ministry of justice were non-noble.[48] Generally, the aristocratic quota decreased the further west one went. The nobility's proportionate share of office was highest in the eastern provinces, reaching over 50 percent in Pomerania or Silesia.[49]

When considering the background of university-educated civil servants in Prussia between 1820 and 1850, it is conspicuous that they recruited them- selves mostly from members of the traditional upper classes. There were few *homines novi*. More than two-fifths, 43.7 percent, came from families of exist- ing higher civil servants, whereas only 14.1 percent rose from the lower and middle ranks of civil servants, the so-called *Subalternbeamte*, who had no university training. A mere 4.2 percent came from families of master crafts- men.[50] Similar figures emerge when examining the background of law students

---

45. The thesis of growing aristocratic influence at German courts, in the army, and in administration after the mid-1820s was also advanced in Ernst Bramsted's *Aristocracy and the Middle Classes in Germany*, 2d ed. (Chicago, 1964), 42.

46. In the Cologne *Regierung*, for example, a councillor was forced to leave active service—despite ministerial intercession on his behalf—for refusing to give satisfaction in an (illegal) duel. See Koselleck, *Preussen zwischen Reform und Revolution*, 245.

47. See Franz Schnabel, *Deutsche Geschichte*, 4:123: "Der untere Beamte sah sich re- spektvoll gegrüsst von Tagelöhnern und Handwerkern, der hohe Beamte kam in der gesellschaftlichen Rangordnung unmittelbar nach dem Offizier und stand weit über dem Kauf- mann und Fabrikanten."

48. Henning, *Beamtenschaft*, 46. In the ministry of finance and the ministry of the interior, bourgeois councillors prevailed as well, though the ratio was not quite as clearly in their favor.

49. While the office of *Landrat* was almost exclusively staffed with aristocratic estate owners in the east, 45–50 percent of *Landräte* in the Rhine Province, Prussia's westernmost province, were bourgeois.

50. Henning, *Beamtenschaft*, 54. Between 1820 and 1850, 7 percent of Prussian higher officials came from families of entrepreneurs, 18.3 percent from the professions, 43.7 percent from university-trained civil servants, 2.8 percent from families of officers, 8.4 percent from gentleman farmers, only 1.5 percent from families of simple farmers, 4.2 percent from master craftsmen, and 14.1 percent from the families of *Subalternbeamte*.

at Halle University between 1820 and 1850, who, for the most part, went on to become Prussian officials.[51] In 1817, the gap between higher civil servants and *Subalternbeamte* was turned into an insurmountable barrier by new regulations concerning rank.[52] The subordinate official became "the soldier without uniform, the reliable man, slavishly following instructions, who did not think for himself, but only executed the orders he received."[53] The *Subalternbeamtentum* was thus turned into an agency for the civilian maintenance of former noncommissioned officers.

The higher civil service gained in prestige and social coherence by dint of its exclusiveness and strict separation from lower bureaucratic orders. This social coherence was augmented further by the high level of recruitment from among its own ranks, for many civil servants had already been socialized in families of officials. New regulations additionally contributed to internal consistency. In 1823, for example, removal from the service became tied to a formal legal procedure, which was meant to constitute a protective shield against random dismissal.[54] Improvements in officials' legal status were supplemented by a standardized retirement and pension plan.[55] Concomitant changes raised entrance requirements and tightened admission to the civil service. From 1834 on, the gymnasium graduation certificate, the *Abitur,* became indispensable to attending a university. Then followed an obligatory three-year course of study at a Prussian university and the long unpaid prepara-

---

51. For the higher civil service the study of jurisprudence was a prerequisite, and the social background of law students therefore serves as an indicator of the social extraction of Prussian officials (see Bleek, *Von der Kameralausbildung zum Juristenprivileg*). One-third of Halle law students came from families where the father had previously studied law; 30.8 percent from families of theologians, university-trained teachers, professors, estate owners, or officers; 10.9 percent from families of *Subalternbeamte* (see Wunder, *Geschichte der Bürokratie,* 56).

52. See Wilhelm Naudé, "Zur Geschichte des preussischen Subalternbeamtentums," *Forschungen zur brandenburgisch-preussischen Geschichte* 18 (1905): 365–86.

53. Ibid., 374. Otto Hintze equally regretted that "able and trustworthy subordinate officials do not have the opportunity to attain higher positions" (see Hintze, "Der Beamtenstand," in *Gesammelte Abhandlungen,* 2:60–125).

54. See Horst Kübler, *Besoldung und Lebenshaltung der unmittelbaren preussischen Staatsbeamten im 19. Jahrhundert* (Nürnberg, 1976), 23. The law of March 29, 1844, concerning "Legal and Disciplinary Penal Procedure Against Civil Servants" also regulated removal from active service.

55. On the basis of obligatory insurance, by which civil servants were bound to enter an insurance company owned by the state (*Pensionsreglement* of April 31, 1825) and pay one-twelfth of their annual salary into the pension fund. This pension regulation of 1825 granted a "legal claim on lifelong pension" for all civil servants after a minimum of fifteen years active service (provided performance was adequate). In regard to old-age pensions the Southern German states blazed the trail for Prussia's regulations. See Kübler, *Besoldung und Lebenshaltung,* 26; Wunder, *Geschichte der Bürokratie;* Henning, *Beamtenschaft.*

tory period of service that could last five years or more.[56] The official could count on receiving a salary only after passing the second state examination. This acted as an effective social filter forestalling any large-scale social mobility into the higher-core bureaucracy, since the prospective official had to be well-off to feed himself during the unpaid preparatory period. The social exclusiveness of the high bureaucracy was further enhanced by an abundance of status symbols that set the official apart from the rest of society. Foremost among these were civil service uniforms, including a civilian épée, the *Zivildegen,* and a special kind of headgear, varying according to rank. Then there were the decorations and badges of honor, which were important for an official's career since they were listed in personal files of conduct, the *Konduitenlisten.*[57] The official also had the moral obligation to maintain a relatively high standard of living (since he represented the state), to keep spacious dwellings and domestic servants, and to entertain at regular intervals.

The funds necessary to meet these obligations often went beyond what the official was able to afford on his initially modest salary.[58] Substantial parental means were therefore a conditio sine qua non for the successful start of a young official's career. Interest on capital investment, a considerable dowry, and finally the inherited family fortune were indispensable for the higher civil servant throughout the nineteenth century, since often a female cook, a governess, and a housemaid were employed simultaneously in his household.[59] In addition to the indispensable household aid, there were the educational journeys, *Bildungsreisen,* and the yearly stay (often stretching over four to six weeks) at a spa with the entire family. But these leisure activities were dictated by convention, and the *"que dirra-t-on"* provided a forceful enough means of coercion to do as everyone else.

56. See Koselleck, *Preussen zwischen Reform und Revolution,* 246. Instructions of October 23, 1817, moreover required a thorough knowledge in ancient and modern languages, in history, mathematics, and *Staatswissenschaften,* a kind of political science. See Clemens von Delbrück, *Die Ausbildung für den höheren Verwaltungsdienst in Preussen* (Jena, 1917).

57. For practical examples see "Acta betreffend die Conduiten-Listen über die Regierungspräsidenten," Staatsarchiv Merseburg, rep. 77, titel 184a, no. 4. In these lists of conduct, there was a column for "Orden und Ehrenzeichen, welche dem Beamten verliehen sind."

58. In his memoirs, Friedrich Meinecke mentioned that the young university-trained civil servant had to keep up appearances if he did not want to be looked down on. Meinecke related his own experiences, mentioning that a young married official had to keep a five-room apartment with expensive *Plüschmöbel,* where he was expected to give soirées for at least eighteen people. Meinecke was only *Archivrat,* which was far below a high bureaucratic rank. Meinecke pointed out that all these customs were relics from the *Biedermeierzeit,* that is, the 1820s and 1830s (see Friedrich Meinecke, *Erlebtes 1862–1901* (Leipzig, 1941).

59. See Kübler, *Besoldung und Lebenshaltung;* Otto Most, *Zur Wirtschafts- und Sozialstatistik der höheren Beamten in Preussen* (Munich and Leipzig, 1916); Johannes Ziekursch, *Beiträge zur Charakteristik der preussischen Verwaltungsbeamten in Schlesien* (Breslau, 1907).

During the first half of the nineteenth century, the higher official was exceptionally well remunerated once he was firmly ensconced in his position. But there was an enormous discrepancy in income between higher and lower officials. Around 1800, for example, the president of a provincial *Kriegs- und Domänenkammer* (comparable to a *Regierung*) had an annual income of 3,026 taler, whereas a document filist (*Aktenhelfer*) and a copyist (*Kopist*), employed at the very same administrative body, earned 50 taler a year, less than one sixtieth of the president's salary.[60] Similar conditions prevailed in Silesia, where (in 1798) the forty-one employees of the *Kriegs- und Domänenkammer* in Breslau earned 20,959 taler altogether, not even twice as much as the president's 10,720 taler.[61] This discrepancy in income between subordinate officials and upper ranks underlined the exalted position of high-echelon bureaucrats. These vast differences were preserved throughout the first half of the nineteenth century and gradually leveled out thereafter.

In relation to the rest of the Prussian population, the entire high-core bureaucracy belonged to the country's highest income group. The following examples illustrate this point. In Cologne with a population of slightly over 80,000 (1845),[62] only 533 people earned the more than 1,200 taler necessary to be part of the first class of constituents.[63] In Koblenz, with 24,245 inhabitants,[64] only 111 individuals surpassed an annual income of 1,200 taler; and in Düsseldorf, with about 25,000 inhabitants, 127 people earned more than the 1,400 taler that was the qualifying income for the first class of constituents there.[65] A yearly income of 1,200–1,400 taler can therefore be considered extraordinarily high in the affluent cities of the Rhine Province, then Prussia's richest. In comparison to these figures, the salaries of higher provincial bureaucrats give a clear indication of the officials' privileged financial standing. According to the pay regulation of the *Regierung* in Düsseldorf, the salaries were:

The president of the *Regierung*	4,000 taler
The directors of the departments (ministerial directors)	3,000 taler
The superior forestry official (*Oberforstmeister*)	2,400 taler

60. Kübler, *Besoldung und Lebenshaltung*, 86.
61. Ziekursch, *Beiträge*, 76.
62. Pierre Ayçoberry, *Cologne entre Napoléon at Bismarck* (Paris, 1981), 396.
63. Kübler, *Besoldung und Lebenshaltung*, 150.
64. See Staatsarchiv Merseburg, rep. 77, titel 94, vol. 4 (1842–53).
65. In Aachen (population 48,557 in 1846), 133 people earned more than 1,600 taler.

| The secret councillors (*Geheime Regierungsräte*) | 1,500–1,800 taler |
| The governmental councillors (*Regierungsräte*) | 900–1,500 taler.[66] |

The Rhineland constituted no exception regarding high salaries. Throughout the kingdom, high officials belonged to the best remunerated group. In 1851, a minister earned 10,000 taler, directors in the ministry 3,500 taler, and ministerial councillors 1,800–2,800 taler. An *Oberpräsident* had an annual salary of 6,000 taler, and even governmental councillors in the *Regierungen* earned 1,000–1,600 taler.[67] As late as 1848, a shift from a leading position in industry to a higher administrative post could mean financial gain.[68] This did not include various fringe benefits that went with high salaries, such as official residences for ministers and *Oberpräsidenten* that were usually paid for by the state. The presidents of *Regierungen* received other emoluments as well, such as remuneration for their rent.[69] In 1854, only 562 individuals in the whole of Prussia earned 6,000 taler or more a year; the eight *Oberpräsidenten* were among them.[70] During the second half of the century, the differences in salary between higher officials and subordinate ones gradually leveled out. As parliament curtailed the power of the bureaucracy, officials eventually had to give up their privileged economic position as well. By the turn of the century, the remuneration of the high civil servants had declined relative to other high income groups as well as to lower-ranking officials.[71]

High-echelon officials were able to make decisions freely and independently by dint of their privileged social and economic status, high income, and social prestige, and because they were removed from the rest of the population through uniforms and other outward insignia of rank. But precisely these paraphernalia of power created a barrier between them and the common people, blinding officials toward the needs and wants of those below them. One reaction to the bureaucracy's loftiness was the severe criticism to which officials

---

66. See Most, *Wirtschafts- und Sozialstatistik*, 8 (the figures for 1816).

67. See Lotz, *Geschichte des deutschen Beamtentums*, 424.

68. See Most, *Wirtschafts- und Sozialstatistik*, 18. Most related the case of a director at the Düsseldorf-Elberfeld Railroad who subsequently became *Regierungspräsident* and earned more money in that position.

69. See Kübler, *Besoldung und Lebenshaltung*, Anhang XI. The rate of exchange for talers to mark is one to three.

70. Kübler, *Besoldung und Lebenshaltung*, 152.

71. The numerous civil servants in the German *Reichstag* made no effort to preserve their privileged financial position. After the foundation of the Empire, it was frequently discussed whether high officials could live *standesgemäss* with their salaries (see Most, *Wirtschafts- und Sozialstatistik*, 11). While in 1875 only 10,000 people earned more than a *Regierungspräsident*, the figure had risen to 63,000 by 1912 (see Kübler, *Besoldung und Lebenshaltung*, 153; Most, *Wirtschafts- und Sozialstatistik*, 17). Salaries of higher civil servants were not directly related to the rise in national wealth: between 1850 and 1910, the number of taxpayers with a higher income than that of a minister increased almost thirtyfold.

were subjected in the 1830s and 1840s. But high officials also acted under constraints and coercions from within the bureaucratic apparatus that could obstruct their decisions or channel them into already established tracks.

In his 1866 study *Der Preussische Beamtenstaat*, the former judicial official Karl Twesten gave an account of the constraints under which civil servants labored.[72] According to the *Allgemeine Landrecht*, the official could be brought before a criminal court for offenses for which a mere reprimand or disciplinary penalty did not seem sufficient. Such offenses included "violation of one's immediate official duties" as well as "vile conduct" in civilian life, "*niederträchtige Aufführung*" as it was put.[73] The disciplinary legislation of 1844 subjected judicial officials to disciplinary proceedings for misdemeanor in office, or disorderly conduct. This led to vociferous protests among judges, for it was rightly feared that judicial magistrates could be subjected to pressure from the state.[74] The disciplinary law of March 29, 1844, supplemented the *Allgemeine Landrecht* insofar as it introduced a cluster of offenses punishable for civil servants only—chief among them, "continually unsatisfactory performance" and "loss of prestige required for official duty."[75]

A decisive tightening of disciplinary legislation occurred in the wake of the revolution. Paradoxically, a first important step toward muzzling politically deviant officials, that is, those not in line with government policies, was an instruction issued by the liberal Hansemann-Auerswald ministry on July 15, 1848, which resulted in the dismissal of three conservative *Oberpräsidenten*.[76] The reactionary régime of the postrevolutionary period gratefully took up the

---

72. Karl Twesten, "Der Preussische Beamtenstaat," *Preussische Jahrbücher* 18 (1866): 1–39, 109–48; reprinted as Twesten, *Der Preussische Beamtenstaat* (Darmstadt, 1979).

73. Twesten, "Der Preussische Beamtenstaat," 138. This meant that officials had to keep up appearances outside office. Being found drunk in the street or leading a "morally questionable" way of life, a pardonable faux pas for the average Prussian citizen, could be of grave consequence for an official's career.

74. During the *Vormärz*, it was a rare event that an official spoke out publicly against the government. Two notable exceptions were *Stadtgerichtsrat* Simon, who protested against the disciplinary legislation of 1844 and was subsequently fired (see Hartung, *Staatsbildende Kräfte*, 250), and Theodor von Schön, whose critical pamphlet *Woher und Wohin* was published in 1842 (against Schön's own intentions). Schön's massive criticism (he compared officials to the Catholic clergy in their unfailing dogmatism) also forced him to resign.

75. See Hartung, *Staatsbildende Kräfte*, 243. According to Hartung, the disciplinary legislation of 1844 was based on the instruction for the *Regierungen* of December 26, 1808. Article 44 of these instructions decreed that officials indifferent toward religion and morality and indulging in drink and gambling must not be tolerated in office.

76. The process was reversed during the period of reaction, when (in 1850–51) the three liberals were superseded by strictly conservative *Oberpräsidenten*. During the New Era (after 1858), the liberals were reinstated in high positions (see Schütz, "Die preussischen Oberpräsidenten," 74).

decree and passed even stricter emergency measures for all nonjudicial officials (July 11, 1849). The significance of the new law was manifold. The official could be discharged from service on the grounds that he had violated his obligation of loyalty toward the government, that he had defiled the "dignity required for office," the *Würde des Amtes,* or that he was guilty of "political partisanship against the state."[77] The "obligation of loyalty by the official," introduced after the revolution, allowed for the new situation created by parliament and political parties. A further corollary of constitutional government was the creation of *"politische Beamte,"* whose immediate removal from service and superannuation could be ordered by the minister, provided he also granted a pension. Removal from active service could be effected without giving compelling reasons for the action and without granting a hearing to the official concerned. The *politische Beamte* included *Oberpräsidenten,* presidents and vice presidents of the *Regierungen* and *Landräte.*[78] The emergency measure of 1849 was further elaborated in the disciplinary law of July 21, 1852, which remained in effect until rendered obsolete by the *Reichsbeamtengesetz* of 1937.

Ironically, it was Karl Marx's brother-in-law, Minister of the Interior von Westfalen, embodiment of the reaction of the 1850s, who exerted formative influence on the political beliefs of the civil service. In his ordinance of January 1, 1851, for the inner administration, he demanded that "one spirit, one will permeate and enliven the entire administration." During the first half of the 1850s, the influence of the higher civil service in the Prussian *Abgeordnetenhaus* was significant. Out of 351 deputies, 175 were active officials and officers, 85 of whom served in the administration. Of these 85 *Verwaltungsbeamte,* 57 belonged in the category of the *politische Beamte* and could therefore be dismissed from active service at any time. The influence the government could bring to bear on this group was considerable, and with one exception, all the *politische Beamte* supported it.

Alongside the obvious coercion of disciplinary decrees, there were more insidious coercive measures emanating from the civil service body itself that exerted invisible control over individual civil servants. The first and foremost means of disciplining the official within the apparatus were the *Konduitenlisten,* records of the official's conduct.[79] These *"geheime Konduitenlisten"* were confidential; the official himself had no access to them.

---

77. Hartung, *Staatsbildende Kräfte,* 253.

78. Ibid., 253. Other *"politische Beamte"* included public prosecutors; *Ministerialdirektoren,* that is, departmental directors at the ministries; and presidents of police authorities.

79. See *Geheimes Preussisches Staatsarchiv Dahlem,* "Preussisches Staatsministerium, General Akten," rep. 90, no. 2318; "Die Konduiten-Listen, Personal-Nachweisungen über die Verhältnisse, Leistungen der Beamten," Staatsarchiv Merseburg, vol. 1, rep. 77, titel 184a, no. 4.

Until abolished during the revolution, on July 14, 1848,[80] they created an atmosphere of fear and intimidation.[81] In addition to providing details on an official's service—that is, how long, where, and in what capacity he had served before attaining his present position—information on religious denomination, and lists of "orders and badges of honor conferred," the *Konduitenlisten* scanned the family affairs and financial circumstances of the official. Together with questions on "the ability to fill the position competently" (*Amtsfähigkeit*) and the "management of the office" (*Amtsverwaltung*), both of which left ample scope for a malevolent superior to ruin any promising career, there were columns on "moral conduct" (*sittlicher Wandel*) and "special observations," which left additional room for arbitrary judgments.[82]

The example of *Regierungspräsident* Carl Ludwig Graf von Fleming shows that harsh assessments were not uncommon even at the highest level. Fleming was characterized as seeing the fulfillment of official duties "only in the observance of outward forms," and the

sterile indifference he displays on every occasion, even during the meetings of the *Collegii*, is so well known throughout the district that confidence in his activities and trust in his effectiveness is out of the question.[83]

In a judgment on the *Regierungspräsident* of Minden in Westfalia, Carl Gottlieb Richer, it was noted that, though being "circumspect" and "orderly," he was "not free, however, of pedantry and vanity, and therefore not generally liked."[84] Especially for younger civil servants, who had their whole careers still ahead of them, secret *Konduitenlisten* served as an ideal means of enforcing conformity and suppressing socially deviant behavior. Whoever wanted to

---

80. Staatsarchiv Dahlem, rep. 90, no. 2318. Before 1848, these confidential lists of conduct were even kept for ecclesiastics; university teachers were among the few civil service categories never to be included.

81. See Twesten, "Der Preussische Beamtenstaat," 139.

82. Staatsarchiv Merseburg, "Acta betreffend die Conduiten-Listen über die Regierungs-Präsidenten," rep.77, titel 184a, no. 4.

83. See Staatsarchiv Merseburg, rep. 77, titel 184a, no. 4, Fleming, 22. Fleming owned "a not inconsiderable fortune" and was married to a countess of Hardenberg, which may have kept him in office. *Konduitenlisten* for councillors of a *Regierung* were written by presidents, vice presidents, or departmental directors; presidents themselves were judged by the *Oberpräsident* of the province.

84. Staatsarchiv Merseburg, rep. 77, titel 184a, no. 4, 40. Negative remarks were not infrequent: e.g., the *Regierungspräsident* of Arnsberg was said to have "a tendency to overestimate his own opinions, not to tolerate contradiction, to demand unquestioning obedience of subordinated authorities, and to vituperate jealously the influence of the superior ones." Overall, positive assessments prevailed with the *Regierungspräsidenten*, which was to be expected, for these high-ranking officials (there were only twenty-seven of them in all Prussia) had already undergone several preselections.

get on and work his way up—and there were few who did not have this desire—was condemned to a career of ingratiation and sycophancy. Opportunities collegial councils provided to speak one's mind were undoubtedly often passed up out of regard for what superiors might write in their confidential reports. And what young official would have wanted to be labeled a liberal when serving under an archconservative president.

A former official who had come into conflict with the bureaucratic apparatus, Karl Heinzen, defined *Konduitenlisten* as "continual reports which, without their knowledge, are written for subordinates by superiors at their own discretion and in secrecy, in order to be handed on to the central authorities in charge." For the official, Heinzen noted, the *Konduitenliste* constituted "the basis for his good or bad luck in office," turning him into the "spineless instrument of his superiors."[85] Heinzen himself had experienced the plight of the junior official in the hierarchy and therefore spoke from firsthand experience when characterizing his lot:

> Through the secret *Konduitenliste,* the subordinate official is completely without any rights. . . . Without any idea of how his superiors are predisposed toward him, without knowing what they intend to do with him, without being able to see the verdict passed on him in black and white, without being in a position to redress the imperfection which places him at a disadvantage, he has to yield blindly to the dark power superiors exert upon him, and it is possible that for half his life he may have to atone for the effect of a confidential report.[86]

In his critical assessment of the Prussian bureaucracy, Heinzen also pointed to the corroding influence of *Konduitenlisten* on the official's character:

> What temptation for domination and injustice on the one hand, what a school for submissiveness and baseness on the other! What instruction to mistrust and deceit, to slander and calumny, for the sepulchre of secrecy put under lock and key everything from which punishment and retribution might spring. How many a superior, who had the courage to blacken his

---

85. Karl Heinzen, *Die preussische Bürokratie* (Darmstadt, 1845), 166–74. Naturally *Konduitenlisten* had a positive aspect as well: notations contained in them were a way of checking on people who normally would not be subject to scrutiny or sanction, even if they did not carry out their duties properly. Existing autobiographies of Prussian civil servants usually point to the repressive aspects of *Konduitenlisten;* contemporary novels, which, with the exception of Karl Immermann's *Die Epigonen* (1835), paid no attention to social and political issues, ignored the subject entirely.

86. See Heinzen, *Die preussische Bürokratie,* 167.

subordinate with a bad report in secret, is too cowardly to adjust his outward behavior accordingly![87]

The servility fostered by these reports undoubtedly effaced many a civil servant's strong personal convictions. This could also affect an official's assessment of social issues. The prevailing opinion within the collegial group, the politically opportune attitude, or the simple attempt to gain the favorable attention of his superiors may have triumphed more than once over practical necessities. The junior members of the bureaucracy in particular may have been reluctant to show their true colors, for they were the ones who had the most to lose. Ministers, *Oberpräsidenten,* and to a certain degree even the *Regierungspräsidenten* could afford to be more candid. In their meetings, they were in a position to speak without restraint. For the more junior members of the bureaucracy, the total supervision within the apparatus, not even sparing their private lives from scrutiny, also meant inner constraints, automatic self-censorship, a pair of scissors in their heads, so that they inadvertently must have shrunk back from decisions that went beyond the well-trodden path of established custom.

Even though officials were sworn to secrecy regarding their official duties, many details about the methods of bureaucratic rule reached the public. Karl Heinzen's critical pamphlet was no exception during the 1840s. Numerous writings, books, tracts, and pamphlets took issue with bureaucratic methods, though they dwelt less on inner problems of the bureaucracy than on its hold over those it administered. And many insiders joined in the criticism, such as Theodor von Schön, for decades *Oberpräsident* of Prussia's largest province, who equally castigated the bureaucratic yoke over the people. Theodor von Schön's *Woher und Wohin* was widely disseminated after it was made public by an indiscretion, which forced Schön to submit his resignation. Coming from Theodor von Schön, renowned throughout the kingdom as a former collaborator of the reformers, reproaches against officials, whom he blamed for curbing social activities and keeping citizens on a leash, cut very close to the bone. Schön characterized officials as "instruments of government, obstructing the cultural development of the people, wanting to keep the people in tutelage."[88]

The geographical center of criticism was the Rhineland, which had become part of Prussia only in 1815.[89] There, the most widely publicized pieces

87. Ibid., 171.

88. Theodor von Schön, "Woher und Wohin," reprinted in Heinzen, *Die Preussische Bürokratie,* 3–10, 8.

89. There is a great deal of literature on the Rhineland between 1815 and 1870 (partly because archival sources were more easily available, i.e., not buried in the formerly East German archives). A noteworthy publication of recent years is Jonathan Sperber's book on the democratic movement before and during the Revolution of 1848, *Rhineland Radicals* (Princeton, 1991).

of criticism were Jacob Venedey's *Preussen und Preussentum* and David Hansemann's *Preussen und Frankreich.*[90] In his *Preussen und Preussentum,* Venedey, who later became one of the leaders of the Catholic party in the Rhineland, maintained that "many thousands of civil servants in Prussia . . . live on the marrow of the people."[91] Venedey's accusations against the bureaucracy were typical of the critical voices raised in the Rhineland.[92] Not only was the bureaucratic apparatus believed to swallow up immense sums (more than the French prefect system under which Rhinelanders had lived during Napoleonic occupation), but the official was also accused of being the "ready defender of decadent absolutism."[93] Venedey asserted that "the impermeable veil of deepest secrecy was cast over all governmental action"—a secrecy that had become "cause for manifold injustice, manifold abuses."[94] A widely disseminated complaint was that the bureaucracy was slow and ineffectual, and that "the complicated bureaucracy amid all its files and documents failed to achieve insight and understanding."[95] Karl Twesten alleged that the Prussian bureaucracy was "fussy and sluggish," that "in unending reports and multifarious instances it exerted everywhere more of an obstructing than a stimulating effect." Twesten maintained that since the 1820s "standstill and stagnation" had become dominant, and that among the public the bureaucracy was seen as "increasingly unwieldy, mechanical, glued to tradition, obstruction, and delay."[96]

---

90. Jacob Venedey, *Preussen und Preussentum* (Mannheim, 1839); David Hansemann, *Preussen und Frankreich* (Leipzig, 1833).

91. Venedey, *Preussen und Preussentum,* 80.

92. Other prominent Rhineland citizens critical of the Prussian bureaucracy included David Hansemann, Gustav Mevissen, and Karl Schorn. See Helene Nathan, *Preussens Verfassung und Verwaltung im Urteile rheinischer Achtundvierziger* (Bonn, 1912).

93. Venedey, *Preussen und Preussentum,* 81; Nathan, *Preussens Verfassung und Verwaltung,* 67–135.

94. See Venedey, *Preussen und Preussentum,* 82, 89; Venedey also opposed the seclusion of the bureaucracy by dint of "a special jurisdiction" (ibid., 88).

95. So, for example, Gustav Mevissen, in Nathan, *Preussens Verfassung und Verwaltung,* 75.

96. Twesten, *Der preussische Beamtenstaat,* 136. Criticism of the bureaucracy was by no means limited to Prussia; it was rampant throughout Germany. A typical example of this was the article by the South German Robert Mohl, "Ueber Bürokratie," published in 1846, in which he summarized the criticism made of the bureaucracy: the noble estate owner feared bureaucratic domination because he was afraid of its leveling mania; the merchant complained about inactivity, on the one hand, and harmful overadministration, on the other; the church maintained that an omnipotent bureaucracy would stifle free and independent religious life; construction engineers and builders of railways and canals deplored the absence of true insight on behalf of the civil servants and lamented repression through needless paperwork and interfering control; communities, finally, complained that flourishing communal life and bureaucracy were incompatible. See Robert Mohl, "Über Bürokratie," *Zeitschrift für die gesamte Staatswissenschaft* 3 (1846): 330–64.

Manifest by the 1840s, the decline of the bureaucracy's image in public perception is reflected in historical research as well. Reinhart Koselleck specified the rapidly dwindling authority of the civil service, which he attributed to the broadening of the intellectual elite in Prussia at the expense of higher civil servants.[97] Fritz Hartung stressed the "expiration of a living creative power," which led "to sterility, to the predominance of a mindless routine, the highest principle of which lay, according to a malicious junior official, in the words '*Es geht auch so.*'"[98] In defense of the bureaucracy, as an extenuating factor, Koselleck asserted that officials had been hopelessly overburdened with work. The number of salaried officials in the provincial and central administration lay only at about 1,600 in 1825;[99] there were about 915 councillors in 1820, a figure that remained stagnant until 1848 for reasons of an economical fiscal policy.[100]

---

97. Koselleck, *Preussen zwischen Reform und Revolution,* 441.
98. Hartung, *Staatsbildende Kräfte,* 244.
99. Koselleck, *Preussen zwischen Reform und Revolution,* 438.
100. Nipperdey, *Deutsche Geschichte 1800–1866,* 325. Koselleck even speaks of an actual decline in numbers. But the most prominent criticism of Prussian officials is found in the literature of Wilhelminean Germany. The "Amtsvorsteher von Wehrhan" in Gerhart Hauptmann's *Der Biberpelz* and the "Oberpräsident von Wulzow" in Heinrich Mann's *Der Untertan* have become well-known stereotypes.

CHAPTER 6

The Bureaucracy and Rural Poverty: Freedom of Movement and the Need to Control

By the 1820s contemporary observers had become keenly aware that rural poverty, a century-old phenomenon, was about to assume new and menacing proportions. In the old days, before the Prussian reforms, the lord of the manor as well as guilds and corporations looked after the poor in case of emergency. By and large, the principle was followed that the *Heimatgemeinde,* the current domicile, had to provide for paupers if need arose. But the impoverished could count on being supported only if they had lived in their community for some time before their impoverishment and shared common burdens with the others. Otherwise they would be sent back to the *Herkunftsgemeinde,* the community of origin. There was no support without previous contribution. The same held true for the peasant villein, whose semifeudal relationship with his manorial lord was also based on a *do ut des:* the estate owner would support only those whose services had previously been useful to him. Therefore, every commune was anxious to rid itself of its poor, sending them back to their place of origin.

The *Allgemeines Landrecht* of 1794 had stipulated that in the final analysis, the state had to provide for the poor. But the provincial poorhouses, which had been established for that purpose, were of only limited significance. They were designed to function as *Arbeitshäuser*—workhouses, prisons, and hospitals of a province—even though their means were miserably inadequate for that purpose due to Prussia's severe financial plight at the beginning of the nineteenth century. The *Landarmenverbände,* established between 1791 and 1804, were largely controlled by the estates; institutional provisions by the state itself were virtually nonexistent—there was no *Armenorganisation.*[1]

---

1. Koselleck observed, "Der staatliche Anspruch für die Armen zu sorgen, stützte sich

Thus, in practice, first the family or the next of kin, then the *"subsidiarische"* obligation of the *Heimatgemeinde* or manorial estate (under the jurisdiction of which most East Elbian peasants lived), and finally the provincial poorhouse were responsible for the paupers' upkeep.

Such a system of poor relief could function only in a socially and geographically immobile society, where subjects remained tied to the soil, where fertility was checked by marriage consents granted by manorial lords, and where town burghers rarely felt tempted to venture beyond familiar walls for fear of having to pay the *"gabella emigrationis."*[2] Before freedom of movement was introduced by the reforms, the potential pauper remained tied to the soil, allowing for the smooth operation of the system: the local lord of the manor was obligated to provide sustenance for his impoverished dependents, and the *Heimatrecht* of the communes functioned without major difficulty, since the future pauper had for the most part earned his upkeep by year-long tax payments. The realization of freedom of movement (in 1816) brought the system to the verge of collapse.[3] Who was now to be responsible for the transient paupers, who had neither been active members of towns or villages, where they might qualify for communal poor relief, nor toiling subjects on an estate, where they might have earned their bread of charity? The separation of manor and commune had freed the manorial lord of any obligation to provide for the welfare of his dependents, and the division of the villages' communal lands, the *Gemeinheitsteilungen,* deprived villages of any means to provide for their own poor. The liberation of the peasantry, the elimination of marriage restrictions, the realization of freedom of movement, and the dissolution of guilds in the towns, along with the reduction of their social functions and the concomitant "decorporation" of societal life in general, resulted in an explosive growth of the landless and propertyless poor.[4] And the growth was steep-

praktisch auf die ständische Selbsthilfe, nur dass er diese in staatliche Verpflichtung nahm und ihre Einrichtungen unter den Schutz und Kontrolle der Verwaltung stellte"; Kosselleck, *Preussen zwischen Reform und Revolution,* 2d ed. (Stuttgart, 1975), 131. On this and the following see Kosselleck, ibid., 129–32, 473–75, 556–57, 620–34; James Sheehan, *German History 1770–1866* (Oxford, 1989), 638–52; Hans-Ulrich Wehler, *Deutsche Gesellschaftsgeschichte* (Munich, 1987), 1:175–76, 198, 335, II: 291–96; Wolfram Fischer, *Armut in der Geschichte* (Göttingen, 1982), 44–49, 56–63.

2. The various poor relief acts that were in effect during the seventeenth and eighteenth centuries were regionally limited. Laws often differed from province to province. For example, the so-called *Abzugssteuer* (*gabella emigrationis*) was dropped in the *Kurmark* in 1718, while it remained in effect in the rest of the monarchy until 1721. See Harald Schinkel, "Armenpflege und Freizügigkeit in der preussischen Gesetzgebung vom Jahre 1842," *Vierteljahreshefte für Sozial- und Wirtschaftsgeschichte* 50 (1963): 459–80.

3. Kosselleck pointed out that freedom of movement was fully realized only in 1816; see Kosselleck, *Preussen zwischen Reform und Revolution,* 58–59, 630–34; Wehler, *Gesellschaftsgeschichte,* 2:292–95.

4. See introduction on the origins of the social question in Prussia.

est in the rural provinces of East Elbian Prussia, for it was there that the abolition of serfdom had brought about the most complete rupture with the past. When searching for remedies, the focus therefore remained on the estates, villages, and small towns of the Prussian countryside.[5] To aggravate matters, the obligation of the state to provide aid in case of emergency, stipulated in the *Allgemeine Landrecht*, had been annulled by the reforms, and communities possessed far-ranging powers to ban "incorrigible, work-shy, and dissolute" persons from their midst. These rights were recorded in local *Armenordnungen* and *Bettlerordnungen* or in *Landarmenreglements*, and one could be sure that communities would make ample use of their power to ward off unwelcome beggars and other paupers who would only act as a drain on village or town resources.

With provincial poorhouses as the only agencies providing for the destitute (and they were, as indicated, largely controlled by the *Stände*), institutional provisions for poor relief were completely insufficient in contrast to the countries of western Europe. Poor relief legislation in England went back to 1360, when a law against vagrancy was passed. The Settlement Act of 1662 contained provisions enabling communities to expel paupers within forty days; and in 1682 freedom of movement was restricted by law, a limitation that was largely abolished in 1785, even though it remained legal to oust the poverty-stricken. The 1834 Poor Law resulted in the establishment of a system of workhouses that became characteristic of the English preference for "indoor relief." In France it was originally the duty of parishes to provide for the poor (1536), until Louis XIV brought ecclesiastical welfare under state control (edicts of 1656, 1693, 1695, and 1705). The revolution introduced the principle that it was the obligation of the state to support the poor (*ateliers nationaux* had been introduced for that purpose in 1789) and that the *domicile de secours* was acquired by birth or a one-year residence. The institutions of poor relief, the

---

5. Prussia's rural population between 1816 and 1846 grew at a faster rate than its urban population. Population increase in the predominantly rural provinces of East and West Prussia, Pomerania, and Posen was faster than that of the more urbanized provinces of the West. See Köllmann, *Quellen zur Bevölkerungs-, Sozial- und Wirtschaftsstatistik Deutschlands 1815–1875* (München, 1985); "Statistische Nachrichten über den preussischen Staat insbesondere über dessen Bevölkerung," *Geheimes Preussisches Staatsarchiv Dahlem*, rep. 84a, no. 4478; "Vergleichende Zusammenstellung der Einwohnerzahl des preussischen Staates in den Jahren 1840–1855," *Archiv für Landeskunde der Preussischen Monarche* 4 (1856); "Historische und statistische Nachrichten über den preussischen Staat," Staatsarchiv Merseburg, rep 77, titel 94, vol. 4 (1842–53), 219, 274.
  Population increase of Prussian provinces, 1816–1846: East Pruss., 874,162–1,468,274 (67.88 percent); West Pruss., 558,242–1,006,281 (80.26 percent); Posen, 813,948–1,350,918 (65.97 percent); Brandenburg, 1,254,176–2,020,424 (61.10 percent); Pomerania, 671,361–1,149,198 (71.17 percent); Silesia, 1,914,093–3,035,781 (58.60 percent); Saxony, 1,180,413–1,718,361 (45,57 percent); Westfalia, 1,057,859–1,436,946 (35.84 percent); Rhine, 1,846,645–2,722,596 (42.10 percent).

hospices, and *bureaux de bienfaisance* remained under the jurisdiction of local communes. In central Europe there were elaborate provisions against mendicancy and vagrancy, which, in the wake of the Thirty Years' War, were more widespread than in either England or France. Punishments were correspondingly harsh: in Bavaria, for example, nonindigenous beggars were branded or, if caught a second time, hanged (1751). In respect to freedom of movement, Prussian legislation was the most liberal among German states; in 1867 the North German Confederation followed the Prussian example and introduced it in its territory, while in Austria the acquisition of *Heimatrecht* became increasingly difficult (residence requirement of ten years in 1896).[6]

At the beginning of the 1820s, therefore, the bureaucracy was compelled to search for new solutions to redress the problem of rural poverty. In 1842, after almost two decades of deliberations, a set of interrelated laws, *"Gesetz über die Verpflichtung zur Armenpflege"* and *"Gesetz über die Aufnahme neu anziehender Personen,"* was passed, which preserved *Freizügigkeit.* That officials resisted the temptation to curtail freedom of movement by introducing barriers to relocation, as Southern German states had done, was subsequently hailed as a great victory of *Beamtenliberalismus.*[7] Harald Schinkel even went so far as to equate the legislation of the Prussian bureaucracy with the French Declaration of the Rights of Man, whereby the bureaucracy was interpreted as an impartial benefactor that stood above societal discord, devoid of interests of its own, permeated by liberality, *Fürsorgedenken,* and a strong ethos of public welfare.[8] This assessment cannot be maintained after a detailed analysis of bureaucratic motivations. Upon thorough scrutiny, economically liberal or humanitarian motivations that have been postulated in respect to the 1842 Poor and Settlement Laws showed themselves eclipsed by different intentions and results. To lay bare and make transparent thought processes within the bureaucracy, the following analysis focuses on the patterns of argumentation and the mode of reasoning as revealed in internal memoranda on the Poor and Settlement Laws.

The need for all-encompassing general legislation regulating poor relief and *Freizügigkeit* was recognized as early as 1824, when the ministry of the

---

6. For a brief orientation on the above see Pauline Gregg, *A Social and Economic History of Britain 1760–1972* 7th ed. (London, 1973), 180–92; "Armenwesen," in *Meyers Konversations Lexikon* (Leipzig, 1902), 1:784–89; Louis Bergeron, François Furet, and Reinhart Koselleck, *Das Zeitalter der europäischen Revolutionen 1780–1848,* Fischer Weltgeschichte 26 (Frankfurt, 1969), 258–61.

7. See Wehler, *Gesellschaftsgeschichte,* 2:295; Koselleck, *Preussen zwischen Reform und Revolution,* 630–34. Wehler mentioned that bureaucratic deliberations dragged on for eighteen years (1824–42), since officials clung to their economically liberal principles even when confronted with great poverty (*Gesellshaftsgeschichte,* 2:293).

8. Harald Schinkel, "Armenpflege und Freizügigkeit."

interior presented the *Staatsministerium* with a legal draft concerning poor relief. From the very beginning of deliberations on a new poor law, valid for all Prussian provinces, the bureaucracy was confronted with two complex issues: (1) Should *Freizügigkeit,* freedom of movement (including *Niederlassungs-, Gewerbe-,* and *Verehelichungsfreiheit*), be maintained, or should subjects be tied to the soil by introducing barriers to relocation, as was the case in Southern Germany? (2) Who was to be responsible for the maintenance of the poor?[9] There was naturally a strong temptation for officials to dispense with *Freizügigkeit* and return to the eighteenth-century practice of tying Prussian subjects to their place of birth. If freedom of movement—which after all constituted a major achievement of the reforms and a basic human right—was to be preserved, other constraints would have to be introduced, namely, the obligation of towns and villages to accept whomever wanted to settle within their territories. This, in turn, meant that towns would forfeit their ancient privilege of excluding undesirable elements—a serious blow to the autonomy and vested rights of local communities.

From the first, officials were unanimous about linking future poor relief legislation with a law concerning *Freizügigkeit* and the obligation of communes to accept newcomers.[10] In the *Staatsrat* session of December 19, 1826, it was hotly debated whether communes and manorial lords had the right to object to the settlement of newcomers on their territories, or whether freedom of movement should prevail.[11] The issue had to be referred back to the bureaucratic committees of the central administration for clarification. Existing legislation, especially the recent *Allgemeines Landrecht für die preussischen Staaten* (1794), favored communes and estate owners. People known as slothful and dissolute could be turned away, and marriage consent could be denied to those stricken with physical disabilities or unable to feed a family.[12]

---

9. "Vortrag über den Gesetzentwurf wegen Verpflichtung der Kommunen, neuanziehende Personen aufzunehmen," Geheimes Staatsarchiv Preussischer Kulturbesitz, Berlin-Dahlem (hereafter cited as *Dahlem*), rep. 84a, no. 10955, Preussisches Justizministerium, *Acta betreffend die Verpflichtung der Kommunen zur Armenpflege und zur Aufnahme neu anziehender Personen, Gesetz vom 31. 12. 1842.*

10. "Vortrag über den Gesetzentwurf . . . , Einleitende Bemerkungen," Dahlem, rep. 84a, no. 10955. Already in the preliminary draft (article 14) that later became law, it was decreed that "no authority [i.e., municipal board] may restrict the liberty of a person to choose his place of residence freely solely on the grounds of his impoverishment; however, a community is only obliged to accept them, if they are able to prove, that the desired change of residence is a means to subsist without charity."

11. "Vortrag über den Gesetzentwurf," 3–5.

12. *Allgemeines Landrecht,* teil 2, titel 7. "Article 65: Der Schulze muss dafür haften, dass fremdes Gesinde oder andere Leute von den Dorfeinwohnern ohne Kundschaft nicht aufgenommen werden. Article 115: Leute, die wegen ihres bisherigen Wandels und Verhaltens sich durch glaubwürdige Zeugnisse nicht ausweisen können, ist die Herrschaft in ihren Schutz aufzunehmen

Bureaucratic discussions on "how far a commune was justified in reject-ing newcomers" were detailed and meticulous: officials scanned an array of provincial ordinances and edicts, from the "*Bauern-, Gesinde-, Hirten- und Schäferordnungen*" of 1639 and 1645 to regulations for the "Marken" (Neu-mark, Altmark, Uckermark), the duchy of Westfalia (1795), and Pomerania.[13] In canvasing the plethora of local, regional, and provincial decrees, laws, edicts, and ordinances, officials tried to do justice to the patchwork of lands that was Prussia, whose regional variety was tremendous. For example, not only were citizens of Trier (Karl Marx's birthplace in the Rhine Province) and Neidenburg in East Prussia separated by a geographical distance of 1,200 kilometers, but their customs, cultural heritage, mental outlook, identity, and even their language were so distinctly different that legislation, which aimed at doing justice to both, had to search painstakingly for the smallest common denominator. It is noteworthy that officials made the effort to take the multitude of regional differences into account.[14] This mode of proceeding would un-doubtedly have astonished the bureaucracy's conservative critics, who had accused officials of not taking into account regional variations.

In bureaucratic discussions of the 1830s and early 1840s, the freedom to choose one's place of residence without interference of municipal authorities and manorial lords prevailed. What had been officials' guiding principles in this decision? In his commentary to the *Gesetzentwurf* (legal draft) on the "Obligation of Communes to Accept Newcomers," Meding, privy councillor and key figure of social policy making, whose opinions can be considered representative for dominant views within the civil service, argued that the numerical increase of the lower classes had to be kept in check. Their rampant growth was "an evil inextricably interwoven with the progress of civilization itself," and the "well-off and properties classes of society" should make an effort to forestall the "moral decay" of the impoverished.[15] Preventive mea-sures, however, would have to be coupled with intuitive understanding of the paupers' plight, since the poor could be wrenched from their fate only if challenged to make full use of their own powers. This could never be accom-plished by allowing communes to lock out individuals whose imminent im-

---

und im Dorfe zu dulden nicht verpflichtet. Article 163: Gesetzmässige Weigerungsursachen sind, wenn die Person, die der Untertan heirathen will, sich grober Verbrechen schuldig gemacht hat. Article 164: Ferner, wenn diese Person wegen Liederlichkeit, Faulheit oder Widerspenstigkeit bekannt ist, und dessen durch glaubwürdige Zeugnisse überführt werden kann. Article 165: In-gleichen, wenn dieselbe wegen körperlicher Gebrechen unfähig ist, den wirtschaftlichen Ar-beiten, deren Verrichtung ihr obliegt, gehörig vorzustehen."

13. "Vortrag über den Gesetzentwurf," 8–10, 38–45.

14. Ibid.

15. "Votum des Coreferenten zu den beiden Gesetz-Entwürfen über die Verpflichtung der Kommunen zur Aufnahme neu anziehender Personen und zur Armenpflege im Allgemeinen, und im Besonderen zu dem ersten Gesetz," Dahlem, rep. 84a, no. 10955, 1–10, 1.

poverishment they feared. By doing so, Meding argued, the better-off would dig their own graves, and "proletarians will enter into a state of war with the propertied classes."[16] This very real danger could be averted only if proletarians were convinced "that the higher classes espoused their cause with benevolence." By allowing communes to follow their own interests, Meding reasoned, they were naturally inclined to shut out foreigners, for their representatives "will always believe it their first duty to look out for themselves."[17] It followed that communal power to lock out potentially parasitic newcomers had to be curtailed.

In the final analysis, poor relief was a question of money—who would pay for those unable to provide for themselves: the local community, the poorhouse of the province, or the state? In monetary matters, especially in a country that had been devastated by the Napoleonic wars, charity began at home.[18] Meding warned that tying Prussian subjects to their place of residence, as communes sometimes advocated, might accelerate impoverishment or even cause it. Therefore, no able-bodied citizen "must be restricted in the choice of his residence."[19] Meding also rejected the argument that *Freizügigkeit* constituted an obstacle to the development of "a corporate life" in towns. In this regard, he adopted a liberal standpoint, defending the achievements of the Reform Era. His liberalism however, was not unqualified, since the town's corporate development, "which cannot be estimated highly enough," should be based solely on "the true members" of communities—as distinguished from mere inhabitants. Meding did not recommend equal access to political power within communities, but leaned toward a social aristocratism that favored

---

16. Ibid., 2. Regarding proletarian dissatisfaction that might translate into violence, Meding feared that "die Verschiedenheit ihres Schicksals kann nicht umhin, in der Seele der Proletarien einen innerlichen Krieg gegen ihre vom Glück mehr begünstigten Mitbürger anzuregen, für dessen Ausbruch die Richtung unserer Zeit, welche jeder Art von Neid so günstig und jeder Autorität so feindselig ist, wahrlich keine geringe Gefahr darbietet" (ibid.).

17. Ibid.

18. On the disastrous state of Prussian finances after 1815 see Wilhelm Treue, *Wirtschafts- und Technikgeschichte Preussens* (Berlin, 1984); Treue, "Preussens Wirtschaft vom Dreissigjährigen Krieg bis zum Nationalsozialismus," in Otto Büsch, ed., *Handbuch der Preussischen Geschichte*, vol. 2 (Berlin, 1992), 449–604, esp. 500–526. Contemporary specialists believed that without Rothschild's loans the Prussian king would have been forced to grant a constitution shortly after 1815, as he would have had to turn to his subjects for financial assistance.

19. In discussions within collegial meetings of ministers, *Freizügigkeit* prevailed by a vast majority. Among the *Provinziallandtage*, most endorsed it; only Westfalia and the Rhine Province raised objections. These provincial diets, established in 1823, were an intrinsically conservative element in Prussia's political landscape, as Herbert Obenaus repeatedly emphasized. See Obenaus, *Die Anfänge des Parlamentarismus in Preussen* (Düsseldorf, 1984), 202, 205, 232. During the discussions on *Freizügigkeit*, there were no rigid voting patterns within the council of ministers. Everyone followed what he thought best. Unanimity was rare and occurred only once in the discussion of five different principles concerning poor relief.

established guild members and men of property.[20] Nevertheless, paupers would account for a substantial portion of the population. With reference to the eighteenth-century conservative Justus Möser, Meding observed that the changed social climate would not permit town populations to be composed of proprietors only: "Now that a daily growing, numerous population of property-less people exists, we have to care for these creatures as well."[21] But caring did not necessarily imply a policy of assimilation. Meding left little doubt that needy newcomers would remain condemned to an existence on the fringes of communal life without a chance to rise in the social hierarchy. This was not necessarily an illiberal attitude by the standards of the age. At least Meding's recommendations manifested compassion with the fate of the poor and downtrodden. But the privy councillor also betrayed the deep-seated fears of a member of the ruling elite, who wanted to avoid social change at all cost. Though seemingly liberal when measured by the standards of eighteenth-century Prussia, Meding's policy guidelines were intrinsically conservative when compared to the views of the reformers, for not only was he averse to social change, but his expert advice was dictated by dread of uncontrollable social uprisings. Viewed in this light, the measures he advocated can only be interpreted as timely concessions to forestall such events.

On the central question of state involvement, "whether the obligation for poor relief could be shouldered by the state," and "whether state-directed poor relief had to be kept strictly separate from foundations or other institutions established by private benefactors," Meding remained strangely obtuse. Poor relief could not be administered solely by private benefactors. Their "sense-lessly practiced charity" might even worsen the disaster into "incalculable proportions." State, communes, and private patrons would have to work to-gether and coordinate their actions by adhering to uniform principles when dealing with the poor. Yet there were no suggestions for concrete measures, only tortuous phrases of admonishment "that activities of authorities and those of private individuals must not be separate from one another" but must be united "in concerted aspiration."[22]

Instructions of local authorities, not generally binding laws, were ulti-mately to regulate poor relief. General laws should merely serve to stake out guiding principles of poor relief, such as, for example, the relationship between church and civic communities. The implementation of these proposals amounted to an extension of competence for local and regional administrative boards, strengthening the bureaucracy's hold over the population, notably its lower orders, and instituting tight supervision, while leaving ample scope for

---

20. One might add that this was typical for members of the upper classes all over Europe.
21. "Votum, des Coreferenten zu den beiden Gesetz-Entwürfen," 3.
22. Ibid., 3–4.

the interpretation of specific details. According to Meding, laws were merely to provide rough guidelines, but how they would be applied was left to the discretion of local officials. It is evident that the natural consequence of these recommendations, the vastly increased authority of local bureaucrats, could have disastrous consequences for paupers in cases where petty officials, who had formerly served in the army, dealt with the destitute. It is difficult to imagine that a subordinate functionary, after having served as sergeant major in the army, would be unbiased when dealing with what to him were but dregs of humanity. In such cases, the degree of the individual pauper's submissiveness, discipline, and order might well decide his access to assistance and the amount of assistance he received.

The potential arbitrariness of officials was enhanced by the provision that the poor had no legal claim to communal or state support. The fact that it lay within the discretion of the *Regierung* to grant aid amounted to an increase of the provincial bureaucracy's power.[23] Meding maintained that *Regierungen,* being in situ, were in a better position to make decisions than the far away ministry. Yet his plea for decentralization was a mixed blessing: ordinances from the center in Berlin may have been unjust by not allowing for local differences, but the regulating and often despotic hand of the state was more immediately felt when administered by local or regional authorities. If the czar was far away in the former case, the knout was close and ubiquitous in the latter. Control was increased in the name of public welfare, the paternalistic and authoritarian side of which later became especially pronounced in the case of Prussia and Germany. The *Meldepflicht,* or obligation to report one's domicile and every change of residence (often within a very short period of time after it had been effected), came to be tightly connected with the poor relief legislation of 1842. The Prussian state's concern for the well-being of its people always entailed a great degree of control over them, and the agents of this "state control" naturally were the officials. Their effectiveness made Prussia the best-administered country in nineteenth-century Europe—but also the most tightly controlled.

But controllers had to control themselves, and their increased role was matched by professional discipline. In order to remain morally unassailable, "official persons,"[24] those representing state, communities, and their organs, had to be model citizens in every respect. Officials committed punishable offenses, where others doing the same merely offended against good form. Meding pointed out, for example, that it had been a frequent occurrence in the past that secret agreements between citizens in small towns succeeded in

---

23. That paupers would have no legal claim to public assistance was one of the few points on which all parties, *Provinziallandtage* as well as officials, were in complete accord.

24. "Votum des Coreferenten zu den beiden Gesetz-Entwürfen," 7.

keeping out unwelcome immigrants. If all proprietors of tenant houses in a community concurred in not admitting aliens, there was little the newcomer could do. To punish simple citizens for agreements that aimed at circumventing the new legislation would be beneath the state's dignity. Officials of any kind, however, such as mayors and town councillors of rural communities, who figured prominently among homeowners, should be seriously taken to task by provincial authorities for similar behavior.

In a second memorandum on the Poor Law,[25] Meding emphasized once more that paupers should not be conceded a legal claim on communes for public assistance; poor relief should merely be seen as an obligation imposed on communes out of "considerations of police surveillance." Only administrative authorities, notably the regional *Regierung,* should be able to enforce its observance. Here it becomes obvious that poor relief was not dictated by humanitarian considerations only. Instead, officials viewed it as a problem of social order, discipline, and control, which was precisely what Meding meant by *landespolizeiliche Rücksichten.* And too great a reliance on state charity, Meding maintained, could stifle the paupers' incentives to exert their own forces.

Each commune naturally had a vital interest in keeping the numbers of its needy citizens as low as possible. Meding related an instance where "a person well advanced in pregnancy" had been forced to change her place of residence several times by communal authorities, who refused to support her; ultimately the town in which she actually gave birth had to provide for her. To avoid such hardships, Meding recommended that paupers who were not accepted by communities should be transferred to the provincial poorhouse. These institutions already existed in the older Prussian provinces and were considered to operate successfully.[26] As indicated, they were administered by the *Stände* and thus considered *ständische Institute.* It is therefore highly unusual for a high official to argue "that this kind of activity of the estates" constituted an "essential element of our present ständisch organism," and that it was to be hoped that estates would augment rather than contract these activities, if given an opportunity. This line of reasoning was remarkable not for its traditional conservatism but because it was reminiscent of the ideas of the *Berliner Politisches Wochenblatt* even though it was advanced by an official.

In pre-March Prussia, bureaucracy and estates were considered antagonistic forces. One may recall that *ständisch*-oriented conservatives, such as the Gerlachs and the early Radowitz, were profoundly hostile toward officials. Meding's policy guidelines were directed toward a strengthening of the

---

25. "Votum des Coreferenten zu dem Gesetz über die Armenpflege," Dahlem, rep. 84a, no. 10955, 12 pp. (following p. 114 of the file).
26. See the beginning of the chapter.

estates—sociologically speaking, the "powers of inertia" deemed to impede progress.[27] This is extraordinary insofar as it runs counter to hitherto prevalent opinions among administrative historians, who view officials as agents of rationalization and modernization, united in their attempt to modernize their country, and thus inclined to weaken and abolish *ständische* institutions rather than to strengthen them. Reinhart Koselleck, for example, described the bureaucracy as the most important progressive force in the transition between the old, primarily *ständisch*-oriented society and the new, bourgeois world of the nineteenth century. Koselleck considered the official to be the catalyst and motor of the profound social and economic processes of modernization, involving, among other things, the modernization of agriculture and the transition of the Junkers into a class of agricultural entrepreneurs. As Jürgen Kocka pointed out, Koselleck's interpretation of the Prussian bureaucracy as a progressive force, at least until the 1830s, was very much in line with the main traditions of German historiography and the majority of West German historians. In this context, Kocka mentioned Heinrich von Treitschke, Franz Schnabel, Werner Conze, Friedrich Lütge, Wilhelm Treue, and Wolfram Fischer, all of whom viewed the state as a driving force behind the process of industrialization and the concomitant socioeconomic modernization.[28] Meding's recommendations, which champion the social status quo, ill fit the official's image as "precursor of a bourgeois public" and advocate of economic, if not always political, liberalism. They suggest that the civil service was more willing to collaborate with the "powers of inertia" than hitherto assumed, and also that there was no unbridgeable gulf of interest dividing Prussia's conservatives from its bureaucracy. Had officials been uncompromisingly bent on modernization, they would have been eager to wrest poor relief from the hands of the *Stände*, putting it firmly under state control, even though monetary considerations (the state was hardly in a position to shoulder another major financial burden) may have been an additional factor determining Meding's reasoning.

The intrinsic conservatism of Meding's proposals became more pronounced still in his examination of the relationship between manorial estates and peasant communities. Even after the reforms, many peasant communities had remained in "manifold dependencies," so that they still had to rely "on the

---

27. The *Berliner Politisches Wochenblatt* propagated the establishment of knights' orders to absorb the poor (see part 1, chapter 1). The article in which this idea was advanced was published in 1841, the final year of the paper's existence. Meding's report was written the same year, suggesting that the social doctrines of the *Wochenblatt* had gained wide currency among the educated public of the time.

28. See Jürgen Kocka, "Preussischer Staat und Modernisierung im Vormärz: Marxistisch-leninistische Interpretationen und ihre Probleme," in *Sozialgeschichte Heute: Festschrift für Hans Rosenberg,* ed. Hans-Ulrich Wehler (Göttingen, 1974), 211–27, esp. 212.

protection, the providence, and the model example of the socially higher-ranking and better-educated social class which owns manorial estates." Far from wishing to dissolve the semifeudal bond between East Elbian estate owners and village communities, the privy councillor wanted to see it consolidated, for "such a relationship of dependence, if viewed correctly and supervised accordingly, is for them [the peasant communities] a very beneficial one."[29] The perpetuation of dependence was moreover imperative for "the higher interest of the state," since social privileges of landowners constituted a cornerstone of the nobleman's self-image, and since every "well-ordered state, above all the monarchial state" needed a strong aristocracy. *Raison d'état* therefore dictated preserving the social privileges of the landowning class. That this was done at the expense of the lower rural classes seemed to matter little. On this issue, Meding is in complete accord with the *Wochenblatt* conservatives—possibly without realizing it. His socially retrogressive recommendations aim at preserving a social order that had already been considered obsolete by the reformers in the first decade of the century.

But there was a practical side to all this as well. By fulfilling their *obrigkeitliche Pflichten,* estate owners served an important administrative function, since no officials were needed for the administration of their territories; and Meding did not fail to mention the monetary benefits for state finances. The financial advantages of *Junkers* control of the villages situated within their estates became manifest after comparing the provinces of Prussia and Silesia with the province of Posen, where the aristocracy was mainly Polish, so that "out of predominantly political considerations, estate owners could not be charged with the exercise of their magisterial rights over their villeins." The administration of Posen was considerably more expensive. Further cultivation of manorial rights and privileges thus presented itself "as one of the foremost duties of the administration." Manors and peasant communities ought to be combined into joint poor relief districts, dominated by estate owners. Meding was, however, quick to emphasize that "the moral foundations" of the traditional relationship between peasants and landowners must not be tampered with; on the contrary, it needed "favorable grooming and provision." In Meding's opinion, it was an important task of the bureaucracy to stabilize the Junker's position and maintain the social status quo.

In this respect Meding's report was representative of the social views of officials in general. Much the same attitudes were expressed at a meeting of eleven higher officials (Meding being one of them) of the ministry of the interior and the ministries of justice and finance held in Berlin on April 10, 1841. The topical focus of the conference was the relationship between estate

---

29. "Votum des Coreferenten zu den beiden Gesetz-Entwürfen," 8.

owners and village communities regarding poor relief.[30] Once more, the importance of "the preservation and consolidation" of the position of estate owners was emphasized.[31] Proponents of both positions—those favoring and those opposing the amalgamation of estates and peasant communities into a common poor relief district—advocated the strengthening of the manorial lord's position.

Opponents of the fusion rejected it because it might diminish the independent position of *Rittergüter* and endanger their "moral preponderance" vis-à-vis communes, thus jeopardizing the magisterial (*ortsobrigkeitliche*) authority of the estate owner. They feared communes would refuse to be subjected to the manorial lord's authority in matters related to poor relief, so that the estate owner would lose his policing powers and become subject to arbitration by *Landrat* and *Regierung*. This argument is remarkable, for it suggests that higher officials themselves wanted to avoid making Junkers accountable to the bureaucracy.[32] They wished to preserve the "moral preponderance" and social privilege of the landed squirarchy. In advocating these views, officials present themselves as a bulwark of social reaction, in sharp contrast to their liberal image. This apparent paradox might become better understandable when allowing for growing aristocratic influence and the increasing "feudalization" of the civil service that took place after 1825. In defending the Junkers' social and political perquisites, officials defended their own, or at least those of their relatives. The mode of reasoning of the part of the collegial group rejecting the merger was reminiscent of the "organic" approach of *Wochenblatt* conservatism: the fusion of estates and communities into common poor relief districts would be artificial they held, as "it would be ordered from above and implemented by force." This would result in a much deeper disruption of relations between manorial lords and communities than "a natural unification without

30. "Vortrag über das Gesetz: Wegen Entstehung und Auflösung des Preussischen Unterthanen- Verhältnisses," Dahlem, rep. 84a, no. 10955, pp. 71–85 (following p. 115 of the file). It may be worth noting that half the officials present were of noble birth. The proceedings were extremely legalistic, that is, in their deliberations, officials paid tribute to spheres of competence of other institutions involved in preparing the Poor Law, such as the *Staatsrat* and the provincial diets (see also the previous conference of March 11, 1841, ibid., pp. 34–42).

31. Participants were familiar with Meding's report, which was praised for having demonstrated "with circumspection and lucidity" how necessary it was to clear away frictions between estate owners and communities over poor relief. Meding had maintained that for the purpose of poor relief, manorial estates and peasant communities should be united, which, in turn, would reestablish the preponderance of estate owners. The argument against the intended merger, which was also advanced during the meeting, ran as follows: though Meding's recommendations would facilitate the administrative process, a merger would be opposed by the *Provinziallandtage*, as it constituted a profound encroachment on currently existing rights. Expected opposition there might give rise to unfavorable judgments on the bureaucracy.

32. The terms *estate owners, manorial lords,* and *Junkers* are used synonymously here.

intervention of public authorities." The separation between manorial lords and communities was based on the "well-founded historical rights" of the former; a "violent dissolution of this division" would engender "numerous justified complaints" by the estate owners.[33]

Officials favoring the union argued that such a merger revitalized mutual interests of estate owners and community members, preventing the emergence of real poverty by careful surveillance of all residents. The stronger partner in the union would naturally be the estate owner, who would be in a position, "by ready concessions, perhaps by offering some small sacrifice, to preserve and newly consolidate his moral preponderance and authority over communities." Those present at the meeting also found words of praise for "our rural Germanic constitution,"[34] an expression otherwise used by conservatives. Further common ground with conservatives consisted in the constant plea to allow for "local differences," a demand often raised in the columns of the *Berliner Politisches Wochenblatt*. With regard to the merger, it was argued that it could be salutary only if matters of local administration, such as the maintenance of roads, fire brigades, and watchmen, were jointly managed as well. It was obvious with whom ultimate say would rest.[35]

An almost inevitable conclusion to be drawn from this was that Prussian conservatives, notably the group around the *Berliner Politisches Wochenblatt* and Radowitz, had been wrong in their assessment of the bureaucracy. Their image of the Prussian state apparatus may have been molded by the officials' actions during the Prussian Reform Era, and they simply failed to adjust it afterward, still judging officials by the measures taken during the reform years. But as revealed in bureaucratic memoranda and meetings on poor relief legislation, times had changed, and the civil service had changed with them.[36] It had

---

33. "Vortrag über das Gesetz: wegen Entstehung," Dahlem, rep. 84a, no. 10955, pp. 71–85, esp. 76–77 (following p. 115 of the file).

34. Ibid., 82.

35. The board of officials finally decided that Meding's proposals concerning the merging of estates and peasant communities into joint poor relief districts should be submitted to the *Staatsrat* for a definitive decision. Final legislation favored joint poor relief districts with some minor modifications. In cases where neither manorial lords nor communes were legally obliged to look after the poor, they became a "provincial burden" and were sent to the *Landarmenverband,* or provincial poorhouse (see, *Gesetz-Sammlung für die preussischen Staaten,* 1843.) At a previous collegial meeting on the Poor Law, it had been established that the obligation of communes to support paupers was only *"subsidiär,"* that is, effective only if there were no family members to look after them. Misuse of funds was to be avoided at all cost; no poverty-stricken persons were to subsist on public money as long as they were able to support themselves. The Poor Law's main concern was to regulate the duties of communities and *Armenverbände* among themselves in respect to the poor; the law did not provide practical details on how the pauperized strata of the population was to be supported.

36. See the detailed discussion of *Beamtenliberalismus* in the historiography on the Prussian bureaucracy (chapter 8).

become infinitely more conservative and backward-oriented than it was during the first decade of the century.

The bureaucracy was not prone to advocate radical solutions. These were more likely to be advanced by the *Provinziallandtage,* two of which, for example, suggested the arrest of all persons without proper domicile.[37] Such propositions were rejected outright by officials. Bureaucrats had no interest in brutally suppressing every movement of the lower classes. They were concerned with order, clear-cut delineations of competence, and rules and regulations that made effective government possible. A part of the civil servant's identity was based on his feeling needed. Officials, therefore, strongly opposed a resolution of the diet of the Rhine Province that advanced the motion that no subsidiary obligation of communes for their poor existed at all. The Rhenish estates argued that neither state nor province nor commune could be called on to provide for the needy.[38] The bureaucracy rejected this, arguing that such a policy could not be applied to "intellectually and industrially advanced countries." In countries where "work and industry have become the general state of affairs," private charity and church welfare have to shrink in importance, to be superseded by the state. It was sheer necessity that compelled the state to take matters in hand. To contain "mendicancy and all mischief connected with it," "public obligation for poor relief had to be recognized."[39] Civil servants also pointed out that "almost all civilized states" had been forced to adopt poor relief as a public obligation.

But the bureaucracy's concept of poor relief was not a liberal one. Surveillance and control were never to be relinquished by officials, whose firm intention it was to keep the poor in servile dependence. Over and over again it was emphasized that there could never be a *Rechtsanspruch,* or legal claim, to public assistance. In the collegial meeting of ministers, participants insisted "that the law itself never must recognize a duty toward the poor, or, what would be the same, a legal claim of paupers for support." Instead, it would have to be distinctly spelled out "that paupers have no right to sue communes for assistance, but can only resort to turning to administrative authorities."[40] This inferior legal status dwarfed the paupers' position as against the bureaucracy,

---

37. "Das Niederlassungs- und Armengesetz betreffend," Dahlem, rep. 84a, no. 10955, 48–55 verso, esp. 54 verso.

38. "Das Gesetz wegen der Verpflichtung zur Armenpflege betreffend," Dahlem, rep. 84a, no. 10955, p. 101 (following p. 110 of the file). The Rhine Province was not only the most advanced, richest, and most industrialized province in the kingdom, it was also the most liberal. The Rhinelanders' insistence on rejecting any sort of state or communal obligation for poor relief germinated from their economic liberalism.

39. Ibid., p. 103. Officials also emphasized that the church had never been able to curb mendicancy and that it was morally untenable to let paupers go hungry or to outlaw begging.

40. "Das Niederlassungs- und Armengesetz betreffend," 52v, 53.

for the poor depended wholly on the grace of the authorities they had to deal
with. Without any rights, as they were, they could never hope to rise socially or
become full citizens.[41] Complete subordination to the direction of the authorities also denied the lower classes the chance of becoming a political
force.[42] Once pauperized, a Prussian subject even lost his *Freizügigkeit,* or
freedom of movement.

Freizügigkeit, however, often hailed as an indicator of the Prussian bureaucracy's liberal predisposition,[43] had its reverse side (which was either
conveniently overlooked or never sufficiently realized): domination of the
countryside could be guaranteed only if a new order was superimposed on the
potential chaos *Freizügigkeit* might engender. Officials knew that the maintenance of *Freizügigkeit* and everything it encompassed meant that hundreds of
thousands of landless and propertyless subjects would be left wandering about
without a proper domicile. Once freedom of movement was granted, authorities had to be in a position to determine how long paupers had been
residents of a place and whether they met the three-year residence requirement
that became the prerequisite for poor relief.[44] Every newcomer would therefore be under obligation to register with the authorities shortly after his arrival.
The registration process was further intensified by stipulations that owners of
tenant houses would be liable for a fine if they failed to register tenants who
later became a burden to the community. Though this latter ordinance was not
fully enforced and had to be tightened during the 1850s, it had now become
virtually impossible for an immigrant to remain unknown to the authorities.
Henceforth, communes and manorial lords were legally obligated to accept
newcomers into their towns and villages unless they were already impoverished or "morally depraved."[45]

---

41. Here lay the decisive difference between the Poor Law of 1842 and Bismarck's social
legislation of the 1880s, which entitled the worker to a state pension. This strengthened not only his
social but also his political position.

42. There were, of course, other reasons preventing the destitute from forming associations.
Foremost among them was the absence of any class-consciousness, the geographic dispersion of
the poor, the absence of a rallying cause, and the paupers' mentality, welded during centuries of
serflike dependence in which revolt was an alien concept.

43. See the beginning of the chapter, especially the above mentioned article by Harald
Schinkel, "Armenpflege und Freizügigkeit," 478–79.

44. See *Gesetzsammlung für die preussischen Staaten* (1842), 8–9.

45. See "Motive zu dem Gesetz-Entwurf wegen Verpflichtung zur Armenpflege," Dahlem,
rep. 84a, no. 10955, p. 43 E: "Everyone wanting to settle somewhere within the land [will be]
compelled to report to the immediate authorities at the place of settlement (magistrate, mayor,
demesne official, etc.) and, on their request, to give evidence insofar as necessary to permit
authorities to judge whether or not legal obstacles for settlement are applicable in his case. . . .
Whoever is unable to procure such evidence can be denied residence. . . . The landlord housing a
newcomer is compelled at peril of police penalty to receive proof that his tenant has registered with
the authorities." The paradox inherent in this legislation produced a cause célèbre in Wilhelminean

As only registered residents could qualify for poor relief, intensification of registration requirements and reporting to police authorities was an automatic corollary of the new poor law. The legislation concerning the *Niederlassungsgesetz*, the "settlement law" that was connected with the poor law, provided additional justification for bureaucratic surveillance and control. It strengthened the civil servant's authority on the regional level, as it authorized the *Regierung* to decide matters in cases of disagreement between local authorities.[46] Yet increased bureaucratic control and surveillance of societal activities seemed perfectly compatible with liberal open-mindedness in economic matters. When the Westfalian *Oberpräsident* Vincke argued that communes should have greater say about whom they were willing to accept, and that *Freizügigkeit* only led to growing atomization among individuals, "dissolving all bonds which bind man to inherited possessions," the central authority's reply to these changes sounded like a clarion call for liberalism.[47] Experience had clearly shown, the ministry argued, that communities often rejected newcomers out of petty reasons—egotistical self-interest and the envy of local craftsmen who merely dreaded competition.[48] The Prussian state of prereform times, impervious to geographical and social mobility, could hardly serve as a model to emulate; it had tied down men and capital instead of letting both circulate freely, which would have been better for society. Thus, it could only be considered beneficial that landed property had become transferable and that everyone was free to pursue the trade he preferred. All these liberal achievements were to the "general public's benefit."

This eminently liberal statement was modified in the response to Vincke's assertion that communities needed the privilege to turn away newcomers "to preserve their personality." Vincke had argued that municipalities had to be in a

---

Germany. The shoemaker Wilhelm Voigt, better known as "Hauptmann von Köpenick," who had spent a number of years in jail for minor theft, found himself unable to get employment after his release, since local authorities refused to register the former prison inmate. Any proper German community naturally had little inclination to enroll an ex-convict in its list of citizens. Without an identity card, however, no employer could or would hire him. Yet to register him, local police authorities requested proof of employment, which Voigt was unable to get without registration papers. To break the vicious cycle, the shoemaker decided to obtain an identity card on his own initiative. He disguised himself as captain of the imperial army (having procured the uniform from a pawn shop) and ordered a small patrol of soldiers, whom he picked up in the street, to occupy the town hall of Köpenick (a small town near Berlin). While his soldiers arrested the local officials and the mayor, the shoemaker issued identity papers to himself. It was only days later, after having successfully carried off the undertaking, that he was found out and arrested. The incident was made famous by Carl Zuckmayer's play *Der Hauptmann von Köpenick*.

46. "Motive zu dem Gesetz-Entwurf wegen Verpflichtung zur Armenpflege."

47. "Das Gesetz wegen der Verpflichtung der Kommunen, neu anziehende Personen aufzunehmen und wegen ihrer Befugnis, dergleichen Aufnahme zu verweigern, betreffend," Dahlem, rep. 84a, no. 10955, pp. 57–97, esp. 61 (following p. 110 of the file).

48. Ibid., 63.

position "to exert decisive influence on the selection of their members." If forced to accept everyone, their *Gemeinsinn*, or civic sense, would be suppressed.[49] For the ministry, such an attitude was profoundly "erroneous." Communes could gain identity and civic sense only by acknowledging their role "as members of a greater whole"—by submitting to the state—not by pursuing their "isolated objectives," which are to be considered selfish per se. Only while serving as a cog in the machinery of the state's greater whole could the civic sense of communes be molded, never in opposition to it.[50]

Here it became obvious that the bureaucracy's liberalism was pervaded by authoritarian streaks. All activities had to be made subservient to the greater whole, and the individual life of localities had to be brought in line with the state, whose activities were *per se* beneficial, while special local rights, which escaped its jurisdiction, were deemed "selfish" and had to be stamped out. The myth of the state as the great benefactor (with officials as its *impartial* agents) served to cement bureaucratic rule. In this point, officialdom was not conservative but, under the guise of *Wohltätigkeit*, potentially totalitarian in character.

After the passing of the Poor Law on December 31, 1842, discussions concerning poor relief continued unabated.[51] Emergencies in Prussia's eastern provinces caused by crop failures and ensuing food shortages found a bureaucracy reluctant to provide substantial grants from the state treasury. In an 1846 memorandum outlining policies on the use of state funds, the minister of the interior and minister of finance pointed out that, in all cases, the means of communes and manorial lords had to be used first. The treasury's resources were insufficient to bear the cost of public assistance, and the state would be able to help only in extraordinary circumstances; the buck was consequently passed on to communes.[52] This placed unusual financial strains on towns and villages, which consequently tried to rid themselves of unpropertied people before the full length of three years to avoid their qualifying for poor relief.[53]

In 1852, a petition to the second Prussian chamber castigated abuses and conspiracies of landlords who had reached clandestine agreements not to rent dwellings to potential paupers. This had resulted in constant expulsions and moving about of poor families, who thus fell victim to misery all the sooner. The petition stated that there was only one possible solution: landlords should

---

49. Ibid., 61.
50. Ibid., 63–64.
51. On deliberations within the civil service concerning public assistance after 1842 see "Acta betreffend die Verpflichtung der Communen zur Aufnahme neu anziehender Personen, 1842–1855," Dahlem, rep. 84a, no. 10956.
52. "Anlage," Dahlem, no. 10956, pp. 84–84 verso.
53. "No. 47, III. Session. Zweite Kammer. Antrag: Gamradt und Genossen (1852)," Dahlem, rep. 84a, no. 10956, 4 pp. (pp. 92–94 of the file).

be made liable to recourse for their unregistered poor, as registration of the destitute could not be enforced by penalties alone.[54] In the past, communes had often chosen not to register the poor, paying instead a token penalty for the landlord. For them it had been financially more expedient to pay this fine than to support the impoverished for years to come. In the future, it was argued, the landlord should therefore have to register his tenants himself, provided he had not received proof of registration within eight days. Failing that, landlords would be forced to reimburse the commune that had to provide for the impoverished.[55]

The immediate response to the 1842 Poor Laws was thus a further tightening of the *Meldepflicht,* or duty of registration. Once firmly institutionalized, it soon encompassed everyone who had moved, regardless of his economic position. This stringent *Meldepflicht,* originally devised to control poverty, was thus ultimately used to monitor the entire population, and it became one of Prussia's authoritarian legacies to Germany. Once in place, the system was an ideal instrument for authoritarian and totalitarian regimes in twentieth-century Germany, and until recently, *Meldepflicht* celebrated new triumphs of perfection in the German Democratic Republic. Every newcomer to a town had to register with the authorities within twenty-four hours, and if hosted by an East German family, he or she had to register in the *Hausbuch* that was kept in tenant houses in East German cities. A ten-day visit to Halle, for example, would thus oblige him or her to go to the police twice, on arrival and prior to departure, and at the same time to record the purpose of the visit in the *Hausbuch.*

By the 1850s it had become clear that dissatisfaction with the 1842 legislation was widespread among municipalities as well. In a memorandum on the modification of poor relief legislation, officials stressed that the law sheltered communes against neither mass invasion of potential paupers nor claims of actual ones.[56] Pauperism, it was maintained, was on the increase, menacing the affluence of towns, while legislation was lopsided, granting virtually unlimited freedom of settlement to the individual, which, in turn,

---

54. Ibid.

55. Existing legislation concerning this point had proved insufficient. In practice, landlords had been obliged to pay only a minor penalty, if their tenants had not reported to the police. Administrative authorities frequently were informed of the missing registration only once the immigrant claimed poor relief. In these cases, communes preferred to defray the cost of the landlord's penalty rather than to support the pauper, for in doing so, they fared better themselves. Future agreements between landlords and communes would now be rendered impossible by making the former liable for poor relief expenses.

56. "Denkschrift betreffend die Abänderung der Armen-Gesetzgebung," Dahlem, rep. 84a, no. 10956, pp. 3–15, esp. 4–5.

often led to potential paupers becoming unwelcome dependents of communes. The communes' right to reject newcomers had, however, been severely curtailed; consequently "the corporate interests" of towns were bound to suffer.[57] Such an analysis pointed to a possible curtailment of *Freizügigkeit,* and future plans to augment communal authority and interdict immigration of aliens were indeed discussed. Ultimately they were rejected on the grounds that petitions pleading for a limitation of *Freizügigkeit* had already been taken into consideration, insofar as towns had been granted the right to levy *Einzugsgeld,* a kind of immigration tax.[58]

That freedom of movement had to be maintained despite the undoubted hardships it entailed was also Meding's opinion, which he expressed in a long 1854 memorandum. If *allgemeine Bevormundung* were to supersede freedom of movement as the guiding principle, grave dangers would follow for "the moral and material well-being of the propertyless classes."[59] Municipal authorities should nevertheless be granted greater powers over whom they admitted to residence, but this could never be carried so far as to let them decide arbitrarily who was and who was not eligible for residence in their community. In the final analysis, "the interest of the state" would always be superior to the *per definition* selfish interest of local communities.[60] The state, as the dominant entity, was always equal to more than the sum of its parts.

---

57. In this *Denkschrift,* officials asserted that poor relief legislation had not sufficiently provided for the corporate interests of towns. Emphasis was again placed on the fact that lower classes must never be granted a legal claim for maintenance from communes. Yet the duty of authorities to provide for the poor was undeniable, for "the state has the obligation to provide for rich and poor, especially for the latter, since they are all the more in need of protection" (ibid., 6).

58. Ibid., 7. Further restrictions on *Freizügigkeit* were rejected as being incompatible with freedom of trade. Limitations on *Freizügigkeit* would only have the effect of impeding the development of trade and industry.

59. "Bemerkungen des Wirklichen Geheimen Raths von Meding zu dem mittelst Allerhöchster Kabinets-Ordre vom 3. Juli d. J. dem engeren Staatsrath zur Begutachtung vorgelegten Gesetz-Entwurf wegen Ergänzung des Gesetzes über die Armenpflege vom 31. Dezember 1842," Dahlem, rep. 84a, no. 10956, pp. 2–11, esp. p. 3.

60. Ibid., p. 6–7. Meding maintained that municipal authorities should be in a position to check whether newcomers were actually able to support themselves. This could be done by requiring paupers to provide a *Verpflichtungsschein* from their former communities, guaranteeing to support the person in question for the duration of one year and to allow the return of the impoverished, if desired.

CHAPTER 7

Social Protest, the Bureaucracy, and the Association for the Welfare of Workers

On June 19, 1844, two weeks after the Silesian weavers' uprising, the *Vossische Zeitung* ran an article on Langenbielau's leading textile manufacturer and the remains of his once stately mansion. Langenbielau had been one of the centers of the uprising.

> No windows, only the debris of the window pane, mullions and transoms of window crosses are broken or pulled out, where windows were barred, the bars are smashed, here and there doors are crashed or broken up, wrecked equipment is piled up in front of houses, walls are strewn with distinct signs of stone throws. . . . We walk on rubble wherever our foot turns. . . . Furniture, hardly recognizable in the small pieces into which it has been smashed, torn papers and torn wallpapers everywhere, beds are cut open, stoves broken apart.

The weavers' accumulated fury had finally exploded. Public attention in the entire German Confederation had been concentrated for months on the misery of Silesian cloth workers, and in the spring of 1844, there was no newspaper of importance that did not discuss their suffering, despair, and agony. To afford the barest necessities, weavers had to toil for twelve hours a day or more, and even this was often no guarantee against hunger.[1] The crisis

---

This chapter appeared in a slightly altered format in *Central European History*, 25, no. 3, published by Humanities Press International, Inc., Atlantic Highlands, NJ 07716.

1. In addition to the Silesian press—i.e., the *Breslauer Zeitung, Privilegierte Schlesische Zeitung*, and the *Schlesische Chronik*—Berlin's traditional papers, the *Vossische Zeitung, Haude- und Spenersche Zeitung*, and *Allgemeine Preussische Zeitung (Staatszeitung)*, related the weavers'

of the textile industries was acutely felt throughout Germany, but it was in Silesia, the center of Prussian cloth manufacturing, where hardship was most severe. Fifty percent of all looms in the entire kingdom were there, so the decline of Prussian homespun fabrics had serious repercussions for the material well-being of large sections of the Silesian population. By the 1840s, misery among weavers was so great that Yorck von Wartenburg, a hero of the Wars of Liberation 1813/14, suggested it might be best "to let some fifty to sixty thousand starve to death, for no other help is possible there; then the rest will have employment."[2]

The Silesian textile industry, which had been blossoming for over a century, was mostly based on outwork, so it was easily outdistanced now by English industrial competition, capable of producing cloth cheaper and faster. And there were no protective tariffs to stem the tide of English cloth inundating German markets. Despite urgent entreaties for customs barriers from Southern German governments, Prussia remained firm in its refusal to establish protective duties and thus depart from the economic liberalism espoused by ruling circles of the bureaucracy in the early decades of the century. Moreover, the politically influential Junkers, exporting timber, cereals, and other agrarian produce to England, acted as a powerful lobby against any tariff for fear of English retaliation. To aggravate matters, lucrative export markets in Portugal, Spain, and their Latin-American dependencies had been lost. Until the late 1830s, Mexicans and West Indians had made their clothing exclusively from Silesian linen, but when Prussia severed all diplomatic ties with Spain after the death of the Spanish king Ferdinand VII, commerce came to a standstill as well.[3] The third misfortune for Prussian cloth manufacturing was high Russian customs barriers, which curbed exports to the East, and thus contributed to the decline of formerly prosperous towns in Silesia and East Prussia, whose affluence had been based on the production of linen since the days of Frederick the Great.[4]

misery and later their uprising in some detail. Other important papers concentrating on events in Silesia were the liberal *Weser-Zeitung* of Bremen, the *Augsburger Allgemeine Zeitung*, which catered to the rising bourgeoisie [Heinrich Heine was their Paris correspondent in the 1840s], David Hansemann's *Aachener Zeitung*, and the *Mannheimer Abendzeitung*, which—under the editorship of Karl Grün—was one of the few radical papers in the German Diet.

2. And this was not said in jest. Wolfgang Büttner, *Weberaufstand im Eulengebirge* (Berlin, GDR, 1982), 12–13.

3. See Heinrich von Treitschke, *Deutsche Geschichte im 19. Jahrhundert*, vol. 4 (Leipzig, 1928), 490–500; Franz Mehring, *Geschichte der deutschen Sozialdemokratie*, 3d ed. (Berlin, 1980), 1:224. The legitimist Frederick William III, cofounder of the Holy Alliance, imbued with strong beliefs in the divine right of kings, was offended by General Espartero's liberal government, which ruled during and after the Carlist Wars in Spain. The king's legitimist policies were thus in part responsible for the weavers' plight.

4. Wilhelm Wolff, "Das Elend und der Aufruhr in Schlesien," in *Deutsches Bürgerbuch für*

Disappointment, frustration, and anger about Prussia's "regimenting caste of officials" that imposed such self-destructive economic policies was widespread among factory owners and textile merchants alike as they saw prices for their linen diminish yearly. Yet most of them were able to cut their losses by lowering the weavers' recompense: men and women working at the loom would henceforth receive less for the products of their labor. Prices for a finished fabric, a "Gewebe von 140 Ellen," were first cut in half and then lowered again.[5]

In 1844, the smoldering crisis gathered momentum. After February hardly a week had passed without disquietening newspaper articles on the plight of poverty-stricken weavers in the Silesian mountains.[6] In the provincial capital of Breslau, merchants and local intellectuals founded associations to support the starving, but the one man who had the actual power to bring immediate relief remained strangely aloof. Friedrich Theodor von Merckel, the Silesian *Oberpräsident* (provincial governor), rejected the offer to head philanthropic associations, and in April 1844, responding to an inquiry of Minister of the Interior Arnim, Merckel played down the urgency and seriousness of the situation. True, conditions in the mountains were bad, but poverty among cloth workers there had been a recurrent phenomenon for decades, and periods of starvation were inevitable. Ten years ago a substantial part of the population in weavers' districts had already been in need, and conditions were unlikely to alter drastically in the future. In any case, Merckel concluded, the press was exaggerating the misery.[7]

1845, ed. Hermann Püttmann (Darmstadt, 1845), 174–202; reprinted in Wolff, *Aus Schlesien, Preussen und dem Reich,* ed. Walter Schmidt (Berlin, 1985), 52–84. On economic hardship in East Prussia, see "Erörterung der Ursachen des in der Provinz Preussen öfters wiederkehrenden Nothstandes," Zentrales Staatsarchiv II, Merseburg, rep. 120, VIII, 1, no. 2.

5. In order to complete a standard size cloth with a length of sixty *Ellen* and a width of 1.5 *Ellen* (one Prussian *Elle* equals 25.5 inches, or 66.69 cm), a weaver needed at least a fortnight, provided the entire family helped. For the finished product, he received one taler and thirteen silbergroschen, which did not even cover half of the three taler and five silbergroschen needed to pay the ground rent he owed his manorial lord (see Wolff, "Elend"). Wilhelm Wolff, himself a native of Silesia and well acquainted with the way of life of entrepreneurs and weavers, wrote that "Der Fabrikant und Leinwandkaufmann magerte trotz der schlechten Konjunktur nicht ab; im Gegenteil, er sah recht munter und behäbig aus, trank seinen Cliquot, ass Austern, gab Feten und hing seiner Gemahlin und Fräulein Töchtern für einige tausend Taler Geschmeide um den Hals, während sich da drüben die von Arbeit erschöpfte Armut im dumpfen, stinkenden Winkel, schlaflos vor Frost und Hunger, auf dem dürftigen Lager der Erschöpfung wälzte" (Wolff, "Elend," 65).

6. A cross section of these is collected in Lutz Kroneberg and Rolf Schlosser, *Weber Revolte 1844* (Cologne, 1980), 68–114. For the most part, reporting was very realistic, and there hardly seemed to have been a voice that did not urge swift action to help the poor.

7. Wolfgang Büttner, *Weberaufstand,* 16.

But Merckel knew better, for in February 1844 he had received a report from Leutmannsdorf, one of the hardest hit communities in the mountains. This account of textile workers' agony and privation was undoubtedly authentic, even to the *Oberpräsident's* critical eye, as it had been drafted by the local parson and a police official. The report bluntly stated that "even with utmost exertion of health, strength, and most enduring industry, even when making use of the evening hours until well after midnight, it was not possible to finish *ein Gewebe von 140 Ellen* in fewer than six working days. For this the factory owner deigns to offer a pittance of 14 Silbergroschen."[8] Why Merckel deliberately minimized the importance of bringing urgent relief to cloth workers remains a matter of conjecture. In all probability he was reluctant to tarnish Silesia's reputation as one of Prussia's most affluent provinces, a reputation in which Merckel, as Silesia's *Oberpräsident* of thirty years, took great pride.[9]

Finally, in May 1844, one month before the uprising, the Breslau-based "Association for the Remedy of Want among Weavers" dispatched one of its members, the junior councillor (*Regierungsassessor*) Alexander Schneer, to collect information and investigate the actual state of affairs on the spot. Schneer's realistic account soon became an invaluable source for all those who were interested in the fate of Silesian cloth workers. Even radicals, such as Wolff, who later became a close collaborator of Karl Marx in his Paris exile, quoted him assiduously, since the account of a civil servant of moderately liberal views was eminently plausible, even though the picture Schneer drew was nothing less than horrifying.[10] According to Schneer, the paupers' clothing often consisted of rags, their dwellings were in a state of dilapidation, their nourishment was made up of black flour and inferior potatoes, normally fed to livestock, and due to recent harvest failures, things seemed to be getting

---

8. Ibid., Franz Mehring, *Geschichte der deutschen Sozialdemokratie,* 3d ed. (Berlin, GDR, 1980), 224–25. There were thirty silbergroschen to one Prussian taler. The provincial governor, the *Oberpräsident,* earned about 6,000 taler annually, while the family of a weaver had hardly more than 60 taler. See Wilhelm Wolff, "Elend." Wolff obtained his information from a report by Eduard Pelz, who, under the pseudonym Treumund Welp, published accounts on weavers' living conditions. According to the Berlin Statistical Bureau, a working-class family of five needed on average 105 taler and 2 silbergroschen annually to cover its most basic needs. Cost of living varied from province to province; it was highest in the Rhine Province with 140 taler, and lowest in Posen with 78 taler. The 93 taler and 10 silbergroschen calculated for Silesia were still more than 50 percent above the weavers' meager earnings. See *Mitteilungen des Statistischen Bureaus in Berlin* (1852), 2:317–19.

9. See "Der Rechenschaftsbericht des Oberpräsidenten von Merckel über den Zustand Schlesiens im Jahre 1840," ed. Karl Wutke, *Zeitschrift des Vereins für die Geschichte Schlesiens* 60 (1926): 210–41.

10. Alexander Schneer, *Über die Not der Leinen-Arbeiter in Schlesien und die Mittel ihr abzuhelfen* (Berlin, 1844). Important sections of Schneer's report are reprinted in Kroneberg and Schlosser, *Weber Revolte,* 114–45.

even worse. Food merchants had long since deserted most of the small mountain villages, for no one had any money left to buy their goods. There were still outdated feudal dues, such as the ground rent, as well as obligatory work on the fields of the manorial lord, all of which weighed heavily on the impoverished and emaciated people. It seemed impossible to meet all obligations and make ends meet at the same time. Schneer noted that a considerable number of Prussian subjects in one of the king's richest provinces were worse off than prison convicts.[11] The chief of local police in a mountain village told Schneer that grinding poverty had deprived the destitute of the physical and mental energy needed to commit a crime or revolt against their fate.[12]

In this conclusion, however, the worthy constable was mistaken. What originally started as a minor riot of discontent, with the principal demand to raise wages, quickly turned into a violent rebellion against exploitation, embodied in Peterswaldau's most powerful and oppressive entrepreneurs, August and Ernst Friedrich Zwanziger.[13] When the Zwanzigers scornfully turned down the cloth workers' request for higher wages, the wave of long repressed fury burst its banks. On June 4, 1844, the Zwanzigers' estate was ravaged by the large crowd of weavers, tile makers, carpenters, coopers, day laborers, and servants who had joined the weavers march. The Zwanziger family escaped by the skin of their teeth, first to the neighboring town of Reichenbach, where they were driven off for fear of reprisals; then to Schweidnitz, the next garrison

---

11. Schneer's research was extensive: with the help of the *Regierung* at Liegnitz (one of the three Silesian districts) and local *Landräte,* he explored dozens of *Kreise,* eleven in the district of Liegnitz alone. According to his own testimony, he visited fifty villages and small towns, in each of which he saw about fifteen to twenty families. Schneer observed that poverty was less grinding in areas where estate owners still exercised their manorial rights fully. For most of Silesia, regular poor relief merely existed on paper, he asserted. Fifteen densely populated villages in the Liegnitz district, all of them hard hit by poverty, received the ridiculous amount of 58 taler poor relief for one entire year. Franz Mehring quotes a contemporary writer who stated that most weavers lived in dwellings "in comparison to which the estate owner's cowshed can be called a state room." See Mehring, *Geschichte,* 225.

12. Schneer, *Über die Not der Leinen-Arbeiter in Schlesien,* 129.

13. For detailed accounts of the insurgency in addition to Wolfgang Büttner and Franz Mehring (*Geschichte,* 225–31), see Karl Obermann, *Deutschland 1815–1849,* 4th ed. (Berlin, 1976), 161–64; Walter Schmidt et al., *Deutsche Geschichte,* vol. 4, 1789–1871 (Berlin, 1984), 251–58; Thomas Nipperdey, *Deutsche Geschichte 1800–1866* (Munich, 1983), 221–23; Wolfgang Büttner, "Der Weberaufstand in Schlesien 1844," in *Demokratische und soziale Protestbewegungen in Mitteleuropa 1815–48/49,* ed. Helmut Reinalter (Frankfurt, 1986), 202–30; Hans-Ulrich Wehler, *Deutsche Gesellschaftsgeschichte,* vol. 2 (Munich, 1987), 654–57; James Sheehan, *German History 1770–1866* (Oxford, 1989), 643–45. The main uprisings took place in Peterswaldau (5,000 inhabitants) and Langenbielau (13,000 inhabitants), two large villages at the foothills of the Silesian Eulengebirge. Subsequently, minor riots occurred in neighboring villages, while in Breslau, Silesia's capital and Prussia's second largest city, "hunger revolts" of pauperized artisans and journeymen took place.

town; and finally to the provincial capital.[14] Wagenknecht and Fellmann, the two other local entrepreneurs, who had been less hard on the weavers, were spared, but the uprising still had not reached its peak. In the morning of the following day, an ever swelling mob of laborers—Franz Mehring speaks of three thousand, which may be too high an estimate—streamed toward the much larger village of Langenbielau, where the brothers Dierig ran one of Silesia's largest industrial estates, employing more than 4,000 workers.[15] There, the insurgents clashed with the military detachment that had been called from the nearby Schweidnitz garrison. Eleven weavers were killed and twenty-four gravely injured in the course of a brief skirmish, but ultimately the soldiers were driven back to the point that the commanding officer was unable to conduct an orderly retreat. The insurgents' triumph proved to be short-lived. Three companies of infantry sufficed to restore order in Langenbielau the next day, and subsequently about a hundred were arrested. Charges were brought against eighty-seven, who, for the most part, disappeared in Prussian prisons and fortresses for years to come.[16]

How did the Prussian state, that is, the all-powerful bureaucracy that had become the uncontested master of Prussia after the reforms,[17] deal with the revolt in Silesia? And how did the often-hailed liberalism of the civil service meet the challenge? In the case of the weavers' uprising, this challenge was

---

14. On social protest in the 1840s see also Manfred Gailus, *Strasse und Brot* (Göttingen, 1990); Helmut Reinalter, ed., *Demokratische und soziale Protestbewegungen in Mitteleuropa 1815–1848/49* (Frankfurt, 1986); Arno Herzig, *Unterschichtenprotest in Deutschland 1790–1870* (Göttingen, 1988). On *Protestforschung* in general see Richard Tilly, ed., *Sozialer Protest, Geschichte und Gesellschaft* 3 (Göttingen, 1977); Werner Giesselmann, "Protest als Gegenstand sozialgeschichtlicher Forschung," in, *Sozialgeschichte in Deutschland*, vol. 3, ed. Wolfgang Schieder and Volker Sellin (Göttingen, 1987), 50–77. See also the essays in Heinrich Volkmann and Jürgen Bergmann, eds., *Sozialer Protest: Studien zu traditioneller Resistenz und kollektiver Gewalt in Deutschland vom Vormärz bis zur Reichsgründung* (Opladen, 1984). On the composition of revolutionary crowds in eighteenth- and nineteenth-century Europe see George Rudé, *The Crowd in History* (London and New York, 1964).

15. There are detailed reports of the events in the June and July issues of the *Deutsche Allgemeine Zeitung, Spenersche Zeitung, Aachener Zeitung, Allgemeine Preussische Zeitung, Triersche Zeitung,* and *Weser-Zeitung.*

16. Prison sentences varied between three and nine years. Altogether, the eighty defendants were sentenced to 203 years imprisonment, 90 years of fortress, and 330 lashes. See Büttner, *Weberaufstand,* 40.

17. Historians are virtually unanimous on this point. Eckhart Kehr, "Zur Genesis der preussischen Bürokratie und des Rechtsstaates," in Kehr, *Der Primat der Innenpolitik,* ed. Hans-Ulrich Wehler (Berlin, 1965), 31–53, even spoke of a "dictatorship," while Hans Rosenberg, *Bureaucracy, Aristocracy and Autocracy* (Cambridge, Mass., 1958), and Hans-Ulrich Wehler, *Gesellschaftsgeschichte,* 2:297–322, characterized the rule of officials as "bureaucratic absolutism." See also chapter 5.

twofold: the bureaucracy was faced not only with an open revolt of the lower classes but also with a stirring of independence by a part of the liberal bourgeoisie, including numerous officials, who soon developed their own ideas of how to deal with the misery of the destitute by founding a large welfare organization, the *Centralverein für das Wohl der arbeitenden Klassen*. How did the bureaucracy react to these independent activities of a nascent civil society threatening to emancipate itself?

How high Prussian officials reacted to an open revolt of the lower classes is not open to question. Relentless suppression was considered the only remedy. But how would officials deal with a societal movement led by the *haute bourgeoisie* that merely attempted to find solutions to social problems so conspicuously neglected by the civil service? Would one not expect that the "bureaucratic modernizer" might join forces with them? The answers to these questions not only will tell us much about the functioning of the bureaucracy during the critical decade of the 1840s but also will cast light on the relationship between the still all-powerful state in Prussia and a society groping to find its identity.

The most detailed study we possess of the Prussian bureaucracy in mid-century, John R. Gillis, *The Prussian Bureaucracy in Crisis 1840–1860*, describes this period as a vital turning point in the history of the civil service.[18] The 1840s, Gillis argues, was a transitional period for the Prussian bureaucracy. A new generation of officials, influenced by the educational reforms and the new spirit of learning and thus imbued by a new spirit of independence, had begun entering the civil service in the 1830s and challenged the rule of the older and more established Prussian officials.[19] The resulting generational conflict that was in full swing by the 1840s was further aggravated by the influx of new social classes into the civil service. The percentage of sons of higher officials steadily declined after the 1830s, while that of "elements of the urban and rural lower classes"[20] as well as, paradoxically, that of sons of the landed aristocracy rose consistently, often for reasons of social and economic necessity. The increasing heterogeneity of the recruitment base, Gillis contends, became an additional cause for tension in the civil service. Moreover, there was an excess of educated men in central Europe in the first half of the nineteenth century, an abundance that was most pronounced in Prussia in the decades

---

18. John R. Gillis, *The Prussian Bureaucracy in Crisis 1840–1860* (Stanford, 1971). The third part of Reinhart Koselleck's *Preussen zwischen Reform und Revolution*, 2d ed. (Stuttgart, 1975), also offers an in-depth analysis of the bureaucracy during the 1830s and 1840s.

19. Gillis, *Prussian Bureaucracy*, 23: ". . . and the distance between their ideas and those of their superiors was so great that conflict was virtually inevitable."

20. Ibid., 39.

before 1848.[21] This was partially due to the marked increase of law students in the 1820s and 1840s who streamed into a civil service that was unable to accommodate the rising number of applicants because of Prussia's strained finances. In 1825 the need to economize had led to a severe reduction of positions in the administrative bureaucracy, cutting the number of officials by about one-fifth.[22] The supply of candidates exceeded demand until the 1860s, and overcrowding led not only to long waiting periods (ten years between the completion of university study and full appointment) but equally to a tightening of admission standards and discipline (the new disciplinary code of March 1844) and to a stricter handling of the infamous *Konduitenlisten*, which laid increasing stress on "moral behavior" inside and outside office.[23] Yet despite internal tensions and the rivalries of competing generations within the apparatus, Gillis maintains that "bureaucratic liberalism remained for the most part unchanged, embracing economic laissez-faire and public welfare measures but excluding political individualism and social equality."[24]

This notion of the "liberal Prussian bureaucracy" in the *Vormärz* has become common coinage among German historians. Already Franz Schnabel devoted a chapter of his four-volume *Deutsche Geschichte im 19. Jahrhundert* to "the liberal bureaucracy,"[25] arguing that the modern official was a creation of the *"liberale Rechtskultur"* and that it was therefore in his own best interest to support the liberal movement and become a spokesperson for the liberal bourgeoisie. In 1937, Wilhelm Treue advanced the concept of a liberal bureaucracy (with a focus on economic liberalism) in his detailed examination of the educational background of fifteen leading officials. And in the same decade, Hans H. Gerth, in his brilliant *wissenssoziologische* study on the preconditions of early liberalism, claimed that "the liberal bureaucracy" constituted "one of the most potent factors of integration of the German *Frühliberalismus.*"[26] Gerth was also one of the first to use the term *Beamtenliberalismus,* which later

---

21. This point is vigorously advanced by Leonore O' Boyle, "The Problem of an Excess of Educated Men in Western Europe, 1800–1850," *Journal of Modern History* 42 (1970): 471–95. Reinhart Koselleck, *Preussen zwischen Reform und Revolution,* 437–42 points to the same problem.

22. See Koselleck, *Preussen zwischen Reform und Revolution,* 438.

23. On the *Konduitenlisten,* see the biting criticism by Karl Heinzen, *Die preussische Bürokratie* (Darmstadt, 1845), 166–75, and, for an example, "Acta betreffend die Conduiten Listen über die Regierungs-Präsidenten," Staatsarchiv Merseburg, rep. 77, titel 184a, no. 4, vol. 1. The section on "sittlicher Wandel" left ample room for criticism. See chapter 5.

24. Gillis, *Prussian Bureaucracy,* 72.

25. First published in 1929–36; see Franz Schnabel, "Das liberale Beamtentum," in *Deutsche Geschichte im 19. Jahrhundert,* vol. 3 (Freiburg, 1964), 247–50.

26. Wilhelm Treue, *Wirtschaftszustände und Wirtschaftspolitik in Preussen, 1815–1825* (Stuttgart, 1937); Hans H. Gerth, *Bürgerliche Intelligenz um 1800: Zur Soziologie des deutschen Frühliberalismus* (Göttingen, 1976), 72; originally Ph.D. diss. (University of Frankfurt, 1935).

became a common label, characterizing officials' political and economic leanings. In the 1950s, Werner Conze asserted that this *Beamtenliberalismus* had remained alive not only in pre-March Prussia but also in the Southern German states;[27] but Heinrich Heffter, in his *Die deutsche Selbstverwaltung im 19. Jahrhundert*, avoided the term when writing about the Prussian *Beamtenstaat* and merely pointed out that the "conservative romantics" in Prussia were strongly opposed to the civil service on account of its "liberal spirit."[28] The *Verfassungshistoriker* Fritz Hartung, one of Otto Hintze's disciples, mentioned the bureaucracy's economic liberalism, but without neglecting the repressive political atmosphere that also characterized bureaucratic rule in the 1820s and 1830s.[29]

In the 1960s, the "liberalism" of the bureaucracy was frequently idealized,[30] until Reinhart Koselleck's *Preussen zwischen Reform und Revolution* (first published in 1967) introduced a more differentiated way of viewing the bureaucracy. According to Koselleck, the modernizing impetus of an originally liberal bureaucracy increasingly gave way to policies hostile to reform and resurgent conservative factions within the apparatus. Still, Koselleck did not negate the basically liberal *Grundhaltung* of the civil service, and when James Sheehan, in his *German Liberalism in the 19th Century*, maintained that "liberalism was widespread in the judicial and administrative bureaucracy," he referred to Koselleck as one of his main sources.[31] As Jürgen Kocka pointed out, Koselleck portrayed "the Prussian *Verwaltungsstaat* as the most important progressive force" in the transition from a prerevolutionary society, based on estates, to the "*bürgerliche Gesellschaft* of the nineteenth century,"[32] and he portrayed the bureaucracy as the "driving force behind a profound process of economic and social modernization." Kocka emphasized that with his interpretation of the Prussian *Beamtenstaat* as a progressive and modernizing force,

---

27. In his seminal article "Das Spannungsfeld von Staat und Gesellschaft im *Vormärz*," in *Staat und Gesellschaft im deutschen Vormärz*, ed. Conze (Stuttgart, 1962), 228. An earlier version of the article was published as "Staat und Gesellschaft in der frührevolutionären Epoche Deutschlands," *Historische Zeitschrift* 186 (1958): 1–35.

28. Heinrich Heffter, *Die deutsche Selbstverwaltung im 19. Jahrhundert* (Stuttgart, 1950), 221.

29. In "Die Blütezeit des bürokratischen Absolutismus von 1815 bis 1848," originally published in the 1940s, and reissued in Fritz Hartung, *Staatsbildende Kräfte der Neuzeit* (Berlin, 1961), 223–48.

30. As, for example, in Harald Schinkel's "Armenpflege und Freizügigkeit in der preussischen Gesetzgebung vom Jahre 1842," *Vierteljahresschrift für Sozial- und Wirtschaftsgeschichte* 50 (1963): 459–79.

31. James Sheehan, *German Liberalism in the Nineteenth Century* (Chicago and London, 1983), 19, 293 n. 4.

32. Jürgen Kocka, "Preussischer Staat und Modernisierung im Vormärz," in *Preussische Reformen*, ed. Barbara Vogel (Königstein, 1980), 49–65, esp. 49–50.

Koselleck's view corresponded with the main traditions of German historiography from Heinrich von Treitschke to Werner Conze and Wolfram Fischer.

In the 1980s the picture became more complex. Thomas Nipperdey, while praising the civil service as a *"diskutierende Verwaltung,"* whose members "expressed their views astonishingly open and liberal with a tendency to lecture to each other,"[33] also pointed to the, as he called it, "Janus face" of the Prussian state after 1815, in which societal reforms were continued (if with reduced vigor) while political restoration, censorship, and repression predominated. In his *Deutsche Gesellschaftsgeschichte,* Hans-Ulrich Wehler underlined the economic liberalism of officials and the existence of a *"sozialökonomisch orientierten Frühliberalismus,"* as well as the great influence wielded by Adam Smith,[34] but he also noted that after the death of *Staatskanzler* Karl August von Hardenberg in 1822, there was a resurgence of a *Beamtenkonservatismus* that superseded the liberalism of earlier years.[35] Wehler's analysis is partly based on Barbara Vogel's perspicacious essay *"Beamtenkonservatismus,"* where she contended that conservative forces had gained the upper hand within the bureaucratic apparatus well before 1820.[36] In an earlier article, Vogel had gone so far as to argue that the reforms were imposed on an overwhelmingly conservative bureaucracy by a small group of men around Hardenberg, such as Christian Scharnweber, Johann Gottfried Hoffmann, and Christian Rother.[37] Bernd Wunder's recent *Geschichte der Bürokratie in Deutschland* also contained a chapter on *Beamtenliberalismus,* even though Wunder largely focused on liberal deputies in Southern German parliaments, paying relatively little attention to Prussia.[38]

The notion of the "liberal bureaucracy" has become a generally accepted axiom in the historiography on the Prussian civil service, which, until very recently, was countenanced by a majority of historians without being questioned. But the bureaucratic response to social problems and the formation of a Prussian society was multifaceted and thus difficult to classify. By the 1840s "bureaucratic liberalism" had clearly fallen by the wayside.

---

33. Thomas Nipperdey, *Deutsche Geschichte 1800–1866,* 333.

34. Hans-Ulrich Wehler, *Gesellschaftsgeschichte,* 1:404–5.

35. Wehler, *Gesellschaftsgeschichte,* 2:442, 313.

36. Barbara Vogel, "Beamtenkonservatismus: Sozial- und verfassungsgeschichtliche Voraussetzungen der Parteien in Preussen im frühen 19. Jahrhundert," in *Deutscher Konservatismus im 19. und 20. Jahrhundert,* ed. Dirk Stegmann, Bernd-Jürgen Wendt, and Peter-Christian Witt (Bonn, 1983).

37. Barbara Vogel, "Reformpolitik in Preussen," in *Preussen im Rückblick,* ed. Hans-Jürgen Puhle and Hans-Ulrich Wehler (Göttingen, 1980), 202–23.

38. Bernd Wunder, *Geschichte der Bürokratie in Deutschland* (Frankfurt, 1986), 60–66.

Viewed from the angle of bureaucratic authorities, intellectual subversion seemed to be the greatest threat to social peace. In his April report to Minister of the Interior Arnim, the Silesian *Oberpräsident* had already pointed to the connection between detailed press accounts on weavers' misery—vastly exaggerated in his estimate—the muckraking of radical intellectuals, and general discontent. For years, long and detailed reports on subversive activities and discontent in the Silesian mountains had been piling up on the desks of the minister of the interior and the Silesian *Oberpräsident.* Already in June 1843, the *Vizepräsident* of the Liegnitz *Regierung* (district) had reported potentially subversive meetings of over 150 teachers to the minister. Due to prevailing discontent among weavers, rebellious movements were particularly dangerous, the official warned, and there had already been instances of bondsmen refusing to perform their services. To make matters worse, elementary education and the ability to read was spreading rapidly, fostering a "tendency to reason about all existing institutions." The minister was informed prophetically that in unsettled times "there will be much revolutionary fuel."[39] And foreign (i.e., non-Prussian) papers, such as the *Lokomotive,* spreading subversive ideas, were devoured "eagerly in the lowest taverns."[40] In August 1844, Berlin's director of police Duncker sent a detailed report to Arnim, describing subversive political activities of a Breslau-based literary association, *Lätitia,* and the connection of its members with Eduard Pelz, who, by that time, was already under arrest. Emphatically, the director of police alerted Arnim to be on his guard, for Silesian authorities underestimated dangers emanating from the oppositional press and intellectuals. Celebrations during the course of which demands for the formation of a journeymen's association had been raised gave cause for concern, for "they only turned the heads of this totally uneducated class, making them dissatisfied with their position in society, . . . creating idlers and malcontent people."[41]

Hardly two weeks after the uprising, Duncker had transmitted another report to the minister of the interior that seemed to confirm his worst fears. And this time, it did not concern Silesia, but the heart of the kingdom, Berlin. "With kind permission I deferentially allow myself to inform your Excellency," Berlin's director of police wrote, "that at the local Café Hollande a gathering of people has taken place . . . discussing the plan to form an association, allegedly

39. See "Akten betreffend Lehrer Wander in Hirschberg wegen politisch verdächtigen Treibens," Zentrales Staatsarchiv II, Merseburg, rep. 77, VI, no. 17, vol. 1 (17.7.1843–1.12.1856), pp. 1–6.

40. Ibid., 3 verso.

41. 17 August 1844, "Duncker an Minister des Innern," Zentrales Staatsarchiv II, Merseburg, rep. 77, VI, no. 125, vol. 1 (22.10.1843–5.4.1845), pp. 236–47 verso ("Akten betreffend den vormaligen Buchhändler, jetzigen Freigutbesitzer Eduard Pelz, in Seitendorf als Verfasser verbreiteter revolutionärer Schriften").

in order to raise the intellectual level of the working classes and promote their material and spiritual well-being."[42] It was probable, Duncker continued with concern, that "communist influences were at work," especially since several of Berlin's most notorious left-wing intellectuals had been present at the meeting, "the literateurs Benda, Dr. Rutenberg, Dr. Meyen, Dr. Theodor Mügge," who already had a reputation for being "among the most active in the party of so-called progress." This was a fact hardly suited to allay Arnim's fears. Moreover, there had been talk of founding a new journal, "calculated to meet the working classes' level of education."[43] For the moment, however, the revolutionary hydra would fortunately remain without a head, for the election of a board of governors, though decided on, had not yet been effected.

There can be no doubt that the meeting at the Café Hollande was a direct outcome of the uprising. Silesian papers had carried the news of the revolt as early as June 6, and Berliners possessed the details of the insurgency no later than June 9, while on June 10 the *Spenersche Zeitung* already published a proclamation by Major von Schlichting, the battalion commander at Langenbielau, to surrender to his military detachment.[44] It was no accident, then, that on June 12, when all Berlin spoke of nothing else but the rebellion in the Silesian mountains, "men from all walks of life, especially teachers and *Literaten,*" convened to found a society for the betterment of the lower classes.[45] There may have been some revolutionary potential in the presence of such men as Eduard Meyen, a member of Berlin's Left Hegelian group *Die Freien;* Theodor Mügge, equally an affiliate of Berlin's Left Hegelian coteries; and Adolf Rutenberg, a member of the so-called *Doktor-Club* and a fellow student of Karl Marx. But the obsessive fears of officials in the ministry of the interior were unwarranted.[46] From the very beginning, radical elements within the

---

42. See Zentrales Staatsarchiv II, Merseburg, rep. 120D, XXII, 1, no. 1, vol. 1 (1844–47), p. 1. ("Akten betreffend die Bildung von Vereinen für das Wohl der arbeitenden Klassen [Hand- und Fabrikarbeiter] sowie die Errichtung eines Centralvereins für solche").

43. Ibid., 2.

44. *Haude- und Spenersche Zeitung* 133 (June 10, 1844). The carefully worded proclamation betrayed clemency and human concern for the local population. It was probably reprinted on government orders in the otherwise strictly censored newspaper to convince Berliners that the armed power of state was proceeding with all the forbearance possible under the circumstances.

45. *Magdeburgische Zeitung* 138 (June 15, 1844).

46. Through Marx, Rutenberg became a member of the editorial staff of the *Rheinische Zeitung.* "Rutenberg weighs on my conscience," Marx wrote in a letter to Ruge on July 9, 1842; "I brought him into the editorial office of the *Rheinische,* and he proves wholly devoid of ideas. Sooner or later, he will get the sack." See Heinz Pepperle and Ingrid Pepperle, eds., *Die Hegelsche Linke: Dokumente zu Philosophie und Politik im deutschen Vormärz* (Leipzig, 1985), 850. In another letter to Ruge on November 30, Marx complained about Rutenberg's "total lack of critical faculties and independence" (ibid., 852), ridiculing the Prussian government for considering Rutenberg a dangerous journalist ("though he wasn't dangerous to anyone except himself and the *Rheinische Zeitung*"). See also Karl Marx and Friedrich Engels, *Der Briefwechsel, 1844–1883,* 4 vols. DTV reprint (Munich, 1983).

association were vastly outnumbered and excluded from participation in the steering committee that set policy guidelines.[47] Members of the association made every conceivable effort to appease the authorities. Judging by detailed press coverage of the first meeting, journalists were asked to attend in order to avoid any appearance of secrecy.[48] Press accounts were mostly favorable, never failing to point out that the authorities had reason to be well disposed toward the new society.[49] In this respect, however, Prussian papers greatly overestimated the threshold of tolerance of the top-echelon officials in the ministry of the interior, who had a decisive say in the matter.

Yet the optimism of the press did not seem wholly unwarranted, for the predispositions of official circles regarding charitable associations could hardly have been more favorable. Frederick William IV possessed far greater ambitions than his father to better the paupers' lot. In a cabinet order of November 1843, the monarch had requested that authorities promote and support organizations founded for the purpose of helping the poor.[50] Frederick William's personal contribution to the problem of poor relief had been the revival of the medieval *Schwanenorden,* meant to stimulate active assistance for the poor. The king himself assumed the grand mastership over the re-established order, hoping that "men and women without regard to religious denomination or social class" would join.[51] Friedrich Wilhelm would soon have further opportunity to give proof of his strong social inclinations, since a much larger association for "The Welfare of Workers" was founded in Berlin on October 7, 1844, the *Centralverein für das Wohl der arbeitenden Klassen,*

---

47. The *Breslauer Zeitung* reported on June 17, 1844 (no. 139) that some of the *Literaten* (the closest English rendition is "free-floating intellectuals") declined participation for fear of retaliatory police measures. See also "Akten betreffend die Bildung von Vereinen," Zentrales Staatsarchiv II, Merseburg, rep. 120D, XXII, I, no. 1, vol. 1, pp. 7–8 verso.

48. Reporting on the first meeting, the *Schlesische Zeitung* 139 (June 17, 1844) emphasized that "there was no shortage of references to communist endeavors in different neighboring countries. Attempts to repel this threat for Germany and especially Prussia were applauded."

49. "That authorities will oppose such an organization by refusing attestation can hardly be expected: in addition to guarantees for strictly legal behavior, provided in the personalities of the elected committee, police authorities will be reluctant to put obstacles in the path of foundation of such a society, since by doing so, it might appear as if lower classes' want and misery were of no concern to them." See *Magdeburgische Zeitung* 138 (June 15, 1844).

50. See Josef Hansen, *Rheinische Briefe und Akten zur Geschichte der politischen Bewegung 1830–1850* (Essen, 1919) 674–75. Jürgen Reulecke, *Sozialer Frieden durch soziale Reform* (Wuppertal, 1983), 60–63. The cabinet order had been circulating among ministers, *Oberpräsidenten,* and other high provincial officials between November 1843 and April 1844, before it was made public in July 1844.

51. See Heinrich von Treitschke, *Deutsche Geschichte,* 5:241. Nothing was said about how and under which conditions this was to be achieved, just as the whole idea seems to have sprung from the king's romantic idealization of the Middle Ages. Treitschke hinted that "the beautiful old tombstones of the Knights of the Swan at the collegiate church at Ansbach" may well have been the crucial factor for the order's reestablishment.

which absorbed all the important members of its modest predecessor.[52] The *Centralverein* originated in the wake of Berlin's great industrial fair (August-October 1844), the largest exhibition of industrial goods ever held on the territory of the German Confederation, with over 3,000 participating firms and a quarter of a million visitors. The two groups that dominated the industrial fair also figured prominently in the *Centralverein:* the new class of industrial entrepreneurs and the established elite of high civil servants, notably from the ministry of finance and commerce department, was part of the ministry of the interior at the time.

Due to the official context in which the foundation took place and the large number of industrialists and civil servants within its ranks, leaders of the new *Centralverein* had good reason to believe that officials in the ministry of the interior would regard the association with a friendly eye. Radical intellectuals, so abhorred by the minister of the interior, had become a *quantité négligeable* in comparison to the vast number of entrepreneurs and high officials who had been instrumental in the organization's foundation and now played a leading role within it. Fourteen entrepreneurs and eight civil servants had signed the "Appeal for the Foundation of the Association of Workers,"[53] and among the seventy-eight members who were Berlin residents, there were nineteen high officials, one subordinate official, seven artisans (most of whom were affiliated with the royal court and thus hardly a revolutionary element), twenty-six entrepreneurs and "factory owners," four "bankers and railroad directors," one officer, one physician, one local politician, four "radical" *Literaten,* and a few persons without specification.[54] The minimal membership fee of four talers was just met by Meyen, Rutenberg, and Nauwerck, who like most other leftist intellectuals were far from affluent, while Secret Councillor von Viebahn, for example, paid twenty talers, some of the industrialists even fifty. It

---

52. It was again a police report prompted by fear of *Literaten* that provided first details of the new foundation. See Zentrales Staatsarchiv II, Merseburg, rep. 120D, XXII, I, no. 1, vol. 1, p. 15. A membership list, dated October 26, showed that the dreaded oppositional intellectuals had joined the new *Centralverein*. In addition to Meyen and Rutenberg, there was Karl Nauwerck, a fellow Left Hegelian and former university lecturer, who had been dismissed from his post for his radical political views by Prussia's conservative culture minister Eichhorn. Nauwerck, who published regularly in the *Hallesche Jahrbücher,* known as the mouthpiece of the radical Left, had been accused of *politische Tendenzschriftstellerei* and was therefore a man to be kept under surveillance. See Max Lenz, *Geschichte der königlichen Friedrich Wilhelms Universität zu Berlin,* 4 vols. (Berlin, 1910–18), 2:73–79. The old *Verein zum Wohl der arbeitenden Klassen* petered out during the early fall of 1844.

53. See "Die Bildung von Vereinen," Zentrales Staatsarchiv II, Merseburg, rep. 120D, XXII, I, vol. 1, pp. 40–40 verso.

54. Ibid., 18 ("Verzeichnis der Mitglieder des Central-Vereins für das Wohl der arbeitenden Klassen").

is difficult to believe that the influence a member could exert and the weight his opinion carried was not connected with his monetary contribution.

As Donald G. Rohr has pointed out, there was a tradition of social liberalism among early German entrepreneurs that accounts for their numerical predominance in the *Centralverein*.[55] These were such men as the Westfalian Friedrich Harkort, who advocated limited state involvement to help the poor, Gustav Mevissen, who, influenced by St. Simon, argued that the upper classes should take the lead in reorganizing society in such a way that all classes could enjoy the benefits of modern industry. To them, restricting free enterprise did not necessarily entail a total surrender to collectivism. Despite the great influence of Adam Smith in Germany, where his ideas were propagated at Göttingen, Königsberg, and Halle, this tradition of social liberalism was widespread. Friedrich Harkort, for example, welcomed the new association and later was counted among its members,[56] though he and other social liberals found themselves in the predicament of having to choose whether constitutional or social reform was to come first. The *Centralverein* was thus firmly controlled by the *juste milieu*. The numbers of high-ranking civil servants alone should have sufficed to allay fears of political subversion, especially since officials already exerted decisive influence within the association.

And indeed, the new association got off to a very good start. Frederick William IV, having heard that a new society had been founded during the *Gewerbeausstellung,* was eager to associate his name with the good cause. He interpreted the foundation as an act of genuine Prussian paternalism in the Frederican tradition and probably overestimated the "official" character of the new society.[57] In a letter to his minister of finance, Eduard Heinrich von Flottwell, the king declared his "great and lively interest in this undertaking" and expressed the wish to support the association financially, for which purpose he asked Flottwell to put 15,000 taler at its disposal.[58] The monarch was hopeful that by "common beneficial work for the welfare of the working classes, a higher consecration would be bestowed on national industry," and he announced his intention to strengthen the association so that it would soon "grow into a tree, covering with its branches the entire fatherland." It had

---

55. See Donald G. Rohr, *The Origins of Social Liberalism in Germany* (Chicago, 1963).
56. Rohr, *Social Liberalism,* 139.
57. Even among historians, there were some who mistook the *Centralverein* for a government foundation. Donald Rohr, for example, wrote that "the Prussian government, after the shock of the Silesian riots, founded in Berlin a "Central Society for the Welfare of the Working Classes" (*Social Liberalism,* 139).
58. Ibid., 17–17 verso. The amount of the donation should not be overestimated, since it was the king's habit to give liberally. To the *Verein für Tierschau und Pferderennen* (Association for Animal Display and Horse Racing), which neither counted needy paupers among its members nor did anything for their benefit, the king donated 30,000 taler. See Wilhelm Wolff, *Aus Schlesien, Preussen und dem Reich.*

indeed been the intention of the *Centralverein's* initiators to set up a network of regional and local societies throughout Prussia, and if possible even beyond. In all of Prussia, notably in the Western provinces Rhineland and Westfalia, where active participation of the citizenry was most highly developed, local *Vereine* soon sprang up like mushrooms.[59] The *Centralverein's* executive board was informed of the royal gift by a joint note of the ministers of finance and the interior, and with the exception of the new society's statutes, which had to be approved by the authorities, there were no further obstacles "to the temporary opening of the association's activities."[60]

Officials in the ministry of the interior, still under the shock of events in Silesia, and thus anxious to suppress potential "intellectual subversion," had quite different ideas about the matter. Decisions concerning the association's future lay largely with them, though any resolution the minister and his councillors arrived at could be made null and void by the king's veto. From the ministry of finance no resistance toward the *Centralverein's* public activities was to be expected, since Flottwell—though notorious for his rigorous policy of germanization during his term as *Oberpräsident* of the largely Polish province of Posen—was otherwise known for his liberal inclinations and his favoring of new ventures.[61] Many officials among the association's members, such as Johann Georg von Viebahn, Erasmus Robert von Patow, Adolf von Pommer-Esche, and its chairman Friedrich Wilhelm Bornemann, had served in the ministry of finance and knew Flottwell personally.[62] The minister of the interior, Adolf Heinrich Graf Arnim Boitzenburg, however, though a nephew of the reformer Freiherr von Stein, had become a symbol of reaction within the bureaucracy through his rigorous suppression of the liberal press. His accession to a ministerial position in 1842 strengthened conservatives in the ministry of the interior, thanks to his deep-seated aversions to liberal stirrings and his obsessive fear of opposition intellectuals. Flottwell once referred to him as "an

---

59. See Nora Stiebel, "Der Zentralverein für das Wohl der arbeitenden Klassen im vormärzlichen Preussen" (Ph.D. diss., University of Heidelberg, 1922).

60. "Die Bildung von Vereinen," pp. 34–35, 23–24 verso. The beginning of public activity seemed imminent, though a submissively worded petition to the authorities, in which the executive board asked for conferment of corporate rights and recognition of its statues, indicated that members of the association expected difficulties from the bureaucracy.

61. See Heinrich von Treitschke, *Deutsche Geschichte*, 4:545–50, 5:589–91. In 1848 Flottwell himself became a member of the *Centralverein.*

62. See Rudolf von Delbrück, *Lebenserinnerungen*, 2 vols. (Leipzig, 1905) 1:131–32, who recounted his dinners at the house of another high official, *Generalsteuerdirektor* Kühne, where, among many others, Patow, Pommer-Esche, and Bornemann were frequent guests, while Flottwell was well known to everyone. Like other officials involved in the association, its chairman, Bornemann, also had a reputation for "his decidedly liberal views" (Treitschke, *Deutsche Geschichte*, 5:204).

entirely aristocratic person," which, in the context it was said, was not meant as a compliment.[63]

The minister himself was naturally too overburdened with other affairs of state to devote much time to the new organization, but it was a man very much after Arnim's heart who was put in charge of dealings with the *Centralverein.* Emil Ludwig Mathis (1797–1874), the descendant of a family of Huguenots, had been influenced by the religious views of his stepfather, the court chaplain Theremin, who like Ernst Wilhelm Hengstenberg and Johann Albrecht Friedrich Eichhorn was one of the ultraconservative pillars of Prussian society.[64] When a relatively young man, Mathis already excelled in the persecution of liberals and "demagogues," when serving as the Prussian member at the *Bundeszentralbehörde* (central authority) in Frankfurt, responsible for the suppression of subversive activities.[65] Due to his religious background, Mathis had close personal relations with the conservatives around the *Berliner Politisches Wochenblatt,* some of whom later became members of the so-called *Kamarilla,* the circle of conservative advisers of Friedrich Wilhelm IV, and exerted considerable influence on Prussian politics in the 1850s.[66] With these conservatives Mathis shared a strong religious commitment, loyalty toward the monarchy, a strictly legalistic conception of the state, and venomous aversion toward liberalism. Mathis wanted to preserve the status quo, not by trying to understand new social and political developments and eventually neutralizing them through timely concessions, as was the intention of the officials involved in the *Centralverein,* but by mustering the full power of the bureaucratic police state against the opponent and by setting constant watch until all weak points were known and the full force of the law could be marshaled against the enemy.

---

63. See Varnhagen, *Tagebücher,* ed. L. Assing (Leipzig, 1861), 2:255. Arnim also knew several officials who were involved in the association, such as Johann Christian Karl Quentin (1810–62), councillor at the Düsseldorf *Regierung,* who had published a treatise on coalitions among workers and had dedicated a copy to Arnim. In the 1830s, Quentin served as junior councillor (*Referendar*) under *Regierungspräsident* Arnim in Aachen. Robert von Patow (1804–90), who held a high position in the ministry of the interior in 1844–45, also knew Arnim.

64. After the revocation of the Edict of Nantes (1685) by Louis XIV, the Great Elector granted asylum to thousands of Huguenots. Many of their descendants later came to occupy prominent positions in Prussian society. The best-known offspring of a Huguenot family is of course Theodor Fontane.

65. Treitschke, *Deutsche Geschichte,* 4:598, 5:511. For Mathis's Frankfurt activities (1835–38), Treitschke finds words of praise, which in itself is telling.

66. In addition to several members of the former *Wochenblatt* group, such as Leopold and Ernst Ludwig von Gerlach, the *Kamarilla* included the conservatives Hans von Kleist-Retzow, Ernst von Senfft-Pilsach, and Edwin von Manteuffel. During the Revolution of 1848 and after, this circle of advisers brought decisive influence to bear on the king.

In his seminal study, *The Genesis of German Conservatism,* Klaus Epstein distinguished three "ideal types" of conservative:[67] the status quo conservative is reluctant to envisage change and stubbornly clings to what he has, but unlike the reactionary, he recognizes the impossibility of moving backward; the reactionary is bitterly hostile to existing society, wishes to undo all change, and usually idealizes the past; and the reform conservative, aware that changes will occur, tries, by gradual reform, to control them—in Burke's words, he has "a tendency to preserve with an inclination to improve."[68] From what we know about the often praised liberalism of the Prussian civil service, it would be reasonable to assume that, after the weakening of liberalism and the resurgence of conservatism, which set in well before 1820,[69] the reform conservative was the prevalent type among officials. Yet in the situation of the 1840s, dominant circles in the bureaucracy were likely to regard any kind of reform as a diminution of their power. In a civil service besieged by a multitude of new challenges, Mathis and his minister tenaciously clung to the status quo.

In an internal memorandum to his minister, Mathis at once expressed his concern about the new association, which could "easily be used by unreliable *Literaten*" for their purposes. The official pointed out that it was high time "to present the king with cautious reservations and ask for precise rules of conduct."[70] In December 1844, Mathis drafted a detailed report for Arnim to submit to the king. In it he vented his doubts about the *Centralverein* on twenty-six tightly argued pages. Mathis wrote that though the idea of helping the lower classes by way of an association was generally to be supported, "an affair like the one at hand, likely to arouse unattainable hopes and expectations, likely to stir up the masses and bring them under the leadership of hotheads, requires the most cautious treatment."[71]

In the report, the statutes were scrutinized with great care, since with the intended branches covering the whole monarchy, the association could wield great power. The ministry therefore argued that it ought to be avoided at all costs that the *Centralverein* be used for "party purposes," which could cause

---

67. See Klaus Epstein, *The Genesis of German Conservatism* (Princeton, 1966), 3–29.

68. Ibid., 9.

69. See Barbara Vogel, "Beamtenkonservatismus."

70. Mathis either shared his minister's idée fixe about intellectuals or adroitly played up to them. In the preparation of reports that Arnim later signed, the minister seemed to have given him free hand. Mathis's acolyte in composing acid memoranda was an official named Wenzel, a former councillor at the *Regierung* at Frankfurt/Oder, who had only recently come to work for the ministry of the interior. Wenzel's political preferences seemed to have been congruent with those of his master.

71. See "Die Bildung von Vereinen," Zentrales Staatsarchiv II, Merseburg, pp. 64–76 verso. After perfunctory introductory phrases, Mathis is quick to point out that "in our time conditions of the lowest classes are often discussed with emotion and glaring exaggeration . . . to spread the opinion that their misery is due to the injustice of others."

"greatest embarrassment" to the government. And it was put to the king that it depended on the association's leadership whether it turned radical or kept in line with governmental policies.[72] Mathis put together a list of potential threats that an all-encompassing network of provincial and local branch associations posed to the state: according to its statutes, membership was unrestricted, contingent only on an annual fee of four reichstaler; in the general assembly, all association members had a vote and, *horribile dictu,* "the majority of votes" decided.[73] The nine-member executive board was to be elected for only three years, and while the board guaranteed political stability, it was impossible to say whether the organization might not be used to serve different political ends in the future. Danger loomed large through the presence of the *Literaten,* "to whom it matters a lot to win over the masses." Worse, the intellectuals seemed to dominate the meetings of the Berlin branch. The unrestricted right of all members to be present at meetings, the report warned, undoubtedly had an adverse effect "on the levelheadedness of discussions, jeopardizing resolutions and opening the way to manifold temptations."[74] Modification of statutes should not, therefore, be solely dependent on the association's resolutions, but should be contingent on the ministry's authorization as well.

In addition to these reservations, significant enough to require observing "future developments carefully" before approving the statutes, Arnim drew the king's attention to the recent meeting of a local association, in which "passions ran so high that authorities were forced to intervene."[75] Those present had mostly elected oppositional intellectuals to represent them, and if newspaper reports could be believed, things had even been worse at another association's gathering in Cologne.[76] While it was true that in the autumn of 1844 newspaper reports had been circulating revealing radical influences at local associa-

---

72. Ibid., 66–66 verso. Arnim explained that the statutes lacked guarantees to frustrate the possibility "that hostile and malicious forces could, sooner or later, seize such a dangerous weapon as the association may prove to be." The potential benefits the association offered were hardly mentioned.

73. Ibid., 67 verso. See also, "Entwurf eines Statuts des Central-Vereins in Preussen für das Wohl der arbeitenden Klassen," ibid., 36–39. "Article 8: Entry into the Association and continuation of membership is contingent on an annual fee of at least four reichstaler." This provision automatically excluded a broad section of the population from membership, notably the working classes. In the 1840s, four reichstaler bought two pigs.

74. Ibid., 71–72.

75. Ibid., 75–76.

76. Ibid. In his recent *Rhineland Radicals: The Democratic Movement and the Revolution of 1848–1849* (Princeton, N.J., 1991), Jonathan Sperber also mentioned the predominance of radical tendencies at local association meetings in Cologne, where "leftist forces outvoted moderates on several occasions, leading them to leave the organization" (119). But then, radicals in Cologne intended to drop the official designation "Association for the Welfare of the Working Classes" and rename their association *"Gegenseitiger Hülfs- und Bildungsverein"* (120).

tion meetings in the Rhineland,[77] notably in Cologne, where socialist demands had been raised, Mathis himself had asked his collaborators to find newspaper articles that would confirm his and Arnim's concerns.[78] Ultimately, these radical stirrings in local associations were passing phenomena and limited to a few places in the Prussian Rhineland and Berlin, but they did lasting damage to the *Centralverein* insofar as they provided a pretext for conservatives in the ministry of the interior to suppress even moderately liberal tendencies.

The overall tone of Arnim's document, its tedious fussiness and fastidiousness in detail, showed all too clearly that officials in the ministry of the interior had little interest in the positive contributions an "Association for the Welfare of the Working Classes" might make. The report was primarily designed to change the king's mind about the *Centralverein* by pointing out the manifold dangers that an independent association of this size might engender. In their dealings with the *Centralverein,* officials not only abandoned all pretense of political liberalism but equally threw overboard any willingness to reform. They had become mere status quo conservatives. Growth of a liberal movement was feared by king and bureaucracy alike, since their power rested on political quietism of the bourgeoisie, not to mention the proletariat. Prussia was after all, politically, still a virtually absolutist state. There was no constitution, no declaration of rights of man and the citizen, no habeas corpus act, and no elected representatives of the people to form a parliament. Thus, whenever the social question threatened to become political, it became dangerous for those in power. Small wonder then that Arnim's entire report breathed fear of agitators, fear of political radicalism, fear of a developing mass movement. In the bureaucracy's perception, the sole remedy was total control: over association meetings, which were to be infested with police spies; over the executive board, whose existence soon depended on official endorsement; and over the statutes, which equally needed the authorities' consent.

Originally the power and identity of the bureaucracy had been based on its claim to restructure society along economically liberal lines, so that every citizen, regardless of his station, would be able to develop his potential fully. After the military collapse of the Prussian state, *raison d' état* had dictated such

---

77. On November 20, 1844, for example, the *Mannheimer Abendzeitung* reported that the Cologne Association had spoken out for the equality of man and for the creation of better working conditions. As if to confirm Arnim's report, Friedrich Engels in Barmen had written to his friend Marx in Paris on November 19, 1844: "Wir haben jetzt überall öffentliche Versammlungen, um Vereine zur Hebung der Arbeiter zu stiften; das bringt Bewegung unter die Germanen und lenkt die Aufmerksamkeit des Philisteriums auf soziale Fragen. . . . In Köln haben wir die Hälfte des Komitees zur Statutenentwerfung mit Unsrigen besetzt, in Elberfeld war wenigstens einer drin, und mit Hülfe der Rationalisten brachten wir in zwei Versammlungen den Frommen eine famose Schlappe bei; mit ungeheurer Majorität wurde alles Christliche aus den Statuten verbannt" (Marx and Engels, *Der Briefwechsel,* 1:5).

78. Reulecke, *Sozialer Frieden,* 92.

a policy, and during the Reform Era, leading circles in the bureaucracy had made a gigantic effort to create a more vigorous Prussia by trying to replace the old *Ständestaat* with a modern *bürgerliche Gesellschaft* likely to meet the challenges of the postrevolutionary age more successfully. Due to a necessary compromise with the Junkers and a resurgence of conservative elements within the apparatus, this grand effort had been partially abandoned, and ultimately it failed.[79] Even after the reforms, the bureaucracy still retained its dominant position, which, as before, rested on its claim to act in the best interest for the development and welfare of society. The source of the official's legitimate authority vis-à-vis the population was his patriarchical *Fürsorgedenken:* his authority and thus his mandate to govern was based on his impartiality and the tacit assumption that what he did was for the good of the state and population. But, as demonstrated by Arnim's reaction, by the mid-1840s disinterestedness had given way to plain indifference and lack of understanding for social problems.[80] The fact that the civil service was hopelessly overburdened after the cuts of 1825 was partially responsible for that. There were simply too few officials for too many tasks, and in the "Hungry Forties," responsibilities had become too manifold to be tackled—not least, as Reinhart Koselleck has argued, because officials proved unable to banish the ghosts they themselves had conjured up during the Reform Era. Once set in motion, the *bürgerliche Gesellschaft,* however stunted in its growth, could not be tamed by its own creator.

After the barrage of Arnim's detailed criticism, the king abandoned the *Centralverein* without further ado. In a cabinet order of January 24, 1845, he agreed with his minister's reservations concerning the *Centralverein*'s statutes and authorized the minister of the interior to examine the statutes of local associations. Arnim and Mathis would now have completely free reign in their dealings with the association.[81] And frequent press reports about seditious

79. On the role of the bureaucracy during the Reform Era, see Rosenberg, *Bureaucracy,* 202–28; Koselleck, *Preussen zwischen Reform und Revolution,* 163–217; Barbara Vogel, *Preussische Reformen 1807–1820* (Königstein, 1980); Thomas Nipperdey, *Deutsche Geschichte 1800–1866,* 33–69; Marion W. Gray, *Prussia in Transition: Society and Politics under the Stein Reform Ministry of 1808* (Philadelphia, 1986); Hans-Ulrich Wehler, *Gesellschaftsgeschichte,* 1:397–486.

80. According to Otto Hintze, disinterestedness together with integrity, a selfless work ethic, and an uncompromising sense of justice had been the salient features of the Prussian bureaucracy. See Otto Hintze "Der Beamtenstand," in Hintze, *Soziologie und Geschichte,* vol. 2 of *Gesammelte Abhandlungen* (Göttingen, 1967), 66–126, esp. 77.

81. Zentrales Staatsarchiv II, Merseburg, rep. 120D, XXII, I, no. 1, vol. 1, p. 126. See also Stiebel, "Zentralverein," 165; Reulecke, *Sozialer Frieden,* 96. Firmness of purpose was not one of Frederick William's salient characteristics, so the king's quick change of heart came as a surprise to no one. As if to substantiate Arnim's charges further, Frederick William had received an urgent report by Count Mirbach, councillor in the Düsseldorf *Regierung,* in which Mirbach complained about local associations' alarming radicalism and about the inability of authorities to intervene,

tendencies at local association gatherings in the Rhineland and Berlin seemed to justify the harshest treatment. At a meeting of the general assembly in Berlin, the Young Hegelian "radicals," such as Rutenberg, Nauwerck, and Meyen, had made an attempt to reassert themselves against moderates like Diesterweg (who had played a leading role in the *Centralverein*'s predecessor that met at the Café Hollande) and the liberal officials in the executive committee.[82] A police report on another general assembly meeting in Berlin distinguished three factions among the members: "the loyal party, the party of law, reason, and intelligence," represented by the executive board and industrial entrepreneurs; "the disloyal party, troublesome and obstructive," opposed to the former, and intent on causing scandal and public unrest, represented "by the most liberal *Literaten*"; and finally the party of "a more moderate progress," which, however, displayed strong affinities to the radical faction.[83]

Meanwhile, officials in the executive board had not remained oblivious to the disapproving attitude of the ministry of the interior. Dreading restrictive instructions to the *Oberpräsidenten*, which were already in preparation, the leaders of the *Centralverein* decided to act. The association's chairman, Friedrich Wilhelm Bornemann, hoped to neutralize crippling instructions to provincial authorities by thorough self-criticism. In a personal letter to Arnim on February 27, 1845, Bornemann conceded that the establishment of provincial branches was indeed inadvisable and that local associations should function under protective tutelage of communal authorities and local notabilities to forestall socialist tendencies. In addition, the *Centralverein*'s executive committee wrote to the ministry, deploring radical developments in some of the branch associations, and enclosing copies of an open letter in which Bornemann had warned his own committee of radical tendencies.[84] All this was

which, the count charged, was partly due to royal protection. See Reulecke, *Sozialer Frieden,* 106; Stiebel, "Zentralverein," 165.

82. There was also a number of publications by radical members, such as Eduard Meyen's, "Der Berliner Local-Verein für das Wohl der arbeitenden Classen," in *Rheinische Jahrbücher zur gesellschaftlichen Reform,* ed. Heinrich Püttman (Darmstadt, 1845), 1:198–214. In the autumn and winter 1844–45, numerous local branch associations in Prussia's Western provinces had been founded.

83. Zentrales Staatsarchiv II, Merseburg, rep. 120D, XXII, I, no. 1, vol. 1, pp. 85–88 verso. The meticulous eight-page report stresses the fact that the radical party was internally divided. Some of its members, Rutenberg and Nauwerck in the present case, supported mutually exclusive motions. The overall impression one gets of the meetings was one of chaos, whereby it was mostly members of the radical faction who were at each other's throats.

84. Zentrales Staatsarchiv II, Merseburg, rep. 120D, XXII, I, no. 1, pp. 90–92, 109–12. The *Centralverein*'s leading officials, notably Bornemann and Patow, anticipating insurmountable difficulties with the ministry of the interior, made every conceivable effort to allay fears and appease the minister. Patow, himself a high official in the ministry of the interior, was familiar with

done to prove to Arnim that the *Centralverein*'s leaders themselves were gravely concerned about radical tendencies in their midst and were ready to resort to stringent measures to eliminate them.

But the minister of the interior was not interested in gestures of good will. He had the whip hand and was in a position to enforce his views. In a circular instruction to Prussia's eight provincial governors, Arnim used the material provided by the *Centralverein*'s executive committee and its chairman Bornemann to tighten the reins even further.[85] The "deviating tendencies" that had sprung up in some local associations harbored great potential danger, Arnim argued, and it was thus of vital importance that local authorities and communal magistrates assumed the leadership of local societies in close association with the *Regierungen* (district authorities). The latter would even be entitled to ban local assemblies. It was the *Oberpräsident*'s task to decide whether magistrates or higher organs of state were to deal with local associations.[86] Arnim was especially concerned about two great risks: the association might raise "wild hopes of the so-called working-classes," and it might eventually digress from its own domain, entering new spheres of operation. Consequently, local associations should be forced to concentrate "on one defined practical subject," such as the establishment of saving banks for the lower classes, and it would be imperative to keep close watch on all assemblies, restrict attendance at public meetings, and limit active membership "to the educated classes of civil society."[87]

That these stringent ministerial guidelines would suffocate all effective work by local associations was obvious to everyone involved. At the end of his memorandum, Arnim emphasized again that officials would have to pay attention to political tendencies of local associations' leaders, for their political persuasions were more important than the wording of statutes. In March 1845, Arnim received further drafts of local associations' statutes, which, together with the report by the Düsseldorf councillor Mirbach to the king (see note 81), rekindled old fears that the active political participation of a wider public with

---

official correspondence and made several futile efforts to get Arnim on his side or at least to predispose him more favorably toward the *Centralverein*.

85. March 16, 1844, Zentrales Staatsarchiv II, Merseburg, rep. 120D, XXII, I, no. 1, pp. 97–107 verso. The following quotations are taken from Arnim's directives to the *Oberpräsidenten*. Together with his instructions, the minister enclosed copies of Bornemann's open letter, which he had received from the *Centralverein*, reassuring the provincial governors that he was acting in accord with the association's leadership.

86. In exceptional cases, namely, in smaller localities, different treatment might be warranted. In these instances, the minister wanted to be consulted for his personal permission (ibid., 105). Of a total of thirty-five branch associations, only three were ultimately granted permission of their statutes. See Reulecke, *Sozialer Frieden*, 108.

87. The minister of the interior did not fail to mention that the "purpose and goals" of the *Centralverein* and those of the bureaucracy were essentially identical (ibid., 100).

the wrong men in steering committees might do great harm to the state. In a second circular instruction to the *Oberpräsidenten,* further constraints were thus introduced.[88] Arnim deemed it intolerable that "all members were conceded more or less direct participation in discussions and resolutions of the association" as envisaged by statutes. He explained that assemblies "comprising hundreds of people of all social classes [Stände] and all educational backgrounds" were not conducive "to correct deliberation of subject matters." Participation of members in discussions should therefore be dispensed with, while their suggestions could be made before or after meetings. Under the pretense of intending the best for the association, the minister of the interior set forth a series of drastic measures: henceforth resolutions could be submitted by leading association members only, participation of rank and file was to be curtailed, decision-making powers of general assemblies were to be restricted to the point that discussions were of no further consequence, and the public was to be excluded from all meetings of the executive committee.[89] Anxiety about subversive intellectuals prompted the minister of the interior to impose his severest measure: since the association's development was essentially preconditioned by the personality of men at the top, it was only appropriate "that it be fixed in the statutes that the election of the respective committee members would be subject . . . to authorization of the *Oberpräsident* or the respective *Regierung.*"[90]

In 1845 the concern of the authorities was not wholly unfounded. In Cologne, other cities of the Rhine Province, and even in Berlin, a multiheaded hydra of Left Hegelians, alleged socialists, and communists seemed to rise.[91] In the imagination of conservative officials, the entire Prussian state might be engulfed by it one day. Yet they exaggerated their destabilizing potential greatly, for the intellectual opposition in Prussia was divided internally and

---

88. April 2, 1845, Zentrales Staatsarchiv II, Merseburg, rep. 120D, XXII, I, no. 1, vol. 1, pp. 121–24.

89. Meetings of the executive board could not be held in public, nor could access to them be open to all members of the association, for "both could only have an unfavorable effect on discipline and levelheadedness of deliberations and resolutions and can thus not be permitted" (ibid., 123 verso).

90. These very harsh policy guidelines were bound to put an end to any independent initiative of local associations. They can be comprehended only in the context of conservative officials' growing fear of radical conspiracies that had recently come to the fore. In Cleves, a town in Prussia's farthest west, an alleged communist circle had been discovered that had attempted to gain a foothold in the local branch of the association, and Arnim feared that other local associations could be affected as well. The minister had good reason for concern, since at Cleves, even state officials had been heard advocating radical opinions. See Zentrales Staatsarchiv II, Merseburg, rep. 120D, XXII, I, no. 1, vol. 1, pp. 116–116 verso; and Reulecke, *Sozialer Frieden,* 106–8. On political radicalism in the Rhineland see also Jonathan Sperber's thorough study, *Rhineland Radicals.*

91. See nn. 76–77 above.

lacked the ability for concerted action. Until the early 1840s, a substantial part of the latter-day radicals had been "orthodoxily Prussian-minded," supporting what they believed to be Prussia's world historical mission, namely, to complete the liberation of the human mind that had begun with the Reformation and was carried further by the Enlightenment.[92] To them Prussia was the manifestation of the Enlightenment tradition embodied by Frederick the Great, and the Prussian state was the incarnation of reason, as Hegel had once celebrated it. They naturally hoped for profound change once the old king had died. Such men as Arnold Ruge, Bruno and Edgar Bauer, Max Stirner, Karl Friedrich Köppen, and Karl Nauwerck had turned against the Prussian state only after the new Minister of Culture Eichhorn made it plain that Hegel's progressive disciples would no longer be tolerated at Prussian universities (Bruno Bauer lost his *venia legendi* in Bonn) and after the government gagged the liberal press anew with the reintroduction of strict censorship in early 1843. Their radicalization and increasing hostility toward Prussia, to which they had once professed deep attachment, thus had largely been caused by repressive state measures. The tighter surveillance and state control grew, the more radical and uncompromising the Left Hegelians became, to the point that they even disavowed common bonds with their former brothers-in-arms, the Königsberg liberals.[93] Oppressive states often create a radical intelligentsia, Czarist Russia being the best case in point. The king and the bureaucracy in Prussia, represented by Eichhorn, Altenstein's successor as minister of culture, had created their own worst enemy.

Disillusionment by the socially conscious officials and entrepreneurs involved in the *Centralverein* was the inevitable result of the repressive measures of the ministry of the interior. It was notably the government's vacillating course, first the king's favorable predisposition and donation, then the minister of the interior's tough stance, that created much ill feeling. Bureaucratic rule was on the verge of bankruptcy: when faced with growing misery and destitution, officials did virtually nothing to relieve poverty—the weavers' uprising being a paradigmatic example. And now that private citizens, mostly men of property in alliance with socially conscious officials, undertook that task, the bureaucracy nipped this promising beginning in the bud. As the bureaucracy seemed unable to meet the obligations that went with the possession of power, that is, to alleviate misery, feed the hungry, and keep citizens generally content, their claim to govern was weakened. Bureaucratic rule increasingly appeared to be nothing other than sheer tyranny.

---

92. See Gustav Mayer, "Die Junghegelianer und der preussische Staat," *Historische Zeitschrift* 123 (1920): 413–40.
93. Ibid., 433.

The stifling of local associations through Arnim's tight regimentation and close surveillance thus brought home to many involved in the *Centralverein* that even modest goals could be pushed through only in opposition to the government, and that their aims could be realized only outside and against the Prussian state and never within it. Contrary to their own intentions, officials in the ministry of the interior who had imposed these measures radicalized part of the moderately liberal bourgeoisie that constituted the bulk of the *Centralverein* membership, which otherwise would have remained a firm supporter of the state. Official policy thus brought about a swing of opinion, as many had to realize that the transformation of the political system had to precede social reform.[94] Arnim and Mathis never took into account the effect their measures might exert on the public mood. Their repressive policies fanned a prerevolutionary mood among association members—not only among radical intellectuals, but also among the liberal members, many of whom were later to participate actively in the Revolution of 1848. Some even emigrated afterward.[95]

Even though Arnim's directives set the tone for the bureaucracy's dealings with the *Centralverein*, the whole story has not yet been told. A flood of official notes, orders, commentaries, reports, and counterreports had to be drafted, corrected, amended, rewritten and dispatched before the statutes were finally approved. It needed the events of February 1848 in France to accelerate official endorsement of the association. The cabinet order of March 31, 1848, making authorization official, was countersigned by the revolutionary ministry of Auerswald and Hansemann. Heinrich von Arnim, sworn enemy of the association from the beginning, had left his post as minister of the interior in June 1845 and was superseded by Ernst von Bodelschwingh, formerly *Oberpräsident* of the Rhine Province and then Flottwell's predecessor as minister of finance. But despite Bodelschwingh's more liberal reputation, the change of ministers did not bring about a change of attitude toward the association in the ministry, since Mathis's influence remained predominant. If it had not been for Flottwell's active intervention, matters would have progressed more hesitatingly still.

From the very beginning to the very end—from October 1844, when first reports on the association disturbed the peace of officials in the ministry of the interior, until final approval of statutes—the bureaucracy's policy had been one

---

94. Further examples are the Rhenish politicians Mevissen and von Beckerath. Nora Stiebel ("Zentralverein," 178) equally made the point that the suppression of the association strengthened opposition movements.

95. There were eleven members of the *Centralverein* in different factions of the Frankfurt national assembly, and numerous other Frankfurt deputies had previously been active in local branch associations. Of the association members, Quentin, Wesendonck, and Groneweg, all civil servants, later emigrated to America.

of procrastination. It took more than half a year, for example, until the *Centralverein* received the first response to its submission of its statutes,[96] and radical tendencies that came to the fore in meetings of local associations provided the pretext needed for further delay. Finally, at a general assembly meeting in December 1845, the members of the *Centralverein*'s executive committee, aware of the seeming futility of their efforts, professed that they intended to resign and dissolve the association.[97] It took all the persuasion of the assembled members to make the committee retain its functions and keep the *Centralverein* in existence.

In late December 1845, Bodelschwingh finally decided to act and inquired about Flottwell's position toward the association. The minister of finance's response was favorable, urging Bodelschwingh not to delay approval of the statutes further. Yet this was precisely what happened. Mathis's influence in the ministry, having outlasted Arnim's tenure of office, undoubtedly also played a role in this. It would lead too far to retrace minutely the sequence of official correspondence. Suffice it to say that in the early spring of 1847, when Bodelschwingh at last seemed to show willingness to approve the statutes, the *Vereinigter Landtag* (United Diet), which congregated in Berlin between April 11 and June 26, 1847, absorbed the minister of the interior's attention, so final authorization was postponed again.

By then all initial enthusiasm connected with the venture had waned. The *Centralverein* would hardly be able "to breathe new life into its numb limbs," the radical Otto Lüning wrote in 1847, as the "flames have subsided."[98] By October 1847, the patience of the association's leaders was completely exhausted, and Patow and Bornemann, who had been driving forces behind the endeavor, had already left office. The remaining members wrote a bitter letter to Bodelschwingh, informing him of the prevailing disillusionment, and charging that due to a long delayed authorization, chances to work successfully had faded away.[99] It must have been humiliating to the officials and entrepreneurs who signed the plaintive letter to couch their indignation in carefully worded euphemisms and to gloss over facts lest the ministerial bureaucracy take of-

---

96. Statutes were submitted on October 27, 1844. For the response see April 4, 1845, Zentrales Staatsarchiv II, Merseburg, rep. 120D, XXII, I, no. 1, vol. 1, pp. 135–45 verso.

97. Zentrales Staatsarchiv II, Merseburg, rep. 120D, XXII, I, no. 1, vol. 1, pp. 208–208 verso, and the long article on the meeting in the *Vossische Zeitung* of December 19, 1845.

98. See *Westfälisches Dampfboot* 3 (1847), 178.

99. See Zentrales Staatsarchiv II, Merseburg, rep. 120D, XXII, I, no. 1, vol. 1, pp. 386–87 verso. Mathis's notes on the margin of nearly every page clearly show that he had been the decisive obstacle all along. His comment to reproaches that "prospects for practical activity, intended with the society's establishment have dwindled due to long procrastination in the approval of the association's statues" was that this was largely "to be blamed on the association itself" (ibid., 386). According to Mathis, the *Centralverein* had pressed its ideas "with little practical sense."

fense and aggravate matters further. In their dealings with the *Centralverein,* the virtually absolute authority of the higher civil service was manifest.[100]

Large numbers of the association's ever growing membership, as well as numerous local associations sprouting up in Prussia's West, testified to the great popular appeal of social and political activity for helping the poor and alleviating their fate. Due to the absence of political life in Prussia, there was, especially among upper-middle classes, great hunger to participate in civic affairs. Among the *Centralverein*'s leaders, there was a genuine readiness to make all the concessions necessary to get their association off the ground. For once, entrepreneurs, officials, and members of the literary intelligentsia were on board the same ship, which, due to the predominance of a loyal *juste milieu,* did not seem in danger of veering off into politically dangerous waters. Paternalistic welfare rather than the emancipation of lower classes was the association's goal. Why were these promising beginnings nipped in the bud; what wrecked a fruitful enterprise that could have drawn part of the bourgeoisie and socially minded liberals closer to the state instead of pushing them into opposition and that could have laid the groundwork for the nascent proletariat's integration into the state, instead of alienating and outlawing it? It was not the economic liberalism instilled in civil servants during the Reform Era, teaching them to refrain from intervention in economy and society, but naked fear of any independent action in the civil sphere, of radical intellectuals who appeared (falsely) to have played so momentous a role in the uprising of Silesian weavers. It was fateful for the *Centralverein* that decisive positions in the ministry of the interior were held by diehard conservatives like Mathis and Arnim. Ultimately it was this supreme arrogance of those in power—more than the actual misery and discontent with social and political conditions—that fanned the flames of revolution.

Between the reform period and the immediate pre-March, the role of the bureaucracy in society had thus changed from an instrument of modernization into one of oppression. After the collapse of the Prussian state in 1806, the civil service had been a progressive element in society, trying to create a more viable, resilient state that was able to withstand the challenges of the new, revolutionary age. By the 1840s, however, it had developed into an obstacle to reform, since it had become clear that further social change would inevitably result in a loss of power for the bureaucracy. Officials' handling of the *Centralverein* also demonstrated that the creation of a sophisticated *Ver-*

---

100. In regard to conservative officials in the ministry of the interior, Varnhagen wrote in his diary on December 25, 1847: "In matters of police supervision they do whatever they want. The minister lends them his reputation, and whoever is in charge of the policing post in the ministry is a pasha who has such powers as if he were not in Prussia but in Turkey" (Varnhagen, *Tagebücher,* 3:488).

waltung was a poor substitute for a constitution.[101] The civil service was unable to bridge the ever widening gulf between state and civil society that had reached a critical point by the late 1840s. With the growing divergence of state and society, officials gradually lost a part of their identity, for they ceased being the "*allgemeine Stand*" (as Hegel once put it) that hovered above societal frictions and represented the general interest. Once officials abandoned the pretension of doing what was best for society at large, they forfeited, in a certain sense, their raison d'être. Reinhart Koselleck has already noted this loss of "impartiality" for the period after 1820, when the bureaucracy relinquished its role as neutral arbiter by increasingly discriminating against the urban bourgeoisie while making concessions to the landed aristocracy. The bureaucracy's handling of the *Centralverein* is a case in point of the destruction of the erstwhile identity between civil service and *Bildungsbürgertum* (another of Koselleck's central arguments) and the concomitantly rising tension between the Prussian bureaucracy and the bourgeois public. During the second half of the 1840s, the bureaucracy had become increasingly alienated from the public, and criticism of bureaucractic policies became one of the salient features of the age, which further undermined the officials' mandate to rule.[102] The bureaucracy failed to tackle the social question successfully, because it refused to acknowledge the political participation of the higher bourgeoisie. This suppression and suffocation of the bourgeois public in Prussia had fateful consequences for the political culture of this state. Elsewhere, particularly in western Europe, the bulk of the *classes politiques* were recruited from the ranks of the higher bourgeoisie, while in Prussia (as later in the German Empire) they continued being in large part identical with the higher civil service.[103]

---

101. Koselleck, *Preussen zwischen Reform und Revolution,* 217–84. Koselleck spoke of a "Behördenausbau von 1815 bis 1825 als verfassungspolitische Vorleistung."

102. See especially, Helene Nathan, *Preussens Verfassung und Verwaltung im Urteil rheinischer Achtundvierziger* (Bonn, 1912); Karl Heinzen, *Die Preussische Bürokratie* (Darmstadt, 1845).

103. In this context, Leonore O'Boyle, "The Middle Class in Western Europe, 1815–1848," *American Historical Review* 72 (1966): 826–45, contended that "an argument might be made that the bureaucracy remained the core of the ruling class in Germany up to 1917" (ibid., 842).

CHAPTER 8

The Bureaucracy and the Urban Proletariat: Economic Liberalism, Conservative Patterns of Argumentation, and the Impossibility of Monolithic Rule

With Hardenberg's liberal trade legislation of 1810–11, the Prussian state renounced active interference in the economy and thereby departed from the legal basis of the *Allgemeines Landrecht,* which had postulated the state's social responsibility for its poor.[1] While the bureaucratic apparatus had become increasingly conservative by the 1840s, laissez-faire liberalism held sway during the early decades of the nineteenth century. Past research on the Prussian bureaucracy has consistently emphasized the economic liberalism of high-ranking officials, a thesis vigorously advanced by Wilhelm Treue, who examined the professional socialization of fifteen leading officials, most of whom later became ministers and provincial governors.[2] According to Treue, their studies at Königsberg with Kant and the economist Kraus and at Göttingen, "the entrance gate of English economic ideas," their long *Bildungsreisen* through England, which had become customary with leading officials, and their thorough study of Adam Smith had turned them into advo-

---

1. Wolfgang Köllmann, "Die Anfänge der staatlichen Sozialpolitik in Preussen bis 1869," in *VSWG* 53 (1966), 28–52; Barbara Vogel, *Allgemeine Gewerbefreiheit: Die Reformpolitik des preussischen Staatskanzlers Hardenberg (1810–1820)* (Göttingen, 1983); Reinhart Koselleck, *Preussen zwischen Reform und Revolution,* 2d ed. (Stuttgart, 1975), 23–143.

2. Wilhelm Treue, *Wirtschaftszustände und Wirtschaftspolitik in Preussen 1815–1825* (Stuttgart, 1937), 121–48; see also chapters 6 and 7.

cates of laissez-faire economics.[3] Since officials trained in Königsberg and
Göttingen were to fill important positions in the civil service after 1815, economic liberalism, Treue argued, persisted even after the victory over Napoleon,
when most of the ambitious reform projects were abandoned. Prussia's liberal
trade policy after 1815 clearly revealed that economic liberalism had permeated the upper echelons of the civil service. What was more, adherents of free
trade succeeded in carrying through their ideas, which was remarkable, given
that Prussia was surrounded by states that protected their commerce by taxes:
France, Bavaria, Württemberg, Belgium, Austria, and Russia defended all
products of their national industries by high customs barriers.[4] With the exception of *Gewerbeförderung,* the specifically Prussian promotion of trade, advanced by officials, such as the Westfalian *Oberpräsident* Vincke, the councillor of state Beuth, and Rother, director of the *Seehandlung,* there was no
state involvement in the economy in the years after 1815.[5]

A comprehensive social policy, which would naturally have implied state
interference in the production process to protect specific groups at high risk,
such as women, children, and workers having met an accident, would therefore
have run counter to contemporary economic concepts of policymakers. Due to
incipient industrialization in the decades preceding the revolution, some protective measures were inevitable, but they remained limited to the banning of
child labor, which had already been put into practice in England. That the
English example blazed the trail for the industrial latecomer on the continent is
made evident by frequent extracts and compilations of English factory legislation in Prussian official documents.[6] Robert Owen, who exerted some influ-

3. Treue, *Wirtschaftszustände und Witschaftspolitik,* 140. Hans-Ulrich Wehler, *Deutsche Gesellschaftsgeschichte,* vol. 1 (Munich, 1987), 405, equally emphasized Adam Smith's influence. According to Wehler, Kant's successor in Königsberg, Kraus, impressed on his listeners that the world had not seen "a more important book" than Smith's *Wealth of Nations.*
4. Prussia's liberal trade policy was epitomized by the elimination of import duties, sanc-tioned by the law of May 26, 1818. This had been pushed through by high-ranking officials. Treue demonstrated that top bureaucrats involved in drafting the law were conditioned by their university education and journeys abroad (mostly to England) and imbued by laissez-faire ideals.
5. On Vincke, Beuth, Rother, and other high officials who actively promoted trade and industry see William O. Henderson, *The State and the Industrial Revolution in Prussia 1740–1870* (Liverpool, 1958); Ulrich Ritter, *Die Rolle des Staates in den Frühstadien der Industrialisierung* (Berlin, 1961); Wolfram Fischer, "Das Verhältnis von Staat und Wirtschaft in Deutschland am Beginn der Industrialisierung," in Fischer, *Wirtschaft und Gesellschaft im Zeitalter der Indus-trialisierung* (Gottingen, 1972), 60–74; Ilja Mieck, *Preussische Gewerbepolitik in Berlin 1806–1844* (Berlin, 1965); Wolfgang Radtke, *Die preussische Seehandlung zwischen Staat und Wirtschaft in der Frühphase der Industrialisierung* (Berlin, 1981).
6. See "Die Beschäftigung jugendlicher Arbeiter in Fabriken, Berg-, Hütten- und Poch-werken," Staatsarchiv Merseburg, rep. 120BB, VII, 3, I, vol. 1 (1835–46), pp. 86–88 verso, "Zusammenfassung über die Gesetzgebung Englands und die Beschäftigung der Kinder in Fabriken."

ence on his own country's factory legislation, related in his autobiography that his *Four Essays on the New Views of Society* was enthusiastically studied in Prussia. Frederick William III himself, having received the treatise from his London ambassador, wrote to Owen to express his approval of the Englishman's ideas. Political and geographic conditions permitting, Owen's ideas would not fail to make an impact on Prussia's national education.[7]

Independent of English influences, there were additional factors that finally led to the passing of the Prussian factory bill, the *Regulativ über die Beschäftigung jugendlicher Arbeiter in Fabriken* of March 9, 1839.[8] Foremost among these was the bureaucracy's deep-seated ethos of paternalism (interspersed with humanitarian ideals, as many would contend) that made it virtually impossible to watch idly the increasing pauperization of broad sections of the population. It was impossible for officials to be indifferent toward new societal developments and to abandon the proletariat to its own fate, especially since periodically arriving reports from the provinces informed officials in Berlin of all ongoing changes. Despite its economic liberalism, members of the core bureaucracy were still pervaded by a patriarchal spirit that had been instilled in them for generations: to them Prussian citizens were, above all, subjects who needed guidance. Politically liberal views of the English and French tradition were uncommon among high officials. If liberal, their liberalism was of a different, more statist kind. The doctrine of the *beschränkten Untertanenverstands* remained thus widespread throughout the bureaucracy in the decades preceding the revolution.[9]

How large a role the great ideal of German Idealism, the "idea of humanity," had played in the making of protective legislation is difficult to assess, for the concept can hardly be distinguished from the traditional, authoritarian view of public welfare. Official documents, too, are not revealing in the matter, since matter-of-fact arguments counted most there, and references to humanitarian considerations may not have been deemed weighty enough. Humanitarian ideals of Wilhelm von Humboldt and other reformers, widely diffused in the early decades of the century, notably at the newly founded University of Berlin

---

7. See Wally Schulze, "Kinderarbeit und Erziehungsfragen in Preussen zu Beginn des 19. Jahrhunderts," *Soziale Welt* 9 (1958): 299–309; Robert Owen, *The Life of Robert Owen written by Himself from his Writings and Correspondence*, vol. 1 (London, 1857), 133–34.

8. *Gesetz-Sammlung für die preussischen Staaten* (1840), 156–58. The essence of the *Regulativ*, which comprised ten articles, was that child labor would be banned for those under the age of nine, and that adolescents under the age of sixteen could work only ten hours a day and could be employed only if proof of three years school attendance could be furnished. In addition, ministries involved in drafting the law reserved for themselves the right to pass further "*sanitäts-, bau- und sittenpolizeiliche Anordnungen*" to preserve "health and morality among factory workers."

9. Rudolf von Delbrück, *Lebenserinnerungen 1817–1867*, vol. 1 (Leipzig, 1905), 183.

(1810), undoubtedly exerted considerable, though hardly measurable, influence on officials.[10]

Child labor, which had become widespread, seemed to undermine two main pillars of the state: education and the military. It has almost become an inexpungible legend that military considerations were instrumental in passing the 1839 *Regulativ*. But this is only part of the truth, and undoubtedly the less important part. It is correct that the report of Lieutenant General von Horn drew attention to the fact that Prussia's more industrialized districts were barely able to levy their army contingent, which provided new impetus to the bureaucracy's discussion on the factory bill, but there were other factors, such as school attendance, that were of equal, if not greater, impact on the realization of the law.[11] The following examination therefore concentrates less on a reconstruction of the sequence of bureaucratic correspondence that eventually led to the passing of the *Regulativ* in 1839 than on what documents reveal about officials' underlying views on social issues. To catch a glimpse of inner moti-

---

10. It is repeatedly emphasized in the literature that high officials were imbued with the idealistic conceptions of the Reform Era and the spirit of German Idealism. See H. Weill, *Die Entstehung des deutschen Bildungsprinzips* (Bonn, 1930); Meinecke, *Weltbürgertum und Nationalstaat*, 4th ed. (Berlin, 1917); Ulrich Preuss, "Bildung und Bürokratie: Sozialhistorische Bedingungen in der ersten Hälfte des 19. Jahrhunderts," *Der Staat* 14 (1975): 371–96; Hans Branig, "Wesen und Geist der höheren Verwaltungsbeamten in Preussen in der Zeit des Vormärz," *Neue Forschungen zur Brandenburgisch-Preussischen Geschichte* 1 (1979): 161–71.

11. The most detailed account on early Prussian factory legislation is Günther K. Anton's, *Geschichte der preussischen Fabrikgesetzgebung*, Staats- und socialwissenschaftliche Forschungen 11 (Leipzig, 1891). Anton's study is exclusively based on primary sources and therefore is still not outdated, despite its age. Anton retraced every step of the legislative process, without however paying much attention to the motivation behind bureaucratic initiatives. Older still, but useful as overview, is Alphons Thun's, "Beiträge zur Geschichte der Gesetzgebung und Verwaltung zu Gunsten der Fabrikarbeiter in Preussen," *Zeitschrift des Königlich Preussischen Statistischen Bureaus* 17 (1877): 59–95. In his short 1954 article "Von den tragenden Ideen der ersten deutschen Sozialpolitik," in *Aus Geschichte und Politik: Festschrift zum 70. Geburtstag von Ludwig Bergstraesser* (Düsseldorf, 1954), 301–11, Ludwig Preller argued that the schoolmaster and not the sergeant major stood at the cradle of the factory bill. Preller convincingly contended that Prussian militarism led to an overestimation of the army's influence in the matter, especially from a twentieth-century vantage point. Yet he failed to produce decisive evidence for humanitarian motives of officials, which he seemed to take for granted. Winfried Feldenkirchen, "Kinderarbeit im 19. Jahrhundert," *Zeitschrift für Unternehmensgeschichte* 26 (1981): 1–42, offered statistical material to bolster his (and Preller's) contention that military influence was not decisive in the making of the law. See also Ruth Hoppe, Jürgen Kuczynski, and Heinrich Waldmann, eds., *Hardenbergs Umfrage über die Lage der Kinder in den Fabriken und andere Dokumente aus der Frühgeschichte der Lage der Arbeiter*, vol. 8 of *Die Geschichte der Lage der Arbeiter unter dem Kapitalismus* (Berlin, 1960); Hans-Joachim Henning, "Preussische Sozialpolitik im Vormärz," *Vierteljahresschrift für Sozial- und Wirtschaftsgeschichte* 52 (1965): 485–539; Koselleck, *Preussen zwischen Reform und Revolution*, 620–28; Florian Tennstedt, *Sozialgeschichte der Sozialpolitik in Deutschland* (Göttingen, 1981), 33–69; Jürgen Kocka, *Lohnarbeit und Klassenbildung* (Berlin and Bonn, 1983), 110–18; Wehler, *Gesellschaftsgeschichte*, 2:254–58.

vations that determined their actions, to find patterns of argumentation that disclosed ways of thought and political preferences otherwise hidden, is the foremost concern.

It began with Hardenberg's degree of September 5, 1817, to the *Oberpräsidenten* of Prussia's industrially more advanced provinces, in which the chancellor expressed his concern that manufacturing industries would produce "a numerous class of people . . . exposed to most miserable poverty."[12] Provincial governors' responses, partly consisting of detailed analyses of childrens' working conditions in industrial establishments, are of no further consequence here. Only Hardenberg himself significantly remarked in his ordinance that "the state has unmistakably means to shelter its youth."[13] Yet the state was not to use its power soon; Hardenberg's foray was not followed up by further measures. What finally set the ball rolling was the discovery that a Rhenish entrepreneur, who had earlier come to the government's attention by founding a factory school, employed hundreds of children during day and night shifts in his spinning mills.

Altenstein, liberal minister of culture, patron of Hegelian philosophy, and promoter of academic freedom at Prussian universities, a man who had done much for the blossoming of cultural life in his country, at once undertook steps to restrict abuses of child labor that had come to his attention.[14] To be effective and to submit a legal draft to the *Staatsministerium,* however, Altenstein needed the support of Schuckmann, the minister of commerce.[15] Schuckmann, "the philistine of old days," as Wilhelm von Humboldt once called him, interested in maintaining Prussia's favorable balance of trade (which he saw jeopardized by government interference with industrial labor policy), delayed the matter, bringing further proceedings to a standstill. Then, in 1828, Altenstein's efforts received new support by a report of Lieutenant General von Horn of the Prussian *Landwehr* that emphasized that child labor, especially labor at night, rendered recruits unfit for military service.[16] The general's report brought the

---

12. Staatsarchiv Merseburg, rep. 74, K 3, VIII, no. 24. Reprinted in Hoppe, Kuczynski, and Waldmann, *Hardenbergs Umfrage,* 1–108, esp. 23.

13. Ibid., 25.

14. For a detailed discussion of Altenstein's activities see Anton, *Geschichte der preussischen Fabrikgesetzgebung* (reprint, Berlin, 1953), 19–24.

15. The ministry of commerce, established in 1817, had lost its independence and become a department of the ministry of interior in 1825. Final discussions of legal drafts took place in the *Staatsministerium.* See chapter 6 above; Ernst Klein, "Funktion und Bedeutung des Preussischen Staatsministeriums," *Jahrbuch für die Geschichte Mittel- und Ostdeutschlands* 9/10 (1961): 195–263.

16. Already in his 1817 memorandum, Hardenberg had emphasized that factory work rendered men unfit "to defend the fatherland in the hour of peril, when not only good will, but physical strength, presence of mind, hardening against the weather . . . are decisive for success . . ." (see Hoppe, Kuczynski, and Waldmann, *Hardenbergs Umfrage,* 24–25). By and large, the

matter to the attention of the king, who, on May 12, 1828, in a directive to his ministers Altenstein and Schuckmann, demanded that measures be considered by which the younger generation could be sheltered from factory work, to exclude the possibility of future generations being even "weaker and more stunted than the present one is believed to be."[17]

In a very comprehensive memorandum to Schuckmann, meant to serve as the basis for a joint ministerial report to the king, Altenstein laid down his ministry's opinion about child labor and his recommendations for measures to redress grievances. The document says much about the elaborate, meticulous, and laborious proceedings of Prussian officialdom, for which thoroughness was more important than speed and efficiency. It also reveals the bureaucracy's approach toward social problems.[18] In his memorandum, Altenstein, champion of culture, education, and humanity, did not question the necessity of child labor. He echoed a prevailing contemporary attitude, when arguing that child labor in factories

> was neither to be avoided, nor to be disapproved of, since production and acquisition are furthered by it, industrialists obtain inexpensive labor, parents the childrens' wages, and the children themselves will early on get accustomed to industry, endurance, and order.[19]

There were other compelling reasons why child labor was indispensable: without it, entrepreneurs would not be able to stand up to foreign competition, and factory workers could not feed all the hungry mouths in their families. Therefore, all schools for children of the poor should be connected with manual work. Yet, the minister conceded, disadvantages predominated. Physical deformities, ill health, and intellectual dullness caused by the mechanical nature of factory work, not to mention loss of youth's carefree cheerfulness, were all inevitable results of hard work at an early age.[20] Worse still were the "moral

---

influence of military considerations on factory legislation has been greatly exaggerated. Except for Horn's report, resulting in a cabinet order that temporarily gave new impetus to attempts favoring a ban on child labor, no official documents contained any trace of further army impact. Winfried Feldenkirchen, "Kinderarbeit..," (cit. ab.) 13–18, has shown that numbers of young men available for compulsory military service far exceeded the number of recruits who were actually drafted (by a ratio of three to one), so concern about the military could indeed have been of only minor importance.

17. Anton, *Geschichte der preussischen Fabrikgesetzgebung,* 51. This was by no means the only occasion on which the king found himself called on to give vent to the low appreciation in which he held his subjects.

18. July 4, 1828, "Die Anordnungen zum Schutze des Lebens und der Gesundheit der Arbeiter in Fabriken, besonders der Kinder," Staatsarchiv Merseburg, rep. 120BB, VII, I, 1, 4, vol. 1, pp. 30–37 verso.

19. Ibid., 30–30 v.

20. Ibid., 31.

damages," toward which Altenstein, classically educated man of letters with the scholar's delicate nature, as Treitschke once characterized him, proved particularly sensitive. He abhorred the "general moral waywardness," the smoking of tobacco, and a precociousness that provoked "misdemeanors of the flesh," all of which were deplorable concomitants of factory work. There could thus be little doubt that steps had to be taken to bring an end to the abuse of children in factories, since industrialists themselves obviously cared very little about the "physical, moral, and intellectual improvement" of those who worked for them.[21] Even though Altenstein was convinced of the necessity of protective legislation, he was reluctant to advocate a general bill valid for all provinces of the state. His mode of reasoning as to why this might not be feasible, doomed to failure even, was closely related to the Prussian conservatives' pattern of thought, as expounded in the *Berliner Politisches Wochenblatt.*

Like the *Wochenblatt* and Radowitz, Altenstein was convinced that legislation would have to take into account the different preconditions prevalent in different regions. "Nature, circumstances, people in different provinces vary so greatly," the minister held, "that restrictive measures may be needed in one province, while promotion and encouragement are needed in another."[22] Altenstein's specific mode of reasoning led him to a flat rejection of generally applicable laws, just as it had led *Wochenblatt* conservatives to the rejection of general laws and a constitution valid for the whole state, for this would have violated idiosyncrasies and historically grown rights of different provinces.[23] This approach to politics and social problems seems to have been the great common denominator between Prussian conservatives and the bureaucracy. And this common mode of reasoning, of viewing the world, often transcended other differences of political outlook. Ruling circles in Prussia shared a preference for piecemeal social engineering. To take into account historically grown differences had originally been an integral part of conservative, antiliberal ideology, which makes it all the more astonishing that officials in the ministry of culture, a bastion of liberal, reformist ideas as long as Altenstein remained at the helm of affairs, subscribed to it.

---

21. Ibid., 31 v.

22. Ibid., 32 v.

23. Why then, one might ask, did the 1839 *Regulativ* not remain restricted to one province? The question to limit it to the Rhine Province, where factories were most numerous and abuses most conspicuous, had indeed been discussed. Yet in the law's final discussion on December 21, 1838, between the *Oberpräsident* of the Rhine Province, Bodelschwingh, and high officials of the ministries of culture, finance, and the interior, the idea was discarded. The ordinance had to be valid for the whole monarchy, it was argued, since otherwise factories in the Rhineland might not be able to compete with those of other provinces.

206 *The Origins of the Authoritarian Welfare State in Prussia*

In this thinking, Altenstein's ministry was not exceptional. There were other significant examples of that "conservative" way of reasoning. Most remarkable among these, and illuminating for bureaucratic views on social issues, was perhaps the memorandum by August von der Heydt, Minister of Commerce between 1848 and 1862, where he expounded on his views on a "Central Commission for the Promotion of Public Welfare," the establishment of which had been proposed.[24] In his memorandum, Heydt avowed "that one of the foremost responsibilities of each government was to bring relief to the people's misery," but he warned against accomplishing this by means of "a simple formula."[25] Great ideas alone would not do "in the face of conditions which are the work of centuries, made up of an immense diversity of relations, which though different from one another are mutually dependent upon one another." To be effective, Heydt maintained, it would be necessary to take into account local differences, allow for "prejudices and errors," and content oneself with very gradual progress. Never would it be possible to apply directly one's theories to reality.[26]

Just as Arnim, Mathis, and other conservative officials had been reluctant to authorize the *Centralverein* for fear of the "exaggerated expectations" connected with it, Heydt, too, when referring to the creation of a "Central Institute for Public Welfare," conceded "that great hopes would be pinned to the creation of such an authority, but exactly these hopes are to feared." Expectations of this kind could only be dangerous, for they were based on the belief "that a system could be invented" that would bring about "fundamental improvement in the present situation of the working classes." According to Heydt, this belief in a general panacea, promising rapid relief, smacked too much of "Baboeuf" and all "false communist and socialist doctrines."

Just as Ludwig von Gerlach, Radowitz, and other Prussian conservatives felt haunted by the memory of the great French Revolution, the specter of liberalism, and demands for a liberal constitution, which, to them, embodied the triumph of abstract principles, Heydt conjured up what was to him the nightmare of the events of February 1848 in Paris. Belief in abstract systems, he claimed, had led to the proclamation of the "*droit du travail*" and later "to

---

24. July 7, 1849, "Vorschläge zur Lösung der sozialen Frage und Massnahmen wegen Abwendung eines Nothstandes, 1848–1860," Staatsarchiv Merseburg, rep. 120BB, VII, 1, no. 2, pp. 84–94. The foundation of such an institute had been suggested by *Landrat* Lavergne-Peguilhen, who had been a member of a committee, set up by the government, to find solutions to recurring misery and hardship in the province of East Prussia in 1846/47; see "Akten betreffend die Erörterung der Ursachen des in der Provinz Preussen öfters wiederkehrenden Nothstandes," Staatsarchiv Merseburg, rep. 120, VIII, 1, no. 2.

25. Staatsarchiv Merseburg, rep. 120BB, VII, 1, no. 2, p. 85–86.

26. Ibid., 86. Unless indicated otherwise, the following quotations are taken from Heydt's memorandum.

the monopolization of all industries and commerce in the hands of the state." Heydt welcomed the Prussian government's decided stance against such tendencies, which had unfortunately also taken root in his country. He strongly condemned all "general formulas of happiness" that promised swift change. Despite great pressure, Heydt argued, the government had followed the right path by confining itself "to keep an eye on the particular, eliminating or mitigating only such grievances by legislative and administrative measures that were recognized as especially ruinous."

With his insistence on the particular—on the uniqueness of circumstance and place—his rejection of abstract ideas and systems and their application to society, and his dismissal of all-encompassing state measures and total organization of available resources, Heydt argued in favor of the very same conservative concepts that had been advocated by the group around the *Berliner Politisches Wochenblatt.* At the root of conservatives' generation-long hostility toward the bureaucracy lay Prussian conservatism's orientation toward organic growth, tradition, and naturally evolved law, with its preference for "piecemeal social engineering," which was juxtaposed with the codified law of the liberal state and the "utopian social engineering" of the bureaucracy. Institutions of state and society had matured only gradually, conservatives argued, just as rights and privileges had developed historically over the course of centuries, and only the gradual process of development could endow legitimacy on them. The Prussian conservatives who advanced such vigorous criticism of the bureaucracy saw themselves divorced from the civil service by their own specific attitude toward political and social problems. They reproved officials for the application of abstract political principles on matters of state and society, and they fought against what they perceived to be the leveling forces of the emerging modern state. Yet the much vilified bureaucracy subscribed to the very same social conceptions as their conservative archenemy.

This convergence of conservative and bureaucratic concepts is surely no accident. Ruling circles in Prussia, be they freelance conservative intellectuals like the *Wochenblatt* group, or high-ranking members of the civil service, shared a common *mode de pensée,* or way of thinking, that transcended institutional barriers and differences in political outlook. This mode of thought also entered their social views, endowing them with a particular slant, an invisible common denominator, so to speak. The common bond of a Prussian *juste milieu* linked conservatives to a substantial part of the civil service and seems to have eclipsed the avowed economic liberalism of many bureaucrats, on the one hand, and the unflinching conservative antiliberalism of such men as Radowitz and the Gerlachs, on the other. This vast conservative-bureaucratic common denominator encompassed the ingredients of authoritarian, patriarchical welfare: patronage, tutelage, and regimentation. These elements were inherent in conservative thought and bureaucratic legislation. The Poor

Laws and the handling of the "Association of the Welfare of Workers" were cases in point. From seemingly opposed starting positions—officials' economic liberalism versus conservatism—they arrived at similar conclusions. The Gerlachs', Radowitz's and Wagener's hostility toward the civil service, based on the assumption that officials were champions of the very principles in which they, the conservatives, had made out a mortal danger for society, rested partly on an error of vision. They had more in common than they realized.

Having emphasized the need to allow for different regional preconditions, Altenstein proposed the establishment of "special commissions" by which this could be accomplished. These committees should serve the purpose of regulating relations between workers and industrialists and should "provide for the physical, moral, and intellectual flourishing of factory children."[27] Two facts are noteworthy in connection with them. First, Altenstein stressed the commission's function of controlling the execution of a prospective factory law, which seemed a special preoccupation with the ministry of culture, for the concept to control protective child legislation reemerged in official documents in an 1844 memorandum of Altenstein's successor, Eichhorn. In it Eichhorn underlined the necessity to "create special organs supervising factories."[28] In final discussions on the factory bill, in which the Rhenish *Oberpräsident* Ernst von Bodelschwingh took an active part, the concept of control never surfaced. The reason why officials in the ministry of culture were so insistent on it was twofold: on the one hand, they did not want to relinquish control in the matter to the ministry of the interior, and control commissions were a means of keeping a foot in the door; on the other, the ministry of culture had a stake in seeing school attendance enforced, which could be accomplished only by controlling organs. Second, the composition of envisaged commissions is worth noting: crucial positions were to be held by school inspectors, members of regional school boards, and medical officers.[29] This was in keeping with the important role education played in contemporary conceptions for the elevation of lower classes. For the 1839 *Regulativ,* school attendance and education in general constituted key factors. *Oberpräsident* Bodelschwingh, instrumental in the final preparation of the law, also emphasized the need to pass "an ordinance to secure sufficient school attendance and religious education for children in factories."[30] More than any other single factor, elementary education for chil-

---

27. July 4, 1828, "Die Anordnungen zum Schutze des Lebens und der Gesundheit der Arbiter in Fabriken, besonders der Kinder" (1822–46), Staatsarchiv Merseburg, rep. 120BB, VII, 1, 4, vol. 1, p. 32 v.

28. December 14, 1844, at "Votum Eichhorns an Flottwell," Staatsarchiv Merseburg, rep. 120BB, VII, 1, 4, vol. 1, pp. 284–86, esp. 284.

29. July 4, 1828, Staatsarchiv Merseburg, rep. 120BB, VII, 1, 4, vol. 1, p. 33.

30. August 14, 1837, "Die Anordnungen zum Schutze des Lebens," Staatsarchiv Merseburg, rep. 120BB, VII, 1, 4, vol. 1, pp. 113–18; esp. 113 verso. One of the main tenets of the

dren, obligatory under the General Code of 1794, was the propelling force behind the law and leitmotif in bureaucratic reports.[31]

Notably, officials in the ministry of culture never tired of pointing out the importance of primary education and compulsory school attendance, which was frequently mentioned in the same breath with "moral protection for children" against the morally corrosive influences of factory life. Officials considered education as a dike against the waywardness and dissolute conduct into which factory life might lure children. When advocating the establishment of factory schools, Sunday schools, or a combination between factory work and school instruction, civil servants paid no attention to the overburdening of children by the double strain. Their situation was indeed far from enviable. Factory *reglements* regimenting every aspect of the workday and imposing penalties on the most trivial transgression inform us of their slavelike lot.[32]

More than ten years since Altenstein's 1828 memorandum had to pass before protective legislation for children in factories became enacted. Militia Lieutenant General von Horn's report, Frederick William's subsequent cabinet order, and Altenstein's fervent advocacy of the urgency of a factory bill had all been to no avail. For almost a decade, Commerce Minister Schuckmann's delaying tactics brought the bureaucratic machine to a standstill. Only Bodelschwingh's initiative—his reports and motions from the Rhine Province to central authorities in Berlin—the activities of the Rhenish industrialist

---

factory bill was to enforce school attendance. Article 2 of the *Regulativ* stated that anyone unable to furnish proof of regular school attendance (of three years), rudimentary knowledge in writing, and fluent reading skills must not be accepted for factory work, unless over sixteen years of age. On May 23, 1840, it was decreed by the school board of the province of Brandenburg that parents who wanted their children to work in factories were obliged to obtain specially prepared forms on which teachers had to certify that the required three years in school had been completed. Certification was indispensable for employment. See "Die Beschäftigung jugendlicher Arbeiter in Fabriken," Staatsarchiv Merseburg, rep. 120BB, VII, 3, 1, vol. 1 (1835–46), p. 130.

31. Even before protective child legislation was passed, school attendance in the industrialized central and western parts of Prussia was already higher than in the agrarian east. In 1816, 61 percent of an age group in East Prussia and Pomerania complied with compulsory school attendance and 42 percent in West Prussia, but over 70 percent in Brandenburg, about 70 percent in Westfalia, and 84.8 percent in the province of Saxony. Figures for the Rhine Province rose from 49 percent in 1816, when the Rhineland had just become part of Prussia, to 86.4 percent in 1846. The sections of the *Allgemeine Landrecht* concerning compulsory school attendance (teil 2, titel 12) were extended to cover newly acquired parts of the monarchy by a cabinet order of May 14, 1825. Even though school attendance increased considerably in all provinces between 1816 and 1846, it remained higher in the central and western parts of the monarchy. The agrarian east continued lagging behind. See *Mitteilungen des Statistischen Bureaus in Berlin* 1 (1849): 47; Ernst Engel, *Beiträge zur Statistik des Unterrichtswesens im preussischen Staat und seinen Provinzen* (Berlin, 1867), 24.

32. See, for example, "Reglement für die Spinnerei Nauendahl," Staatsarchiv Merseburg, rep. 120BB, VII, 1, 4, vol. 1, p. 192. Most factory *reglements* contained such a multitude of rules and regulations that it was virtually impossible to pay heed to all of them.

Schuckmann (his publication of an article about the suicide attempt of a young girl working in a factory), and the subsequent proposition of the Rhenish Diet of which Schuchard was a member gave the final impulse for the enactment of the law.[33]

Official correspondence on the new regulation's effectiveness and on whether it needed to be amended (arrangements for that had already been made under article ten) continued unabated throughout the 1840s.[34] The *Regulativ* was widely publicized to guarantee its effectiveness; regional *Regierungen* reprinted it in their *Amtsblätter* (gazettes) supplemented by *Ausführungs-verordnungen* (ordinances of execution), in which police authorities were instructed to supervise compliance with the law and undertake audits once every three months, while *Landräte* were instructed to submit yearly reports on the matter.[35] These controls resulted in the discovery of a number of abuses and violations of the law, which soon raised doubts among officials in the responsible ministries of culture, the interior, and finance about whether existing legal provisions were sufficient. But it was only after the Revolution of 1848, and then under substantial participation of the newly established Prussian parliament, that further industrial legislation was passed.[36]

Nevertheless, the Prussian factory bill of 1839 had an undeniable effect. Numbers of children employed in factories sank continually after the mid 1840s—from 31,064 in 1846, accounting for 6.45 percent of the work force, to 29,149 in 1849 and 21,945 in 1852, a mere 3.3 percent of all those industrially employed.[37] The decrease of numbers of children employed in iron, steel, and textile industries has equally been attributed to technical progress. Yet this

33. See "Die Anordnungen zum Schutze des Lebens und der Gesundheit," Staatsarchiv Merseburg, rep. 120BB, VII, 1, 4, vol. 1; "Die Beschäftigung jugendlicher Arbeiter in Fabriken, Berg-, Hütten- und Pochwerken, 1835–1846," Staatsarchiv Merseburg, rep. 120BB, VII, 3, 1, vol. 1; Anton, *Geschichte der preussischen Fabrikgesetzgebung,* 19–77.

34. See "Die Beschäftigung jugendlicher Arbeiter in Fabriken, Berg-, Hütten- und Pochwerken, 1835–1846," Staatsarchiv Merseburg, rep. 120BB, VII, 3, 1, vol. 1; "Akten betreffend die Beschäftigung jugendlicher Arbeiter in Fabriken..," Staatsarchiv Merseburg, rep. 120BB, VII, 3, 1, vol. 2 (July 1846–March 15, 1848).

35. See "Die Beschäftigung jugendlicher Arbeiter," Staatsarchiv Merseburg, rep. 120BB, VII, 3, 1, vol. 1 (1835–46), pp. 244–45, "Amtsblatt der Regierung Aachen zu Fabrikarbeiten vom 20. Juni 1844."

36. See Heinrich Volkmann, *Die Arbeiterfrage in preussischen Abgeordnetenhaus 1848–1869* (Berlin, 1968). The law of May 16, 1853, raised the minimum age for factory work from nine to twelve years and reduced working hours from ten to six for those under the age of fourteen. Factory inspection to supervise enforcement of ordinances was equally introduced.

37. See *Mitteilungen des Statistischen Bureaus in Berlin* 5 (1852): 249–51; Gladen, *Geschichte der Sozialpolitik in Deutschland,* (Wiesbaden, 1974), 40; Feldenkirchen, "Kinderarbeit," 18. After the 1853 legislation, numbers sank further to 16,147 in 1856 and 12,592 in 1858. This drop in the workforce was compensated by increasing employment of women in factories (from about 57,000 in 1846 to almost 89,000 in 1858).

accounted at best for a small portion of the fall, since in England and the kingdom of Saxony, numbers of children employed in the very same industries rose during that time period. While 7.27 percent of all factory workers in the kingdom of Saxony, where child labor was not restricted until 1861, were under the age of fourteen (1846), the percentage for the adjacent Prussian province of Saxony lay at 2.1 percent.[38] Prussian factory legislation not only had an effect reflected in these numbers but it also broke the path for similar laws in other states of the German Confederation: the Southern German states of Baden and Bayern followed suit with similar legislation in 1840.[39] Even in comparison to industrially more advanced states, the Prussian factory act was relatively progressive. English factory legislation had been a model and example for Prussian officials, as long compilations in official records document.[40] Though English industry was older, more highly developed, and had changed the landscape and society more profoundly than Prussia's, the 1839 *Regulativ* was in a sense more comprehensive than English factory acts. While English legislation was limited to children working in textile industries, the Prussian law was all-encompassing.[41]

Despite their belief in economic laissez-faire, Prussian officials had passed protective legislation for children in factories at a time when Prussian industry was still in its infancy. As official documents clearly show, the 1839 *Regulativ*, relatively progressive even in comparison with more advanced countries, was an offspring of the authoritarian welfare state and was created by a mixture of educational and moral considerations that were so typical for the bureaucracy. That officials needed incentives other than mere humanitarian ones to intervene on behalf of factory workers became evident from their inactivity regarding the banning of the *Trucksystem,* a system of exchange and barter under which workers were forced to accept the industrialists' goods in

38. In the kingdom of Saxony, over 1 percent of all children under the age of fourteen were employed in factories, while respective figures for the Prussian province of Saxony lay at a fifth of 1 percent. See *Mitteilungen des Statistischen Bureaus in Berlin* 2 (1849): 263–64; Feldenkirchen, "Kinderarbeit," 20–22.

39. That Prussia was a precursor in factory legislation was all the more astonishing when considering its image as the model state of economic liberalism in the German Confederation. Prussia was often perceived as a country with a strange amalgamation of economic liberalism and political repression, a thesis also advanced by Werner Conze, "Das Spannungsfeld von Staat und Gesellschaft im Vormärz," in *Staat und Gesellschaft in Deutschen Vormärz* (Stuttgart, 1962), 243.

40. See "Die Beschäftigung jugendlicher Arbeiter," Staatsarchiv Merseburg, rep. 120BB, VII, 3, 1, vol. 1 (1835–46), 86–88 verso, "Zusammenfassung über die Gesetzgebung Englands über die Beschäftigung der Kinder in Fabriken."

41. See Anton, *Geschichte der preussischen Fabrikgesetzgebung,* 76–78; Feldenkirchen, "Kinderarbeit," 12. English laws, however, were more specific, banning work for children under nine (just as in Prussia), and setting a limit of forty-eight hours per week for children under thirteen and sixty-nine hours for youths under eighteen. But these restrictions applied only to children and adolescents working in cotton, flax, and silk factories.

return for their labor. Since commodities obtained rarely constituted the true equivalent of actual wages, workers' petitions to local and regional authorities were quite frequent.[42] Despite motions of the Westfalian (1837) and Rhenish provincial diets (1843), and despite petitions of the Rhenish *Fabrikengericht*'s president (1844) and the Düsseldorf *Regierung* (1844–45), central authorities refused to prohibit the *Trucksystem.* The final *Truckverbot,* frequently discussed during the 1830s and 1840s, but always postponed with reference to the economy's self-regulating mechanism, was not passed until 1849. And then it was enacted not as separate law but in the larger frame of revised general regulations of trade.[43]

Despite long hesitation to ban payment by goods, the heyday of laissez-faire was over by the 1840s. Growing pauperism and the increasing hardships of the 1840s, an emergency situation in East Prussia, misery in the Silesian mountains followed by the weavers' uprising, and the new king's seeming interest in social issues and growing public concern about pauperism (where possible combined with participation in social policy matters) pushed officials into more active involvement in social questions. In addition to laws on "Poor Relief and Freedom of Movement" (1842/43) for rural paupers, the 1839 *Regulativ* for industrial laborers, and the bureaucracy's disputes with the "Association for the Welfare of Workers," there remained the question of trading regulations for Prussian craftsmen.

Freedom of trade had not been popular everywhere, least of all among established master craftsmen organized in guilds.[44] Before the introduction of freedom of trade in 1810, guilds had regulated every aspect of the artisan's existence. Training of apprentices, admission of new masters in towns, "moral" conduct of journeymen and masters, and even provisions of deceased craftsmen's impoverished widows had to be sanctioned by the guild.[45] In provinces where the new trade laws were applied, these corporations threatened to lose their function. After 1815, freedom of trade was in force in the Rhine Province

---

42. See "Die Entlöhnung der Fabrikarbeiter mit Waren," Staatsarchiv Merseburg, rep. 120BB, VII, 3, 4, vol. 2 (1835–47). The file is replete with petitions to the authorities to abolish the *Trucksystem.* See also Anton, *Geschichte der preussischen Fabrikgesetzgebung,* 157–86.

43. "Allgemeine Gewerbeordnung vom 9. Februar 1849," in *Gesetz-Sammlung für die königlich Preussischen Staaten* (1849). Articles 50–55 and article 75 of the "Verordnung, betreffend die Errichtung von Gewerberäthen und verschiedene Abänderungen der allgemeinen Gewerbeordnung." See also Thun, "Beiträge zur Geschichte," 68–71.

44. See Nipperdey, *Deutsche Geschichte 1800–1866* (Munich, 1983) 210–19; Koselleck, *Preussen zwischen Reform und Revolution,* 596–600; Otto Büsch, *Industrialisierung und Gewerbe im Raum Berlin/Brandenburg 1800–1850* (Berlin, 1971); Jürgen Bergmann, "Das Zunftwesen nach der Einführung der Gewerbefreiheit," in *Preussische Reformen 1807–1820* ed. Barbara Vogel (Königstein, 1980), 150–68; Ilja Mieck, *Preussische Gewerbepolitik in Berlin 1806–1844* (Berlin, 1965).

45. See part 1, chapter 1 above, on the *Berliner Politisches Wochenblatt.*

(due to French influence), in parts of Westfalia, and in the old provinces of Brandenburg, Silesia, and East and West Prussia; but in the provinces of Posen, Saxony, and parts of Pomerania and Westfalia, traditional guild codes still regulated trade. The bureaucracy refrained from imposing freedom of trade on all territories, in part because of the strong resistance of provincial diets and towns, even though freedom of trade became more widely accepted after the foundation of the German Custom's Union (1834). Yet continued demands for strengthening and reviving of old guild ties were not completely wasted on officials, since the trading regulations of 1845 reflected some of these concerns.[46] There, provisions were made for the formation of new guildlike corporations, the *Innungen*, without, however, making membership obligatory as it had been in the old days. Craftsmen did not have to be affiliated with them to carry on their trade. The objective of the new corporations was to supervise "admission, training, and conduct of apprentices and journeymen," to help widows and orphans of deceased members, and to administer the various funds set aside for needy members.[47]

Overall, the *Allgemeine Gewerbeordnung* of 1845 was a compromise between the town burghers' demands for restoration of guilds and the ideas of economically liberal officials who favored freedom of trade. Though freedom of trade had been maintained in principle, the *Gewerbeordnung* set the course for increasing state interference. The 1849 amendment to the *Gewerbeordnung* that contained the prohibition of the *Trucksystem* restricted freedom of trade further by strengthening the positions of new corporations, which obtained the right to control admission and examination of all apprentices, and by raising necessary qualifications for journeymen and masters. A renaissance of the venerable guild age seemed almost possible.[48] Demands of master craftsmen and journeymen, who feared pauperization and yearned for the corporation's protective shelter, had played an important part in this; it could even be argued that officials yielded to popular pressure by strengthening *Innungen*. Among craftsmen—at midcentury all trades combined employed a million men in a country of sixteen and a half million—demands to keep corporations going,

---

46. "Allgemeine Gewerbeordnung vom 17. Januar 1845," in *Gesetz- Sammlung für die königlich Preussischen Staaten* (1845). The Prussian *Staatsrat* strongly favored corporations, since they were believed to counteract "antisocial tendencies of so-called proletarians" (see Koselleck, *Preussen zwischen Reform und Revolution,* 599).

47. *Allgemeine Gewerbeordnung,* titel VI, article 104. Corporations were to be set up in close collaboration with municipal authorities, "under supervision of the government," while their statutes had to be approved by the bureaucracy (article 105). Overall, motives of order and control, though never spelled out, were an important underlying factor in the trade regulations. The *Allgemeine Gewerbeordnung* also led to the establishment of many new corporations.

48. See also Mack Walker, *German Home Towns* (Ithaca, 1971), 307–404; Margret Tilmann, "Der Einfluss des Revolutionsjahres 1848 auf die preussische Gewerbe- und Sozialgesetzgebung" (Ph.D. diss., University of Berlin, 1935).

dispense with freedom of trade, maintain strict aptitude tests to control admission to corporations, and make membership in *Innungen* compulsory remained strong.

In 1861, fifteen corporations of the city of Görlitz in Silesia sent a petition to the upper chamber of the Berlin Parliament, which constitutes an eloquent and concise summary of arguments against freedom of trade. Petitioners protested against the threatening reintroduction "of total freedom of trade," as this would "lead to certain ruin of the already declining artisanage."[49] Masters of corporations maintained that freedom of trade, introduced in 1810, had brought in its wake "unrestricted, anarchic freedom, which for well-nigh forty years has oppressed tradesmen and the general public alike."[50] And was it not a well-established fact that ever since 1824, vociferous complaints had been launched against freedom of trade, for it destroyed the craftsman's dignity by making certificates of qualification redundant, undermined the "inner discipline" of the entire profession, and corrupted professional competence, efficiency, and morale, since ever swelling numbers of men flocking into the trades brought about oppressive competition?[51] Did not lawyers and doctors have their qualifying tests, indispensable for practicing their professions, and did not "the ordinary salaried clerk" need his license, which was part of his professional honor? By opening up the trades to everyone regardless of qualification, the artisan's product, an object of sincere pride under the old system, would suffer immeasurably, as the craftsman, to withstand stiff and unfair competition, would be forced to use inferior materials and thus to manufacture goods of poor quality.[52] This, petitioners were convinced, would be doubly harmful—to the general public, which would obtain low quality products, and to the artisan profession in general, which would lose all public esteem. Imperfect manufacturing of certain goods, "of a boiler, a wheel, a lock, an anchor, a rope," might be of fatal consequence to the user. In addition, a great influx of unskilled and unqualified newcomers into the profession could only have the result that "the so-called proletariat grows excessively."[53] With wife and child, they will end up becoming a burden on public poor relief, the Görlitz master craftsmen predicted. They would contribute to the proletarization of an entire professional class and thus only harm artisans' public reputation further. The undersigned craftsmen therefore insisted on retaining corporations for tradesman. Should parliament deem a change of current legislation necessary, it ought to

---

49. February 1, 1861, "Akten betreffend die gewerbliche Verordnung vom 9. Februar 1849 und die Anträge auf eine Ausführung, Revision, Ergänzung," Staatsarchiv Merseburg, rep. 120B, I, 1, vol. 6, no. 62, pp. 51–61 verso, "Petition von 15 Innungen der Stadt Görlitz," esp. p. 51 v.
50. Ibid., 53.
51. Ibid., 54, 56 v., 58.
52. Ibid., 57–57 v.
53. Ibid., 59.

consider introducing compulsory *Innungen,* so that "every tradesman be placed under obligation to enter a corporation."[54]

Just as conservatives of the *Berliner Politisches Wochenblatt,* the representatives of the corporations favored the reestablishment of obligatory guilds, for "organic control of all members of the artisan class" would go beyond the professional sphere and encompass surveillance of "conduct of this class [artisans] outside regular business activities."[55] That corporations would contribute their share to the maintenance of "law and order" as the Görlitz guildsmen promised must have struck a sympathetic cord in many officials, and the relicensing of corporations in 1845 and further consolidation of their position in 1849 must be seen in this context. Order, control, and surveillance had always been major concerns of the Prussian civil service, and if the bureaucracy found itself unable to perform these tasks adequately due to the shortage of its staff, which was acute in the 1840s, other organizations were naturally welcome to share the burden, especially if they were as loyal to the state as artisan guilds were generally believed to be.

The emergency situation in East Prussia caused by successive harvest failures in 1844/45 offers one final telling example of the conflict between those officials favoring a laissez-faire approach and those advocating that the state was responsible for alleviating the plight of paupers.[56] The committee of inquiry, set up to analyze causes of the disaster and submit recommendations for improvement, was chaired by the *Oberpräsident* of the province. It consisted of eight high officials and seven *ständische Mitglieder,* mostly *Landräte* and estate owners.[57] Between December 3, 1846, and January 15, 1847, when the final report was submitted, the commission met at regular intervals in the royal castle of the East Prussian capital, Königsberg.

Manifold causes for recurring misery in the province were soon established. East Prussia still suffered from the immense drain on resources it had sustained during the Napoleonic Wars, when parts of the province had been turned into a desert by the Grande Armée on its march to Russia. There was acute shortage of roads and other means of communication, resulting in a scarcity of internal markets and vast price differences, while high Russian customs barriers since 1821 had strangled trades in the smaller towns, notably

---

54. Ibid., 61.
55. Ibid., 60–61.
56. "Akten betreffend die Erörterung der Ursachen des in der Provinz Preussen öfters wiederkehrenden Nothstandes, 1847–1866," Staatsarchiv Merseburg, rep. 120, VIII, 1, no. 2, pp. 10–82 verso. See also Rolf Engels, *Die Preussische Verwaltung von Kammer und Regierung Gumbinnen 1724–1870* (Cologne and Berlin, 1974), 108–16.
57. Staatsarchiv Merseburg, rep. 120, VIII, 1, no. 2, pp. 10–10 v.

linen manufacturing.[58] Among further causes cited for East Prussia's depression was a lack of capital, generally low industrial and mercantile standards, and increasing proletarization of the formerly unfree peasantry, who had lost their shelter together with their shackles when liberated. There was the pitifully low level of elementary education among peasants, rapid population increase brought about by "the all too thoughtless conclusion of bonds of matrimony" among the "uncultivated classes,"[59] and finally a shortage of towns. In contrast to other provinces, none of East Prussia's rural communities had attained town status, though the rural population had swollen considerably.[60]

The commission's findings were unambiguous: East Prussia needed better roads, improvement of its elementary schools, and marriage restrictions for the poor. In short, remedies were suggested for each of the numerous defects. But who was to be responsible for the elimination of these countless shortcomings? Who would foot the undoubtedly substantial bill to set all grievances right? Was it the state, as the General Code of 1794 decreed, or the commune and the provincial poor house, as the Poor Laws of 1842 suggested?[61] The matter was discussed in the session of December 14, 1846, which ended in insoluble disagreement. The *Allgemeine Landrecht*, it was held, dated from the last century, when emergencies comparable to the one at hand were unknown; therefore it could not constitute a legal basis. But was it in doubt that the state had the obligation "to make provisions for the maintenance of needy citizens," and was not the family, the commune, and the provincial poorhouse part of the state's organism?[62] If the state had helped overcome an internal state of emergency in the past, "considerations of higher state policy," not legal obligations, had been responsible for that.[63] When it came to the final vote on who was legally obliged to help in emergencies, the committee was split right down the middle. Eight opted that the state was legally bound to help, one member argued that it was the duty of regular poor relief to cover the emergency, and the remaining seven maintained that there was a loophole in legislation. Unfor-

---

58. Ibid., 13 v.–16.

59. Ibid., 20. To obtain a complete picture of the situation, local merchants and businessmen from Königsberg were consulted to report to the commission "on matters of commerce and trade" (ibid., 19 v.).

60. Ibid., 16 v.–33 v. In East Prussia, the rural population had been growing twice as fast as the population in towns since 1819 (ibid., 60). The province had the lowest density of artisans among all Prussian provinces; in the kingdom of Saxony, for example, there were three times as many craftsmen per 1,000 inhabitants (see also Nipperdey, *Deutsche Geschichte 1800–1866*, 213). According to commission findings, the fragmentation of formerly large holdings into small plots of land in the wake of the Prussian reforms was responsible for the tremendous increase of agrarian paupers.

61. Staatsarchiv Merseburg, rep. 120, VIII, 1, no. 2, pp. 40–43.

62. Ibid., 40–41.

63. Ibid., 40 v.

tunately, the minutes of the proceedings fail to indicate whether the officials on the committee voted differently from the *ständisch* members.

The committee then questioned whether it was necessary to introduce legal requirements to aid depressed areas in emergency situations. Again the commission was divided. Some emphasized that automatic state help was bound to exert a demoralizing influence on the population's work ethic. Would not the knowledge that maintenance was furnished by authorities in any event have a paralyzing effect on paupers' own activities? This eminently liberal argument that the most effective help was self-help, that provisions made by the state only had the effect of stifling the will and activity of the needy, who were thus deprived of incentives to work, was advanced by several committee members.[64] Yet, others objected, in past emergencies, the state had always shouldered relief willingly, mostly because the means of provinces and communes proved insufficient and because communal funds would be critically depleted in deprived areas. Therefore, state help, be it only in the form of a onetime donation to a province, would have to be mandatory in the future as well. Most of the already impoverished communes would hardly be in a position to help, it was argued, and they had a right to be sheltered from the onslaught of the poor. Committee members never conjured up the specter of communism, never saw in rural proletarians more than a threat to the province's affluence, never sensed the danger of political upheaval as the result of mass proletarization. Masses of paupers were innocuous, the men convened in Königsberg's castle believed, as long as they were not led by "subversive *Literaten*," whom officials had come to dread so much in the wake of the weavers' uprising.

To these arguments, other committee members retorted that the state should be entirely liberated of any obligation for emergency aid, which ought to be assumed solely by communes, districts, and provincial poorhouses. Such a solution would give communes a great deal of control over its poor and strengthen their communal spirit and the *ständisch* element—suggestions already familiar from deliberations on the Poor Laws of 1842. The final vote reflected the divisiveness of the discussion: seven committee members argued that communes ought to be bound by law to help in emergency situations, while nine held that this was the obligation of the state.

The committee's work proved to be of little avail. Part of the blame for the failure could be attributed to East Prussia's woefully incompetent *Oberpräsident* Bötticher and to the outbreak of the revolution one year after the committee finished its work, but the main reason for the failure lay somewhere else.

---

64. Ibid., 41. Automatic state help would lead to a situation where people "would fail to save for the winter, never strive to earn their livelihood away from home, nor pursue it with the necessary zeal, and await the future in dull, weary inactivity" (ibid).

True, the ambiguous legal situation led to the mutual blocking of decisions, and Prussia still suffered from an acute shortage of financial resources; money was a scarce commodity, and parsimonious economic policy was therefore imperative. Nevertheless, major causes for bureaucratic inefficiency lay within the civil service itself. In the case of the East Prussian emergency, there were two opposing schools of thought in the apparatus regarding social policy measures: adherents of economic laissez-faire, favoring self-help and state abstinence; and supporters of state intervention. This opposition consisted of deep-seated liberal convictions, on the one hand, and the notion that the state had the duty to intervene and alleviate social misery, on the other. In the interbureaucratic disputes over the *Centralverein* statutes, the dividing lines had been determined by different issues, but in each instance, the salient fact was the same, namely, the profound division within the bureaucracy itself. Thus it was ultimately the divisions within the apparatus itself that incapacitated the Prussian bureaucracy.[65]

Reinhart Koselleck once argued that the civil service, with the vast spectrum of different opinions represented in it, resembled a kind of parliament.[66] But the bureaucracy was no parliament, where conflicting opinions might be fruitful. Disagreement among officials could result in gridlock, since there was no modus operandi to break the stalemate. Besides, both the conflicts of ideology, however veiled, that have been noted in the case of the *Centralverein* and the mutually exclusive views in the East Prussian emergency went beyond stimulating exchange. They cast doubt on the implicitly postulated monolithic character of the bureaucracy. In past research on the Prussian civil service, a corollary to the axiom of impartiality was the more or less implicit assumption that the bureaucracy formed a socially homogeneous entity, internally united, and imbued with a strong sense of collective identity.

Otto Hintze, in his numerous studies on the Prussian bureaucracy, constantly emphasized independence of judgement, esprit de corps, and the "*un-bedingte Sachlichkeit*" of a civil service, which he portrayed as a monolithic bloc, coherent in itself, and invested with the strong common ideal of service for the people without regard for inequalities.[67] In Hintze's understanding, the

---

65. Efficiency of bureaucratic intervention could additionally be hampered by scruples to make introduced measures applicable to all situations and valid for all provinces, as in the case of the 1839 *Regulativ,* where officials had argued that legislation had to allow for specific regional features and do justice to historic circumstance.

66. See Koselleck, "Staat und Gesellschaft im preussischen Vormärz," in *Moderne Preussische Geschichte 1648–1947,* 3 vols. ed. Otto Büsch and Walter Neugebauer (Berlin and New York, 1981), 379–415 (see also part 2, chapter 5, on the bureaucracy in general).

67. See Otto Hintze's numerous articles on the Prussian bureaucracy in his *Gesammelte Abhandlungen,* 3 vols. (Göttingen, 1962–67), notably his long essay "Der Beamtenstand," in *Soziologie und Geschichte,* vol. 2 of *Gesammelte Abhandlungen,* 66–126; Jürgen Kocka, "Otto

bureaucracy stood morally far above the divisions of society. Hintze's ideal-typical view, his constant emphasis on the "integrity, sense of duty, selfless work ethic, public spirit, uncompromising sense of justice, and unassuming loyalty," and on the "patriae inserviendo consumor," naturally favored his tendency to view the bureaucracy as a monolithic bloc.[68] This premise of the monolithic nature of the Prussian civil service, which ultimately goes back to Hegel's notion of officials as the universal estate, was naturally perpetuated by historians who viewed the bureaucracy with a kindly eye. Even Reinhart Koselleck, notwithstanding his differentiated and detailed examination of the apparatus, described the bureaucracy as "a socially homogenous and intellectually closely aligned group, possessing through its collegial organization a strong sense of collective identity."[69] Ironically, this concept of the bureaucracy's monolithic nature was never questioned by such historians as Eckhart Kehr and Hans Rosenberg, who achieved fame as uncompromising critics of the Prussian state apparatus, but it was perpetuated by them, only this time with reversed premises.[70] Only in the last few years has our image of the civil service become more complex. Barbara Vogel underscored the influence of a strong conservative group in the civil service before 1820, and Hans-Ulrich Wehler highlighted the antagonism of liberal and conservative groups within the apparatus.[71] Ideological and political conflicts persisted as long as the bureaucracy remained "in power," that is, until the constitutional state that emerged after the revolution put an end to bureaucratic rule. The exigencies of government were bound to create chasms among administrators. Plato's guardian class, with which Prussian officials have occasionally been compared, was spared the harsh test of reality. It, too, would have foundered on the stern rock of real issues.

Hintze, Max Weber, und das Problem der Bürokratie," in *Otto Hintze und die moderne Geschichtswissenschaft,* ed. Otto Büsch and Michael Erbe (Berlin, 1983), 150–89, esp. 154.

68. "Rechtschaffenheit, Pflichtgefühl, uneigennütziger Fleiss, Gemeinsinn, unbeugsames Rechtsgefühl, und schlichte Treue," in Hintze, "Der Beamtenstand," 77.

69. See Jonathan Sperber, "State and Civil Society in Prussia: Thoughts on a New Edition of Reinhart Koselleck's *Preussen zwischen Reform und Revolution," Journal of Modern History* 57 (1985): 278–97, esp. 278.

70. See Eckhart Kehr, "Zur Genesis der preussischen Bürokratie und des Rechtsstaates," in Kehr, *Der Primat der Innenpolitik: Gesammelte Aufsätze zur preussisch-deutschen Sozialgeschichte,* ed. Hans-Ulrich Wehler (Berlin, 1965); Rosenberg, *Bureaucracy, Aristocracy, and Autocracy: The Prussian Experience, 1660–1815* (Cambridge, Mass., 1958). Even though both stressed the repressive character of the Prussian state apparatus, their examinations were still based on the assumption that the bureaucracy was monolithic in character.

71. Barbara Vogel, "Beamtenkonservatismus: Sozial- und verfassungsgeschichtliche Voraussetzungen der Parteien in Preussen im frühen 19. Jahrhundert," in *Deutscher Konservatismus im 19. und 20. Jahrhundert,* ed., Dirk Stegmann, Bernd-Jürgen Wendt, Peter-Christian Witt (Bonn, 1983), 1–33; Hans-Ulrich Wehler, *Deutsche Gesellschaftsgeschichte,* 2:297–322.

CHAPTER 9

The Bureaucracy and Social Legislation after the Revolution

The position of the bureaucracy changed fundamentally with the transition to the constitutional state after the revolution. The civil service, which formerly had possessed legislative and executive functions, was now relegated to an organ of the executive, charged only with implementing government orders.[1] Before the revolution, "bureaucracy" had virtually been synonymous with the state per se. But in the 1850s, it was only an important component of the state. There are occasional references to the "absolutist bureaucratic regime" of the *Reaktionszeit* in Prussia (1850–58), but these are merely due to the fact that the Prussian prime minister of the reactionary period, Otto von Manteuffel, is commonly regarded as a champion of the Prussian administration, since he was less concerned with the resurrection of *ständisch* privileges than with the consolidation of firm state authority, manifested in kingdom, bureaucracy, and army. The authority of the bureaucracy in shaping domestic politics had been lost for good after 1848. Moreover, the postrevolutionary bureaucracy lacked the will to form and remodel the state from its very foundations, a will once found in leading bureaucratic circles after Prussia's military collapse in 1806–7. The defeat by French armies at Jena had discredited monarchy and army; the Revolution of 1848 signified the failure of restoration and pre-March Prussia. The blame for that failure was squarely laid at the doorstep of the civil service, which, after all, had run the country after 1815. The successful initial stage of the revolution and the events of March 1848 in Berlin, the most humbling

---

1. See Günther Grünthal, *Parlamentarismus in Preussen 1848/49–1857/58* (Düsseldorf, 1982); Grünthal, "Grundlagen konstitutionellen Regiments in Preussen 1848–1867: Zum Verhältnis von Regierung, Bürokratie und Parlament zwischen Revolution und Reichsgründung," in *Regierung, Bürokratie und Parlament in Preussen und Deutschland von 1848 bis zur Gegenwart,* ed. Gerhard A. Ritter (Düsseldorf, 1983), 41–56; Fritz Hartung, *Staatsbildende Kräfte der Neuzeit* (Berlin, 1961), 223–75.

hours in the history of the Hohenzollern monarchy,[2] clearly demonstrated the failure of bureaucratic rule. The grand dream of the reformers to create a new Prussia from the ashes of the old had not been realized. After 1848 political leadership devolved on the crown, especially the so-called *Kamarilla* around Frederick William IV (which partly consisted of the erstwhile members of the circle around the *Berliner Politisches Wochenblatt*),[3] Prime Minister Otto von Manteuffel and the heads of the various ministries, united in the *Staatsministerium*. This latter body continued initiating legislation, but the formulation and passing of laws was now largely in the hands of the lower chamber of parliament, the *Abgeordnetenhaus* (or *Landtag*), where legal drafts submitted by the *Staatsministerium* were debated and modified.

After the revolution, Prussia became a *Parteienstaat*, which introduced the problem of the political legitimacy of higher officials. From now on, the civil service (at least in its higher ranks) was expected to support the general political course of the government and to enforce its measures. This also meant that the idealism that many claimed had once pervaded the Prussia of the reformers now became immaterial, viewed as merely unnecessary baggage. In its stead, a functional state-centeredness characterized the civil service.[4] A bureaucracy that formerly governed was superseded by one that only administered.

The politics of high-echelon officials first presented a problem for the liberal Auerswald-Hansemann ministry (June 25–September 20, 1848), which was determined to remove dyed-in-the-wool conservatives from office. During the revolution, on July 14, 1848, the secret *Konduitenlisten* were abolished,[5] and three conservative *Oberpräsidenten* were removed from office on political grounds.[6] This forcible retirement created a precedent for the introduction of stricter disciplinary legislation for civil servants, first by ordinance in 1849,

---

2. See Hagen Schulze's vivid description of the humiliation of Frederick William IV in his *Der Weg zum Nationalstaat: Die deutsche Nationalbewegung vom 18. Jahrhundert bis zur Reichsgründung* (Munich, 1985), 9–49.

3. This circle of conservative advisers consisted of Leopold and Ernst Ludwig von Gerlach, Edwin von Manteuffel, Hans von Kleist-Retzow, and Senfft von Pilsach.

4. Ernst Rudolf Huber, *Deutsche Verfassungsgeschichte seit 1789*, 3d ed., vol. 3 (Stuttgart, 1988); Hagen Schulze, "Preussen von 1850 bis 1871: Verfassungsstaat und Reichsgründung," in *Handbuch der Preussischen Geschichte*, vol. 2, ed. Otto Büsch (Berlin, 1992), 303–71.

5. See "Die Konduitenlisten, Personal-Nachweisungen über die Verhältnisse und Leistungen der Beamten," Geheimes Staatsarchiv Dahlem, rep. 90, no. 2318, vol. 1 (1800–May 1916).

6. On *politische Beamte* in general see Hartung, *Staatsbildende Kräfte*, 248–50; John R. Gillis, *The Prussian Bureaucracy in Crisis, 1840–1860* (Stanford, 1971), 89–91; Schütz, "Die Preussischen Oberpräsidenten von 1815 bis 1866," in *Die preussischen Oberpräsidenten 1815–1945*, ed. Klaus Schwabe (Boppard, 1981), 74–75.

then by law in 1852.[7] According to the new disciplinary legislation, judges had to undergo a formal disciplinary procedure before being punished, which essentially improved their overall position as compared to the disciplinary laws of 1844. Higher *Verwaltungsbeamte* could be retired immediately with no explanation. This pertained primarily to *Oberpräsidenten, Regierungspräsidenten,* and *Landräte.*[8]

In Prussian political life of the reactionary 1850s, this disciplinary legislation for civil servants created a paradoxical situation, since state officials, notably the *Landrat,* organized the elections for the conservative governmental party. This meant that the state official, obligated to treat citizens of all classes and political persuasions equitably, was called on to organize and run the elections in Prussia's rural east for the party of the government. It was clear that the aristocratic *Landrat* would seek to influence elections in favor of the conservatives,[9] since the much vaunted *Junkerliberalismus* had petered out with the revolution.[10] Especially in East Prussia, the liberal movement of the early 1840s was supported by the aristocracy. It has even been alleged that East Prussian Junkers formed the vanguard of the liberal opposition movement, which set in after the disillusionment following the accession of Frederick William IV, before the economically more advanced Rhine Province replaced East Prussia as the center of the liberalism of the monarchy.[11] Contemporaries of the 1840s spoke of the liberal *"Flügelprovinzen der Monarchie,"* whereby the situation in the province of Prussia (i.e., East and West Prussia) was exceptional in that the aristocracy of the province largely shaped the liberal movement and, in contrast to other provinces, willingly cooperated with the bourgeoisie.[12] The unruliness of the bourgeoisie and the lower classes, how-

7. See chapt... ...the workings of the bureaucratic apparatus.

8. Public prosecutors, *Ministerialdirektoren,* directors of police, and members of the diplomatic service were affected as well. See Harro-Jürgen Rejewski, *Die Pflicht zur politischen Treue im preussischen Beamtenrecht 1850–1918* (Berlin, 1973); Bernhard Steinbach, *Die politische Freiheit der Beamten unter der konstitutionellen Monarchie in Preussen und im Deutschen Reich* (Bonn, 1962).

9. See Hubertus Fischer, "Konservatismus von unten: Wahlen im ländlichen Preussen 1849/52—Organisation, Agitation, Manipulation," in *Deutscher Konservatismus im 19. und 20. Jahrhundert,* ed. Dirk Stegmann, Bernd-Jürgen Wendt, and Peter-Christian Witt (Bonn, 1983), 69–129.

10. On *Junkerliberalismus* see the articles by Peter Schuppan, "Ostpreussischer Junkerliberalismus und bürgerliche Opposition um 1840," in *Bourgeoisie und bürgerliche Umwälzung in Deutschland 1789–1871,* ed. Helmut Bleiber (Berlin, GDR, 1971), 65–100; Herbert Obenaus, "Gutsbesitzerliberalismus: Zur regionalen Sonderentwicklung der liberalen Partei in Ost- und Westpreussen während des Vormärz," *Geschichte und Gesellschaft* 14 (1988): 304–28.

11. See Schuppan, "Ostpreussischer Junkerliberalismus," 65–100.

12. Herbert Obenaus, "Gutsbesitzerliberalismus." There are different explanations for the East Prussian peculiarities (none of which is wholly satisfying), such as the high percentage of non-noble estate owners, which may have led to a "gentrification" of the upper class, or the

ever, which had become manifest during the revolution, forced the aristocracy and monarchy into a closer alliance. The revolution had thus made it clear to the Prussian nobility that they had grown dependent on an alliance with the monarchy.

The situation became more paradoxical still in cases where high-ranking officials served as deputies in the *Abgeordnetenhaus,* a frequent occurrence for which the constitution had made special provisions.[13] The government supported or opposed the candidacy of an official for parliamentary office according to the official's politics. Between 1855 and 1858, for example, 215 of 352 deputies (61 percent) were "active state officials," and 125 of these belonged to the category of the *politische Beamte,* who could be retired forcibly at any time.[14] Disciplinary legislation made it possible to turn the deputy official into a willing tool of the government, unless he was willing to risk his entire career.[15] For the official who became a parliamentarian, a conflict in allegiance was thus built in his two roles. In accordance with article 108 of the constitution, the state official was sworn to constitutional *"gewissenhafte Beobachtung"* (duty to obey the letter of the law). Yet at the same time, he had vowed to serve the monarch obediently.[16] On the one hand, the official was forced to take a constitutional oath that obligated him to protest any violation of the law during elections; on the other, this righteous protest could well be construed as a violation of loyalty against his supreme worldly master, the king. The deputy official was therefore caught in the throes of an inescapable predicament.

There were, however, some officials who, as deputies, were prepared to support openly the liberal opposition. Willing to risk forced retirement on the basis of their convictions, these officials shine as examples of what had become a rare breed by the 1850s—an official who followed the counsel of his own conscience.[17] The inherent deficiencies of the system must have been apparent to the high officials who served as parliamentarians, as they labored daily under its contradictions. Despite constitutional provisions, which may have been devised to allow greater governmental control over the *Abgeordneten-*

---

possibility of grain exports contributing to a more capitalist organization of production and a liberal "free trade" outlook (so argues the East German historian Peter Schuppan), or finally the continuity of the reform spirit as embodied in the province's longtime *Oberpräsident* Theodor von Schön.

13. Grünthal, *Parlamentarismus in Preussen,* 106–8, 254–64, 395–400.

14. Grünthal, "Grundlagen," 51.

15. For the number of officials in parliament see Grünthal, *Parlamentarismus in Preussen,* 108–9.

16. See Wilhelm Claus, *Der Staatsbeamte als Abgeordneter in der Verfassungsentwicklung der deutschen Staaten* (Karlsruhe, 1906).

17. Grünthal, "Grundlagen," 52.

haus, the duties of state official and parliamentarian proved to be mutually exclusive.

The contradictory legal and constitutional positions of civil servants serving as deputies led to profound disillusionment and demoralization during the years of the *Verfassungskonflikt* after 1862. The potentially dangerous mood did not remain hidden to the *Staatsministerium,* which took steps to exert more stringent control over the bureaucracy as a whole. A further tightening of disciplinary laws would hardly have been possible during the *Konfliktzeit,* since the *Abgeordnetenhaus* would not have endorsed it. Stricter control, therefore, had to be imposed over the bureaucracy itself. In a confidential memorandum of April 20, 1863, the ministry requested *Oberpräsidenten* to report on "the attitude of officials" in their provinces.[18] Detailed information was needed to discipline the wayward official. During the constitutional conflict after 1862, the loyalty of the civil service was essential if the government was to succeed in implementing the measures it had imposed, such as the collection of taxes. It was clear to the *Staatsministerium* that judicial officials were more inclined to recalcitrance than were *Landräte,* for example, on whose loyalty the ministry counted. Even though the survey reports indicated that the majority of civil servants would remain loyal to the crown, provided the government continued pursuing a firm line in its policies, ambiguity in the position of the bureaucracy remained.[19] This equivocality was produced by an inexplicit constitution, one which left ample scope for politically expedient interpretation.

The revised constitution that came into force in 1850 was stripped of the liberal components of its predecessor, the so-called *oktroyierte Verfassung* of December 5, 1848. The amended constitution's conservative clauses included a replacement of the originally envisaged universal manhood suffrage with a three-class franchise based on tax revenue, and the transformation of parliament's upper chamber into a *Herrenhaus,* the members of which were not elected as originally designed but appointed by the king.[20] The fact that the constitution contained a series of basic human rights (articles 3–43) and postulated equality of all citizens before the law (article 4) made it appear more liberal than it was, for the constitution lacked an *Ausführungsgesetz* to enforce these progressive provisions.[21] The constitution was based not on the principle of popular sovereignty but on the monarchical principle as established in the

18. Ibid., 53.
19. Ibid., 54.
20. See Jacques Droz, "Liberale Anschauungen zur Wahlrechtsfrage und das preussische Dreiklassenwahlrecht," in *Moderne deutsche Verfassungsgeschichte 1815–1918,* ed. Ernst-Wolfgang Böckenförde (Cologne, 1972), 195–214.
21. See H. Schulze, "Preussen von 1850 bis 1871," in *Handbuch,* ed. Büsch, 2:304; Hans Boldt, "Die Preussische Verfassung vom 31. Januar 1850," in *Preussen im Rückblick,* eds. Hans-Jürgen Puhle and Hans-Ulrich Wehler (Göttingen, 1980), 224–46.

Wiener Schlussakte (1820) for the member states of the German Confedera-tion. Accordingly, all state power remained indivisibly united in the mon-arch.[22] The monarch's power thus remained rooted in the divine right of kings, while the legitimacy of representative bodies rested on the constitution. The king remained inviolate in his retention of all executive power. His military role as commander-in-chief of the army was supplemented with significant influence over the government. He appointed and dismissed the heads of ministries, and even though all government ordinances (with the exception of those pertaining to army and church) had to be countersigned by a minister, the king enjoyed executive prerogative.

The legislative, in like measure, was moving in a conservative direction. The upper chamber of parliament had originally been designed to function as an elective institution with suffrage based on a high census. The *Herrenhaus*, which eventually emerged in 1854, included aristocrats—whose membership was hereditary—and high officials, officers, or clergymen—who were ap-pointed for life—as well as representatives of Prussia's larger cities. Overall, the preponderance of conservative forces was ensured.[23] The main function of the *Abgeordnetenhaus* was the elaboration of laws, though both chambers of parliament as well as the crown and the *Staatsministerium* had the right to initiate legislation. Financial plans and the annual budget were compiled by the government, though the latter was subject to the approval of both houses of parliament and to the consent of the crown.

The *Herrenhaus* and *Abgeordnetenhaus* were on an equal footing. Both had to countersign new legislation for laws to become effective. Elections to the second chamber, or *Abgeordnetenhaus*, were based on a three-class fran-chise, or *Dreiklassenwahlrecht*, that had been introduced by emergency ordi-nance on May 30, 1849.[24] According to election procedure, the *Urwähler* (who had to be at least twenty-four years old) elected the *Wahlmänner*, who, in turn, elected the deputies. The *Urwähler* were divided into three classes, each of which accounted for one-third of tax revenues and elected one-third of the *Wahlmänner*. Elections were thus indirect and unequal.[25] Moreover, elections were held in public so that those hostile to the government remained easily

---

22. Heinrich-Otto Meisner, *Die Lehre vom monarchischen Prinzip im Zeitalter der Restau-ration und des deutschen Bundes* (Breslau, 1913).

23. See Grünthal, *Parlamentarismus in Preussen*, 295–316.

24. See H. Schulze, "Preussen von 1850 bis 1871," 305; Egid Beitz, *Die Ver-fassungsurkunde vom 31. 1. 1850 und die Wahlordnung vom 30. Mai 1849 in Preussen* (Cologne, 1907).

25. In 1850, for example, 4.7 percent of the population voted in the first class of voters, 12.6 percent in the second, and 82.7 percent in the third. The vote of a citizen in the first class thus carried over seventeen times the weight of a voter in the third. With the increasing discrepancy of wealth that developed in the course of industrialization, the weight was shifted further in favor of the first class of voters.

identified. A substantial part of the rural proletariat of East Elbian Prussia continued following the lead of their estate owner. Voter turnout of the third class was therefore excessively low, in some regions under 20 percent.[26]

As a result of restrictive suffrage, low voter turnout, and active manipulation of elections by the *Landrat,* the conservative party emerged as the largest party in the *Abgeordnetenhaus.* Local officials were instructed by the government to influence the outcome of elections in favor of the conservatives, while the liberals frequently boycotted elections.[27] This, together with the pervasive conservative *Zeitgeist,* ensured the preponderance of conservative forces until the beginning of the New Era. With the accession of a new, more liberal-minded ministry in 1858, which, among other things, prohibited manipulation of elections, it soon became evident that the plutocratic three-class franchise actually favored the liberal bourgeoisie.[28]

Despite their initial numerical superiority in parliament, the conservatives were divided into a number of *Fraktionen,* which made concerted action difficult, if not impossible. The most influential conservative group was the extraparliamentary *Kamarilla* around Leopold von Gerlach, which exerted great and lasting influence on the king. All its clout evaporated, however, once Frederick William's unstable mental condition forced him from office in 1858. The regent (and later king) William I preferred to lend his ear to other advisers. In the *Abgeordnetenhaus,* Ludwig von Gerlach figured prominently as leader of the strongest conservative faction, the *Hochkonservativen* (or ultraconservatives), who, at the beginning of the reactionary period, continued advocating the reintroduction of the *Ständestaat.* Conservative aristocrats had an intrinsic disdain for political parties, as party affiliation was bound to cause a conflict of loyalty to the king.[29] Party politics and monarchical government seemed therefore mutually exclusive, as representative institutions would reduce the king to nothing more than, in conservative parlance, a Monsieur Veto. The unassailable position of the Manteuffel government, which conservatives viewed as the epitomy of bureaucratic rule, and the corresponding fear of "bureaucratic absolutism" finally led to the reconciliation of the *Hochkonservativen* with the

---

26. See H. Schulze, "Preussen von 1850 bis 1871," 307; Johannes Ziekursch, *Politische Geschichte des neuen deutschen Kaiserreiches,* vol. 1 (Frankfurt, 1925), 43–72.

27. See Ludwig Bergstraesser, *Geschichte der politischen Parteien in Deutschland,* 11th ed. (Munich and Vienna, 1960), 89; Helga Grebing, *Geschichte der deutschen Parteien* (Wiesbaden, 1962), 46–55; Hans-Jürgen Puhle, "Konservatismus," in *Die deutschen Parteien im Überblick,* ed. Walter Schlangen (Königstein, 1979), 32–37.

28. Bismarck therefore counted among the diehard opponents of the *Dreiklassenwahlrecht* and insisted on the introduction of universal and equal manhood suffrage for the *Reichstag* of the North German Confederation.

29. See Sigmund Neumann, *Die Stufen des preussischen Konservatismus* (Berlin, 1930); Marjorie Lamberti, "The Rise of the Prussian Conservative Party, 1840–1858" (Ph.D. diss., Yale University, 1966), 178–283.

constitutional state. Others, such as Viktor A. Huber, continued rejecting the
constitutional arrangement and Gerlach's all too concessionary policies.[30] In
addition to Gerlach's *Hochkonservative,* other conservative factions in the
Abgeordnetenhaus included the *Fraktion* of Arnim and Heinrichsdorf,[31] which
supported the Manteuffel government unquestioningly; the *Fraktion* of Alexander and Moritz von Lavergne-Peguilhen, which evinced strong interest in
social questions; and finally the liberal-conservative *Fraktion* around the legal
scholar August von Bethmann-Hollweg, which gained notoriety under the
epithet *Wochenblattpartei.* Several members of the *Wochenblattpartei* later
became ministers during the New Era.[32] The *Wochenblattpartei* had many
supporters in diplomatic circles and the bureaucracy. In stark contrast to the
group around Gerlach, which championed an alliance with Russia in foreign
policy, the *Partei Bethmann-Hollweg* was intent on casting off Russian tutelage and advanced the idea of an alliance with England.[33] In the *Landtag,*
Bethmann-Hollweg's supporters frequently cooperated with the (small) liberal
and Catholic factions.

With the beginning of the regency of William I (1858), which ended the
reactionary era and its manipulated elections, conservative dominance in parliament ceased. The number of conservatives was quickly reduced from 224 to
47, while the "alt-liberale" *Fraktion* Vincke received 151 seats, and the liberal-
conservative *Wochenblattpartei* received 44.[34] Since the left liberals continued
their boycott of the elections, the moderate and constitutional liberals enjoyed a
clear majority in the *Abgeordnetenhaus.* It was only after the outbreak of the
constitutional conflict that the weight within the liberal camp shifted in favor of
the left liberals. The left wing of the *Altliberalen* had risen in protest against the
moderate's conciliatory delaying tactics. They split from the party, forming the
Fortschrittspartei. This new progressive party was successful from its inception, obtaining 104 (of 352) seats in the elections of December 6, 1861, and 133
seats during the elections of May 19, 1862. Together with the left center, which
had received 96 mandates, the opposition parties thus enjoyed a clear majority,
as the *Altliberale* held a mere 19 seats to the conservatives' 11. This was the
distribution of power when Bismarck was appointed prime minister.

---

30. On the changing attitude of Prussian conservatives toward the constitutional state see
Lamberti, "Rise of the Prussian Conservative Party," 215–22; on Huber see Sabine Hindelang,
Konservatismus und soziale Frage (Frankfurt, 1983), 128–43.

31. See Bergstraesser, *Geschichte der politischen Parteien,* 91; Grünthal, *Parlamentarismus in Preussen,* 404–5.

32. Michael Behnen, *Das Politische Wochenblatt 1851–1861: Nationalkonservative Publizistik gegen Ständestaat und Polizeistaat* (Göttingen, 1971).

33. See Bergstraesser, *Geschichte der politischen Parteien,* 92; Hans-Joachim Schoeps,
Das andere Preussen, 5th ed. (Berlin, 1981), 110–17.

34. See H. Schulze, "Preussen von 1850 bis 1871," 325.

With the consolidation of the constitutional state, parliament became instrumental in drafting social policy measures. Between the revolution and *Reichsgründung*, it was the *Abgeordnetenhaus* that debated social policy measures, and the few (mostly older) monographs available on the social policies of the 1850s and 1860s focus accordingly on parliamentary proceedings.[35] Legislative debates over a series of social policy measures from 1850 to 1870 can be divided into roughly two phases.

The first phase, which culminated during the third legislative period between 1852 and 1855, was the most active in the consideration of social policies prior to Bismarck's program of social legislation.[36] Especially noteworthy were the measures concerning the extension of protective legislation for children in factories (1853) and the amendment of the Poor Law in 1855, which led to a further tightening of *Meldepflicht*.[37] There were further measures extending *Arbeiterschutz,* including the introduction of factory inspectors. The lively debates over social policies in the reactionary period were dictated by fear of renewed revolutionary social unrest.[38] In 1848, the urban and rural proletariat had figured prominently in the revolutionary uprisings and made their existence felt more powerfully than ever before in the nineteenth century. The social measures of the reactionary period were mainly designed to alleviate misery, to ease the burden of communities, and, where possible, to elevate the educational level of the proletariat. Thus, the social policies of the 1850s were consistent with the period's conservatism; their main goals were to blunt the proletariat's revolutionary edge, eliminate discontent, and avoid further revolutionary upheavals. What was essentially new was the sharpened awareness of impending social dangers, which many had experienced in 1848. Among other things, the revolution had been instrumental in sensitizing and alerting public consciousness toward the potential dangers emanating from the

35. See, for example, Carl-Valerius Herberger, *Die Stellung der preussischen Konservativen zur sozialen Frage 1848–1862* (Meissen, 1914); Adolf Richter, *Bismarck und die Arbeiterfrage im preussischen Verfassungskonflikt* (Stuttgart, 1935); and especially Heinrich Volkmann, *Die Arbeiterfrage im preussischen Abgeordnetenhaus 1848–1869* (Berlin, 1968). Little is known about the civil service in the decades preceding 1870. While there is an exhaustive recent study on the civil service during the empire, Tibor Süle's *Preussische Bürokratietradition: Zur Entwicklung von Verwaltung und Beamtenschaft in Deutschland, 1871–1918* (Göttingen, 1988), and a good chapter on "Verwaltung" in Thomas Nipperdey's *Deutsche Geschichte 1866–1918: Machtstaat vor Demokratie* (Munich, 1992), 109–40, John R. Gillis's study is still the only one to cover the 1850s.

36. See Heinrich Volkmann, 93–111.

37. Ibid., 102.

38. Yet the number of deputies who showed interest in social policy was small; the majority barely took notice of social issues. Among conservatives, it was mostly Hermann Wagener, Ludwig von Gerlach, and Moritz von Blanckenburg; in the Catholic faction, deputies with social concerns included Peter Reichensperger and Hermann Joseph von Mallinckrodt; and Friedrich Harkort and Karl Degenkolb were among the more active liberals. See Grünthal, *Parlamentarismus in Preussen,* 284–90; Volkmann, *Arbeiterfrage,* 104.

proletariat. The order of the day now was to arrest these forces that threatened to undermine the social edifice.

The most important measure in the field of factory legislation, the protective law of May 16, 1853, which went far beyond the 1839 *Regulativ* by raising the minimum age for child labor from nine to twelve and by curtailing working hours from ten to six for those under the age of fourteen, was also affected by the revolution, since revolutionary events had brought in their wake a reassessment of child labor. In 1845, authorities had deemed the protective clauses of the 1839 *Regulativ* as sufficient, but new governmental inquiries at *Regierungen* and *Oberpräsidien,* conducted by Minister of Commerce August von der Heydt in 1851, brought in very different results. Now the shortcomings of the old *Regulativ* had become so self-evident that a complete overhaul of the old law was deemed necessary, despite the fact that the number of children working in Prussian factories had fallen from 31,035 to 21,945 between 1846 and 1852.[39] The debate on child labor in the *Abgeordnetenhaus* was essentially different from that within the bureaucracy in the 1820s and 1830s in that industry's demand for child labor had ceased being a central topic. Nevertheless, due to their all-pervasive economic liberalism, most of the liberal minority voted against the bill. Fear of growing dereliction among adolescents, since their exclusion from factory work meant the end of supervision, also prompted members of other parties to vote against the new factory bill. The law was passed only with the votes of the conservative majority, who followed the government's lead.

Though conservatives were ideologically more predisposed toward endorsing state interference and social policy measures than their liberal counterparts, who preferred to see the economy treated as a self-regulating mechanism, the conservatives in the *Abgeordnetenhaus* showed little interest in social matters (among the few exceptions, Hermann Wagener was by far the most noteworthy).[40] As soon as their own material interests were affected (as happened with the amendment of the Poor Law in 1855), the unity of conservative factions foundered. The amendment had become necessary, since through the maintenance of *Freizügigkeit* in the Poor Law of 1842, larger towns and industrial centers, which attracted vast numbers of immigrants from the rural east, had to shoulder an ever heavier burden of poor relief. The gist of the

---

39. Karl-Heinz Ludwig, "Die Fabrikarbeit von Kindern im 19. Jahrhundert: Ein Problem der Technikgeschichte," *Vierteljahreshefte für Sozial- und Wirtschaftsgeschichte* 52 (1965): 63–85, esp. 78.

40. In the 1850s, the focus of the *Soziale Frage* largely shifted to the industrial proletariat and gradually turned into the *Arbeiterfrage,* with which the landed squire was unfamiliar as it primarily concerned the industrialized western and central areas of Prussia. Nevertheless, conservatives supported the social legislation submitted by the government, with the exception of the poor law revisions, in which case their votes were dispensable.

revision was to limit the towns' duty of maintenance and place a heavier burden on the pauper's commune of origin. A natural result of this was to take financial pressure off the larger towns at the expense of rural communes and estates, as the flow of migration moved unilaterally from the rural east to the more industrialized provinces of the western and central parts of Prussia. As part of the substantiation of the new law, the state's obligation to provide for the poor was emphasized, a stipulation against which even conservatives vehemently protested.[41] The liberals were more favorably disposed toward the law, since freedom of movement remained largely untouched. While the liberal opposition was united in supporting the amendment, conservatives were divided in "town" and "countryside" factions. It was self-interest that drove estate owners into opposition, since the new bill promised additional burdens for an already impecunious rural east. Tangible material interests thus transcended party loyalty and ultimately decided the individual deputy's political stance. But that was hardly surprising in an age when parliamentary factions, which were named after their respective leaders, were made up of independent-minded individuals who would have found the concept of *Fraktionszwang* anathema. The amendment of the Poor Law thus saw a curious reversal of fronts. To eschew incurring the expense, some conservatives even pleaded liberal positions, while the liberals, who naturally favored the interests of industrial development, strongly supported the new Poor Law and even advocated a certain legal constraint, whereas otherwise they had defended freedom from state interference. Especially the *Hochkonservativen* around Leopold von Gerlach, together with their mouthpiece, the *Kreuzzeitung,* rejected outright any state obligation for the poor.[42] Realizing, however, that they were hopelessly outnumbered, as the government, the liberals, and other conservative factions supported the bill, the agrarian conservatives renounced active opposition.

The period of constitutional conflict represented the second phase of an increasingly animated debate on social policies. The motivation behind social legislation had, however, changed fundamentally. Now it was the wooing of the proletariat that prompted liberals and conservatives alike to champion *Koalitionsfreiheit,* or the freedom to form associations. During the constitutional conflict, social issues were bound to become politicized; that is, social

---

41. Hermann Wagener—before his unconditional endorsement of state involvement—claimed that "the principle of the current poor law is decidedly socialistic," while Peter Reichensperger, a prominent member of the Catholic faction, concurred with Wagener, arguing that the state's obligation "proclaimed an axiom . . . , as it could not be demanded more stringently by communism." See Volkmann, *Arbeiterfrage, 84.*

42. After the law was passed, the *Kreuzzeitung* wrote, "Our current poor relief system is too costly, while it often neglects those needing help most urgently; on the whole it has a demoralizing effect." *Neue Preussische Zeitung,* October 20, 1855.

programs and bills were now used as strategic devices in strengthening one's political position. Social policy had become a lever in the day-to-day struggle of party politics. Wagener's (and Bismarck's) temporary wooing of Lassalle was the most illustrative case in point (see chapter 4). An envisaged political alliance with the workers now forced politicians of all parties to abandon social discrimination as politically unwise. Never before and not for a long time in the future (until 1933) had the working class been as *salonfähig* as it was in the first half of the 1860s. Especially the conservatives were willing to use the industrial proletariat for tactical purposes to further conservative ends. The decision to legalize workers' associations as well as the famous audience of the Waldenburg weavers with King William must be interpreted in this light. Bismarck insisted that the king receive the weavers to illustrate to the wider public the self-appointed social mission of the Hohenzollern.

After the election disaster at the beginning of the New Era (1858), as a result of Regent William prohibiting undue influencing of elections, Hermann Wagener was widely seen as a potential rejuvenator of conservative politics by dint of his social program.[43] Wagener's influence thus temporarily grew as a result of the conservative election defeat, to reach its height during the constitutional conflict. After Bismarck's foreign policy successes, however, Wagener's "domestic solution" to the conflict, never popular with the traditional members of the conservative party, was quietly discarded. Wagener's most interesting memoranda to Bismarck originated accordingly in the years 1862–64. Pressure to collaborate with the national-minded forces of liberalism after 1866 further eroded the feasibility of Wagener's intrinsically illiberal program and weakened his standing within conservative party ranks. Königgrätz was thus also a decisive defeat for social politics, as Bismarck's foreign success preempted the outcome of the domestic conflict and made sweeping social reform, at least for the time being, unnecessary.

Once the constitutional conflict between monarchy and parliament was resolved in favor of royal authority in 1866, social legislation once again abated, though *Koalitionsfreiheit* became law in 1869. The political affiliations and coalitions that began to emerge after 1866 were markedly different from those of the preceding period. In Imperial Germany, for example, the liberal parties are generally regarded as being outrightly opposed to the interests of the industrial proletariat, while earlier liberals, such as Harkort and Mevissen, displayed active concern over the amelioration of the lower classes' lot. With the foundation of the Social Democratic party in Eisenach (1869), the social question ultimately turned into a political one, so that political consideration prevailed even in debates on issues of a purely social nature.

---

43. Adalbert Hahn, *Die Berliner Revue* (Berlin, 1934), 91.

An interesting characteristic of bureaucratic behavior was the toleration of coalitions among workers, even though they had been theoretically declared illegal by the *Allgemeine Gewerbeordnung* of 1845. The unrestricted freedom to form coalitions that came with the introduction of freedom of trade in 1810–11 had been curtailed in 1845. The *AGO* eliminated *Koalitionsfreiheit* and strikes. There was no immediate political reason for this prohibition in Prussia itself; it was due solely to industrial disputes in England and France. Even in instances of strikes, the bureaucracy reacted with extraordinary forbearance.[44] Officials largely ignored existing prohibitions of strikes as well as the *Koalitionsverbot*,[45] though there was a series of strikes in the 1850s and 1860s. After 1863, workers' associations began to form without the intervention of officials. When the *Oberpräsidenten* sent in their reports concerning workers' associations, they favored *Koalitionsfreiheit* without exception.[46]

That these prohibitions were ignored has little to do with the often postulated philanthropic attitude of the bureaucracy. It ties in with the phenomenon of not reporting incidents of social unrest in one's own province. Richard Tilly has argued that during the 1840s, newspapers were often a more reliable source of information than government reports, as it frequently happened that reports on local incidents were dismissed as unimportant, to avoid reprimands or unwelcome investigation.[47] It was Bismarck's government that finally seized the initiative to do away with the prohibition of workers' coalitions at the height of the struggle with the liberal majority in the *Abgeordnetenhaus*. Bismarck's politics was modeled on Bonapartist France, where any restrictions on the freedom to form coalitions had just been abolished.[48] After 1867 Bismarck's enthusiasm for such a policy waned as the first socialist deputies made their appearance in the North German Diet, while in France the working classes turned from supporters into opponents of the Bonapartist regime.

The historiography of social policy measures between the revolution and *Reichsgründung* is an interesting chapter all by itself. Surprisingly few monographs dealing with pre-Bismarckian social legislation appeared in post–Second World War West Germany. One may have expected that social policies

---

44. On the *Koalititonsverbot* see Wolfgang Köllmann, "Die Anfänge der staatlichen Sozialpolitik in Preussen bis 1869," *Vierteljahresschrift für Sozial- und Wirtschaftsgeschichte* 53 (1966): 28–52; on the behavior of the bureaucracy see Karl E. Born, "Sozialpolitische Probleme und Bestrebungen in Deutschland von 1848 bis zur Bismarckschen Sozialgesetzgebung," *VSWG* 46 (1959): 29–44.

45. See Born, "Sozialpolitische Probleme," 43.

46. Horst Kollmann, *Die Entstehungsgeschichte der deutschen Koalitionsgesetzgebung* (Breslau, 1916), 235–37.

47. Richard Tilly, "Unruhen und Protest in Deutschland im 19. Jahrhundert: Ein erster Überblick," in *Staat, Kapital, und sozialer Protest in der deutschen Industrialisierung* (Göttingen, 1980), 143–74, esp. 147.

48. See Born, "Sozialpolitische Probleme," 39.

enacted before 1862, still largely free of tactical party politics, would have offered themselves as pillars of strength to a new West German national identity, just as the radical democratic forerunners of the labor movement served as pillars to cement the *Staatsautorität* of the German Democratic Republic. Instead, Prussia's early *Sozialpolitik* was discarded in favor of other, seemingly more pressing topics, such as Prussian militarism or issues of foreign policy. Walter Vogel's *Bismarck's Arbeiterversicherung*,[49] one of the few studies based consistently on primary sources, was largely completed during the war, so that Heinrich Volkmann's investigation remained virtually the only major monograph on the subject.[50] Early Prussian social policies had attracted more interest in Wilhelminean Germany, when a whole series of dissertations dealt with individual measures of social policy legislation.[51]

The strongest interest in the social legislation of the *Reichsgründungszeit* was developed during the Third Reich. Historians drew up explicit parallels between their own time (1933–36) and the 1850s and 1860s, which appeared as an age in which the social kingdom was about to become a reality, as conservatives and liberals vied with equal fervor for the soul of the worker (before the advent of an independent working class party). It was an age that seemed to promise the realization of a true *Volksgemeinschaft*. In this context, the studies by Adalbert Hahn and Adolf Richter are worthy of note.[52] In the preface to his book, for example, Hahn wrote that while his study was originally designed as a contribution to the history of the conservative party, "it became evident during the course of the investigation that the circle of men and ideas under scrutiny signified the first emergence of national socialist ideas in German politics."[53] And Adolf Richter (whose study was published in 1935) wrote, when dealing with Hermann Wagener, that "when we survey Wagener's ideas as a whole, comparisons with the present become perfectly obvious."[54]

---

49. Walter Vogel, *Bismarck's Arbeiterversicherung: Ihre Entstehung im Kräftespiel der Zeit* (Braunschweig, 1951).

50. Volkmann, *Arbeiterfrage*. For his analysis, Volkmann perused the parliamentary proceedings of the Prussian *Abgeordnetenhaus* and the diet of the North German Confederation.

51. See, e.g., Elisabeth von Richthofen, "Über die historischen Wandlungen in der Stellung der autoritären Parteien zur Arbeiterschutzgesetzgebung und die Motive dieser Wandlungen" (Ph.D. diss., University of Heidelberg, 1901); Hugo Müller, "Der preussische Volks-Verein" (Ph.D. diss., University of Greifswald, 1914); and, though from a later period, Karl Edmund Femerling, "Die Stellung der konservativen Partei zur gewerblichen Arbeiterfrage in der Zeit von 1848 bis 1880" (Diss. jur., University of Halle, 1927).

52. Hahn, *Die Berliner Revue;* Adolf Richter, *Bismarck und die Arbeiterfrage im preussischen Verfassungskonflikt* (Stuttgart, 1935).

53. Hahn, *Die Berliner Revue*, 4.

54. Richter, *Bismarck und die Arbeiterfrage*, 35. Richter went on to deplore the fact that in the 1860s the time had not yet been "ripe" for Wagener's ideas.

Throughout his work, Richter favorably compared his own time, the early phase of the Third Reich, with the 1860s, expressing his hope that the present regime would be more successful in winning the worker's support for "the national idea."[55]

---

55. So, e.g., ibid., 23, 33.

Social Conservatism, the Prussian Bureaucracy, and the Question of Continuity in German History

German administrative historians, from Otto Hintze to Hans Rosenberg, have tended to assume that the Prussian civil service constituted a monolithic bloc. It is understandable that such historians as Otto Hintze, who was sympathetic toward the civil service, would examine this professional class as a coherent, unified entity, imbued by a strong ideal of service to all citizens, regardless of social status or class. It is ironic, however, that this approach of the bureaucracy constituting a monolithic entity was never seriously questioned by such historians as Eckhart Kehr and Hans Rosenberg, who achieved fame as uncompromising critics of the Prussian state apparatus. Indeed, while reversing Hintze's premise that the civil service was an ideal-oriented, altruistic "guardian class," they perpetuated the myth of a monolithic bureaucratic machinery. This myth might arguably go back to Hegel's depiction of officials as an *allgemeiner Stand,* which hovered above the rest of society. This supposition was taken for granted and never seriously scrutinized; to contemporaries it may indeed have seemed that "one spirit and one will" permeated the Prussian civil service.

Yet the Prussian civil service was far from a monolithic apparatus. Competing political interests within the bureaucracy produced opposing forces and internal dissension despite the common social background of the bureaucracy as a class. Officials did not always assume the mantle of their office but acted as individuals with opposing interests. The struggle over the *Centralverein's* statutes, for example, resulted in internal bureaucratic conflict: the conservatives Arnim and Mathis in the ministry of the interior tried to suppress an association led by Bornemann, Viebahn, and Patow, officials who had served in the ministries of finance and the interior, and who were personally known to their

opponents. Top level civil servants, even ministers, were pitted against one another on many issues: Ministers Altenstein and Schuckmann openly disagreed with one another about the necessity of introducing protective legislation for children; Flottwell and Arnim were at loggerheads over how to deal with the *Centralverein;* and committee members investigating the emergency in East Prussia disagreed about whether the state or local communities should help the poor—indeed, about whether active intervention was necessary at all. In each case, the inevitable consequence was obstruction that resulted in procrastination and delay and seriously jeopardized the much vaunted efficiency of the Prussian civil service.

On questions of social policy, disagreements often boiled down to a debate over active state intervention versus laissez-faire and self-help. Proponents of a strong, responsible (and paternalistic) state, advocating active state participation in social matters, were pitted against champions of economic liberalism, generally officials of a reformist orientation, whose views had been shaped during their *Bildungsreisen* in England. This latter type of civil servant, quite common during the first decades of the century, had become a rare breed by the 1840s, when a broad conservative consensus permeated ever wider circles of the bureaucracy. Several factors working together explain this conservatism. A deep-seated fear of leftist intellectuals had been kindled by recurrent reports of the intelligentsia's subversive activities and alleged conspiracies. This fear was aggravated, no doubt, by the weavers' uprising, for which intellectuals had been blamed as convenient scapegoats. One result of the obsessive dread of intellectual subversion was a pronounced shift to the right: conservatives in the civil service now had a compelling excuse to tighten the reins of bureaucratic control. Economic liberalism, moreover, seemed to have lost its attraction soon after the reforms, and (as Barbara Vogel has demonstrated) officials were increasingly influenced by the conservative ideas of Savigny's historical school of law in the decade after 1807.[1] After 1820, conservative tendencies became even more pronounced.

The second part of this study on the social policies of the Prussian bureaucracy has focused on the convergence of conservative social thought and bureaucratic patterns of argumentation: their common intellectual approach to social realities, their preference for piecemeal social engineering, and their joint aversion to general laws that would be applicable without distinction to all citizens and provinces alike. Like conservative thinkers, officials rejected sweeping social reform and were opposed to the "general formulas of happiness" that August von der Heydt had written about in his memorandum. In drafting new legislation, officials tried to account for existing differences with

---

1. See also Lothar Dittmer, *Beamtenkonservatismus und Modernisierung: Untersuchungen zur Vorgeschichte der konservativen Partei in Preussen 1810–1848/49* (Wiesbaden, 1992).

an eye toward preserving cultural idiosyncrasies of each province. When investigating the issue of a community's right to reject newcomers, for example, officials perused all existing edicts, regulations, and ordinances on the subject. Their methods were essentially conservative and existed side by side with economic liberalism and social paternalism. When in conflict, ingrained cultural heritage usually prevailed over ideology. Even economically liberal officials were greatly influenced by the ideals of eighteenth-century Prussia and its strong paternalistic state. Many seemingly liberal policies, like the Poor Laws and their controversial retention of *Freizügigkeit,* had authoritarian undertones. A corollary of the *Freizügigkeit* legislation was the intensification of registration procedures and the enforcement of a citizen's duty to report to authorities upon arrival in a new town or village. Maintenance of *Freizügigkeit* did not mean that officials favored an open society; quite to the contrary, they were mostly concerned with social control.

The profound social changes that came in the wake of the reforms, and the widespread poverty of the 1830s and 1840s, called for a socially active civil service. But officials were ill prepared to play this role. The Prussian bureaucracy constituted too much of an elite, and its members were too detached from the rest of society to understand the significance of social issues and to be sympathetic toward the plight of the lower classes. Despite conflicting political opinions within the bureaucracy that prevented the emergence of a single political "spirit and will," officials did have salient traits in common that set them distinctly apart as a professional class and led them to support (consciously or not) the social status quo. The higher civil service was relatively homogeneous in terms of social standing and background. Highly privileged as a group, set apart from the rest of the population by rank and the corresponding insignia, and with the advantage of a privileged social background, high officials were naturally loathe to adopt policies that were likely to result in profound social change. With no blueprint of how to cope with the multitude of new problems, no past experience to draw from, and no tested measures of swift reform, officials tended to fall back on the proven panacea of social control. Peasants, if actually set free and released from century-old bondage, often exchanged one yoke for another: estate owners were replaced by a bureaucracy in which neo-feudal, authoritarian elements were strong, and which purported to act as guardian for society by keeping the lower orders in tutelage. The multitude of police reports in official documents, the close supervision of the Association for the Welfare of Workers, the intensification of the *Meldepflicht,* and the registration procedures in the Poor Laws all testify to that.

When understaffing of the bureaucracy had become a problem by the 1840s, officials were even prepared to strengthen the *Stände* and revive the artisan guilds abolished during the reforms to help monitor the population. By

thus consolidating the relationship of dependence between peasants and estate owners, as happened as a corollary of the Poor Laws, and by giving the *Innungen* supervisory powers over journeymen and apprentices, officials turned the wheel of time backward and reversed measures taken during the reforms.[2] By stressing the *obrigkeitlichen Pflichten* of the Junkers in the deliberations on poor relief and *Freizügigkeit*, bureaucrats shook off social obligations and saved public money, which was a scarce commodity in Prussia, but they also cemented the social dominance of the East Elbian aristocracy. And this was in flagrant contradiction to their policy measures earlier in the century, when modernization of state and society and the creation of a modern *Rechtsstaat* seemed the bureaucracy's foremost concern. Official documents reveal that this was done intentionally, in full view of the consequences. It can be argued that the socially retrogressive policies of Prussian officials benefited the bureaucracy as a class, for the percentage of aristocrats in the highest ranks of the administrative branch of the civil service was substantial, and key administrative positions, such as those of the *Landrat, Regierungspräsident,* and *Oberpräsident,* constituted virtually an aristocratic preserve.[3]

Still, quite apart from the lack of financial resources and the acute shortage of manpower in the Prussian administration, the failure of officials to pursue a more active social policy remains to be explained. The notion of a *fürsorgliche* bureaucracy, a civil service geared toward public relief and welfare, has become too widely accepted to be lightly dismissed by reference to an empty treasury. Why were decisive steps not taken earlier to alleviate the weavers' suffering? Why was the factory bill passed only in 1839 and not a decade before? Why was the *Truckverbot* enacted only after the revolution?

The most obvious of answers is also the most plausible: there were many officials who simply did not care about the plight of the lower classes. Merckel and his subordinates were well informed of the cloth workers' misery yet refused to recognize it as a serious problem. They took no steps even after countless petitions concerning abuses of the *Trucksystem* had been dispatched to central authorities in Berlin. It could certainly be argued that the prevailing mood of laissez-faire dictated nonintervention, but in the cases of Silesia and factory legislation, for example, this argument explains little. A more feasible

---

2. The socially retrogressive measures taken during the 1840s shed a different light on the bureaucracy's role as a "modernizing force," which, if viewed as a whole, was contradictory.

3. In his analysis of the nineteenth-century French state, Theodore Zeldin argued that "the civil service is another of the professions where expansion is usually equated with the increase in the power of the bourgeoisie" (Zeldin, *Ambition and Love* [Oxford, 1979], 113). In Prussia, however, the increasing sophistication of the administrative bureaucracy was not accompanied by a growth of bourgeois power, since bourgeois influence within the apparatus was receding after 1825.

explanation is that the suffering of the lower classes was beyond the range of vision of an elitist professional civil service. This added to the inertia of the civil service on a policy-making level: the ambiguous legal situation, as illustrated by the East Prussian emergency; a strong mutual distrust among officials, which, for example, prevented the certification of the *Centralverein;* a blinding fear of intellectual subversion and democratic stirrings, which made officials in the ministry of the interior overlook the potential benefits of the Association for the Welfare of Workers; and finally, the all too laborious bureaucratic process, which included an endless, prolonged interchange of official correspondence.

When officials did act on social legislation, their motivations were not of a humanitarian nature, as is often ascribed to them. Maintenance of social order and control was the paramount consideration in discussion of the Poor Law, for example. And when it came to drafting a factory bill, civil servants were unmoved by hair-raising accounts of child labor but shocked and outraged over the "moral damages" factory life inflicted on society—its "morally corrosive influence," as Altenstein put it. Authoritarian paternalism, characteristic of Prussian officials' social policies, was indeed interspersed with humanitarian ideals, but these remained the ideals of their particular *Bildung*—abstract and divorced from the policy implications of real-life social problems. It was only natural for civil servants to treat members of the lower orders of Prussian society as subjects, whose legal claim to welfare benefits they strongly disavowed. Public assistance had to be granted as a favor and could never be claimed as a right.

The conservative swing within the bureaucratic apparatus during the 1840s naturally influenced the bureaucracy's social policies, which, as indicated, were geared toward solidifying the social status quo, strengthening the aristocracy's social position, intensifying social surveillance and control, and suppressing social movements that, once fully developed, might potentially elude the bureaucratic grasp. But even before key administrative positions became occupied by conservatives in the 1840s—long before Eichhorn became minister of culture or Arnim the minister of the interior—many official memoranda were couched in terms of supervision, control, and stifling regimentation. Lothar Dittmer recently documented the conservative tendencies that prevailed long before the 1840s.[4] And despite controversies within the civil service on issues of social reform, there was a common mode of reasoning, a common approach to social problems, to which even liberals, such as Altenstein, subscribed. As the second part of this study has shown, patterns of bureaucratic argumentation were pervaded by conservative assumptions, and the officials' approach toward the world and its problems was virtually con-

---

4. Dittmer, *Beamtenkonservatismus und Modernisierung.*

gruent with the conservative understanding of political and social issues: both favored a gradual, historical approach to social questions, emphasized the necessity of integrating and assimilating the individual into a larger whole, and rejected a holistic approach to social problems. This combination of conservative and bureaucratic social thought (and action) thus created a *Preussische Staatsgesinnung,* or state ideology, which provided a deeply rooted foundation for the future Prussian (and subsequently German) state-society relationship— a conservative-bureaucratic consensus that transcended narrowly drawn party lines. This conservative-bureaucratic *Staatsgesinnung* later permeated the entire *juste milieu.* It formed the basis of a profound consensus among the *classes politiques* that became a manifestation of the Prussian spirit.

Hugo von Hofmannsthal, comparing Prussia with Austria, once remarked that Prussia, in contrast to his native Austria, was a country in which an *aktuelle Gesinnung,* a "current mood," was continually prevalent: cosmopolitan in the early 1800s, liberal around 1848, Bismarckian in the latter part of the nineteenth century, and "devoid of remembrance for past phases."[5] According to Hofmannsthal, Prussians were *"konsequent"* (i.e., consistent in logic and action) but unable *"sich in andere hineinzuversetzen"* ("to put themselves into the position of others and understand their hidden motives"). They were geared toward functionalism and thus operationalized every activity; and, of course, they consistently acted according to *Vorschriften*—rules, regulations, and instructions. These insightful remarks of a well-informed observer make one wonder what could have been the *ruhende Pol* (stable rock) in the sea of movement of this seemingly so artificial and forced (*"gewollt,"* as Hofmannsthal puts it) Prussian world. One possible answer is that a substantial component of the Prussian identity, which later left such a strong imprint on the German Empire, was formed by the confluence of conservative social thought and bureaucratic policy making during the least eventful decades in the history of Prussia. Between the 1820s and the early 1860s, Prussian soldiers fought few battles, no great king spread the country's fame, and Bismarck was still a Junker among many others. But these decades, these quiet years, these *"halkyonischen Jahre"* as Leopold von Ranke once referred to the pre-March period, were critical in the formation of the Prussian spirit.

The Sonderweg

Trends in Prussian conservative social thought and bureaucratic responses to social problems laid the foundation of a social conservatism that remained influential until well into the twentieth century. In some respects, notably in the renewed blossoming of conservative concepts during the so-called conserva-

---

5. Hugo von Hofmannsthal, *Prosa,* vol. 3 (Frankfurt, 1964), 404–10.

tive revolution at the end of the Weimar Republic, they came into their own only after the First World War.[6] The social views of Radowitz had lost none of their topicality eighty years after his death, while the cultural criticism levied by him and his former collaborators at the *Berliner Politisches Wochenblatt* promoted a continuity in conservative thought that gathered full momentum only during the Empire.[7] Rodbertus's state socialism, outlined in his 1839 essay, already pointed to pronounced state interference and the "organized capitalism" that became the hallmark of the German economy after 1900,[8] while Hermann Wagener appeared as a precursor of the radical conservatism that came into its own first in France and then in Austria after the mid-1880s.[9] In contrast to later radical conservatives, however, Wagener was neither a nationalist nor an avowed anti-Semite. In the same vein of continuity, the shared mentality between conservatives and officials, which has been described above as a unifying *Staatsideologie,* contributed to the basic consensus among the conservative elite. These issues are directly related to the problematic of continuity in German history and its role in Germany's "special path" to modernity.

The idea of the peculiarity of the German path of political, social, and economic development goes back to the early nineteenth century, when German romantics and proponents of the German national movement opposed first the French Revolution and then Napoleonic rule in Germany. According to early German nationalists, such as Johann Gottlieb Fichte, the formation of the

---

6. See Arnim Mohler, *Die Konservative Revolution in Deutschland 1918–1932,* 2 vols., 3d ed. (Darmstadt, 1989; first published in 1950); Klemens von Klemperer, *Germany's New Conservatism* (Princeton, 1957); Fritz Stern, *The Politics of Cultural Despair* (Berkeley and Los Angeles, 1961); Kurt Sontheimer, *Antidemokratisches Denken in der Weimarer Republik* (Munich, 1968); Herman Lebovics, *Social Conservatism and the Middle Classes in Germany 1914–1933* (Princeton, 1969); Stefan Breuer, *Anatomie der Konservativen Revolution* (Darmstadt, 1993).

7. See Fritz Stern, *Politics of Cultural Despair;* David L. Gross, *"Kultur* and Its Discontents: The Origins of a 'Critique of Everyday Life' in Germany, 1880–1925," in *Essays on Culture and Society in Modern Germany,* ed. Gary D. Stark and Bede K. Lackner, (College Station, Tex., 1982), 70–98.

8. Though the model of "organized capitalism" came under severe criticism shortly after its inception, it proved useful in the debate of the late 1970s. See Heinrich A. Winkler, ed., *Organisierter Kapitalismus: Voraussetzungen und Anfänge* (Göttingen, 1974); Winkler, *Liberalismus und Antiliberalismus* (Göttingen, 1979), 259–71; Wolfgang Mommsen, "Gegenwärtige Tendenzen in der Geschichtsschreibung der Bundesrepublik," *Geschichte und Gesellschaft* 7 (1981): 149–89, esp. 173–75.

9. On France see Zeev Sternhell, *Maurice Barrès et le Nationalisme Français* (Paris, 1972); Sternhell, *La Droite Révolutionaire 1885–1914* (Paris, 1978), 245–348; Eugen Weber, "Nationalism, Socialism, and National-Socialism in France" (1962), reprinted in *My France* (Cambridge, Mass., 1991). On Austria see Carl Schorske, "Politics in a New Key: An Austrian Trio," in *Fin-De-Siècle Vienna: Politics and Culture* (New York, 1980), 116–81; John Boyer, *Political Radicalism in Late Imperial Vienna* (Chicago, 1981).

German nation state was to take place under entirely different auspices.[10] Germans took pride in the fact that their development differed from that of Western nations; Germany's uniqueness was perceived as an asset rather than a liability.[11] In Germany itself this positive connotation of the nation's historic peculiarities was preserved until the Weimar Republic and then revived again during the Third Reich, while in the period leading up to the First World War, Germany's western neighbors tended to emphasize negative continuities, such as traditions of militarism and autocracy.[12]

After the unification of Germany in 1871, German social scientists, such as Gustav Schmoller and Werner Sombart, insisted on the innate superiority of German political institutions and argued that Germany had to pursue its own path of economic development.[13] German historians canonized the path to unification, as Bernd Faulenbach once put it, arguing that the Empire not only constituted a solution that was fully in keeping with the course of German history but also was better equipped to deal with the social and administrative problems of a great power than were the political systems of Western Europe.[14]

---

10. Recent publications dealing specifically with the notion and historiography of the German *Sonderweg* include: Bernd Faulenbach, *Ideologie des deutschen Weges: Die deutsche Geschichte in der Historiographie zwischen Kaiserreich und Nationalsozialismus* (Munich, 1980); Bernd Faulenbach, "Deutscher Sonderweg: Zur Geschichte und Problematik einer zentralen Kategorie des deutschen geschichtlichen Bewusstseins," *Aus Politik und Zeitgeschichte* 27, no. 33 (1981): 3–21; Jürgen Kocka, "Der 'deutsche Sonderweg' in der Diskussion," *German Studies Review* 5 (1982): 365–79; Dieter Groh, "Le *Sonderweg* de l' Histoire Allemande: Mythe ou Réalité," *Annales* 38 (1983): 1166–87; Helga Grebing, *Der deutsche Sonderweg in Europa 1806–1954: Eine Kritik* (Stuttgart, 1986); Jacques Droz, "Postface," *Le Mouvement Social* 136 (1986): 125–35; Wolfram Fischer, "Wirtschafts- und sozialgeschichtliche Anmerkungen zum 'deutschen Sonderweg,'" *Tel Aviver Jahrbuch für deutsche Geschichte* 16 (1987): 96–116; Bernd Faulenbach, "Eine Variante europäischer Normalität? Zur neuesten Diskussion über den 'deutschen Weg' im 19. und 20. Jahrhundert," *Tel Aviver Jahrbuch für deutsche Geschichte* 16 (1987): 285–309; Jürgen Kocka, "German History before Hitler: The Debate about the German *Sonderweg*," *Journal of Contemporary History* 23 (1988): 3–16; Gerhard A. Ritter, "Die neuere Sozialgeschichte in der Bundesrepublik Deutschland," in *Sozialgeschichte im internationalen Überblick,* ed. Jürgen Kocka (Darmstadt, 1989), 19–89, esp. 52–58.

11. According to Johann Gottlieb Fichte, the German people were "das ursprüngliche, das unverfälschte Volk, das gegen die militärische wie kulturelle Unterjochung durch Frankreich um seine Freiheit und Identität kämpft und dabei im Dienste eines höheren geschichtlichen Auftrags handelt." Quoted in Hagen Schulze, *Der Weg zum Nationalstaat: Die deutsche Nationalbewegung vom 18. Jahrhundert bis zur Reichsgründung* (Munich, 1985), 63.

12. See Claude Digeon, *La Crise allemande de la Pensée Française, 1870–1914* (Paris, 1959); Günther Blaicher, *Das Deutschlandbild in der englischen Literatur* (Darmstadt, 1992).

13. See also Kocka, "Der 'deutsche Sonderweg' in der Diskussion," 366; and Pauline R. Anderson, "Gustav von Schmoller," in *Deutsche Historiker,* vol. 2, ed. Hans-Ulrich Wehler (Göttingen, 1971), 39–65; Bernhard vom Brocke, "Werner Sombart," in *Deutsche Historiker,* vol. 5 (Göttingen, 1972), 130–48.

14. Bernd Faulenbach, "Deutscher Sonderweg," 3–21, esp. 6–7. Only the left liberals and Social Democrats considered the development of western Europe as a model to be emulated.

A strong and efficient, but at the same time benevolent, monarchical power, an efficient and seemingly incorruptible bureaucracy, and the most advanced social legislation of the times accounted for the strength of the German model, which, it was claimed, afforded a far better integration of the lower classes than the Western democracies. Before the First World War, Germans saw themselves as having established a viable third path between the Western democracies and Czarist despotism. The German *Sonderbewusstsein* remained strong and increased with Germany's growing international isolation after 1905.[15] The awareness of a special development was kept alive, and a majority of Germans took pride in what they perceived as their special mission.[16]

When war came in 1914, a war that had been prepared ideologically by all sides,[17] Germany's intellectuals were as ready to defend their country's cultural achievements and national idiosyncrasies as her soldiers. The "ideas of 1914" were thus often tantamount to a manifesto for German uniqueness. Historians—such as Friedrich Meinecke and Ernst Troeltsch—journalists, and writers—Thomas Mann is among the better known—took up the pen to defend the cause of their country in the ideological struggle with the enemy, primarily England and France.[18] They did this by emphasizing Germany's divergence from the West. Profound German *Kultur* was juxtaposed with superficial English "civilization."[19] The deeply felt *Gemeinschaft* of German society was considered superior to the loose bonds that connected individuals in Western *Gesellschaften.* And what appeared to be the manifest disadvantage of Germany's political system, namely, its lack of democratic institutions, was turned into an intrinsic asset of the German state, which, though authoritarian, shouldered the material responsibility for even its lowliest citizens. The pathbreaking social legislation in Germany, which, according to the historian Ernst Troeltsch, created a "magnificent special variety of *Volksfreiheit...,*

---

15. On the term *Sonderbewusstsein* see Karl Dietrich Bracher's contribution in *Deutscher Sonderweg—Mythos oder Realität?* Kolloquien des Instituts für Zeitgeschichte (Munich, 1982), 46–53.

16. Bernd Faulenbach emphasizes that the idealization of the German path also served to conceal tensions, conflicts, and problems of integration within the Empire, contributing to the greater harmony of the fate-ordained German solution. Faulenbach, "Deutscher Sonderweg," 8.

17. Today one often tends to forget the role popular literature played in fanning national hatreds during the decade and a half before 1914. Erskine Childers's *The Riddle of the Sands,* for example, is only the best-known title among a plethora of books dealing with the growing German menace. See the excellent treatment of this issue in the first part of Marc Ferro's *The Great War* as well as in Samuel Hynes's *The Edwardian Turn of Mind* (Princeton, 1968), 35–38.

18. See Hermann Lübbe, "Die philosophischen Ideen von 1914," in *Politische Philosophie in Deutschland,* DTV paperback (Munich, 1974), 171–237; Klaus Schwabe, "Die politische Haltung der deutschen Professoren im ersten Weltkrieg," *Historische Zeitschrift* 193 (1961): 601–34; Schwabe, *Wissenschaft und Kriegsmoral* (Göttingen, 1969).

19. Treitschke's famous dictum that the English confounded soap with civilization had not been forgotten.

forcing the whole world to emulate it," was especially extolled.[20] The superiority of the Prussian-German *Beamtenstaat,* with its ethos of service and its intrinsic social-mindedness over Western plutocracy and eudaemonism, was evoked again and again.[21] Germany's superiority to Western Europe was felt even by the "unpolitical man," the title of Thomas Mann's famous book. In the ideological campaign waged during the first years of the First World War lie the origins of the more recent comparison between Germany's development and that of her Western neighbors that has occasioned so much controversy in the *Sonderweg* debates of the early 1980s.

After the First World War, in a republic disdained by its conservative elites, German historians continued positively emphasizing Germany's idiosyncrasies.[22] Studies claimed the continuity of "the German character" from old Germanic times, comparing it favorably to the French and English national character.[23] In the same vein, the uniqueness of the "German mind" was stressed, as was the importance of Luther's Reformation and German idealism and historicism for the formation of the German identity.[24] It was Hitler's assent to power that radically turned the argument against Germany. At this point the nature of the debate and the foundations of the *Sonderweg* question underwent a profound change. Through the emigré historians who fled Nazi Germany, the *Sonderweg* debate began to assume its present-day form. Once the ruthlessness of the Nazi dictatorship became fully evident (which did not take long), people questioned how a people that took such ostentatious pride in its culture could so willingly, cheerfully, and blindly follow a dictator who made no bones about his ultimate goals. Not only German emigré scholars but also journalists, intellectuals, and politicians in the West asked themselves how a movement as unrefined, uncouth, and violent as national socialism could rise to national prominence and captivate a civilized and educated nation.

During the 1930s, and then with increased intensity during the Second World War, the success of national socialism in Germany was explained with reference to German history. Such books as *From Luther to Hitler* were written for a popular audience, to warn an unsuspecting public of the German danger.

---

20. Ernst Troeltsch, "Der Ansturm der westlichen Demokratien," in *Die deutsche Freiheit,* ed. Bund deutscher Gelehrter und Künstler (Gotha, 1917), 79–114 (quoted in Faulenbach, "Deutscher Sonderweg," 8).

21. Lübbe, "Die philosophischen Ideen von 1914," in *Politische Philosophie in Deutschland,* 171–235; Schwabe, "Zur politischen Haltung der deutschen Professoren im ersten Weltkrieg," 601–34; Karl-Dietrich Bracher, *Zeit der Ideologien* (Stuttgart, 1982), 135.

22. See especially Bernd Faulenbach, *Ideologie des deutschen Weges* (Munich, 1980).

23. Germans were alleged to be "religiös-introvertiert, philosophisch spekulativ begabt, individuell freiheitsliebend, arbeitsam, ordnungsliebend und tapfer, nicht zuletzt aber unpolitisch." See Faulenbach, ibid., 31.

24. Faulenbach, ibid., 122–41.

Serious scholars also examined German prewar history with reference to the present (e.g., Ergang's biography of Frederick William I, entitled *The Potsdam Führer*) or explained Hitler's success as the continuity of authoritarian tendencies.[25] Ever since, the *Sonderweg* concept has implicitly been connected with 1933; it has been virtually impossible to analyze German history without reference to the Third Reich. German history prior to 1933 would henceforth be seen either as a long prelude to the following twelve years (by historians subscribing to the *Sonderweg* thesis) or as completely disconnected from the "aberration" of the Third Reich. For many historians the concept remained an implicit assumption underlying their writing, even when they were working on the history of the eighteenth or nineteenth century. The failure of the Revolution of 1848, for example, foreshadowed the weakness of the liberal bourgeoisie in Germany, which, in turn, became a structural precondition to Hitler's rise to power. Historians writing about Frederick the Great often studiously avoided the obvious military aspects of his reign, lest the Prussian king be seen in the light of a continuity of Prussian-German militarism that so often had been conjured up by the allies in the Second World War.

It is ironic that the propaganda of the Third Reich made every effort to integrate the national socialist movement into the course of German history. What were regarded as positive traditions, images, and achievements, from those of Luther to those of Frederick the Great and Bismarck, including those of Goethe, Schiller, Beethoven, and Wagner, were embraced as precursors of the Nazi regime.[26] Nazi propaganda toward this end was active and vociferous. During the Third Reich, the German past was made serviceable to the present to an extent hitherto unprecedented. Until then, the concept of Germany's special development was an ideology adopted mainly by the elites and the *Bildungsbürgertum*. But during the Third Reich, it was made palpable to the *Volksgemeinschaft* at large. History was reinterpreted in monumental motion pictures to suit the needs of the moment. In a series of films on Frederick the Great,[27] the Prussian king provided a model example of how tenacity, austerity, and the willingness to sacrifice could overcome even the greatest odds

---

25. For example, Edmond Vermeil argues in *Les Doctrinaires de la Révolution allemande* (Paris, 1939) that Hitler's path to power was blazed by a continuity of authoritarian thought. See Lucien Febvre's perspicacious criticism of this approach in his review, "Sur la doctrine Nationale-Socialiste," *Annales d' Histoire Sociale* 1 (1939): 426–28.

26. This often accounted for their negative image after the war. Some German writers and composers, such as Friedrich Nietzsche and Richard Wagner, were to remain permanently tainted. Works or persons not fitting Nazi ideology, e.g., Lessing's *Nathan der Weise* or Heinrich Heine's works, were quickly eliminated. For a full collection of who counted among the German Pantheon after 1933 see Willy Andreas and Wilhelm von Scholz, *Die Grossen Deutschen,* 5 vols. (Berlin, 1935–37), which contains about two hundred biographies.

27. Johannes Meyer's *Fridericus* (1937), Veit Harlan's *Der grosse König* (1942) and *Der Choral von Leuthen* (1933), and the earlier *Das Flötenkonzert von Sanssouci* by Gustav Ucicky.

stacked against his country. In Wolfgang Liebenheiner's *Bismarck* (1940), the Prussian prime minister was turned into the protagonist of the German national movement. And in Veit Harlan's *Kolberg* (1944–45), the popular upswell underlying the Wars of Liberation in 1813 was distorted to prepare the ground for a general popular uprising to counter Germany's immanent invasion by the allies.[28] Propaganda thus made a gigantic effort to identify national socialism with specifically Prussian values, such as thrift, austerity, frugality, integrity, tenacity in pursuit of even seemingly unattainable goals, and self-reliant composure in the face of adversity. These virtues were meant to become part of the foundation on which the new national socialist character would be formed.[29]

The image of a strong welfare-state tradition that had already been emphasized during the Empire was revived as a centerpiece of German particularities to stress the traditional social responsibility for the lower orders that the state had taken on itself. Prussian conservatives' concern for the lower classes was applauded, in particular their specifically "Prussian socialism," whereby the industrial worker attained the place that was his due while being integrated into the national community. Between 1933 and 1939, the Prussian social policies that foreshadowed Bismarck's all-encompassing program of social reform attracted much interest.

Major studies on the 1840s through the 1860s, such as Walter Früh's *Radowitz als Sozialpolitiker,* Adalbert Hahn's analysis of the social conservatism of the *Berliner Revue,* and Adolf Richter's *Bismarck und die Arbeiterfrage im preussischen Verfassungskonflikt,* were written during the early stages of the Third Reich.[30] It is revealing that a topic that met with scant interest after 1945 enjoyed great popularity during the Third Reich. The parallels the authors of these studies drew between their own time and the Prussia of the 1850s and 1860s were critical to the question of continuity in German historical development.[31] Walter Früh, for example, emphasized that Radowitz's view of social problems had become especially timely "today"

---

28. There was also a multitude of films on famous German writers (e.g., Herbert Maisch's *Friedrich Schiller—Triumph eines Genies*), musicians (Traugott Müller's *Friedemann Bach*), and doctors (G. W. Papst's *Paracelsus*).

29. On the use of Prussian symbols and values in national socialist propaganda see Manfred Schlenke, "Das 'Preussische Beispiel' in Propaganda und Politik des Nationalsozialismus," *Aus Politik und Zeitgeschichte* 27 (1968): 16–23; Schlenke, "Nationalsozialismus und Preussen/Preussentum," in *Das Preussenbild in der Geschichte,* ed. Otto Büsch (Berlin, 1981), 247–64; Wolfgang Wippermann, "Nationalsozialismus und Preussentum," *Aus Politik und Zeitgeschichte* 52–53 (1981): 13–22; Konrad Barthel, *Friedrich der Grosse in Hitlers Geschichtsbild* (Wiesbaden, 1977).

30. See Walter Früh, "Radowitz als Sozialpolitiker" (Ph.D. diss., University of Berlin, 1937); Adalbert Hahn, *Die Berliner Revue* (Berlin, 1934); Adolf Richter, *Bismarck und die Arbeiterfrage im preussischen Verfassungskonflikt* (Stuttgart, 1935).

31. See also chapter 9.

(i.e., 1937).[32] In regard to social issues, Früh equated his own time with nineteenth-century Prussia:

> Present-day German socialism, the revival of the irrational, organic forces of the *Staats-* and *Volksgemeinschaft,* the endeavors to realize the restructuring of the whole people along *ständisch* lines—these factors are suited [*geeignet*] to a rekindling of interest in the ideas of German social conservatives in the age of early capitalism [*Frühkapitalismus*] and the March revolution on the basis of a new appreciation.[33]

Adalbert Hahn admitted that while his analysis of the *Berliner Revue* was originally meant as a contribution to the history of the conservative party, "it became evident in the course of the investigation that the men and ideas under consideration were a product of [*handelten vom*] the first appearance of national socialist reasoning in German politics." Putting it even more bluntly, he expressed the hope that his examination of conservative ideas would contribute "to advance the understanding of this great movement of freedom and rejuvenation" (i.e., national socialism).[34] The social ideas of the *Reichsgründungszeit* in Prussia were viewed as both forerunners of and a model for national socialism. But the national socialist present had the decisive advantage over the Prussian past in that the working class was now fully integrated into the state, whereas in the past, as a result of Wagener's failure to implement his social program "the mass of workers had been alienated from national ideas for a long time."[35]

The constant appeal by the German elite to the values of the German past undoubtedly contributed to the tendency of the Western powers during the Second World War to interpret pre-1933 German history as a long prelude to Nazi dictatorship.[36] Hitler's seizure of power was interpreted as the logical conclusion of German historical development. In the West, as in the Nazi Empire, German history thus became a history of continuities, from Luther, to Frederick the Great, to Bismarck, and finally to Hitler. In Western eyes, the vaunted Prussian virtues, which were assessed positively within Germany, assumed purely negative qualities. Prussia became synonymous with degrad-

---

32. See Früh, "Radowitz," 8, "Seine heute wieder besonders zur Geltung kommende Auffassung von der Gesellschaft als einem organischen Ganzen."

33. Ibid., 7.

34. Hahn, *Die Berliner Revue,* 4.

35. Richter, *Bismarck und die Arbeiterfrage,* 259. Richter also emphasized the common ground between Hermann Wagener's ideas and the present (34).

36. See, for example, William M. McGovern, *From Luther to Hitler: The History of Fascist Nazi Philosophy* (London, 1946); Rohan D'O. Butler, *The Roots of National Socialism 1783–1933* (London, 1942).

ing humiliation of the individual, spineless obedience, contempt for human life, humorlessness, militarism, and inhuman severity.

While the boundaries between propaganda and historical scholarship had become fluid during the war, a new generation of emigré historians continued the *Sonderweg* line of inquiry with greater sophistication in the 1950s and 1960s. George L. Mosse, Fritz Stern, and Leonard Krieger were the most prominent among those historians who focused on laying bare the traditions and intellectual trends in the German past that facilitated Hitler's rise to power. These included the *völkisch* nationalism of the German youth movement, examined in Mosse's *Crisis of German Ideology;* the antimodernism and anti-intellectualism among right-wing intellectuals in the Empire and the Weimar Republic, emphasized by Fritz Stern's *The Politics of Cultural Despair;* and the peculiar understanding of a liberalism that was perfectly compatible with the authoritarian *Obrigkeitsstaat,* found in Krieger's *The German Idea of Freedom.*[37] Most of these studies were highly sophisticated and drew attention to tendencies in the German past that hitherto had been little noticed. Their common denominator was an emphasis on ideas and intellectual movements, and accordingly they employed the methods and sources of intellectual history rather than those of social or political history. In contrast, the next generation of German historians who became associated with the *Sonderweg* (e.g., Hans-Ulrich Wehler and Jürgen Kocka) primarily focused on structures (bureaucracy), social classes (*Mittelstand*), and organizations (*Interessenverbände*) representing special interests. In the English literature, they are often referred to as social historians of politics.[38]

In the 1950s and the first half of the 1960s, analyses bearing a direct relationship to the *Sonderweg* were limited to Anglo-Saxon scholars. In the fifteen years after the Second World War, historians in Germany reacted defensively to the wholesale condemnation of the German past. Instead, they upheld the conservative traditions of the Empire. Since the more progressive historians of the Weimar Republic had been forced into emigration and did not return to Germany after the war, the prevailing mood in the German historical profession was more conservative in the 1950s than it had been during the early 1930s.[39] The prevalent consensus among the older generation of historians (as

---

37. George L. Mosse, *The Crisis of German Ideology* (London, 1964); Fritz Stern, *Politics of Cultural Despair;* Leonard Krieger, *The German Idea of Freedom: History of a Political Tradition* (Boston, 1957). Other studies focus on ideological filiations, such as Hans Kohn's *The German Mind.*

38. See, for example, Georg Iggers, *The Social History of Politics* (Leamington Spa, 1985).

39. The German historical establishment of the 1950s was, as George Iggers remarked, more conservative than that of Weimar, since the liberals had been forced into either emigration or retirement. Such historians as Hans Rosenberg, Felix Gilbert, Arthur Rosenberg, Erich Eyck, and Hajo Holborn left Germany, while Johannes Ziekursch and even Friedrich Meinecke were forced into retirement.

embodied by Gerhard Ritter) was that Hitler had been an aberration rather than the logical outcome of German history. The older generation of German historians thus fought against the condemnation of their past and found themselves in a position of permanent defensiveness.

This changed dramatically in the wake of the Fischer controversy. Fritz Fischer, a member of the establishment itself, broke ranks and left the united front of the profession by arguing that German elites had deliberately provoked (and accelerated) the outbreak of war in 1914 to salvage the privileges offered them by an outmoded political and social system. Though the content of Fischer's arguments was revolutionary, Fischer continued to use methods and sources of traditional historiography, namely, documents on foreign policy. By implicitly postulating a continuity of foreign policy from Imperial Germany to the Third Reich, Fischer naturally raised the possibility of a corresponding continuity in domestic politics.[40] If there were similarities between Hitler's foreign policy and that of Wilhelm II, then comparable similarities might be found between the domestic policies of the Third Reich and that of the Empire. The origins of the Third Reich might then precisely be found in the domestic development of late nineteenth- and early twentieth-century Germany.[41] To a younger generation of historians, the unabashed authoritarian behavior of their elders and of German elites in general must have strengthened the case for the continuity thesis. Partially as a result of Fisher's heresy, which had cleared the way for a new generation of historians born after 1930, Germany's historiographical landscape altered drastically by the end of the 1960s.[42] Somewhat

---

40. As Fischer wrote in the introduction, "The book points beyond its own limits, in that it demonstrates certain ways of thought and formulation of aims of German policy in the First World War, which have continued to remain active. From this point of view it may also be a contribution to the problem of continuity in German history from the First to the Second World War." Quoted in James Joll, "The 1914 Debate Continues: Fritz Fischer and his Critics," *Past and Present* 34 (1966): 100–113. See also Wolfgang J. Mommsen, "The Debate on German War Aims," *Journal of Contemporary History* 1, no. 3 (1966): 47–72. Both Joll and Mommsen emphasize the importance of Fischer for the continuity thesis. According to Mommsen, Fischer's book triggered off a whole series of investigations on the constitutional, political, and social structure of the Empire (71). For Fischer's importance for the problem of continuity see also Wolfgang Jäger, *Historische Forschung und politische Kultur in Deutschland: Die Debatte 1914–1980 über den Ausbruch des Ersten Weltkrieges* (Göttingen, 1984).

41. This had already been postulated by Helmut Plessner in his book *Die verspätete Nation* (1959).

42. This "paradigm change" in German historiography, as some historians have called it, was due also to the influx of many new historians in the course of the expansion of the universities after 1960. See Werner Conze, "Die deutsche Geschichtswissenschaft seit 1945," *Historische Zeitschrift* 225 (1977): 1–28, esp. 18–21; Hans-Ulrich Wehler, "Geschichtswissenschaft heute," in *Stichworte zur 'Geistigen Situation der Zeit,'* ed. Jürgen Habermas (Frankfurt, 1979), 709–53; Ernst Schulin, "Zur Restauration und langsamen Weiterentwicklung der deutschen Geschichtswissenschaft nach 1945," in *Traditionskritik und Rekonstruktionsversuch* (Göttingen, 1979), 133–43.

misleadingly, these historians have become known under the label of the "Bielefeld School" or, by their Anglo-Saxon detractors, as "Kehrites,"[43] after Eckhart Kehr, who inaugurated the tradition followed by the Bielefelders (among others, Hans-Ulrich Wehler, Jürgen Kocka, Hans-Jürgen Puhle, Helmut Berding, Heinrich August Winkler, Reinhard Rürup, and Hans and Wolfgang Mommsen).

The Bielefeld historians had strong theoretical interests and put forth a relatively coherent *Geschichtsbild*. They shared a pronounced emphasis on theory insofar as they usually interconnected their empirical studies with theoretical models that were often borrowed from Max Weber or Karl Marx. And some have argued that they shared an often impenetrable writing style of long involved nominal constructions to which the German language lends itself.[44] Two additional factors were constitutive in forming the Bielefeld historical paradigm. The first and most important factor was undoubtedly the shared experiences and views of German history that had shaped their generation. Born shortly before or during the Third Reich and forced to witness the disintegration of a world around them, expelled (in several cases) from their native homelands and having spent their formative years in ruins in an often alien environment, they were less likely to fall victim to any saving belief; on the contrary, they became fiercely critical of traditional ideologies. The second factor was the Bielefeld group's common reaction to the traditional conservatism of their mentors, for whom the values of the Kaiserreich had still provided the guiding yardsticks of proper behavior. In reacting to this standpoint, the new generation of historians fell into the opposite extreme: instead of excusing the Third Reich as a mere accident in the German past, as several of the older historians were tempted to do, they tended to view German history prior to 1933 as a prehistory of the Third Reich. They never explicitly stated that the course of German history would inevitably lead to Hitler, but they implicitly interpreted important periods in German history before the Third Reich from the standpoint of what followed 1933 and not in their own right.

The most prominent example of this approach is Hans-Ulrich Wehler's *The German Empire,* which treats the Empire as a prelude to the Third Reich. Wehler selected and structured his material according to this assertion. He thus focused exclusively on the negative features, that is, on structures of Imperial German history that facilitated Hitler's rise to power. Due to his perspective,

---

43. The term itself was coined by Wolfgang Mommsen, "Domestic Factors in German Foreign Policy before 1914," *Central European History* 6 (1973): 3–43, in the context of his analysis of different "approaches in recent research on Wilhelmine Germany by Western historians" (7). Mommsen distinguished between the socio-Marxist, moralistic, Kehrite, and functional-structural approaches.

44. In light of their more recent publications in the 1980s, most of which are superbly readable (e.g., Wehler's *Gesellschaftsgeschichte*), this contention is simply incorrect.

Wehler was bound to overemphasize the authoritarian aspects of political life in the Empire, such as political repression, the weight of the neofeudal Junker class, and the semiconstitutional makeup of the state.[45] The image Wehler put forth was thus too neat, too model-oriented, too free of contradictions, and too logical; his argument was too coherent in its formidable one-sidedness, focusing solely on the continuities between the *Kaiserreich* and the Third Reich. Wehler's point of view becomes understandable (and his work a considerable achievement) when taking into account the political atmosphere surrounding West German historiography, but one can rightly accuse him of simplifying a multifaceted German past, because by consciously dispensing with the contradictions and imponderables of complex historical development, he channeled the vagaries of history into the strictures of a more accurate science. Like most iconoclasts, he exaggerated to make his point and painted the new image without shades of gray, in colors too stark, to shatter the old one all the more effectively.

A salient feature of Bielefeld historiography was its political mission. History, in Wehler's telling phrase, was the *Lehrmeister* of life (*Historia Magistra Vitae*), providing yardsticks for political orientation. An effective attack on Wehler's view could not come from within Germany, for anyone sharing his political views would necessarily have shied away from criticizing his historiographical assumptions, and conservative critics of his politics would have been accused of political motives for any attack on his historiography. Correspondingly, Bielefeld historiography became heavily politicized. Its most unfortunate by-product was that a sort of "political correctness" became a *conditio sine qua non* for practicing history. The left-liberal Bielefelders began to practice a kind of reverse discrimination vis-à-vis their more conservative colleagues, which, in an antagonistic political climate, may well be said to have

---

45. The constitution of the Empire was labeled "pseudoconstitutional semiabsolutism"; Bismarckian Germany was seen as a "plebiscitary dictatorship" (along the lines of Napoleon III); Bismarck's ruling technique was characterized as "Bonapartism"; and civil rights and freedoms were drastically curtailed. To remain in power, the elites employed tactics of manipulation (as when Bismarck split the liberals in 1866 and 1878/79). To foster loyalty among the masses, they were mobilized behind a program of national enthusiasm that deflected attention from real social problems (social imperialism), while the ruling elites themselves remained welded together, despite divergent economic interests, by constant fear of internal subversion emanating from groups such as Social Democrats, Catholic South Germans, and national minorities (negative integration). The *staatserhaltende* groups of the right were bound together by *Sammlungspolitik* (heavy industry and landed aristocracy). Ideologically the bourgeoisie was feudalized (*Reserveoffizier*) and made every effort to ape the Junkers. The German Empire as a whole was depicted as a mixture of highly successful capitalist industrialization and socioeconomic modernization on the one hand and of surviving preindustrial institutions on the other: an unstable edifice whose internal tensions led to oppression and manipulation.

been part of regular discourse.[46] It was quite possible, especially in the 1970s, that a historian's political views might have some bearing on the ultimate evaluation of his scholarly work.[47]

The angle under which German history was viewed, that of 1933, predetermined, to a certain extent, its selection and content. The knowledge of the crimes of the national socialist regime exerted moral pressure on the historian to deal severely with the German past. German history became the history of negative continuities leading up to Hitler's seizure of power. Especially in the 1970s, when the real and imagined opposition to the history the Bielefelders preached was strong, it must have been difficult for their own followers to escape from their excessively narrow *Geschichtsbild.* Still attacked from a more traditional historical point of view by historians who stressed the primacy of foreign policy (e.g., Andreas Hillgruber and Klaus Hildebrand), the Bielefelders turned with indignation against their critics from the Left, such as Geoff Eley and David Blackbourn. The latter were initially dismissed as orthodox Marxists, since the Bielefelders believed that someone from their own political camp would hardly have dared be critical of their historiography. What aggravated the situation further was that Eley's and Blackbourn's criticism of the Bielefelders was originally welcomed by conservatives in Germany, who mistakenly ascribed a conservative approach to the two British historians, since they so unashamedly attacked the Bielefeld dogma. German conservatives also rejected the notion of a "negative" *Sonderweg,* but on the basis of a significantly different set of assumptions. Blackbourn and Eley were just as critical of the authoritarian and undemocratic streaks of Imperial German society as the Bielefelders, but they denied their all-pervasiveness and their uniqueness when compared to Western Europe. They were far from agreeing with the traditionally conservative assertion that the Third Reich was but an aberration in German history. One also tends to overlook the fact that they had a certain debt of gratitude to the Bielefelders, since, as Blackbourn, Eley, and Richard Evans have repeatedly emphasized, it was because of the works of Wehler, Böhme, Puhle, Berghahn, and others that there was a sense of "freshness and excitement" surrounding the historiography of the *Kaiserreich* that prompted them to select Imperial Germany as their scholarly pursuit.[48]

---

46. The fact that scholarship had acquired political overtones was not a purely negative phenomenon, since it also provided incentives for empirical research to buttress one's own position.

47. See Karl-Georg Faber's pertinent criticism of Wehler's "Geschichtswissenschaft heute," in Faber, "Geschichtswissenschaft als retrospektive Politik," *Geschichte und Gesellschaft* 6 (1980): 574–85; Thomas Nipperdey, "Unter der Herrschaft des Verdachts," in *Historikerstreit* (Munich, 1987), 215–19.

48. See Richard Evans, "Introduction: Wilhelm II's Germany and the Historians," in *Society and Politics in Wilhelmine Germany* (London, 1978), 11–39; the introduction to Evans,

Bielefeld historians could always defend their concept of the *Sonderweg* by pointing out that short-term factors hardly sufficed to explain Nazism. The lost war, the oppressive Versailles Treaty, the inflation of 1923, and the Great Depression of the late 1920s could explain much. But to appreciate fully why the most radical of fascist ideologies took root in Germany, how Hitler could come to power legally, and why his regime enjoyed such great popularity (especially before 1938), more fundamental causes had to be found. The most obvious explanation seemed to be that national socialism could draw on traditions ingrained in the German past, which Hitler, in turn, shrewdly exploited. In searching for these traditions, Bielefeld historians were interested not so much in the intellectual forerunners of Nazism (as, for example, Leonard Krieger, Fritz Stern, and George Mosse had been) or in a filiation of ideas from Luther to Hitler, but in an examination of the social, economic, and structural preconditions of German history that made Hitler possible. Toward this end, they focused on institutions, social classes, and modernization processes. Bielefeld historiography has been aptly summarized and interpreted too often to be discussed again in detail.[49] Much of it concentrated on the German Empire. Like Thorstein Veblen and Ralf Dahrendorf before them,[50] Bielefeld

---

Rethinking German History (London, 1987), 1–20; David Blackbourn, *Populists and Patricians* (London, 1987), 1–29; Geoff Eley, *From Unification to Nazism: Reinterpreting the German Past* (London, 1986), 1–20. In recounting his intellectual *Werdegang,* Eley writes that with his dissertation, he originally (before going to the archives) meant to "add one more building block to the emerging revisionist [i.e., "Bielefeld"] edifice" (8). See also Eley's originally positive assessment of Wehler in "Some Recent Tendencies in Social History," in *International Handbook of Historical Studies: Contemporary Research and Theory,* ed. Georg G. Iggers and Harold T. Parker (Westport, Conn., 1979), 66 n. 4. The reception of Bielefeld historiography in Anglo-Saxon countries, especially in the United States, was facilitated by the fact that much of their scholarly audience was already familiar with the basic theme of a negative continuity in German history. German emigré scholars had blazed the trail.

49. See especially Irmeliné Veit-Brause, "Zur Kritik an der 'Kritischen Geschichtswissenschaft': Tendenzwende oder Paradigmawechsel?" *Geschichte in Wissenschaft und Unterricht* 31 (1984): 1–24; James Retallack, "Social History with a Vengeance? Some Reactions to H.-U. Wehler's 'Das Deutsche Kaiserreich,'" *German Studies Review* 7 (1984): 423–50; Roger Fletcher, "Recent Developments in West German Historiography: The Bielefeld School and Its Critics," *German Studies Review* 7 (1984): 451–80; Robert G. Moeller, "The Kaiserreich Recast? Continuity and Change in Modern German Historiography," *Journal of Social History* 17 (1984), 655–83; David Blackbourn and Geoff Eley, *The Peculiarities of German History* (Oxford, 1984). See also the surveys by Georg G. Iggers: *The German Conception of History,* rev. ed. (Hanover, 1983), 269–93; *New Directions in European Historiography,* rev. ed. (Hanover, 1984), 80–122; and, most recently, *Geschichtswissenschaft im 20. Jahrhundert* (Göttingen, 1993), pp. 54–62. See also Wehler, "Geschichtswissenschaft heute"; Wolfgang Mommsen, "Gegenwärtige Tendenzen in der Geschichtsschreibung der Bundesrepublik"; Gerhard A. Ritter, "Neuere Sozialgeschichte in der Bundesrepublik."

50. Thorstein Veblen, *Imperial Germany and the Industrial Revolution* (New York, 1915); Ralf Dahrendorf, *Gesellschaft und Demokratie in Deutschland* (Munich, 1968).

historians emphasized the discrepancy between Germany's economic transformation into a great industrial power and its stultified social and political system—that is, the fact that hand in hand with industrialization, Germany did not develop into a democratic state. In contrast to England and France, Germany modernized without experiencing a successful social or political revolution.[51]

In response to the central arguments and underlying assumptions of Bielefeld historiography (as exemplified in Wehler's *Das deutsche Kaiserreich*) and the Bielefeld concept of the *Sonderweg*, Hans-Günther Zmarzlik and Thomas Nipperdey in Germany and David Blackbourn, Geoff Eley, and Richard Evans in England raised a series of objections.[52] The starting point of Blackbourn's and Eley's criticism was a distrust, nourished by experience, of the idealized liberalism of English society that was inherent in the *Sonderweg* concept. As English leftists, they knew instinctively that the *Sonderweg* thesis painted an idealized image of their native England. Their ingrained knowledge of "the undemocratic and illiberal side of Victorian and Edwardian Britain" caused a feeling of unease that Richard Evans encapsulated when he wrote that "it seemed absurd to those of us brought up in the decades of British decline that modern British history should be held up by historians of Germany as an example from which it was Germany's entire misfortune to have deviated."[53] David Blackbourn emphasized the strength of the German bourgeoisie, and Eley's main concern was "both to loosen the deterministic grip of the 'road to 1933' on our perceptions of the period before 1914 and to render the imperial German experience more constructively comparable to that of its peer societies west of the Rhine."[54] In his earlier criticism, Hans-Günther Zmarzlik had equally demanded "a more 'open' historiography" that did not treat the Empire solely as a "forecourt" of the Third Reich,[55] while Thomas Nipperdey had pointed out that there were many continuities in German history before 1933 that mutually overlapped. Wehler had overemphasized the "deterministic ele-

---

51. Already Theodore Hamerow had written that "the mistakes of 1848 had to be paid for not in 1849, but in 1918, 1933 and 1945." See Hamerow, *Restoration, Revolution, Reaction* (Princeton, 1958), viii.

52. See Hans-Günther Zmarzlik, "Das Kaiserreich in neuer Sicht?" *Historische Zeitschrift* 222 (1976): 105–26; Thomas Nipperdey, "Wehlers 'Kaiserreich': Eine kritische Auseinandersetzung," *Geschichte und Gesellschaft* 1 (1975): 539–60; Blackbourn and Eley, *Peculiarities of German History.* See also the collections of essays by David Blackbourn, *Populists and Patricians;* Geoff Eley, *From Unification to Nazism;* and Richard Evans, *Rethinking German History.*

53. Evans, *Rethinking German History,* 8.

54. Eley, *From Unification to Nazism,* 12.

55. Zmarzlik, "Das Kaiserreich in neuer Sicht?" 125, 106.

ment;"[56] German history before Hitler's rise to power was more than a pre-history of the Third Reich.[57]

The accumulated weight of the combined criticism fundamentally questioned the validity of the *Sonderweg* thesis. The problem of continuity in German history, as expressed in the *Sonderweg* thesis, was originally defined as Germany's divergence from the West. But was there really a normal path from which Germany's development diverged? Could the Western path of development be taken as the norm, or might it not be better to formulate the question differently (as Ralf Dahrendorf did, for example, in asking why Germany failed to become a liberal democracy and in examining the structural impediments on the road to a liberal democratic state)? And why should the West be used as a model?[58] Why not compare Germany to Russian or Polish constitutional development?[59] A comparison of the resistance to liberalism in Germany and Russia might prove as instructive as a comparison of German and Russian conservatism. But then the very nature of a theory of continuity is problematic since, as Thomas Nipperdey has argued, it is bound to relate past reality in a polarized fashion, thereby not only doing injustice to a complex reality but also destroying the claim of a universally valid *Wissenschaft* by explicitly introducing value judgments.[60] An extreme instance of this was presented by Kurt Sontheimer in a 1982 colloquium on the *Sonderweg,* where he insisted that the *Sonderweg* concept be retained in its present form (even if falsified empirically) since it constitutes "a necessary function of post–World War II German political identity."[61] According to Sontheimer, the thesis of the German *Sonderweg* must maintain the character of a moral appeal. Relinquishing the *Sonderweg* concept would break the spine of German political consciousness as it had evolved after 1945 and would "tempt us on to *falsche politische Wege.*"[62] In Sontheimer's estimation, the theory of the *Sonderweg*

---

56. Nipperdey, "Wehler's 'Kaiserreich,'" 544.

57. See also Thomas Nipperdey, "1933 und die Kontinuität der deutschen Geschichte," *Historische Zeitschrift* 227 (1978): 86–111.

58. Thomas Nipperdey justifiably argued that since the second half of the nineteenth century, Germany was more directly comparable with western Europe than with the countries of southern and eastern Europe in regard to legal systems, culture, and bourgeois mentality. See Nipperdey's commentary in *Deutscher Sonderweg—Mythos oder Realität?* Kolloquien des Instituts für Zeitgeschichte (Munich, 1982), 19.

59. See, for example, Otto Hintze's essays in *Staat und Verfassung* (Göttingen, 1962).

60. See Thomas Nipperdey's article, "1933 und die Kontinuität der deutschen Geschichte," in which he disputes the validity of the "critical continuity theory." For a less critical overall assessment of the continuity theory see his commentary in *Deutscher Sonderweg—Mythos oder Realität?* 16–27, where he does not question the basic usefulness of the concept.

61. *Deutscher Sonderweg—Mythos oder Realität?* 30 (27–33 for the full text).

62. Ibid., 32–33.

was therefore to be retained at all cost for reasons of moral and political expediency, an intellectual position that (despite the genuine moral concern that looms large behind it) renders social science as we know it superfluous.

Gerhard A. Ritter's argument that the *Sonderweg* debate should not be limited to Germany's divergence from the West with the sole aim of explaining the success of the Nazi regime is especially convincing.[63] While the origins of national socialism will always remain one of the *Sonderweg*'s central tenets, the concept could successfully be used to highlight other idiosyncrasies of German historical development that need not be solely negative. The *Sonderweg* concept can serve to make historians more receptive to special features of the German past by focusing on the innate peculiarities of German history and their long-term effect on later developments (such as, for example, the Thirty Years' War, the social impact of the Reformation, or the constitutional dilemmas posed by countless principalities). So far we have little more than sweeping generalizations devoid of empirical substantiation, such as claims of the nefarious effects of authoritarian Prussian Protestantism on the shaping of the German *Untertanenmentalität*.

The most portentous peculiarity of the German past lies possibly in Prussia's overpowering influence on Germany's political and social development after 1871. Historians have speculated on the importance of the Prussian legacy for twentieth-century German history, a heritage occasionally summarized under the heading "Preussentum und Nationalsozialismus."[64] The importance of Prussian symbols and values for national socialist propaganda is beyond dispute; Goebbels's and Hitler's allusions to Prussian history, especially Frederick the Great, are virtually innumerable.[65] In the day-to-day propaganda of the Third Reich, references to Prussian history served as a basis of legitimation, as Manfred Schlenke has demonstrated so impressively.[66] At the same time, it

---

63. Gerhard A. Ritter, "Neuere Sozialgeschichte in der Bundesrepublik," 55.

64. See Manfred Schlenke, "Nationalsozialismus und Preussen/Preussentum"; Wolfgang Wippermann, "Nationalsozialismus und Preussentum"; Johannes Rogalla von Bieberstein, "Preussen und Preussentum," *Aus Politik und Zeitgeschichte* 2 (1980): 26–38.

65. See Konrad Barthel, *Friedrich der Grosse in Hitlers Geschichtsbild* (Wiesbaden, 1977).

66. The integration of the Prussian past into the national socialist state is best embodied in the symbolism surrounding the opening of parliament at the "Tag von Potsdam" after the 1933 March election. There the identity of national socialism and Prussianism became virtually complete. So, for example, on a postcard commemorating the event, the images of Frederick the Great, Bismarck, and Hindenburg were superimposed on the photograph of their "legitimate heir," Hitler. The caption on the card, which circulated by the millions, read: "Was der König eroberte, der Fürst formte, der Feldmarschall verteidigte, rettete und einigte der Soldat" (Schlenke, "Nationalsozialismus und Preussen/Preussentum," 252). Very much in the same vein, Goebbels stated in a speech during the election campaign for the Prussian Diet (April, 1932): "Der Nationalsozialismus darf mit Fug und Recht von sich behaupten, dass er Preussentum sei. Wo immer wir Nationalsozialisten auch stehen in ganz Deutschland, sind wir Preussen. Die Idee, die wir

is obvious that the real historical links between republican Prussia, a bastion of democracy during the Weimar Years, and the Third Reich are extremely tenuous. There are, however, ideological connections between Prussianism and national socialist ideology[67] that were more than tenuous. The social policy conceptions of Radowitz and Hermann Wagener in the 1840s through 1860s, greatly praised and held up as models by historians after 1933, indeed foreshadow ideas or even foster a sociopolitical discourse that gained renewed significance after 1933. The ideas of Prussia's social conservatives were conceived before the time of rigid party constellations and before social democracy had established itself as a strong independent force. Viewed through the lens of the 1930s, the decades between 1840 and 1870 seemed a period when the industrial laborer could still be won over by a conservative state and used as a tool to combat the liberal challenge (as best exemplified in the "Social Kingdom").

During those decades in the middle of the nineteenth century, social conservatives finally turned away from the old ideal of the *Ständestaat* and began fully to endorse state power, realizing that the remnants of their own power were vested in the state. In their affirmation of a strong state lies the explanation for their surprising affinity toward socialism, especially with Radowitz and Wagener. In their amalgamation of conservative and socialist ideas, their opposition to industrial capitalism, their emphasis that property entailed an inherent obligation and was morally untenable without it, and their intellectual anti-intellectualism, they were ideological precursors of the radical conservatism of the twentieth century and even of fascism.

But their ideas were only one ingredient of the authoritarian welfare state. The other essential component was provided by the long-standing Prussian tradition of bureaucracy. This bureaucratic tradition in Prussia, going back to Frederick William I, in some respects even to the Great Elector, facilitated the rise of the welfare state; in stronger terms, the establishment of the welfare state would have been impossible without this tradition. The strength and early consolidation of an entrenched bureaucracy is another pivotal feature of Germany's special development. In this regard one could say that Germany was a more "modern" state than any of the states in Western Europe. The early development of a sophisticated bureaucracy had, however, its own inherent dichotomy of welfare for the citizens, on the one hand, and the mailed fist of an authoritarian state, on the other.

---

tragen, ist preussisch. Die Wahrzeichen, für die wir fechten, sind von Preussengeist erfüllt, und die Ziele, die wir zu erreichen trachten, sind in verjüngter Form die Ideale, denen Friedrich Wilhelm I., der grosse Friedrich und Bismarck nachstrebten" (ibid., 248).

67. Wolfgang Wippermann speaks of "ideologiegeschichtliche Verbindungen" (Wippermann, "Nationalsozialismus und Preussentum," 20).

The old question of whether the Third Reich represented continuity in Prusso-German history or departed significantly from the mainstream of historical development certainly cannot be answered with a simple "yes" or "no." There were elements of both continuity and discontinuity. The emphasis on continuity or deviation ultimately depends on the individual historian's perspective, that is, on the specific questions asked which, in turn, predetermine the selection of the historian's sources. Within the context of conservative ideas and policies it can be argued that the image of a certain continuity was emphasized during the Third Reich, a continuity that did not, in fact, exist as distinctly in the actual theory or practice of conservative politics. As has been shown above, this was accomplished by tailoring proven and tested conservative concepts from the nineteenth century to the specific socio-political circumstances of the 1930s.

Bibliography

Archival Sources

Zentrales Staatsarchiv II, Merseburg (The archival sources listed under Merseburg were transferred to the Geheimes Staatsarchiv Preussischer Kulturbesitz in Berlin-Dahlem between 1992 and 1994.)

Rep. 77. Ministerium des Innern

Sammmlung der für die verschiedenen Territorien in den Provinzen Rheinland und Westfalen erlassenen Provinzial- und Partikulargesetze, vol. 2 (1837–47), no. 39.

Historische und statistische Nachrichten über den preussischen Staat, vol. 4 (1842–53), titel 94, no. 14.

Die Conduitenlisten über die Regierungspräsidenten, Beamtensachen CB, vol. 1 (1844–47), titel 184a, no. 4.

Acta betr. Lehrer Wander in Hirschberg wegen politisch verdächtigen Treibens, vol. 1 (1843–56), 6, no. 117.

Acta betreffend den vormaligen Buchhändler, jetzigen Freigutbesitzer Eduard Pelz, vol. 1 (1843–45), 6, no. 125.

Die Marktpreise des Getreides, der Hülsenfrüchte, des Fleisches, Branntweins in den vorzüglichsten Städten der preussischen Staaten, titel 94, no. 23.

Vorschläge zur Verbesserung der Staatsverwaltung, vol. 2 (1841–49) 5, 36, no. 4.

Das Verhalten der katholischen Geistlichen und der Beamten in der Provinz Posen in Bezug auf den polnischen Aufstand (1831–35), titel 503, no. 5.

Die politischen und Volksvereine der Stadt Berlin und deren Umgebung, vol. 1 (1844–50), titel 1072, no. 1.

Die Gründung einer neuen Politischen Zeitung in der Rheinprovinz, vol. 1 (1842–44), titel 864, no. 1.

Volksaufstände und Tumulte, Königsberg, vol. 1 (1831–51), titel 504, no. 6.

Die gegen Volksaufstände und Tumulte in der Provinz Preussen zu nehmenden Sicherheitsmassregeln (1830–52), titel 504, no. 1.

Die geselligen Vereine in der Provinz Preussen in Verfolgung politischer Zwecke (1846), titel 504, no. 7.

Die Bildung von Vereinen für das Wohl der arbeitenden Klassen, vol. 3 (1848–63), titel 1104, no. 1.

Rep. 92. Nachlässe
Nachlass Zitelmann, no. 91.
Nachlass Radowitz, no. 56.
Nachlass Carl von Voss-Buch, no. 32.
Nachlass Rodbertus-Jagetzow, no. 17.
Nachlass Hansemann, no. 15.

Rep. 120. Ministerium für Handel und Gewerbe
Vorschläge zur Lösung der sozialen Frage und Massnahmen wegen Abwendung eines Nothstandes, rep. 120 BB, VII, 1, no. 2.
Massregeln zur Steuerung des Missbrauchs der Ablöhnung mit Waren, vol. 2 (1835–47), rep. 120 BB, VII, 3, no. 4.
Beschäftigung und Beaufsichtigung der jugendlichen Fabrikarbeiter, vols. 1–2, rep. 120 BB, VII, 3, no. 1.
Die Anordnungen zum Schutze des Lebens und der Gesundheit der Arbeiter in Fabriken, insbesondere der Kinder, vol. 1 (1822–46), rep. 120 BB, VII, 1, no. 4.
Beschäftigung jugendlicher Arbeiter in Fabriken, Berg-, Hütten- und Pochwerken, vol. 1 (1828–46), vol. 2 (1846–48), rep. 120 BB, VII, 3, no. 1.
Erörterung der Ursachen des in der Provinz Preussen öfter wiederkehrenden Nothstandes (1847–66), rep. 120 A, VIII, 1, no. 2.
Anträge der gewerbetreibenden und arbeitenden Klassen auf Abhilfe ihrer bedrängten Lage durch Abänderung der bestehenden Gewerbepolizeigesetze, vols. 5–7, rep. 120 B, I, 1, no. 60.
Bestimmungen über die Verhältnisse der Fabrikarbeiter und Gewerbegehilfen, vol. 2 (1839–49), rep. 120 B, V, 33, no. 4.
Acta betreffend die gewerbliche Verordnung vom 9.2.1849 und die Anträge auf deren Ausführung, Revision und Ergäzung, rep. 120 B, I, 1, no. 62.
Acta betreffend die Aufsicht auf die Handwerksgesellen und das Wandern derselben, rep. 120 B, III, 1, no. 3.
Die Bildung von Vereinen für Hand- und Fabrikarbeiter sowie die Errichtung eines Centralvereins für das Wohl der arbeitenden Klassen, vol. 1 (1844–47), vol. 3 (1851–55), rep. 120 D, XXII, 1, no. 1.
Vereine für das Wohl der arbeitenden Klassen in den einzelnen Provinzen, 10 vols. (1830–50), rep. 120 D, XXII, 2–11.
Die Leinwandfabrikation in Schlesien und die Massnahmen zu ihrer Erhaltung, vols. 3–7, rep. 120 D, V, 2c, no. 3.
Bestimmungen für die Verhältnisse der Fabrikarbeiter und Gewerbegehilfen, vols. 1–2 (1812–49), rep. 120 B, V, 33, no. 4.
Aufsicht über die Handwerksgesellen, vols. 1–3 (1813–67), rep. 120 B, III, 1, no. 3.

Zentrales Staatsarchiv I, Potsdam (now Bundesarchiv)

Nachlass Hermann Wagener 90 Wa 3.

Geheimes Staatsarchiv Preussischer Kulturbesitz, Dahlem

Rep. 90. Preussisches Staatsministerium. Abteilung C: Reichs- und Staatsbeamte

Konduitenlisten, vol. 1 (1800–1916), no. 2318.

Das politische Verhalten der Beamten, vol. 1 (1847–70), no. 2322.

Grundsätze für Ernennung und Beförderung (1810–60), no. 2336.

Rang, Titel der preuss. Beamten, vol. 1 (1809–1920), no. 541.

Rang, Titel der höheren Beamten der Ministerien sowie der Chefs und höheren Beamten der Ministerialverwaltung, vol. 1 (1817–1922), no. 543.

Vernehmung der Beamten als Zeugen vor Gericht, vol. 1 (1808–1931), no. 616.

Gesetz über das gerichtliche und Disziplinierungsstrafverfahren gegen Beamte, vol. 2 (1841–44), no. 644.

Einstweilige Versetzung der Beamten in den Ruhestand unter Gewährung von Wartegeldern, vol. 1 (1818–66), no. 814.

Personalien, Oberpräsidenten, vol. 1 (1817–39), no. 983, vol. 2 (1840–48), no. 984.

Die allgemeinen Jahresberichte, Verwaltungsbeamte, no. 1321.

Registratur des Geheimen Oberjustizrats Voss, rep. 90, annex C, no. 15.

Abteilung U: Erlass von Polizeiverordnungen, vol. 1 (1808–1931), no. 1808.

XIV. Hauptabteilung, Westpreussen

Streitigkeiten zwischen Dienstherrschaften und Instleuten, Landratsamt Neustadt (1838–63), rep. 191, no. 163.

Geheime Verbindungen in Könitz, Kreis Marienwerder (1833), no. 545.

Der letzte Hexenprozess (1836–95), rep. 192, no. 23.

Die Wahl des Landrates, Stargard (1847–77), rep. 193, no. 38.

Nachweisung über die Dienstalters- und Besoldungsverhältnisse der Landräte im Regierungsbezirk Danzig (1840–1920), rep. 180, no. 17501.

Rep. 84a. Preussisches Justizministerium

Acta betreffend die Verpflichtung der Communen zur Armenpflege und zur Aufnahme neu anziehender Personen (1837–42), no. 10955.

Die Verpflichtung der Communen zur Armenpflege und zur Aufnahme neu anziehender Personen (1842–55), no. 10956.

Betreffend die erlaubten Vereine im preussischen Staat (1811–45), no. 5410.

Die Ernennung der Oberpräsidenten und Chefpräsidenten bei den Regierungen (1816–98), no. 4183.

Statistische Nachrichten über den preussischen Staat, insbesondere über dessen Bevölkerung (1810–49), no. 4478.

Bestrafung der Duelle, vol. 1 (1791–1844), no. 8034.

Published Primary Sources

Allgemeines Landrecht für die preussischen Staaten. 1794. Reprint, Berlin, 1862.

Ammon, Friedrich v. *Lebenserinnerungen von Friedrich von Ammon.* Cologne, 1937.

Arnim, Bettina v. *Briefe und Werke.* Vol. 3. Munich, 1963.

Bauer, Bruno. *Vollständige Geschichte der Parteienkämpfe in Deutschland.* Charlottenburg, 1847.

———, ed. *Allgemeine Literaturzeitung.* Charlottenburg, 1843.

Bergius, Carl J. *Preussische Zustände.* Münster, 1844.

Berliner Politisches Wochenblatt. 1832–41.

Biedermann, Karl. *Vorlesungen über Sozialismus und Soziale Frage.* Leipzig, 1847.

Bodelschwingh, Ernst v. *Leben des Oberpräsidenten Freiherr von Vincke.* Berlin, 1853.

Born, Stefan. *Erinnerungen eines Achtundvierzigers.* Leipzig, 1893.

Breslauer Zeitung. 1844.

Buhl, Ludwig. *Die Herrschaft des Geburts- und Bodenprivilegiums in Preussen.* Mannheim, 1844.

Bülow-Cummerow, E. v. *Preussen, seine Verfassung, seine Verwaltung und sein Verhältnis zu Deutschland.* Berlin, 1842.

Carové, Friedrich W. *Mitteilungen aus und über Frankreich.* Leipzig, 1838.

Cieszkowski, A. v. *Prolegomena zur Historiographie.* Berlin, 1838.

De la Prusse et de sa domination sous les rapports politiques et religieux, spécialement dans les nouvelles provinces par un inconnu. Paris, 1842.

Delbrück, Rudolf v. *Lebenserinnerungen.* Vol. 1. Leipzig, 1905.

Deutsche Jahrbücher für Wissenschaft und Kunst, ed. Arnold Ruge and Theodor Echtermeyer. 1841–43.

Diest, Gustav v. *Aus dem Leben eines Glücklichen.* Berlin, 1904.

Dieterici, C. F. W. *Geschichtliche und statistische Nachrichten über die Universitäten im Preussischen Staate.* Berlin, 1836.

Dronke, Ernst. *Berlin.* 2 vols. Frankfurt, 1846. Reprint, Berlin, GDR, 1987.

Eberty, Felix. *Jugenderinnerungen eines alten Berliners.* Berlin, 1878.

Eilers, Gerd. *Meine Wanderung durchs Leben: Ein Beitrag zur Geschichte des 19. Jahrhunderts.* Leipzig, 1858.

"Einwohnerzahlen preussischer Städte." *Archiv für Landeskunde der preussischen Monarchie* 4 (1856).

Engel, E. *Beiträge zur Statistik des Unterrichtswesens im preussischen Staat und seinen Provinzen.* Berlin, 1867.

Ernsthausen, Ernst v. *Erinnerungen eines preussischen Beamten.* Bielefeld and Leipzig, 1894.

Evangelische Kirchenzeitung. 1842–44.

Gans, Eduard. *Rückblicke auf Personen und Zustände.* Berlin, 1836.

Gerlach, Ludwig v. *Aufzeichnungen aus seinem Leben und Wirken.* Vol. 1 (1795–1848). Ed. J. v. Gerlach. Schwerin, 1903.

Gesetz-Sammlung für die preussischen Staaten. 1830–50.

Grävell, M. F. W. C. *Der Staatsbeamte als Schriftsteller oder der Schriftsteller als Staatsbeamter im Preussischen.* Stuttgart, 1820.

———. *Über höhere, geheime und Sicherheitspolizei.* Sondershausen, 1820.

Grün, Karl. *Die soziale Bewegung in Frankreich und Belgien.* Darmstadt, 1848.

Haller, Carl Ludwig v. *Restauration der Staatswissenschaft.* Winterthur, 1820.

Hallesche Jahrbücher für deutsche Wissenschaft und Kunst. 1838–41.

Handatlas des preussischen Königreiches. Glogau, 1846.

Hansemann, David. *Preussen und Frankreich.* Leipzig, 1833.

Hansen, Joseph. *Rheinische Briefe und Akten zur Geschichte der Politischen Bewegung 1830–1850.* Essen, 1919. Reprint, Osnabrück, 1967.

Harkort, Friedrich. *Die Vereine zur Hebung der unteren Volksklassen nebst Bemerkungen über den Centralverein in Berlin.* Elberfeld, 1845.

Haude- und Spenersche Zeitung. 1830–48.

Hegel, G. F. W. *Grundlinien der Philosophie des Rechts.* Frankfurt, 1972.

Heinzen, Karl. *Die preussische Bürokratie.* Darmstadt, 1845.

Herwegh, Georg. *Einundzwanzig Bogen aus der Schweiz.* Zürich and Winterthur, 1843.

Historisch-Politische Blätter für das katholische Deutschland 27 (1838).

Hoffmann, Johann G. *Die Bevölkerung des preussischen Staates nach den Ergebnissen der zu Ende des Jahres 1837 amtlich aufgenommenen Nachrichten.* Berlin, 1839.

Huber, Viktor A. *Die englischen Universitäten.* 2 vols. Kassel, 1839–40.

———. *Über die Elemente, die Möglichkeit oder Notwendigkeit einer konservativen Partei in Deutschland.* Marburg, 1841.

———. *Die Opposition: Ein Nachtrag zu der conservativen Partei.* Halle, 1842.

———. *Bruch mit Revolution und Ritterschaft.* Berlin, 1852.

Jacoby, Johann. *Briefwechsel 1816–1849.* Ed. E. Silberner. Hannover, 1974.

Janus: Jahrbücher deutscher Gesinnung, Bildung und Tat. Ed. Viktor A. Huber. Berlin, 1845–48.

Kertbeny, C. v. *Berlin wie es ist.* Berlin, 1831.

Königlich privilegierte Zeitung von Staats- und gelehrten Sachen, Vossische Zeitung. 1835–48.

Köppen, Karl F. *Friedrich der Grosse und seine Widersacher.* Leipzig, 1840.

Leo, H. *Die Hegelingen.* Halle, 1838.

Lerminier, J. L. *Au delà du Rhin.* Brussels, 1835.

Lette, Wilhelm. *Über die Verfassungszustände in Preussen.* Berlin, 1842.

Mannheimer Abendzeitung. 1841–49.

Marx, Karl, and Friedrich Engels. *Der Briefwechsel, 1844–1883.* 4 vols. DTV reprint, Munich, 1983.

Marx-Engels Werke. Vols. 1–10 (Berlin, GDR, 1960).

Michelet, Carl L. *Zur Verfassungsfrage.* Frankfurt/O. and Berlin, 1848.

Mitteilungen des statistischen Bureaus in Berlin. Vols. 1–5. Berlin, 1848–52.

Mohl, Robert. "Über Bürokratie." *Zeitschrift für die gesamte Staatswissenschaft* 3 (1846).

Müllensiefen, Peter E. *Ein deutsches Bürgerleben im 19. Jahrhundert.* Ed. F. v. Oppeln-Bronikowski. Berlin, 1931.

Neue Preussische Zeitung: Kreuzeitung. Berlin, 1848–70.

Oppenheim, Heinrich B. *Philosophie des Rechts und der Gesellschaft.* Vol. 5 of *Neue Enzyklopädie für Wissenschaft und Künste.* Stuttgart, 1850.

———. *Vermischte Schriften aus bewegter Zeit.* Leipzig, 1866.

Owen, Robert. *The Life of Robert Owen written by Himself from his Writings and Correspondence.* Vol. 1. London, 1857.

Parumer, F. v. *Lebenserinnerungen und Briefwechsel.* Leipzig, 1861.

Perthes, Clemens T. *Der Staatsdienst in Preussen: Ein Beitrag zum deutschen Staatsrechte.* Hamburg, 1838.

———. *Friedrich Perthes Leben nach dessen schriftlichen und mündlichen Mitteilungen aufgezeichnet.* Vols. 1–2. 6th ed. Gotha, 1872.

Prutz, R. *Zehn Jahre. Geschichte der neuesten Zeit 1840–1850.* Vols. 1–2. Leipzig, 1850–56.

Puttkammer, A. v., ed., *Staatsminister von Puttkammer: Ein Stück preussischer Vergangenheit 1828–1900.* Leipzig, 1929.

Püttmann, Heinrich, ed. *Rheinische Jahrbücher zur gesellschaftlichen Reform.* Vol. 1. Darmstadt, 1845.

Radowitz, Josef M. v. *Gespräche aus der Gegenwart über Kirche und Staat.* 4th ed. Stuttgart, 1851.

———. *Neue Gespräche aus der Gegenwart über Kirche und Staat.* 2 vols. Stuttgart, 1851.

———. *Gesammelte Schriften.* Vols. 1–4. Berlin, 1852–53.

———. *Ausgewählte Schriften.* Ed. W. Corvinius. Vols. 1–3. Regensburg, 1911.

Reichensperger, Peter. *Erlebnisse eines alten Parlamentariers im Revolutionsjahr 1848.* Berlin, 1882.

Richter, Eugen. *Jugenderinnerungen.* Berlin, 1893.

Rodbertus-Jagetzow, Carl. *Briefe und sozialpolitische Aufsätze von Dr. Rodbertus-Jagetzow.* Ed. R. Meyer. Berlin, 1895.

———. *Schriften von Dr. Carl Rodbertus-Jagetzow.* 4 vols., ed. A. Wagner. Berlin, 1899.

———. *Die Forderungen der arbeitenden Klassen.* Frankfurt, 1946.

Rosenkranz, Karl. *Aus einem Tagebuch.* Leipzig, 1854.

———. *Politische Briefe und Aufsäze 1848–1856.* Ed. P. Herre. Leipzig, 1919.

———. *Von Magdeburg bis Königsberg.* Königsberg, 1873.

———. *Briefwechsel zwischen Karl Rosenkranz und Varnhagen von Ense.* Königsberg, 1926.

Ruge, Arnold. *Zwei Jahre in Paris: Studien und Erinnerungen.* 2 vols. Leipzig, 1846.

———. *Polemische Briefe.* Mannheim, 1847.

———. *Geschichte unserer Zeit: Von den Freiheitskriegen bis zum Ausbruch des deutsch-französischen Krieges.* Leipzig, 1881.

———. *Briefwechsel und Tagebuchblätter aus den Jahren 1825–1880.* 2 vols. Berlin, 1886.

Sass, Friedrich. *Berlin in seiner neuesten Zeit und Entwicklung.* Leipzig, 1846.

Schmitthenner, F. *Über Pauperismus und Proletariat.* Frankfurt, 1848.

Schneer, Alexander. *Über die Zustände der arbeitenden Klassen in Breslau.* Berlin, 1844.

Schoefert, J. G. *Der preussische Beamte oder die Kenntnis der preussischen Gesetze und Verordnungen über die Befähigung der höheren und niederen Verwaltungs-, Justiz-, Bau- und Eisenbahnbeamten.* Glogau, 1852.

Schön, Theodor v. *Woher und Wohin.* Strassburg, 1843.

Schorn, Karl. *Lebenserinnerungen.* 2 vols. Bonn, 1898.

Schraepler, Ernst. *Quellen zur Geschichte der sozialen Frage in Deutschland.* Vol. 1. Frankfurt, 1955.

Stein, Lorenz v. "Der Sozialismus in Deutschland." *Die Gegenwart* 7 (1849).

———. *Proletariat und Gesellschaft.* Ed. E. Hahn. Darmstadt, 1971.

———. *Schriften zum Sozialismus.* Darmstadt, 1974.

Temme, Jacodus D. *Erinnerungen.* Ed. S. Born. Leipzig, 1883.

Unruh, Hans V. v. *Erinnerungen aus dem Leben von Hans Viktor von Unruh.* Ed. H. Poschinger. Stuttgart, 1895.

Varnhagen von Ense, Karl. *Tagebücher.* Vols. 2–4. Ed. L. Assing. Leipzig, 1861.

Venedey, Jacob. *Preussen und Preussentum.* Mannheim, 1839.

————. *Vierzehn Tage Heimatluft.* Mannheim, 1847.

"Vergleichende Zusammenstellung der Einwohnerzahlen des preussischen Staates in den Jahren 1840–1855." *Archiv für Landeskunde der Preussischen Monarchie* 4 (1856).

Vincke, K. v. *Die Patrimonial- und Polizeigerichtsbarkeit auf dem Lande.* Breslau, 1847.

Wagener, Hermann. *Die Lösung der sozialen Frage.* Berlin, 1878.

————. *Erlebtes: Meine Memoiren.* Berlin, 1884.

————. *Die kleine aber mächtige Partei.* Berlin, 1885.

————. *Die Mängel der christlich-sozialen Bewegung.* Berlin, 1885.

Wehler, Hans-Ulrich, ed. *Friedrich Knapp, Briefe 1846–1884.* Bonn, 1969.

Westfälisches Dampfboot. Vol. 3. 1847.

Secondary Literature

Abel, Wilhelm. "Der Pauperismus in Deutschland." In *Wirtschaft, Geschichte und Wirtschaftsgeschichte: Festschrift für Friedrich Lütge.* Stuttgart, 1966.

————. *Massenarmut und Hungerkrisen im vorindustriellen Deutschland.* 2d ed. Göttingen, 1977.

Adler, Georg. *Rodbertus, der Begründer des wissenschaftlichen Sozialismus.* Leipzig, 1883.

Agulhon, Maurice. *Le Cercle dans la France bourgeoise.* Paris, 1977.

Andreas, Willy, and Wilhelm v. Scholz. *Die Grossen Deutschen.* 5 vols. Berlin, 1935–37.

Anton, Günther K. *Geschichte der preussischen Fabrikgesetzgebung.* Staats- und sozialwissenschaftliche Forschungen 11. Leipzig, 1891. Reprint, Berlin, GDR, 1953.

Arnold, Robert "Die Aufzeichnungen des Grafen von Voss-Buch über das Berliner Politische Wochenblatt." *Historische Zeitschrift* 106 (1911).

Avineri, Shlomo. *The Social and Political Thought of Karl Marx.* Cambridge, 1968.

————. *Hegel's Theory of the Modern State.* Cambridge, 1972.

Ayçoberry, Pierre. "Der Strukturwandel im Kölner Mittelstand." *Geschichte und Gesellschaft,* vol. 1 (1975).

————. *Cologne entre Napoleon et Bismarck.* Paris, 1981.

Bär, Max. *Die Behördenverfassung der Rheinprovinz seit 1815.* Bonn, 1919.

Barthel, Konrad. *Friedrich der Grosse in Hitlers Geschichtsbild.* Wiesbaden, 1977.

Baxa, Jacob. "Romantik und konservative Politik." In *Konservatismus in Europa,* ed. G. Kaltenbrunner. Freiburg, 1972.

Beck, Hermann. "The Social Policies of Prussian Officials: The Bureaucracy in a New Light." *The Journal of Modern History* 64 (June 1992).

————. "State and Society in pre-March Prussia: The Weavers' Uprising, the Bureaucracy and the Association for the Welfare of Workers." *Central European History* 25:3 (July 1992).

————. "Conservatives and the Social Question in Nineteenth-Century Prussia." In *Between Reform, Reaction, and Resistance: Studies in the History of German Con-*

servatism from 1789 to 1945, eds. Larry E. Jones and James Ratallack. London: Berg, 1993.

Behnen, Michael. *Das Politische Wochenblatt 1851–1861: Nationalkonservative Publizistik gegen Ständestaat und Polizeistaat.* Göttingen, 1971.

Beitz, Egid. *Die Verfassungsurkunde vom 31. 1. 1850 und die Wahlordnung vom 30. Mai 1849 in Preussen.* Cologne, 1907.

Belke, Hans-Joachim. *Die preussische Regierung zu Königsberg, 1808–1850.* Cologne and Berlin, 1976.

Berdahl, Robert M. *The Politics of the Prussian Nobility: The Development of a Conservative Ideology 1770–1848.* Princeton, 1988.

Berger, Irene. *Die preussische Verwaltung des Regierungsbezirks Bromberg.* Cologne and Berlin, 1966.

Bergeron, Louis et al. *Das Zeitalter der europäischen Revolutionen 1780–1848.* Frankfurt, 1969.

Bergmann, Jürgen. "Das Zunftwesen nach der Einführung der Gewerbefreiheit." In *Preussische Reformen 1807–1820,* ed. B. Vogel. Königstein, 1980.

Bergmann, Jürgen, and Heinrich Volkmann. *Sozialer Protest.* Opladen, 1984.

Bergstraesser, Ludwig. *Geschichte der politischen Parteien in Deutschland.* 11th ed. Munich and Vienna, 1960.

Bieberstein, Johannes R. v. "Preussen und Preussentum." *Aus Politik und Zeitgeschichte* 2 (1980).

Bigler, Robert M. *The Politics of German Protestantism: The Rise of the Protestant Church Elite in Prussia, 1815–1848.* Berkeley and Los Angeles, 1972.

———. "The Social Status and Political Role of the Protestant Clergy in Pre-March Prussia." In *Sozialgeschichte Heute,* ed. H.-U. Wehler. Göttingen, 1974.

Bitter, v. *Handbuch der preussischen Verwaltung.* 2 vols. Leipzig, 1911.

Blackbourn, David, and Geoff Eley. *The Peculiarities of German History: Bourgeois Society and Politics in Nineteenth-Century Germany.* Oxford, 1984.

———. *Populists and Patricians.* London, 1987.

Blaicher, Günther. *Das Deutschlandbild in der englischen Literatur.* Darmstadt, 1992.

Blasius, Dirk. "Lorenz von Stein und Preussen." *Historische Zeitschrift* 212 (1971).

———. *Bürgerliche Gesellschaft und Kriminalität: Zur Sozialgeschichte Preussens im Vormärz.* Göttingen, 1976.

———. *Kriminalität und Alltag: Zur Konfliktgeschichte im 19. Jahrhundert.* Göttingen, 1978.

Bleek, Wilhelm. *Von der Kameralausbildung zum Juristenprivileg: Studium, Prüfung und Ausbildung der höheren Beamten.* Berlin, 1972.

Bleiber, Helmut. *Zwischen Reform und Revolution: Lage und Kampf der schlesischen Bauern und Landarbeiter im Vormärz 1840–1848.* Berlin, GDR, 1966.

Blum, Jerome. *The End of the Old Order in Rural Europe.* Princeton, 1978.

Bock, Helmut. *Unzeit des Biedermeier.* Leipzig, 1985.

Böckenförde, Ernst-Wolfgang, ed. *Moderne deutsche Verfassungsgeschichte 1815–1918.* Cologne, 1972.

Boehn, Max v. *Biedermeier: Deutschland von 1815 bis 1847.* Berlin, 1911.

Böhme, Helmut. *Probleme der Reichsgründungszeit 1848–1879.* Cologne and Berlin, 1968.

Boldt, Hans. *Deutsche Verfassungsgeschichte: Von 1806 bis zur Gegenwart.* 2 vols. Munich, 1990.

Bonham, Gary. "Bureaucratic Modernizers and Traditional Constraints: Higher Officials and the Landed Nobility in Wilhelmine Germany, 1890–1914." Ph.D. diss., University of California at Berkeley, 1985.

Born, Karl E. "Sozialpolitische Probleme und Bestrebungen in Deutschland von 1848 bis zur Bismarckischen Sozialgesetzgebung." *Vierteljahresschrift für Sozial- und Wirtschaftsgeschichte* 46 (1959).

Botzenhart, Manfred. *Reform, Restauration, Krise: Deutschland 1789–1847.* Frankfurt, 1985.

Boyer, John. *Political Radicalism in late Imperial Vienna.* Chicago, 1981.

Bracher, Karl-Dietrich. *Zeit der Ideologien.* Stuttgart, 1982.

Bramsted, Ernst. *Aristocracy and the Middle Classes in Germany.* 2d ed. Chicago, 1964.

Branig, Hans. "Wesen und Geist der höheren Verwaltungsbeamten in Preussen in der Zeit des Vormärz." *Neue Forschungen zur Brandenburgisch-Preussischen Geschichte* 1 (1979).

Braun, Rudolf, ed. *Industrielle Revolution.* Cologne, 1972.

Bredendieck, Walter. *Christliche Sozialreformer des 19. Jahrhunderts.* Leipzig, 1953.

Breuer, Stefan. *Anatomie der Konservativen Revolution.* Darmstadt, 1993.

Broch, Rudolf. *Grenzenloses Wachstum? Das rheinische Wirtschaftsbürgertum und seine Industrialisierungsdebatte 1814–1857.* Göttingen, 1991.

Bruch, Rüdiger v. *Weder Kommunismus noch Kapitalismus: Bürgerliche Sozialreform in Deutschland vom Vormärz bis zur Ära Adenauer.* Munich, 1985.

Brunschwig, Henri. *La Crise de l'Etat Prussien à la Fin du XVIIIe Siècle et la Genèse de la Mentalité Romantique.* Paris, 1947.

Burg, Peter. *Der Wiener Kongress.* Munich, 1984.

Büsch, Otto. *Militärsystem und Sozialleben im Alten Preussen.* Berlin, 1962.

———, ed. *Untersuchungen zur Geschichte der frühen Industrialisierung im Wirtschaftsraum Berlin-Brandenburg.* Berlin, 1971.

———, ed. *Das Preussenbild in der Geschichte.* Berlin, 1981.

———, ed. *Handbuch der Preussischen Geschichte.* Vol. 2. Berlin, 1992.

Büsch, Otto, and Walter Neugebauer, eds. *Moderne Preussische Geschichte 1648–1947.* 3 vols. Berlin and New York, 1981.

Buttlar, Madelaine v. *Die politischen Vorstellungen des F.L.A.v.d. Marwitz.* Frankfurt, 1980.

Büttner, Wolfgang. *Weberaufstand im Eulengebirge.* Berlin, GDR, 1982.

Carsten, Francis L. *Geschichte der preussischen Junker.* Frankfurt, 1989.

Chevalier, Louis. *Laboring Classes and Dangerous Classes in Paris during the First Half of the Nineteenth Century.* Princeton, 1981.

Christoph, Siegfried. "Hermann Wagener als Sozialpolitiker." Ph.D. diss., University of Erlangen, 1950.

Claus, Wilhelm. *Der Staatsbeamte als Abgeordneter in der Verfassungsentwicklung der deutschen Staaten.* Karlsruhe, 1906.

Conrad, Johannes. *Das Universitätsstudium in Deutschland während der letzten 50 Jahre.* Sammlung nationalökonomischer und statistischer Abhandlungen. Vol 3. Berlin, 1884.

Conze, Werner. "Vom Pöbel zum Proletariat." *Vierteljahresschrift für Sozial- und Wirtschaftsgeschichte* 41 (1954).

———. "Das Spannungsfeld von Staat und Gesellschaft im Vormärz." In *Staat und Gesellschaft im Deutschen Vormärz*, ed. W. Conze. Stuttgart, 1962.

———. "Die deutsche Geschichtswissenschaft seit 1945." *Historische Zeitschrift* 225 (1977).

———. "Proletariat, Pöbel, Pauperismus." In *Geschichtliche Grundbegriffe*, vol. 4, ed. O. Brunner, W. Conze, R. Koselleck. Stuttgart, 1984.

Conze, Werner, and Ulrich Engelhardt, eds. *Arbeiterexistenz im 19. Jahrhundert*. Stuttgart, 1981.

Craig, Gordon. *The Politics of the Prussian Army*. Oxford, 1964.

———. *The End of Prussia*. Madison, 1984.

Dahrendorf, Ralf. *Gesellschaft und Demokratie in Deutschland*. Munich, 1968.

Delbrück, Clemens v. *Die Ausbildung für den höheren Verwaltungsdienst in Preussen*. Jena, 1917.

Deutscher Sonderweg—Mythos oder Realität? Kolloquien des Instituts für Zeitgeschichte. Munich, 1982.

Dietzel, Hermann. *Carl Rodbertus*. 2 vols. Berlin, 1886.

Digeon, Claude. *La Crise Allemande de la Pensée Française*. Paris, 1959.

Dilcher, Liselotte. "Der deutsche Pauperismus und seine Literatur." Ph.D. diss., University of Frankfurt, 1957.

Dinges, Martin. *Stadtarmut in Bordeaux 1525–1675: Alltag, Politik, Mentalitäten*. Bonn, 1988.

Dipper, Christof. *Die Bauernbefreiung in Deutschland*. Stuttgart, 1980.

Dittmer, Lothar. *Beamtenkonservatismus und Modernisierung*. Wiesbaden, 1992.

D'O. Butler, Rohan. *The Roots of National Socialism 1783–1933*. London, 1942.

Doege, Michael. *Armut in Preussen und Bayern (1770–1840)*. Munich, 1991.

Dönhoff, Marion, Gräfin v. *Namen die keiner mehr kennt*. Cologne, 1962.

———. *Preussen: Mass und Masslosigkeit*. Berlin, 1987.

———. *Kindheit in Ostpreussen*. Berlin, 1988.

Dorn, Walter L. "The Prussian Bureaucracy in the Eighteenth Century." *Political Science Quarterly* 46 (1931).

Dorwart, Reinhold A. *The Administrative Reforms of Frederick William I of Prussia*. Cambridge, Mass., 1953.

Droz, Jacques. "Préoccupations Sociales et Préoccupations Réligieuses aux Origines du Parti Conservateur Prussien." *Revue d'Histoire Moderne et Contemporaine* 2 (1955).

———. *Le Libéralisme Rhénan 1815–1848*. Paris, 1957.

———. *Le Romantisme Allemand de l'Etat*. Paris, 1966.

———. "Postface." *Le Mouvement Social* 136 (1986).

Droz, Jacques, and Pierre Ayçoberry. "Structures sociales et courants idéologiques dans l'Allemagne prérévolutionaire 1835–1847," in *Annali*, vol. 4. Milan, 1963.

Eley, Geoff. *From Unification to Nazism: Reinterpreting the German Past*. London, 1986.

Elvers, Rudolf. *Viktor Aimé Huber: Sein Werden und Wirken*. Bremen, 1872.

Engelberg, Ernst. *Bismarck: Urpreusse und Reichsgründer*. Berlin, 1985.

Engels, Rolf. *Die preussische Verwaltung von Kammer und Regierung Gumbinnen 1724–1870.* Cologne and Berlin, 1974.

Engelsing, Rolf. *Zur Sozialgeschichte deutscher Mittel- und Unterschichten.* Göttingen, 1973.

Epstein, Klaus. *The Genesis of German Conservatism.* Princeton, 1966.

Evans, Richard, ed. *Society and Politics in Wilhelmine Germany.* London, 1978.

———. *Rethinking German History.* London, 1987.

Evans, Richard J., and W. R. Lee. *The German Peasantry: Conflict and Community in Rural Society from the Eighteenth to the Twentieth Centuries.* London, 1986.

Faber, Karl-Georg, "Verwaltungs- und Justizbeamte auf dem linken Rheinufer während der französischen Herrschaft," *Aus Geschichte und Landeskunde.* Bonn, 1960.

———. *Die Rheinlande zwischen Restauration und Revolution.* Wiesbaden, 1966.

———. "Geschichtswissenschaft als retrospektive Politik." *Geschichte und Gesellschaft* 6 (1980).

Fann, Willard R. "The Rise of the Prussian Ministry 1806–1827." In *Sozialgeschichte Heute: Festschift für Hans Rosenberg,* ed. Hans-Ulrich Wehler. Göttingen, 1974.

Faulenbach, Bernd. *Ideologie des deutschen Weges: Die deutsche Geschichte in der Historiographie zwischen Kaiserreich und Nationalsozialismus.* Munich, 1980.

———. "Deutscher Sonderweg: Zur Geschichte und Problematik einer zentralen Kategorie des deutschen geschichtlichen Bewusstseins." *Aus Politik und Zeitgeschichte* 33 (1981).

———. "Eine Variante europäischer Normalität? Zur neuesten Diskussion über den 'deutschen Weg' im 19. und 20. Jahrhundert." *Tel Aviver Jahrbuch für deutsche Geschichte* 16 (1987).

Feldenkirchen, Winfried. "Kinderarbeit im 19. Jahrhundert." *Zeitschrift für Unternehmensgeschichte* 26 (1981).

Femerling, Karl E. "Die Stellung der konservativen Partei zur gewerblichen Arbeiterfrage 1848–1880." Ph.D. diss., University of Halle, 1927.

Fischer, Ferdinand. *Preussen am Abschlusse der ersten Hälfte des 19. Jahrhunderts.* Berlin, 1876.

Fischer, Fritz. "Der deutsche Protestantismus und die Politik im 19. Jahrhundert." *Historische Zeitschrift* 171 (1951).

Fischer, Wolfram. *Wirtschaft und Gesellschaft im Zeitalter der Industrialisierung.* Göttingen, 1972.

———. *Armut in der Geschichte.* Göttingen, 1982.

———. "Wirtschafts- und sozialgeschichtliche Anmerkungen zum deutschen Sonderweg." *Tel Aviver Jahrbuch für deutsche Geschichte* 16 (1987).

Fischer, Wolfram et al., eds. *Sozialgeschichtliches Arbeitsbuch: Materialien zur Statistik des deutschen Bundes 1815–1870.* Munich, 1982.

Fletcher, Roger. "Recent Developments in West German Historiography: The Bielefeld School and Its Critics." *German Studies Review* 7 (1984).

Frauendienst, Werner. "Das preussische Staatsministerium in vorkonstitutioneller Zeit." *Zeitschrift für die gesamte Staatswissenschaft* 1 (1960).

Frevert, Ute. *Krankheit als politisches Problem, 1770–1880: Soziale Unterschichten in Preussen zwischen medizinischer Polizei und staatlicher Sozialversicherung.* Göttingen, 1984.

Früh, Walter. "Radowitz als Sozialpolitiker." Ph.D. diss., University of Berlin, 1937.

Gailus, Manfred. "Zur Politisierung der Landbevölkerung in der Märzbewegung von 1848." In *Probleme politischer Partizipation im Modernisierungsprozess,* ed. P. Steinbach. Stuttgart, 1982.

————. *Strasse und Brot: Sozialer Protest in den deutschen Staaten unter besonderer Berücksichtigung Preussens, 1847–1849.* Göttingen, 1990.

Gall, Lothar. *Bürgertum in Deutschland.* Berlin, 1989.

Geremek, Bronislaw. *Geschichte der Armut.* Munich, 1991.

Gerth, Hans. *Bürgerliche Intelligenz um 1800.* 2d ed. Göttingen, 1976.

Giese, F. *Preussische Rechtsgeschichte.* Berlin and Leipzig, 1920.

Gillis, John R. *The Prussian Bureaucracy in Crisis, 1840–1860.* Stanford, 1971.

————. "Aristokratie und Bürokratie im Preussen des 19. Jahrhunderts." In *Preussische Reformen,* ed. B. Vogel. Königstein, 1980.

Gladen, Alphons. *Geschichte der Sozialpolitik in Deutschland.* Wiesbaden, 1974.

Goetting, Hildegard. "Die sozialpolitische Idee in den konservativen Kreisen der vormärzlichen Zeit." Ph.D. diss., University of Berlin, 1920.

Göhre, Paul. *Die evangelisch-soziale Bewegung.* Leipzig, 1896.

Görlitz, Walter. *Die Junker: Adel und Bauer im deutschen Osten.* 2d ed. Glücksburg, 1957.

Gray, Marion W. *Prussia in Transition: Society and Politics under the Stein Reform Ministry of 1808.* Philadelphia, 1986.

Grebing, Helga. *Geschichte der deutschen Parteien.* Wiesbaden, 1962.

————. *Der Deutsche Sonderweg in Europa 1806–1954: Eine Kritik.* Stuttgart, 1986.

————. *Arbeiterbewegung: Sozialer Protest und kollektive Interessenvertretung bis 1914.* Munich, 1985.

Grebing, Helga et al., eds. *Konservatismus—Eine deutsche Bilanz.* Munich, 1971.

Gregg, Pauline. *A Social and Economic History of Britain 1760–1972.* London, 1973.

Greiffenhagen, Martin. *Das Dilemma des Konservatismus in Deutschland.* Munich, 1977.

Griewank, Karl. *Gneisenau: Ein Leben in Briefen.* 3d ed. Leipzig, 1939.

Grimm, Dieter. *Deutsche Verfassungsgeschichte 1776–1866.* Frankfurt, 1988.

Groh, Dieter. "Le *Sonderweg* de l'Histoire Allemande: Mythe ou Réalité." *Annales* 38 (1983).

Grolle, Joist. "Lorenz von Stein als Preussischer Geheimargent." *Archiv für Kulturgeschichte* 50 (1968).

Grünthal, Günther. *Parlamentarismus in Preussen 1848/49–1857/58.* Düsseldorf, 1982.

————. "Grundlagen konstitutionellen Regiments in Preussen 1848–1867." In *Regierung, Bürokratie und Parlament in Preussen und Deutschland von 1848 bis zur Gegenwart,* ed. G. A. Ritter. Düsseldorf, 1983.

Guillaumin, Emile. *The Life of a Simple Man.* Middletown, Conn., 1986.

Habermas, Jürgen, ed. *Stichworte zur 'Geistigen Situation der Zeit.'* Frankfurt, 1979.

Hagen, William. "How Mighty the Junkers? Peasant Rents and Seigneurial Profits in Sixteenth-Century Brandenburg." *Past and Present* 108 (1985).

————. "The Junkers' Faithless Servants: Peasant Insubordination and the Breakdown of Serfdom in Brandenburg-Prussia, 1763–1811." In *The German Peasantry,* ed. R. J. Evans and W. R. Lee. London, 1986.

————. "Working for the Junkers: The Standard of Living of Manorial Laborers in Brandenburg, 1584–1810." *Journal of Modern History* 58 (1986).

————. "Seventeenth-Century Crisis in Brandenburg: The Thirty Years' War, the Destabilization of Serfdom, and the Rise of Absolutism." *American Historical Review* 94 (1989).

————. "Descent of the *Sonderweg:* Hans Rosenberg's History of Old-Regime Prussia." *Central European History* 24 (1991).

Hahn, Adalbert. *Die Berliner Revue.* Berlin, 1934.

Hamerow, Theodore S. *Restoration, Revolution, Reaction.* Princeton, 1958.

————. *The Social Foundations of German Unification, 1858–1871.* 2 vols. Princeton, 1969–72.

Hansen, Joseph. *Gustav von Mevissen: Ein rheinisches Lebensbild.* 2 vols. Berlin, 1906.

Harden, Maximilian, ed. *Die Zukunft,* vol. 12. Berlin, 1895.

Hardtwig, Wolfgang. *Vormärz: Der monarchische Staat und das Bürgertum.* Munich, 1985.

Hartung, Fritz. *Staatsbildende Kräfte der Neuzeit.* Berlin, 1961.

Hassel, Paul. *Josef Maria von Radowitz, 1797–1848.* Berlin, 1905.

Hattenhauer, Hans. *Geschichte des Beamtentums: Handbuch des öffentlichen Dienstes.* Vol. 1. Cologne and Berlin, 1980.

Heffter, Heinrich. *Die deutsche Selbstverwaltung im 19. Jahrhundert.* Stuttgart, 1950.

Henderson, William O. *The State and the Industrial Revolution in Prussia 1740–1870.* Liverpool, 1958.

Henning, Hans-Joachim. "Preussische Sozialpolitik im Vormärz." *Vierteljahresschrift für Sozial- und Wirtschaftsgeschichte* 52 (1965).

————. *Die deutsche Beamtenschaft im 19. Jahrhundert.* Wiesbaden, 1984.

Herberger, Carl-Valerius. *Die Stellung der preussischen Konservativen zur sozialen Frage 1848–1862.* Meissen, 1914.

Herzfeld, Hans. *Berlin und die Mark Brandenburg im 19. und 20. Jahrhundert.* Berlin, 1968.

Herzig, Arno. *Unterschichtenprotest in Deutschland 1790–1870.* Göttingen, 1988.

Hildebrand, Bruno. *Die Nationalökonomie der Gegenwart und Zukunft und andere gesammelte Schriften.* Jena, 1922.

Hindelang, Sabine. *Konservatismus und soziale Frage: Viktor Aimé Hubers Beitrag zum sozialkonservativen Denken im 19. Jahrhundert.* Frankfurt, 1983.

Hinrichs, Carl. *Preussen als historisches Problem.* Berlin, 1964.

Hintze, Otto. *Die Hohenzollern und ihr Werk.* Berlin, 1915.

————. *Gesammelte Abhandlungen.* 3 vols. Göttingen, 1962–67.

Höffner, J. *Die deutschen Katholiken und die soziale Frage im 19. Jahrhundert.* Paderborn, 1954.

Holzapfel, Karl. *Die Lyoner Arbeiteraufstände 1831 und 1834.* Berlin, GDR, 1984.

Hubatsch, Walter. *Die Stein-Hardenbergschen Reformen.* 2d ed. Darmstadt, 1989.

Huber, Ernst-Rudolf. *Deutsche Verfassungsgeschichte seit 1789.* 4 vols. Stuttgart, 1957–69.

Hübner, H. *Lage und Kampf der Landarbeiter im ostelbischen Preussen.* Vol. 1. Berlin, GDR, 1977.

Husung, Hans-Gerhard. *Protest und Repression im Vormärz: Norddeutschland zwischen Restauration und Revolution.* Göttingen, 1983.

Iggers, George G. *The German Conception of History.* Rev. ed. Hanover, N.H., 1983.

———. *New Directions in European Historiography.* Rev. ed. Hanover, N.H., 1984.

———, ed. *The Social History of Politics.* Leamington Spa, 1985.

———, ed. *Ein anderer historischer Blick: Beispiele ostdeutscher Sozialgeschichte.* Frankfurt, 1991.

———. *Geschichtswissenschaft im 20. Jahrhundert.* Göttingen, 1993.

Iggers, George, and Harold T. Parker, eds. *International Handbook of Historical Studies: Contemporary Research and Theory.* Westport, Conn., 1979.

Ipsen, Gunther. "Die preussische Bauernbefreiung als Landesausbau." *Zeitschrift für Agrargeschichte und Agrarsoziologie* 1–2 (1954).

Isaacsohn, Siegfried. *Geschichte des Preussischen Beamtentums.* Vols. 2–3. Berlin, 1884.

Jäger, Wolfgang. *Historische Forschung und politische Kultur in Deutschland: Die Debatte 1914–1980 über den Ausbruch des Ersten Weltkrieges.* Göttingen, 1984.

Jansen, Hans-Ernst. "Das Proletariat im Vormärz in den Anschauungen deutscher Denker." Ph.D. diss., University of Kiel, 1928.

Jantke, Carl, and Dietrich Hilger. *Der vierte Stand.* Freiburg, 1955.

———. *Die Eigentumslosen.* Freiburg, 1965.

Joll, James. "The 1914 Debate Continues: Fritz Fischer and his Critics." *Past and Present* 34 (1966).

Jones, Larry, and James Retallack, eds. *Between Reform, Reaction, and Resistance: Studies in the History of German Conservatism from 1789 to 1945.* Providence and London, 1993.

Jordan, Erich. *Die Entstehung der konservativen Partei und die preussischen Agrarverhältnisse von 1848.* Munich and Leipzig, 1914.

Jütte, Robert. *Obrigkeitliche Fürsorge in den deutschen Reichsstädten der frühen Neuzeit: Städtisches Armenwesen in Frankfurt am Main und Köln.* Cologne and Vienna, 1984.

Kaeber, Ernst. *Berlin, 1848.* Berlin, 1948.

———. *Beiträge zur Berliner Geschichte.* Berlin, 1964.

Kaehler, Siegfried A. *Wilhelm von Humboldt und der Staat.* 2d ed. Göttingen, 1963.

Kaelble, Hartmut. *Berliner Unternehmer während der frühen Industrialisierung.* Berlin, 1972.

Kaltenbrunner, Gerd-Klaus, ed. *Konservatismus in Europa.* Freiburg, 1972.

Kaschuba, Wolfgang. *Lebenswelt und Kultur der unterbürgerlichen Schichten im 19. und 20. Jahrhundert.* Munich, 1990.

Kaufmann, Walter. *Hegel's Political Philosophy.* New York, 1970.

Kehr, Eckart. *Der Primat der Innenpolitik: Gesammelte Aufsätze zur preussisch-deutschen Sozialgeschichte.* Ed. H.-U. Wehler. Berlin, 1965.

Kettler, David, et al., eds. *Karl Mannheim: Konservatismus.* Frankfurt, 1984.

Klein, Ernst. "Funktion und Bedeutung des preussischen Staatsministeriums." *Jahrbuch für die Geschichte Mittel- und Ostdeutschlands* 9–10 (1961).

Klemperer, Klemens v. *Germany's New Conservatism.* Princeton, 1957.

Knapp, Georg F. *Die Bauernbefreiung und der Ursprung der Landarbeiter in den älteren Teilen Preussens.* Vol. 1. Leipzig, 1887.

Koch, Rainer. *Deutsche Geschichte 1815–1848: Restauration oder Vormärz?* Stuttgart, 1985.

Kocka, Jürgen. "Capitalism and Bureaucracy in German Industrialization before 1914." *Economic History Review,* 2d ser., no. 33 (1981).

⸻. "Der 'deutsche Sonderweg' in der Diskussion." *German Studies Review* 5 (1982).

⸻. *Lohnarbeit und Klassenbildung: Arbeiter und Arbeiterbewegung in Deutschland 1800–1875.* Berlin and Bonn, 1983.

⸻. *Bürgertum und Bürgerlichkeit im 19. Jahrhundert.* Göttingen, 1987.

⸻. "German History before Hitler: The Debate about the German *Sonderweg.*" *Journal of Contemporary History* 23 (1988).

⸻, ed. *Sozialgeschichte im internationalen Überblick.* Darmstadt, 1989.

⸻. *Weder Stand noch Klasse: Unterschichten um 1800.* Berlin, 1990.

Koigen, Detlev. *Zur Vorgeschichte des modernen philosophischen Sozialismus in Deutschland.* Bern, 1901.

Kollmann, Horst. *Die Entstehungsgeschichte der deutschen Koalitionsgesetzgebung.* Breslau, 1916.

Köllmann, Wolfgang. "Industrialisierung, Binnenwanderung und Soziale Frage." *Vierteljahresschrift für Sozial- und Wirtschaftsgeschichte* 46 (1959).

⸻. *Sozialgeschichte der Stadt Barmen im 19. Jahrhundert.* Tübingen, 1960.

⸻. "Die Anfänge der staatlichen Sozialpolitik in Preussen bis 1869." *Vierteljahresschrift für Sozial- und Wirtschaftsgeschichte* 53 (1966).

⸻. *Bevölkerung in der industriellen Revolution.* Göttingen, 1974.

⸻. ed., *Quellen zur Bevölkerungs-, Sozial- und Wirtschaftsstatistik Deutschlands 1815–1875.* Munich, 1985.

Kondylis, Panajotis. *Konservatismus: Geschichtlicher Gehalt und Untergang.* Stuttgart, 1986.

Koselleck, Reinhart. *Preussen zwischen Reform und Revolution: Allgemeines Landrecht, Verwaltung und soziale Bewegung von 1791 bis 1848.* 2d ed. Stuttgart, 1975.

Köster, Johanna. *Der rheinische Frühliberalismus und die soziale Frage.* Berlin, 1938.

Köster, Ulrich *Literarischer Radikalismus.* Frankfurt, 1972.

⸻. *Literatur und Gesellschaft in Deutschland 1830–1848.* Stuttgart, 1984.

Kraus, Antje. *Die Unterschichten Hamburgs in der ersten Hälfte des 19. Jahrhunderts.* Stuttgart, 1965.

Krause, Hans. "Die demokratische Partei von 1848 und die sociale Frage." Ph.D. diss., University of Breslau, 1921.

Krieger, Leonard. *The German Idea of Freedom.* Boston, 1957.

Kroll, Frank-Lothar. *Friedrich Wilhelm IV und das Staatsdenken der deutschen Romantik.* Berlin, 1990.

Kroneberg, Lutz, and Rolf Schlosser. *Weber Revolte 1844.* Cologne, 1980.

Kuczynski, Jürgen. *Die Geschichte der Lage der Arbeiter unter dem Kapitalismus.* Vols. 1, 8–9, 11. Berlin, GDR, 1960.

Kübler, Horst. *Besoldung und Lebenshaltung der unmittelbaren preussischen*

Staatsbeamten im 19. Jahrhundert. Nürnberg, 1976.

Küther, Carsten. *Räuber und Gauner in Deutschland.* Göttingen, 1976.

Lamberti, Marjorie E. "The Rise of the Prussian Conservative Party 1840–1858." Ph.D. diss., Yale University, 1966.

Langewiesche, Dieter. "Republik, konstitutionelle Monarchie und soziale Frage." In *Die deutsche Revolution von 1848,* ed. D. Langewiesche. Darmstadt, 1983.

————. *Europa zwischen Restauration und Revolution 1815–1849.* Munich, 1985.

Langner, Albrecht, ed. *Katholizismus, konservative Kapitalismuskritik und Frühsozialismus bis 1850.* Paderborn, 1975.

Lebovics, Herman. *Social Conservatism and the Middle Classes in Germany 1914–1933.* Princeton, 1969.

Lee, Lloyd E. *The Politics of Harmony: Civil Service, Liberalism and Social Reform in Baden, 1800–1850.* Newark, 1980.

Lenk, Kurt. *Deutscher Konservatismus.* Frankfurt and New York, 1989.

Lenz, Max. *Geschichte der Friedrich Wilhelms Universität zu Berlin.* Vols. 1–2. Berlin, 1910–18.

L' Homme, Jean. *La Grande Bourgeoisie au Pouvoir.* Paris, 1960.

Lincoln, Bruce W. *In the Vanguard of Reform: Russia's Enlightened Bureaucrats, 1825–1861.* De Kalb, Illinois, 1982.

Lindemann, Mary. *Patriots and Paupers: Hamburg 1712–1830.* New York and Oxford, 1990.

Loening, Edgar. *Gerichte und Verwaltungsbehörden in Brandenburg-Preussen.* Halle, 1914.

Lotz, Albert. *Geschichte des deutschen Beamtentums.* Berlin, 1909.

Löwith, Karl. *Gesammelte Abhandlungen.* Stuttgart, 1960.

————. *Von Hegel bis Nietzsche.* 8th ed. Hamburg, 1981.

Lübbe, Hermann. *Die Hegelsche Rechte.* Stuttgart, 1962.

————. *Politische Philosophie in Deutschland.* Munich, 1974.

Lüdtke, Alf. *Police and State in Prussia, 1815–1850.* Cambridge, 1989.

————. "Der starke Staat." In *Bürgerliche Gesellschaft in Deutschland,* ed. L. Niethammer. Frankfurt, 1990.

Ludwig, Karl-Heinz. "Die Fabrikarbeit von Kindern im 19. Jahrhundert: Ein Problem der Technikgeschichte." *Vierteljahreshefte für Sozial- und Wirtschaftsgeschichte* 52 (1965).

Lütge, Friedrich. *Die wirtschaftliche Situation in Deutschland und Österreich um di Wende vom 18. zum 19. Jahrhundert.* Stuttgart, 1964.

————, ed. *Geschichte der deutschen Agrarverfassung vom frühen Mittelalter bis zum 19. Jahrhundert.* 2d ed. Stuttgart, 1967.

Lutz, Heinrich. *Zwischen Habsburg und Preussen: Deutschland zwischen 1815 und 1866.* Berlin, 1985.

Marquardt, Frederick D. "Pauperismus in Germany during the Vormärz." *Central European History* 2 (1969).

————. "A Working Class in Berlin in the 1840s?" In *Sozialgeschichte Heute,* ed. H.-U. Wehler. Göttingen, 1974.

————. "Sozialer Aufstieg, sozialer Abstieg und die Entstehung der Berliner Arbeiterklasse 1806–1848" *Geschichte und Gesellschaft* 1 (1975).

Marschalk, Peter. *Bevölkerungsgeschichte Deutschlands im 19. und 20. Jahrhundert.* Frankfurt, 1984.

Martiny, Fritz. Die Adelsfrage in Preussen als politisches und soziales Problem. Halle, 1938.

Matz, Klaus-Jürgen. *Pauperismus und Bevölkerung.* Stuttgart, 1980.

Mayer, E. W. *Das Retablissement Ost- und West-Preussens unter der Mitwirkung und Leitung Theodor von Schöns.* Jena, 1916.

Mayer, Gustav. "Die Anfänge des politischen Radikalismus im vormärzlichen Preussen." *Zeitschrift für Politik* 6 (1913).

————. "Die Junghegelianer und der preussische Staat." *Historische Zeitschrift* 123 (1920).

————. *Bismarck und Lassalle: Ihr Briefwechsel und Ihre Gespräche.* Berlin, 1928.

————. *Radikalismus, Sozialismus und bürgerliche Demokratie.* Ed. H.-U. Wehler. Frankfurt, 1969.

Mayntz, Renate, ed. *Bürokratische Organisationen.* 2d ed. Cologne and Berlin, 1971.

McGovern, William M. *From Luther to Hitler: The History of Fascist Nazi Philosophy.* London, 1946.

Mehring, Franz. *Geschichte der deutschen Sozialdemokratie.* 3d ed. Berlin, GDR, 1980.

Meinecke, Friedrich. *Radowitz und die deutsche Revolution.* Berlin, 1913.

————. *Weltbürgertum und Nationalstaat.* 4th ed. Berlin, 1917.

————. *Erlebtes 1862–1901.* Leipzig, 1941.

Meisner, Heinrich-Otto. *Die Lehre vom monarchischen Prinzip im Zeitalter der Restauration und des deutschen Bundes.* Breslau, 1913.

Meyer, Dora. *Das öffentliche Leben in Berlin im Jahr vor der Märzrevolution.* Berlin, 1912.

Mieck, Ilja. *Preussische Gewerbepolitik in Berlin 1806–1844.* Berlin, 1965.

Mies, Horst. *Die preussische Verwaltung des Regierungsbezirks Marienwerder 1830–1870.* Cologne and Berlin, 1972.

Moeller, Robert G. "The Kaiserreich Recast? Continuity and Change in Modern German Historiography." *Journal of Social History* 17 (1984).

Mohler, Arnim. *Die Konservative Revolution in Deutschland 1918–1932.* 3d ed. Darmstadt, 1989.

Mollat, Michel. *Die Armen im Mittelalter.* Munich, 1984.

Mombert, Paul. "Aus der Literatur über die soziale Frage und über die Arbeiterbewegung in Deutschland in der ersten Hälfte des 19. Jahrhunderts." *Archiv für die Geschichte des Sozialismus und der Arbeiterbewegung* 9 (1921).

Mommsen, Hans, and Winfried Schulze. *Vom Elend der Handarbeit: Probleme historischer Unterschichtenforschung.* Stuttgart, 1981.

Mommsen, Wolfgang J. "The Debate on German War Aims." *Journal of Contemporary History* 1 (1966).

————. "Domestic Factors in German Foreign Policy before 1914. *Central European History* 6 (1973).

————."Gegenwärtige Tendenzen in der Geschichtsschreibung der Bundesrepublik." *Geschichte und Gesellschaft* 7 (1981).

Mommsen, Wolfgang J., and G. Hirschfeld, eds. *Sozialprotest, Gewalt, Terror.* Stuttgart, 1982.

Mooser, Josef. *Ländliche Klassengesellschaft 1770–1848: Bauern und Unterschichten, Landwirtschaft und Gewerbe im östlichen Westfalen.* Göttingen, 1984.

Mosse, George L. *The Crisis of German Ideology.* London, 1964.

Most, Otto. *Zur Wirtschafts-und Sozialstatistik der höheren Beamten in Preussen.* Munich and Leipzig, 1916.

Müller, Hugo. "Der Preussische Volks-Verein." Ph.D. diss., University of Greifswald, 1914.

Nathan, Helene. *Preussens Verfassung und Verwaltung im Urteil rheinischer Achtundvierziger.* Bonn, 1912.

Naudé, Wilhelm. "Zur Geschichte des preussischen Subalternbeamtentums." *Forschungen zur brandenburgisch-preussischen Geschichte* 18 (1905).

Neumann, Sigmund. *Die Stufen des preussischen Konservatismus.* Berlin, 1930.

Nipperdey, Thomas. *Die Organisation der deutschen Parteien vor 1918.* Düsseldorf, 1961.

———. "Wehlers 'Kaiserreich': Eine Kritische Auseinandersetzung." *Geschichte und Gesellschaft* 1 (1975).

———. "1933 und die Kontinuität in der deutschen Geschichte." *Historische Zeitschrift* 227 (1978).

———. *Deutsche Geschichte 1800–1866.* Munich, 1983.

———. "Unter der Herrschaft des Verdachts." In *Historikerstreit: Die Dokumentation der Kontroverse um die Einzigartigkeit der nationalsozialistischen Judenvernichtung.* Munich, 1987.

———. *Deutsche Geschichte 1866–1918.* 2 vols. Munich, 1990–92.

Nolte, Ernst. *Marxismus und Industrielle Revolution.* Stuttgart, 1983.

Noyes, Paul. *Organization and Revolution.* Princeton, 1966.

Obenaus, Herbert. *Die Anfänge des Parlamentarismus in Preussen bis 1848.* Düsseldorf, 1984.

———. "Gutsbesitzerliberalismus: Zur regionalen Sonderentwicklung der liberalen Partei in Ost- und Westpreussen während des Vormärz." *Geschichte und Gesellschaft* 14 (1988).

Obermann, Karl. "Die Volksbewegung in Deutschland von 1844 bis 1846." *Zeitschrift für Geschichtswissenschaft* 5 (1957).

———. "Wirtschafts- und sozialpolitische Aspekte der Krise von 1845–1847 in Deutschland, insbesondere in Preussen." *Jahrbuch für Geschichte* 8 (1972).

———. *Deutschland 1815–1849.* 4th ed. Berlin, GDR, 1976.

O' Boyle, Leonore. "The Democratic Left in Germany in 1848." *Journal of Modern History* 33 (1961).

———. "The Middle Class in Western Europe, 1815–1848." *American Historical Review* 72 (1966).

———. "The Problem of an Excess of Educated Men in Western Europe, 1800–1850." *Journal of Modern History* 42 (1970).

Oncken, Hermann. *Lassalle: Eine politische Biographie.* 3d ed. Stuttgart and Berlin, 1920.

Orr, William J. "The Prussian Ultra Right and the Advent of Constitutionalism in Prussia." *Canadian Journal of History* 11 (1976).

———. "East Prussia and the Revolution of 1848." *Central European History* 13/14 (1980).

Pankoke, Eckart. *Sociale Bewegung—Sociale Frage—Sociale Politik: Grundfragen der deutschen "Socialwissenschaft" im 19. Jahrhundert.* Stuttgart, 1970.

Paulsen, Friedrich. *Geschichte des gelehrten Unterrichts.* Leipzig, 1885.

Paulsen, Ingwer. *Viktor Aimé Huber als Sozialpolitiker.* 2d ed. Berlin, 1956.

Pepperle, Heinz, and Ingrid Pepperle, eds. *Die Hegelsche Linke.* Leipzig, 1985.

Peradovich, Nikolaus von. *Die Führungsschichten in Österreich und Preussen 1815– 1918.* Wiesbaden, 1955.

Peter, Klaus, ed. *Die Politische Romantik in Deutschland.* Stuttgart, 1985.

Plathner, Günther. *Der Kampf um die richterliche Unabhängigkeit bis zum Jahre 1848.* Berlin, 1935.

Preller, Ludwig von. "Von den tragenden Ideen der ersten deutschen Sozialpolitik." In *Aus Geschichte und Politik: Festschrift zum 70. Geburtstag von Ludwig Berg- straesser.* Düsseldorf, 1954.

Preuss, Ulrich. "Bildung und Bürokratie: Sozialhistorische Bedingungen in der ersten Hälfte des 19. Jahrhunderts." *Der Staat* 14 (1975).

Price, Roger. "Poor Relief and Social Crisis in Mid-Nineteenth-Century France." *European Studies Review* 4 (1983).

Puhle, Hans-Jürgen. "Conservatism in Modern German History." *Journal of Contemporary History* 13 (1978).

Puhle, Hans-Jürgen, and Hans-Ulrich Wehler, eds. *Preussen im Rückblick.* Göttingen, 1980.

Quarck, Max. *Die erste deutsche Arbeiterbewegung.* Leipzig, 1924.

Radtke, Wolfgang. *Die Preussische Seehandlung zwischen Staat und Wirtschaft in der Frühphase der Industrialisierung.* Berlin, 1981.

Raeff, Marc. *The Well-Ordered Police State.* New Haven and London, 1983.

Reif, Heinz. *Westfälischer Adel 1770–1860: Vom Herrschaftsstand zur regionalen Elite.* Göttingen, 1979.

Reinalter, Helmut, ed.. *Demokratische und soziale Protestbewegungen in Mitteleuropa 1815–1848/49.* Frankfurt, 1986.

Rejewski, Harro-Jürgen. *Die Pflicht zur politischen Treue im Preussischen Beamtenrecht 1850–1918.* Berlin, 1973.

Retallack, James. "Social History with a Vengeance? Some Reactions to H.-U. Wehler's 'Das Deutsche Kaiserreich.'" *German Studies Review* 7 (1984).

———. *Notables of the Right.* London, 1988.

Reulecke, Jürgen. *Sozialer Frieden durch soziale Reform.* Wuppertal, 1983.

———. *Geschichte der Urbanisierung in Deutschland.* Frankfurt, 1985.

Rexroth, Frank. "Recent British and West German Research on Poverty in the early Modern Period." *Bulletin of the German Historical Institute in London* 12 (1990).

Ribhegge, Wilhelm. *Konservative Politik in Deutschland: Von der französischen Revolution bis zur Gegenwart.* Darmstadt, 1989.

Richter, Adolf. *Bismarck und die Arbeiterfrage im preussischen Verfassungskonflikt.* Stuttgart, 1935.

Richthofen, Elisabeth v. "Über die historischen Wandlungen in der Stellung der autoritären Parteien zur Arbeiterschutzgesetzgebung und die Motive dieser Wandlungen." Ph.D. diss., University of Heidelberg, 1901.

Ritter, Gerhard. *Die preussischen Konservativen und Bismarcks deutsche Politik 1858 bis 1876.* Heidelberg, 1913.

————. *Stein: Eine politische Biographie.* Stuttgart and Berlin, 1931.

Ritter, Gerhard A. *Sozialversicherung in Deutschland und England.* Munich, 1983.

————. *Die deutschen Parteien 1830–1914.* Göttingen, 1983.

————. "Die Entwicklung des Sozialstaates in vergleichender Perspektive." *Historische Zeitschrift* 243 (1986).

Ritter, Peter U. *Die Rolle des Staates in den Frühstadien der Industrialisierung: Die preussische Industrieförderung in der ersten Hälfte des 19. Jahrhunderts.* Berlin, 1961.

Rohr, Donald G. *The Origins of Social Liberalism in Germany.* Chicago, 1963.

Rörig, Anton. "Die Ansichten über den Pauperismus in der ersten Hälfte des 19. Jahrhunderts." Ph.D. diss., University of Cologne, 1921.

Rosenberg, Hans. *Bureaucracy, Aristocracy, and Autocracy: The Prussian Experience, 1660–1815.* Cambridge, Mass., 1958.

————. *Politische Denkströmungen im Vormärz.* Göttingen, 1972.

————. *Die Weltwirtschaftskrise von 1857–1859.* 2d ed. Göttingen, 1974.

Rössler, Helmut, ed. *Deutscher Adel 1555–1740.* Darmstadt, 1965.

Rothfels, Hans. *Theodor Lohmann und die Kampfjahre der staatlichen Sozialpolitik.* Berlin, 1927.

————. *Theodor von Schön, Friedrich Wilhelm IV und die Revolution von 1848.* Schriften der Königsberger gelehrten Gesellschaft. Geisteswissenschaftliche Klasse, no. 13. Halle, 1937.

Rudé, George. *The Crowd in History.* London and New York, 1964.

Rüfner, W. *Verwaltungsrechtsschutz in Preussen von 1749–1842.* Bonner rechtswissenschaftliche Abhandlungen, no. 33. Bonn, 1962.

Rürup, Reinhard. *Deutschland im 19. Jahrhundert.* Göttingen, 1984.

Runge, Wolfgang. *Politik und Beamtentum im Parteienstaat.* Stuttgart, 1965.

Sachsse, Christoph, and Florian Tennstedt. *Geschichte der Armenfürsorge in Deutschland: Vom Spätmittelalter bis zum Ersten Weltkrieg.* Stuttgart, 1980.

Saile, Wolfgang. *Hermann Wagener und sein Verhältnis zu Bismarck.* Tübingen, 1958.

Salomon, Felix. *Die deutschen Parteiprogramme.* Vol. 1, 2d ed. Leipzig & Berlin, 1907.

Salomon, Ludwig von. *Geschichte des deutschen Zeitungswesens.* Vol. 3. Oldenburg and Berlin, 1906.

Scheel, Wolfgang. *Das Berliner Politische Wochenblatt.* Göttingen, 1964.

Schieder, Wolfgang. *Die Anfänge der deutschen Arbeiterbewegung.* Stuttgart, 1963.

————. "Die Rolle der deutschen Arbeiter in der Revolution von 1848/49." In *Die deutsche Revolution von 1848/49,* ed. Dieter Langewiesche. Darmstadt, 1983.

Schieder, Wolfgang, and Volker Sellin, eds. *Sozialgeschichte in Deutschland.* Vol. 3. Göttingen, 1987.

Schinkel, Harald. "Armenpflege und Freizügigkeit in der preussischen Gesetzgebung vom Jahre 1842." *VSWG* 50 (1963).

Schissler, Hanna. *Preussische Agrargesellschaft im Wandel.* Göttingen, 1978.

Schlangen, Walter, ed. *Die deutschen Parteien im Überblick.* Königstein, 1979.

Schlenke, Manfred. *England und das friderizianische Preussen 1740 bis 1763.* Freiburg, 1963.

———. "Das friderizianische Preussen im Urteil der englischen öffentlichen Meinung 1740–1763." *Geschichte in Wissenschaft und Unterricht* 14 (1963).

———. "Das 'Preussische Beispiel' in Propaganda und Politik des Nationalsozialismus." *Aus Politik und Zeitgeschichte* 27 (1968).

Schmidt, Walter, et al. *Deutsche Geschichte 1789–1848.* Berlin, 1984.

Schmitt, Carl. *Politische Romantik.* 3d ed. Berlin, 1968.

Schmoller, Gustav. *Zur Geschichte des deutschen Kleingewerbes im 19. Jahrhundert.* Halle, 1870.

Schnabel, Franz. *Deutsche Geschichte im 19. Jahrhundert.* 4 vols. Herder Tb. Freiburg, 1965.

Schneider, Hans. *Der preussische Staatsrat 1817–1918.* Munich and Berlin, 1952.

Schoeps, Hans-Joachim. "Hermann Wagener: Ein konservativer Sozialist." *Zeitschrift für Religions- und Geistesgeschichte* 8 (1956).

———. "Neue Briefe zur Gründung des Berliner Politischen Wochenblattes." *Zeitschrift für Religions- und Geistesgeschichte* 13 (1961).

———. *Das war Preussen.* 3d ed. Berlin, 1966.

———. *Üb' immer Treu' und Redlichkeit: Preussen in Geschichte und Gegenwart.* Düsseldorf, 1978.

———. *Deutsche Geistesgeschichte.* 5 vols. Frankfurt, 1980.

———. *Das andere Preussen.* 5th ed. Berlin, 1981.

Schorske, Carl. *Fin-de Siècle Vienna: Politics and Culture.* New York, 1980.

Schramm, Percy E. *Neun Generationen.* 2 vols. Göttingen, 1964.

Schuecking, L. E. *Die Reaktion der Inneren Verwaltung.* Berlin, 1908.

———. *Die innere Demokratisierung Preussens.* Berlin, 1919.

Schulin, Ernst. "Zur Restauration und langsamen Weiterentwicklung der deutschen Geschichtswissenschaft nach 1945." In *Traditionskritik und Rekonstruktionsversuch.* Göttingen, 1979.

Schulte, Wolfgang. *Volk und Staat: Westfalen im Vormärz und in der Revolution 1848/49.* Münster, 1954.

Schulze, Friedrich, and Paul Ssymank. *Das deutsche Studententum von den ältesten Zeiten bis zur Gegenwart.* 4th ed. (Munich, 1931).

Schulze, Hagen. *Der Weg zum Nationalstaat: Die deutsche Nationalbewegung vom 18. Jahrhundert bis zur Reichsgründung.* Munich, 1985.

Schulze, Wally. "Kinderarbeit und Erziehungsfragen in Preussen zu Beginn des 19. Jahrhunderts." *Soziale Welt* 9 (1958).

Schuppan, Peter. "Ostpreussischer Junkerliberalismus und bürgerliche Opposition um 1840." In *Bourgeoisie und bürgerliche Umwälzung in Deutschland 1789–1871,* ed. H. Bleiber. Berlin, GDR, 1971.

Schwabe, Klaus. "Die politische Haltung der deutschen Professoren im ersten Weltkrieg." *Historische Zeitschrift* 193 (1961).

———. *Wissenschaft und Kriegsmoral.* Göttingen, 1969.

———, ed. *Die preussischen Oberpräsidenten 1815–1945.* Boppard, 1981.

Schwenke, Elisabeth. "Friedrich der Grosse und der Adel." Ph.D. diss., University of Berlin, 1911.

Schwentker, Wolfgang. *Konservative Vereine und Revolution in Preussen 1848/49: Die Konstituierung des Konservatismus als Partei.* Düsseldorf, 1988.

Shanahan, William O. *German Protestants face the Social Question*. Notre Dame, 1954.

Sheehan, James. "Liberalism and Society in Germany 1815–1848." *Journal of Modern History* 45 (1973).

———. *German Liberalism in the Nineteenth Century*. Chicago, 1978.

———. *German History 1770–1866*. Oxford, 1989.

Siemann, Wolfgang. *Gesellschaft im Aufbruch: Deutschland 1849–1871*. Frankfurt, 1990.

Simon, Walter. *The Failure of the Prussian Reform Movement 1807–1819*. Ithaca, 1955.

Slack, Paul. *The English Poor Law 1531–1782*. London, 1991.

Sontheimer, Kurt. *Antidemokratisches Denken in der Weimarer Republik*. Munich, 1968.

Spencer, Elaine G. *Police and the Social Order in German Cities: The Düsseldorf District 1848–1914*. De Kalb, Ill., 1992.

Spengler, Oswald. *Preussentum und Sozialismus*. 2d ed. Munich, 1924.

Sperber, Jonathan. *Popular Catholicism in Nineteenth-Century Germany*. Princeton, 1984.

———. "State and Civil Society in Prussia: Thoughts on a new edition of Reinhart Koselleck's *Preussen zwischen Reform und Revolution*." *Journal of Modern History* 57 (1985).

———. *Rhineland Radicals: The Democratic Movement and the Revolution of 1848–1849*. Princeton, 1991.

Spreng, Karl. *Studien zur Entwicklung der sozialpolitischen Ideen in Deutschland auf Grund der Schriften Franz von Baaders und Franz Josef von Buss*. Giessen, 1932.

Stadelmann, Rudolf. *Soziale und Politische Geschichte der Revolution von 1848*. Munich, 1948.

Stark, Gary D., and Bede K. Lackner, eds. *Essays on Culture and Society in Modern Germany*. College Station, Tex., 1982.

Stegmann, Dirk, et al., eds. *Deutscher Konservatismus im 19. und 20. Jahrhundert*. Bonn, 1983.

Stegmann, Franz Josef. *Von der ständischen Sozialreform zur staatlichen Sozialpolitik*. Munich, 1965.

Stein, Lorenz v. *Geschichte der sozialen Bewegung in Frankreich von 1789 bis auf unsere Tage*. Ed. Gottfried Salomon. Munich, 1921.

Steinbach, Bernhard. *Die politische Freiheit der Beamten unter der konstitutionellen Monarchie in Preussen und im Deutschen Reich*. Bonn, 1962.

Stern, Fritz. *The Politics of Cultural Despair*. Berkeley and Los Angeles, 1961.

Sternhell, Zeev. *Maurice Barrès et le Nationalisme Français*. Paris, 1972.

———. *La Droite Révolutionaire 1885–1914: Les Origines Françaises du Fascisme*. Paris, 1978.

Stiebel, Nora. "Der Zentralverein für das Wohl der arbeitenden Klassen im vormärzlichen Preussen." Ph.D. diss., University of Heidelberg, 1922.

Stiller, F. "Das ältere Berliner Armenwesen bis zur Einführung der Selbstverwaltung im Jahre 1820." Ph.D. diss., University of Heidelberg, 1908.

Stillich, Oscar. *Die politischen Parteien in Deutschland: Die Konservativen*. Leipzig, 1908.

Stuke, Horst. *Philosophie der Tat: Studien zur Verwirklichung der Philosophie bei den Junghegelianern.* Stuttgart, 1963.

Süle, Tibor. *Preussische Bürokratietradition: Zur Entwicklung von Verwaltung und Beamtenschaft in Deutschland, 1871–1918.* Göttingen, 1988.

Tennstedt, Florian. *Sozialgeschichte der Sozialpolitik in Deutschland.* Göttingen, 1981.

Teuteberg, Hans-Jürgen. *Geschichte der industriellen Mitbestimmung.* Tübingen, 1961.

Thier, Erich. *Rodbertus, Lassalle, Adolph Wagner: Ein Beitrag zur Theorie und Geschichte des deutschen Staatssozialismus.* Jena, 1930.

Thomas, Hinton. *Liberalism, Nationalism, and the German Intellectuals, 1822–1847.* Cambridge, 1951.

Thun, Alphons, "Beiträge zur Geschichte der Gesetzgebung und Verwaltung zu Gunsten der Fabrikarbeiter in Preussen." *Zeitschrift des Königlich statistischen Bureaus* 17 (1877).

Tilly, Charles, et al. *The Rebellious Century.* Cambridge, Mass., 1975.

Tilly, Richard. *Industrialisierung und Raum.* Stuttgart, 1979.

———. *Kapital, Staat und sozialer Protest in der deutschen Industrialisierung.* Göttingen, 1980.

———. *Vom Zollverein zum Industriestaat.* Munich, 1990.

———, ed. *Sozialer Protest: Geschichte und Gesellschaft.* Vol. 3. Göttingen, 1977.

Tilmann, Margret. "Der Einfluss des Revolutionsjahres 1848 auf die preussische Gewerbe- und Sozialgesetzgebung: Die Notverordnung vom 9. Februar 1849." Ph.D. diss., University of Berlin, 1935.

Torke, H. J. *Das Russische Beamtentum in der ersten Hälfte des 19. Jahrhunderts.* Forschungen zur osteuropäischen Geschichte, no. 13. Berlin, 1967.

Treitschke, Heinrich v. *Deutsche Geschichte im 19. Jahrhundert.* 5 vols. Leipzig, 1879–97.

Treue, Wilhelm. *Wirtschaftszustände und Wirtschaftspolitik in Preussen.* Stuttgart, 1937.

———. *Wirtschaftsgeschichte Preussens.* Berlin, 1984.

———, ed. *Geschichte als Aufgabe: Festschrift für Otto Büsch.* Berlin, 1988.

Troeltsch, Ernst. "Der Ansturm der westlichen Demokratien." In *Die Deutsche Freiheit,* ed. Bund deutscher Gelehrter und Künstler. Gotha, 1917.

Trox, Eckhard. *Militärischer Konservatismus: Kriegervereine und "Militärpartei" in Preussen zwischen 1815 und 1848/49.* Stuttgart, 1990.

Tschirch, Otto. *Geschichte der öffentlichen Meinung in Preussen vom Baseler Frieden bis zum Zusammenbruch des Staates.* 2 vols. Weimar, 1934.

Twesten, Karl. "Die Preussische Beamtenstaat." *Preussische Jahrbücher* 18 (1866).

Varrentrap, Carl. "Rankes historisch-politische Zeitschrift und das Berliner Politische Wochenblatt." *Historische Zeitschrift* 99 (1907).

Veblen, Thorstein. *Imperial Germany and the Industrial Revolution.* New York, 1915.

Veit-Brause, Irmeliné. "Zur Kritik an der 'Kritischen Geschichtswissenschaft': Tendenzwende oder Paradigmawechsel?" *Geschichte in Wissenschaft und Unterricht* 31 (1984).

Vermeil, Edmond. *Les Doctrinaires de la Révolution allemande.* Paris, 1939.

Vetter, Klaus. *Kurmärkischer Adel und Preussische Reformen.* Weimar, 1979.

Vierhaus, Rudolf, ed. *Der Adel vor der Revolution.* Göttingen, 1971.

Vogel, Barbara. *Allgemeine Gewerbefreiheit: Die Reformpolitik des preussischen Staatskanzlers Hardenberg 1810–1820.* Göttingen, 1983.

———. "Beamtenkonservatismus: Sozial- und verfassungsgeschichtliche Voraussetzungen der Parteien in Preussen im frühen 19. Jahrhundert." In *Deutscher Konservatismus im 19. und 20. Jahrhundert: Festschrift für Fritz Fischer.* Bonn, 1983.

———, ed. *Preussische Reformen 1807–1820.* Königstein, 1980.

Vogel, Walter. *Bismarcks Arbeiterversicherung: Ihre Entstehung im Kräftespiel der Zeit.* Brunswick, 1951.

Volkmann, Heinrich. *Die Arbeiterfrage im preussischen Abgeordnetenhaus.* Berlin, 1968.

Wagner, A. *Der Kampf der Justiz gegen die Verwaltung in Preussen.* Hamburg, 1936.

Wagner, Adolph, ed. *Aus dem literarischen Nachlass von Dr. Carl Rodbertus-Jagetzow.* Berlin, 1913.

Wahl, Adalbert. *Beiträge zur deutschen Parteiengeschichte im 19. Jahrhundert.* Munich and Berlin, 1910.

Walker, Mack. *Germany and the Emigration, 1816–1885.* Cambridge, Mass., 1964.

———. *German Home Towns: Community, State, General Estate, 1648–1871.* Ithaca, 1971.

———. *Johann Jakob Moser and the Holy Roman Empire of the German Nation.* Chapel Hill, 1981.

Weber, Eugen. *My France.* Cambridge, Mass., 1991.

Wegmann, Dietrich. *Die leitenden staatlichen Verwaltungsbeamten der Provinz Westfalen 1815–1918.* Münster, 1969.

Wehler, Hans-Ulrich. *Deutsche Gesellschaftsgeschichte.* Vols. 1–2. Munich, 1987.

———, ed. *Moderne deutsche Sozialgeschichte.* Königstein, 1966.

———, ed. *Deutsche Historiker.* Vols. 2 and 5. Göttingen, 1972.

———, ed. *Sozialgeschichte Heute: Festschrift für Hans Rosenberg.* Göttingen, 1974.

Weill, H. *Die Entstehung des deutschen Bildungsprinzips.* 2d ed. Bonn, 1967.

Wenger, Klaus R. *Preussen in der öffentlichen Meinung Frankreichs 1815–1870.* Göttingen, 1979.

Wilhelm, Theodor. *Die Idee des Berufsbeamtentums.* Tübingen, 1933.

Winkler, Heinrich A. *Liberalismus und Antiliberalismus.* Göttingen, 1979.

———, ed. *Organisierter Kapitalismus: Voraussetzungen und Anfänge.* Göttingen, 1974.

Wippermann, Wolfgang, "Nationalsozialismus und Preussentum." *Aus Politik und Zeitgeschichte* 52–53 (1981).

Wirth, Max. *Bismarck-Wagener-Rodbertus.* Berlin, 1883.

Wolff, Kurt H., ed. *From Karl Mannheim.* New York, 1971.

Wolff, Wilhelm. *Aus Schlesien, Preussen und dem Reich.* Ed. Walter Schmidt. Berlin, GDR, 1985.

Wunder, Bernd. *Privilegierung und Disziplinierung: Die Entstehung des Berufsbeamtentums in Bayern und Württemberg 1770–1825.* Munich, 1978.

———. *Die Geschichte der Bürokratie in Deutschland.* Frankfurt, 1985.

Wutke, Karl, ed. "Der Rechenschaftsbericht des Oberpräsidenten von Merckel über

den Zustand Schlesiens." *Zeitschrift des Vereins für die Geschichte Schlesiens* 60 (1926).

Zeldin, Theodore. *Ambition and Love*. Oxford, 1979.

Ziekursch, Johannes. *Beiträge zur Charakteristik der preussischen Verwaltungsbeamten in Schlesien*. Breslau, 1907.

———. *Politische Geschichte des neuen deutschen Kaiserreiches*. Vol. 1. Frankfurt, 1925.

———. *Hundert Jahre schlesischer Agrargeschichte*. 2d ed. Breslau, 1927.

Zmarzlik, Hans-Günther. "Das Kaiserreich in Neuer Sicht?" *Historische Zeitschrift* 222 (1976).

Zunkel, Friedrich. *Der rheinisch-westfälische Unternehmer 1834–1879*. Cologne and Opladen, 1962.

———. "Beamtenschaft und Unternehmertum beim Aufbau der Ruhrindustrie 1849–1880." *Tradition* 9 (1964).

Zwahr, Hartmut. *Zur Konstituierung des Proletariats als Klasse: Strukturuntersuchungen über das Leipziger Proletariat während der industriellen Revolution*. Berlin, 1978.

Index

and *Biedermeier,* 38
Frondienste, 22n.83

Gabella emigrationis, 100
Gans, Eduard, 102n.1
Gemeinheitsteilungen, 150
Gerlach, Leopold von, 42. See also *Kamarilla*
Gerlach, Ludwig von, 66, 67, 101, 102
  conception of property, 80–81, 119
  and conservative party, 79, 227–28
  member of circle around the *BpW,* 42, 44
  and proletariat, 80–81
  and Radowitz, 80
  and *Ständestaat,* 79–80, 107, 116
  as Wagener's mentor, 102
German Custom's Union, 213
German Idealism
  influence on officials, 201, 202n.10
Gerth, Hans H.
  on bureaucracy, 176
Gesinde, 23
Gewerbeförderung, 73, 200
  literature on, 73n.41
Gewerbeordnung
  amendment of 1849, 213–14
  of 1845, 213
  prohibition of *Trucksystem,* 213
Gillis, John R.
  on bureaucracy, 175–76
Görlitz
  petition of town's craftsmen, 214
Growth of rural proletariat
  reasons for, 25–27
Guilds, 50–53. See also *Berliner Politisches Wochenblatt*
  in late medieval town, 51–52
  loss of function, 212
  power of, 50–53
  regulating town life, 50, 212
  as social network, 51–52
Gutswirtschaft, 19

Haller, Karl Friedrich von, 41
  member of "*Maikäferei,*" 41
Hamerow, Theodore S.
  interpretation of pauperism, 7–8
Hansemann, David
  criticism of bureaucracy, 146
Hardenberg, Karl August von, 124, 126, 178
  and factory legislation, 203

Harkort, Friedrich, 183
Hartung, Fritz
  on bureaucracy, 125, 147, 177
Heffter, Heinrich
  on bureaucracy, 177
Hegel, Georg Wilhelm Friedrich, 51, 54n.63
  on bureaucracy, 219, 237
  and the state, 92
Heidelberger Romantik, 38
Heinzen, Karl
  criticism of bureaucracy, 144, 145
  on *Konduitenlisten,* 144
Hengstenberg, Ernst Wilhelm, 43, 185
Herrenhaus, 225–26
Heuerlinge, 23
Heydt, August von der, 92
  rejection of abstract ideas, 206–8
  on social policy, 206–8, 238
Hintze, Otto
  on bureaucracy, 218–19, 237
Historiography
  of pauperism in Central Europe, 5–10
Hitler, Adolf, 122, 246–59 passim
Hochkonservative
  disdain for parliamentary politics, 227–28
  hostility to Manteuffel government, 227
  opposition to Poor Law, 231n.41
  reconciliation with constitutional state, 228
Hofmannsthal, Hugo von
  on *Bindung,* 53
  on "Prussian spirit," 242
Huber, Viktor A., 81–93
  on association, 72n.35, 85, 86, 90
  on atomization, 86
  background, 82
  and *BpW,* 91
  on bureaucracy, 91
  and conservative party, 83
  early works, 82–83
  and England, 86
  and French socialists, 85, 88, 88n.53
  on industrialization, 90–91
  literature on, 81nn.9, 10
  moralizing approach to social problems, 86–87
  and other conservatives, 81, 85–89, 90–91, 101
  and Radowitz, 83, 84, 89, 90, 91
  and rural proletariat, 87–88
  on property, 91